American Pragmatism
and Communication Research

LEA'S COMMUNICATION SERIES
Jennings Bryant/Dolf Zillmann, General Editors

Selected titles in Communication Theory and Methodology subseries (Jennings Bryant, series advisor) include:

Berger • *Planning Strategic Interaction: Attaining Goals Through Communicative Action*

Dennis/Wartella • *American Communication Research: The Remembered History*

Ellis • *Crafting Society: Ethnicity, Class, and Communication Theory*

Greene • *Message Production: Advances in Communication Theory*

Heath/Bryant • *Human Communication Theory and Research: Concepts, Contexts, and Challenges, Second Edition*

Olson • *Hollywood Planet: Global Media and the Competitive Advantage of Narrative Transparency*

Riffe/Lacy/Fico • *Analyzing Media Messages: Using Quantitative Content Analysis in Research*

Salwen/Stacks • *An Integrated Approach to Communication Theory and Research*

For a complete list of titles in LEA's Communication Series, please contact Lawrence Erlbaum Associates, Publishers.

American Pragmatism
and Communication Research

Edited by

David K. Perry
The University of Alabama

LEA LAWRENCE ERLBAUM ASSOCIATES, PUBLISHERS
2001   Mahwah, New Jersey   London

Lawrence Erlbaum Associates, Inc., Publishers
10 Industrial Avenue
Mahwah, New Jersey 07430

Cover design by Kathryn Houghtaling Lacey

Library of Congress Cataloging-in-Publication Data

American pragmatism and communication research / David K. Perry, ed.
   p.   cm. — (LEA's communication series)
   Includes bibliographical references and index.
   ISBN 0-8058-3590-3
   1. Pragmatism.   2. Communication—Research.   I. Perry, David K.
II. Series.
B832.A44   2000
144'.3'0973—dc21   00-034735
                                                                  CIP

Printed in the United States of America
10 9 8 7 6 5 4 3 2 1

Contents

v

Preface

This book concerns the past, present, and potential relationships between American pragmatism and communication research. Pragmatism is a pluralistic concept. According to one version, for example, it is a philosophical worldview, of which change is a categorical feature (Pepper, 1942). According to another, it is a method of settling philosophical disputes such as monism versus pluralism by examining their observable consequences (James, 1907), including those that guide research practice. At various points, this volume focuses on various forms. For most of these, its influence across a broad range of scholarly disciplines, including communication, continues to grow (e.g., see chap. 1, this volume).

Unfortunately, many misconceptions and exaggerations about pragmatism remain as well. Here, I attempt to dispel these instead of presenting a formal essentialist definition. The Darwinian roots of pragmatism might discourage the latter. As time passes, pragmatism is apt to evolve.

First, pragmatism is not a Machiavellian philosophy of expedience, which casts principles aside. Instead, it demands that we judge principles by their broad consequences. In this light, no contradiction need exist between morality and expediency. Second, pragmatists do not inherently oppose theory. In fact, for me, social psychologist Kurt Lewin's famous statement that nothing is so practical as a good theory summarizes its orientation quite well. Scientific theories have revolutionized our lives, and philosophical ones condition the ways that human societies operate. Expediency versus principle and theory versus practice are two oppositions that pragmatists often try to overcome. In fact, rejection of a theory–practice dualism may be the closest thing to an essential characteristic that pragmatists share (see Mounce, 1997). I agree with Kaplan (1964) that to focus on expediency and reject all theory is to embrace a *vulgar* pragmatism. That has little to do with the ideas of John Dewey, William James, and so on. One finds many vulgar pragmatists both within and outside of academia. Allegations concerning contemporary pragmatists to the contrary, such ideas really do not appear in this book.

Third, in light of what I have already said, pragmatism is not the philosophy of the U.S. businessperson. For some reason, Europeans sometimes describe it thusly. I hope that Thomas Jacobson's chapter in this volume (chap. 11), which links leftist German philosopher Jurgen Habermas with pragmatism, helps put such notions to rest. Fourth, pragmatism is no philosophy of the political left either. Of course, many of its adherents, both historically and among contributors to this volume, fall to the left of a conservative–liberal median. John Dewey was a well-known social democrat. His student, Sidney Hook, may have been the first Marxist philosopher in the United States. Yet other pragmatists, such as C. I. Lewis and W. V. Quine, have held clearly conservative views. Hook became a well-known anticommunist during the last five decades of his long life. Of course, pragmatists judge political ideas by their consequences. In this light, the left has not always passed muster. Indeed, pragmatists often may appear inconsistent ideologically. My favorite illustration here concerns Hook. In 1972, he believed the foreign policy views of Democratic presidential nominee George McGovern to be extremely naïve. He was torn between endorsing Richard Nixon as a lesser evil or recommending that voters cast a protest ballot for the DeLeonist Socialist Labor Party!

The chapters in this volume also are diverse and perhaps even occasionally contradictory. Certainly, no one, myself included, will agree with every point included herein. To a degree, I have tried to arrange them in order from the general to the specific. In chapter 1, Simonson has accomplished perhaps the most difficult task—that of introducing the links between pragmatism and communication. Cronen and Chetro-Szivos discuss in chapter 2 how a pragmatic, Darwinian approach to inquiry has guided and might further guide communication research. Although at times they focus on the Coordinated Management of Meaning (CMM) theory, their ideas deserve all our attention. In chapter 3, Woodward advocates a functional view of communication based on Dewey's mature notion of transaction. He takes care to distinguish it from certain forms of structural/functionalism in social science today. The ideas of William James, including their applicability to postmodern notions of communication, constitute the subject of Leonhirth's chapter 4. Leonhirth also discusses the influences of James on early communication scholars. In chapter 5, Jensen articulates a pragmatist aesthetics and connects it to Deweyan democracy. Many of us who have read Dewey might benefit from her warnings about possible misinterpretations of these ideas.

In chapter 6, Craig discusses the similarities and differences between Dewey's notion of inquiry and the philosophical hermeneutics of Hans-Georg Gadamer, especially as they apply to his influential conception of communication as a practical discipline. Many of the classical pragmatists, especially Dewey, concerned themselves with ethics and values. In this light, Horne's discussion in chapter 7 of the ethical ideas of neopragmatist Richard Rorty is especially significant. Her rhetorical discussion of Rorty's ironic self is especially intriguing. In chapter 8, Meyer applies accommodation theory, linked to symbolic interactionism and more generally to the social behaviorism of George H. Mead and his followers, to media research. He focuses especially on the possibilities created by the Internet. Chapter 9 interprets media-effects evidence, an exemplar of quantitative social research, in light of pragmatist ideas about inquiry. I hope that it encourages other empirical researchers to consider the ideas of Dewey, James, Quine, and so on, as they apply to their work. Shuler and Tate discuss in chapter 10 the often unacknowledged affinity between pragmatism and feminist communication inquiry. They also explore why the two have developed in relative isolation from each other. In chapter 11, Jacobson argues that Habermas' work resembles scientific forms of pragmatism. He also suggests that we can look on the theory of communicative action as a contemporary articulation of a number of Deweyan themes. Finally, in chapter 12, Shepherd draws on a young William James' bout with suicidal feelings to articulate a vision of the relation between pragmatism and communication. He argues that pragmatism theorizes about despair and life's sense of the tragic. To him, communication provides us with a rationale for continuing in the face of this. When employed as a form of active resistance, he reminds us, it can change the universe.

In summary here, I draw from Richard Rorty, a pragmatist with whom I sometimes disagree. He often has argued that diverse scholars, including analytic philosophers and postmodernists, will find Dewey waiting at the end of the roads they are traveling. I chose to create this volume because of a similar feeling. In communication, Rorty's idea may apply whether we employ qualitative or quantitative methods, whether we believe in rules or laws, whether we base human behavior on reasons or causes. It may apply even if we believe in all of these together. As our research progresses and we cover more ground, the more affinity we may find between ourselves and the classical and contemporary pragmatists.

ACKNOWLEDGMENTS

Many thanks are due to the collectivity of persons without whom this volume could not exist. I can mention only a few individuals. First, Jennings Bryant, general editor of Lawrence Erlbaum Associates' communication series, encouraged me to pursue the concept from the time I first discussed it with him. Lawrence Erlbaum Associates editors Linda Bathgate and Corin Huff provided invaluable guidance and displayed considerable patience with the inevitable delays that arose. Vernon Cronen's affirmative voice mail response one Friday to my letter seeking a contribution restored my hope that I might find a critical mass of scholars willing to participate. Some early difficulties had left me wondering. My skilled research assistants, Beverly Piotrowski and Megan Walde, made many helpful contributions in helping me prepare this volume.

—*David K. Perry*

REFERENCES

James, W. (1907). *Pragmatism: A new name for some old ways of thinking*. New York: Longmans, Green.
Kaplan, A. (1964). *The conduct of inquiry*. San Francisco: Chandler.
Mounce, H. O. (1997). *The two pragmatisms: From Peirce to Rorty*. London: Routledge.
Pepper, S. C. (1942). *World hypotheses*. Berkeley, CA: University of California Press.

Chapter 1

Varieties of Pragmatism and Communication: Visions and Revisions From Peirce to Peters

Peter Simonson
University of Pittsburgh

During the past two decades, literature on pragmatism has exploded. From philosophy to film studies, from law to literary criticism, and from history to religion to communication studies, pragmatism has a new generation of defenders and interpreters. This sometimes breathtaking array of thought should remind us that pragmatism is, as it has always been, a many splendored thing.

Amid plurality, pragmatism has always concerned itself with communication. The current revival offers communication studies an opportunity to rethink and creatively revise its canon. This chapter aims to contribute to that process by revisiting first-generation pragmatism and reviewing revivalist work relevant to the field. I draw attention to pragmatist studies in communication from the late 19th century through the contemporary revival, and I highlight the exciting new intellectual lineage established by revisionist work. This is a project of excavation and review intended to make overlooked texts available as resources for theory, criticism, and other practices within the field. Communication studies would be richer, I argue, if we revisited classic texts and expanded our intellectual canons.

Pragmatism can be approached as a doctrine or a historical tradition. As a doctrine (or method or habit of thought), it typically has advanced the notion that the consequences of their adoption determines the meaning of ideas, truth of propositions, or value of proposed actions. Thus, pragmatism has often tied knowledge to social practices and ethics, taken inquiry as communal and historically situated, and held that the world is open ended and in process. It also typically has rejected hard dualisms of mind and body, knowledge and action, fact and value, individual and society.

However, one must tread cautiously with generalizations. From the beginning, pragmatism has been pluralistic.

Alternatively, one can understand pragmatism as a tradition that is partly constituted by arguments about its meaning and historical lineage. I favor this tack. As a tradition, certain recurring themes, including the idea of communication and allied concepts, have marked it. Like doctrinal pragmatism, however, the deeply plural tradition resists overarching characterizations. The misleading idea exists that pragmatism is distinctly American, but from the beginning, encounters with Continental thought have fundamentally shaped its arguments. Moreover, Continental thinkers have defended it staunchly. Views colored by American exceptionalism are simply inadequate.

I break the tradition down into three main categories. It was classically articulated by Peirce, James, Dewey, and Mead,[1] each of whom formulated ideas and habits of inquiry relevant to contemporary communication studies. Pragmatism then moved beyond that core and in the first half of the 20th century had important defenders not always recognized as pragmatists. This group included Jane Addams, George Santayana, W. E. B. Du Bois, Alain Locke, Walter Lippmann, and C. Wright Mills. Together they pushed the tradition beyond the Protestant Yankee establishment of White males and developed pragmatism's aesthetics, criticism, sociology, politics, and racial theory. Finally, pragmatism has experienced an energetic revival in the late 20th century, and the final section of the chapter sketches some of its most important theorists. Like their precursors, the revivalists are a diverse lot collectively concerned with communication. Their work ranges from the grand German philosophy of Jürgen Habermas and Karl-Otto Apel to Stanley Fish's literary antitheory to the varied, politically accented work of Richard Rorty, Richard Bernstein, Nancy Fraser, and Cornel West. They also include three heavyweight theorists in the field of communication—James Carey, Michael Schudson, and John Peters. Together they have replayed the intellectual roles of Dewey, Lippmann, and James and given the tradition a high-profile presence in American communication studies.

PRAGMATISM AND COMMUNICATION
IN THE FIRST GENERATION

Pragmatism emerged between the Civil War and World War I paradigmatically in the work of Charles Sanders Peirce (1839–1914), William

---

[1]Because space is limited, I ignore Oliver Wendell Holmes (1841–1935) and the tradition of legal pragmatism. Readers interested in that area might begin with Grey (1989), Posner (1992), and Brint and Weaver (1991).

James (1842–1910), John Dewey (1859–1952), and George Herbert Mead (1863–1931). This was a group of cultural insiders. All were Yankee WASPs trained in or with sympathy for science, with deep interest in Charles Darwin and serious, although varied, encounters with religion. In their milieu, agnosticism was establishing its first cultural beachheads, the academy was becoming professionalized, modern social science was taking root, and positivism was vying for intellectual hegemony with a revived Absolute Idealism. All of these things shaped first-generation pragmatism.

Despite similarities, the classic pragmatists forged distinct and sometimes competing modes of thought, and they bear different legacies for communication studies. One can begin by distinguishing Cambridge from Chicago pragmatism, with Peirce and James in the former camp, Dewey and Mead in the latter. The Cambridge duo was half a generation older, sat uneasily with the emerging research university, and was never attracted to Hegel in the way Dewey and Mead once were. Although the Chicago pragmatists eventually rejected philosophical Idealism, they brought from Hegel a communitarian social ontology that eventually led them to give the idea of communication a central place in their thought. Although attentive to communication, the Cambridge pragmatists never gave the term the same explicit attention. Still they offer important things to communication studies: Peirce a highly sophisticated semiotic theory and links between knowledge, reality, and communicative practices; and James a mode of inquiry open to the radically other and unwilling to reduce pluralistic truths to a singular system.

Cambridge Beginnings

Pragmatism traces its roots to an early 1870s reading group that half ironically called itself *The Metaphysical Club*. The Harvard-based group included James, Peirce, Nicholas St. John Green, Oliver Wendell Holmes, and Chauncey Wright. All had either legal or scientific training, and each wanted to explore the implications of Darwinian theory. Green, largely forgotten today, urged the others to examine the practical significance of every proposition and, according to Peirce, insisted belief was "that upon which a man is prepared to act." Here appeared one important element of pragmatist thought (Kuklick, 1977, pp. 48–54; Peirce, 1906, p. 270; see also Brent, 1993, chap. 2; Wiener, 1949, chap. 2).

As a *material souvenir* of the group, Peirce wrote an essay in 1872 (published as "How to Make Our Ideas Clear") that set out key principles later associated with pragmatism. Attacking Cartesian introspective inquiry, Peirce (1878/1955a) argued that "the whole function of thought is to produce habits of action" and "what a thing means is simply what habits it involves" (p. 30). In much of Peirce's work, the key habit was disciplined scientific investigation. Inquiry was a decidedly communal affair, so communication was central. He defined *truth* and *reality* as "the opinion which is fated to be ultimately agreed to by all who investigate" (p. 38). Logic was also "rooted in the social principle" (1878/1955b, p. 162) and inquiry conducted not by solitary thinkers but rather "for the community of philosophers" (1868/1955, p. 229). Peirce offered an anti-Cartesian philosophy opposed to monological reason and the introspective method and committed instead to communication as the basis of truth, logic, and, in Peirce's (e.g., 1893/1955) grander religious moments, *evolutionary love*.

Peirce began developing his important semiotic theory in the late 1860s. As James Hoopes has pointed out, it offers an alternative to the Continental tradition that emerged from Ferdinand de Saussure's lectures on linguistics (1906–1911) that subsequently shaped poststructuralism and Marxian cultural studies. While Saussure posited two elements arbitrarily connected with one another, signifier and signified (elements Derrida destabilized into endless free play), Peirce's system had three elements: object, sign, and interpretant (see e.g., Peirce, 1868/1955, 1873/1991, 1897/1955; Hoopes, 1991). A sign stands for an object to an interpretant, which is a subsequent thought or action that determines the meaning of the sign. Thoughts are themselves signs that give rise to other signs, including the sign that is the *self*.[2] The interpretant anchors the signifying process with disciplined habits of thought and action. As a result, "Peirce's semiotic was constructive rather than deconstructive" (Hoopes, 1991, p. 3; see also Eco, 1995; Habermas, 1995, Liszka, 1996, chap. 1; Lyne, 1980).

Although Peirce probably coined the word *pragmatism*, culling it from Immanuel *Kant's Critique of Pure Reason*, the term did not appear in print until William James' 1898 "Philosophical Conceptions and Practical Results," a work that represents the first rupture in pragmatism. James credited Peirce with the principle, but quickly added that pragmatism "should be expressed more broadly." For James (1898/1992),

> the effective meaning of any philosophical proposition can always be brought down to some particular consequence, in our future practical experience, whether active or passive; the point lying rather in the fact that the experience must be particular, than the fact that it must be active. (p. 1080)

This call to particularity departed from Peirce, who in 1903 distanced himself from James by dubbing his own doctrine *pragmaticism* (see Apel,

---

[2]Although poststructuralism has given it new resonance, the trope of the self as sign has a long history of Christian expression; Royce used Peirce's semiotics for explicitly religious ends in *The Problem of Christianity* (1918/1968, chaps. 11, 14), the last important idealist work in the United States.

1981, chap. 8; cf. Hookway, 1985, 1997). James gave the doctrine a public face in 1906 to 1907, delivering lectures at the Lowell Institute in Boston that would become *Pragmatism* (1907/1981), arguably the most important first-generation document. Soon after, Arthur Lovejoy (1908) counted no less than 13 pragmatisms in circulation. Meanwhile, James defended himself in an overlooked article called "The Pragmatist Account of Truth and its Misunderstanders" (1908/1987). There he pushed the idea of particularity more explicitly, saying pragmatism was about pragmata, "things in their plurality" (p. 931). James was developing a kind of nominalism—an emphasis on particulars at odds with Peircean system and grander semiotic theory. Although Peirce had seen pragmatism as a principle of logic that might aid science, James moved the doctrine in more modernist directions and took it as a philosophical *attitude* instead (Hookway, 1997).

Chicago Pragmatism and the Idea of Communication

Although Cambridge pragmatism had roots in the Metaphysical Club, the grandest metaphysician of all—G. W. F. Hegel—infected neither Peirce nor James. This was not true of Dewey and Mead. Their Chicago social pragmatism owed much to what Dewey later called the *Hegelian bacillus*, which was widespread in the Anglo-American world between the Civil War and World War I. Jamesian pluralism, on the other hand, was forged in what he called a *death grapple of an embrace* with his idealist colleague Josiah Royce (cited in Conant, 1997), as well as criticisms of other Hegelianisms from the 1880s on (see also Kuklick, 1977; Sprigge, 1997). Royce was just one of many important idealists of a period that also included the old Walt Whitman, Charles Horton Cooley, and the British philosophers T. H. Green and F. H. Bradley. In the first generation, idealism served as a rhetorical counterforce shaping pragmatism.

For Dewey and Mead, however, Hegel served a positive resource. Both men drew deeply from the idealist well before renouncing its drink in the mid-1890s.[3] Their mature social theories can be read as Hegel decapitated, lopping off Absolute Spirit but maintaining a social ontology where individuals are always already social beings. In places, the mystic term *communication* plays the part of Hegelian spirit, and Dewey's and Mead's use of it owes more to Hegel than to anything Peirce or James said. From this perspective, the fact that James rarely used the words *communication* or *community* is of a piece with his rejection of Hegel (but see McDermott, 1986).

---

[3]For good accounts of Dewey's encounters with Hegel, see Westbrook (1991), Coughlan (1973), and Kuklick (1985). For Mead, see Joas (1991) and Cook (1993). For idealism's encounters with communication, see Peters (1999b, chap. 5).

Jamesian psychology (e.g., 1890) helped turn Dewey in more naturalistic, less idealistic directions,[4] but the two men had important differences. Dewey appreciated the biological basis of Jamesian psychology, along with the contention that the mind is a "fighter for ends" in purposeful action (Westbrook, 1991, p. 66f). At the same time, James had Emersonian appreciation for individual experience and the depths of privacy, and Dewey criticized what he saw as dualism and subjectivism in the older man's thinking. Although James (and Peirce) affirmed or left open belief in the supernatural, "Dewey often wrote as if no educated twentieth-century man or woman who understood the scientific method and trusted experience could responsibly give credence to the idea of the transcendental" (Rockefeller, 1991, pp. 370–380). Although Dewey wrote about religion, he domesticated and naturalized it and was never disposed to study the lonely, extraordinary phenomena James chronicled in *Varieties of Religious Experience* (Coughlan, 1973, pp. 67–68, 111–112; Rockefeller, 1998).

James' attitude toward the supernatural was at bottom an openness to the radically other, something Dewey rarely displayed. As Cavell (1998) wrote, "William James characteristically philosophizes off of the language of the street, which he respects and wishes to preserve." In Dewey, by contrast, "the speech of others, whose ideas Dewey wishes to correct, or rather to replace . . . hardly appears—as though the world into which he is drawn to intervene suffers from a well-defined lack or benightedness" (p. 75). James' openness to the language of the street and the experiences of mystics displayed an intellectual cosmopolitanism that Dewey never approached.

If Dewey was open to mysticism, it was mysticism in the service of *communication*—a term he began using in the mid-1890s. In 1920, for instance, blissfully removed from the postwar cynicism affecting others, Dewey (1920/1948) wrote that,

> when the emotional force, the mystic force one might say, of communication, of the miracle of shared life and shared experience is spontaneously felt, the hardness and crudeness of contemporary life will be bathed in the light that never was on land or sea. (p. 211)

In that same work, he suggested that, "distance is an obstacle, a source of trouble," a condition that communication technologies aimed to overcome (pp. 118–119). If mystery appears in Dewey, it is that of social communion. He stresses closeness, not distance, and arguably collapses the world into the social.

---

[4]This turn is often marked with reference to Dewey's important 1896 essay, "The Reflex Arc Concept in Psychology" (Westbrook, 1991, pp. 65–77; Coughlan, 1973, pp. 138–142).

Together with his colleague, Mead, Dewey developed a social pragmatism that by 1903 was linked to "the Chicago school."[5] Mead studied under both Royce and James at Harvard in the late 1880s. Like Dewey, he remained an idealist in the early 1890s. Mead quickly fell under Dewey's spell when the two taught at Michigan. "I have gained more from him than from any one man I ever met," Mead said of Dewey in 1892 (cited in Cook, 1993, p. 32). In 1894, both moved to Chicago, where they participated in the Settlement House movement of Jane Addams and in other Progressive social reform causes. There they developed a pragmatism distinct from those of James and Peirce.[6]

Communication was one key element of Chicago-school pragmatism. Dewey remembered later that reading James' *Psychology* led him "straight to the perception of the importance of distinctive social categories, especially communication and participation" (Dewey, 1930/1962, p. 25). Nonetheless, Dewey's earliest use of communication draws as much on Hegelian social ontology as Jamesian theory of the mind or the social self. His first treatment of the concept probably occurred in an unpublished paper from around 1895, "Plan of Organization of the University Primary School." Addressing a subject that would long concern him, Dewey wrote, "The ultimate problem of all education is to co-ordinate the psychological and the social factors. . . . [T]he child [needs] be capable of expressing himself, but in such a way as to realize social ends" (Dewey, 1895/1972, p. 224; see also 1899/1976, pp. 29–31). *Communication* named one important mode for this socially anchored expressiveness. For Dewey, it included speech, writing, reading, drawing, molding, modeling, and literature. Together with carpentry, sewing, and cooking, which he called *direct modes of expression*, communication lay at the heart of Dewey's socially organic curriculum (1895/1972, p. 231 passim).

---

[5]James began an appreciative review of a 1903 Chicago publication of Dewey, Mead, and others, *Studies in Logical Theory*, with a wry remark that revealed some of the different intellectual disposition between himself and Dewey: "Chicago has a School of Thought!—a school of thought which, it is safe to predict, will figure in literature as the School of Chicago for twenty-five years to come. Some universities have plenty of thought to show, but no school; others plenty of school, but no thought. The University of Chicago, by its Decennial Publications, shows real thought and a real school. Professor John Dewey, and at least ten of his disciples, have collectively put into the world a statement" (James, 1903/1987, p. 1136).

[6]Mead and Dewey rarely criticized each other, and both were critical of what they saw as the remnants of individualism and dualism in James: "His individual had that in him which was not fashioned in the living process," Mead wrote in 1930 (in 1964, p. 386). For accounts of the relation between Dewey and Mead, see Cook (1993, pp. 27–47, 68–70, 161–166), Coughlan (1973, pp. 112–134, 143–150), and Joas (1985, pp. 33–39, 64–68). For Dewey's and Mead's social reform efforts and relation to Jane Addams, see Westbrook (1991, chap. 4), Ryan (1995, chap. 4), Rockefeller (1991, pp. 205–212, 228f), Deegan (1988, chap. 5), Cook (1993, chap. 7), and Shalin (1991).

Dewey's first extended treatment of communication did not come until 1916, however. By then, both Mead and Michigan's Charles Horton Cooley had made important statements of the concept. Idealism was an important backdrop for each. Communication technologies had resonated with Mead during his Hegelian days. In 1892, he wrote a friend that "the telegraph and locomotives are the great spiritualizers of society because they bind man and man so close together . . . bringing the day when every man will be my neighbor . . . and acts shall be not simply ours but the processes of the great body politic which is God revealed in the universe" (cited in Cook, 1993, p. 31). Cooley, an unreformed idealist who, like Mead, contributed to the nascent field of social psychology, had been writing about communication since his 1894 dissertation, *The Theory of Transportation*. His 1909 *Social Organization* remains one key document of the first era that explicitly theorized communication (see Czitrom, 1982; Peters, 1999b, pp. 184–188 passim).

Contemporaneously with Cooley, Mead turned to *communication* more explicitly in a series of articles beginning in 1909. The term helped him fill in his anti-Cartesian view of a social self fundamentally forged in relationship with others. As Leys (1994) showed, Mead's theory drew on James' writings on the social self, the 1890s revival of Adam Smith's *Theory of Moral Sentiments* and its account of sympathy, and Gabriel Tarde's (1890) *Laws of Imitation*. Against Tarde, Mead argued that society and self grew out of "ceaseless interaction," not imitation—out of communication, a social process that originated in "cooperation, . . . where conduct differed and yet where the act of the one answered to and called out the act of the other" (Mead, 1909/1964, pp. 98, 101).[7]

During the next several years, Mead developed his social-self concept and added key notions of *roles* and *taking the attitude of the other*. These influenced symbolic interactionism and shaped both Burke's dramatism and Habermas' theory of communicative action and discourse ethics. In "The Social Self" Mead (1913/1964) called thought "an inner conversation" generated developmentally as children internalized the dramatic stage of actor and accompanying chorus (pp. 146–147). By 1922, he wrote of a "generalized other," whereby the individual addresses himself from the perspective of the whole group—a stance that opens out into a moral and social universalism (Mead, 1922/1964, pp. 245–246; see also 1927/1964, pp. 312–313; 1934/1962, pp. 152–164). In short, Mead tied social communication back to internalized voices and conversations. Out of that, he generated principles of cooperation, group identification, and moral life.

---

[7]For good discussions of Mead's thought and its development in this period, see Joas (1985) and Cook (1991, 1993, chap. 4). For Mead's relation to symbolic interactionism, see Blumer (1969) and Maines and Couch (1988).

Although Mead is often considered to have followed Dewey's intellectual lead, that flow was reversed with regard to the concept of communication. Dewey wrote intermittently about communication from the mid-1890s, but his first extended treatment of the idea did not occur until 1916, seven years after Mead's had begun serious treatment of it. At the time, Dewey was 12 years out from leaving Chicago and Mead for Columbia, and to be sure, he added his own stamp to the concept—*the experiment of communication*, he called it, using his favorite scientific trope.[8] However, when Dewey described communication as a process for getting outside one's experience and "seeing it as another would see it, considering which points of contact it has with the life of another," his views were very much consonant with Mead's (1916/1980, p. 8). Both offered philosophies for Progressive politics in which communication was the stuff of morally authentic communities pursuing common ends and cognizant of themselves as a collective.

Communication was most significant to Dewey during the interwar period, from *Reconstruction in Philosophy* (1920/1948) to *Logic: The Theory of Inquiry* (1938/1986). As he made clear in a critical response to Bertrand Russell, Dewey saw communication as central to the pragmatist doctrine, a doctrine he equated with "a belief that we do not fully know the meaning of anything till it has been imparted, shared, made common property" (1922/1983, p. 308). As Dewey made clear in *Reconstruction*, a series of lectures delivered in Tokyo in 1919, communication formed the foundation of "the modern sense of humanity and democracy" (1920/1948, p. 206). This was the land of social caste, emperor cults, and grand military symbols (Westbrook, 1991, pp. 240–242), and Dewey served as a kind of Progressive intellectual carpetbagger who preached the gospel of communication. For him, communication lay at the heart of knowledge, politics, morals, and social being.

Between 1925 and 1934, Dewey published four significant books that extended this project and added an aesthetic dimension. In *Experience and Nature* (1925/1981), he sometimes waxed rhapsodic, "That the fruit of communication should be participation is a wonder by the side of which transubstantiation pales" (p. 132). He also explored there the central issues for cultural studies of communication: communication as a mode of

---

[8]Dewey's account of communication has received much attention. Carey's work in the mid-1970s is key here, especially his essay "Communication and Culture" (1975; reprinted in 1988). He made a strong impression on Daniel Czitrom, then a graduate student, whose *Media and the American Mind* (1982) still offers one of the best accounts of communication in the Progressive Era (see also Czitrom, 1990). Carey wrote two other important essays canonizing Dewey in 1982 and 1986 (1988, chaps. 3–4), and treatments of communication in Dewey followed (see e.g., Peters, 1989a, 1989b, 1999a, 1999b; Carey, 1988; Hardt, 1992; Jensen, 1995; Langsdorf & Smith, 1995; Schudson, 1998; Simonson, 1996).

generating meaning, establishing social order, and creating human experience, including aesthetic experience. *The Public and Its Problems* (1927/ 1984) responded to Walter Lippmann's *Public Opinion* (1922/1997). It made communication a central component of democratic life, with "the winged words of conversation" giving breath to newspaper discourse in an early version of the two-step flow.[9] *Art as Experience* (1934/1987) offered a democratic aesthetic theory and argued that all human activity could be artistic. Art was the consummation of experience and the enactment of social communion. It was an expressive and creative act of communication with the power "to merge different individualities in a common surrender, loyalty and inspiration" (1934/1987, p. 335). Finally, *Logic: The Theory of Inquiry* (1938/1986), the culmination of 40 years work in the theory of knowledge, portrayed inquiry as a social activity for which language, culture, and communication structure conditions of possibility (chap. 3).

REVISING THE TRADITION, EXPANDING THE ANCESTRY

When John Dewey died in 1952 at age 92, his influence was near its low point. Pragmatism always had critics, but by the 1940s it had fewer heavyweight defenders. Writers such as Will Durant and Irwin Edman (Cotkin, 1994) had popularized pragmatism between the wars, and it was still "almost the official philosophy of America," in Henry Commager's (1950) words. Nonetheless, its day seemed to have passed (see Diggins, 1994, chap. 10; Westbrook, 1991, p. 537f). In 1980, Hollinger declared that " 'pragmatism' is a concept most American historians have proved they can get along without" (p. 88; see also Hollinger, 1995; Kloppenberg, 1996). Since Hollinger's appraisal, however, pragmatism has become a concept that neither history nor any other field apparently can get along without.

From philosophy to criticism to literary, political, and legal theory, aesthetics, and communication, pragmatism has enlisted a new corps of defenders and interpreters. Largely absent from this list, however, are the social sciences (Wolfe, 1998). This is one sign of the revival's distance from the first generation. Most revivalists are also long removed from the questions of religious belief that haunted the late Victorians, Darwin rarely echoes through their theories, and defenses of science are generally lacking. However, the tradition continues as this generation calls out the names of the ancestors, quotes from their texts, and embraces the pragmatist mantle.

---

[9]On Dewey and Lippmann, see Carey (1988, chap. 3), Peters (1989a), Lasch (1991, pp. 363–368), Westbrook (1991, pp. 293–306), and Schudson (1998, p. 211f).

The revival is marked by new (and contested) accounts of the tradition—revisionist tales that have broadened the pragmatist ancestry and resuscitated Dewey and others. West's (1989) *American Evasion of Philosophy*, for example, offers a creative genealogy that begins with Ralph Waldo Emerson (a move Cavell [1998] resisted) and includes figures like W. E. B. Du Bois, Lionel Trilling, and C. Wright Mills. For West's teacher, Richard Rorty, meanwhile, Friedrich Nietzsche and Michel Foucault count as pragmatists. Dewey is the patron saint of the tradition for both West and Rorty, although it is a Dewey not everyone recognizes. Indeed, some revisionist accounts have been criticized for "all but making it up" (Hollinger, 1995, pp. 32–33; see also Haack, 1997; Kloppenberg, 1994; Rorty, 1998, chap. 15; Westbrook, 1998).

Revisionist histories have moved pragmatism beyond its traditional origins in the Protestant philosophizing of White Yankee males. They have drawn in writings by African Americans like Du Bois and Alain Locke, women such as Jane Addams and Charlotte Perkins Gilman, the novelist Henry James, and Catholic-born cultural outsiders like Mills and George Santayana. Others can also be included, even Walter Lippmann, sometimes portrayed as Dewey's antipragmatist foil.

The revised pragmatist ancestry provides new openings for communication studies. Du Bois, Locke, and Santayana offer aesthetic theories that supplement Dewey's often plodding accounts, and they point toward and exemplify pragmatist modes of criticism. Locke and Du Bois also theorize race and thus fill a clear void in first-generation pragmatism. They offer insights about intercultural communication and point toward social theories of communication attentive to difference. Meanwhile, Addams' (1911) *Twenty Years at Hull House* should be seen as the founding document in the community studies tradition, while Lippmann's *Public Opinion* should be brought back where it belongs—squarely within the pragmatist fold. There it might remind us that participatory democracy is not the only mode of pragmatist politics. Collectively, this ancestry shows us that pragmatism did not die with Dewey and wait for Rorty to be resuscitated.

Pragmatism, Race, Aesthetics: Du Bois, Locke, and Literary Pragmatism

Both West and Ross Posnock have argued that Du Bois (1868–1963) was a pragmatist. A Harvard PhD, Du Bois remembered in his autobiography that he had been "a devoted follower of James at the time he was developing his pragmatic philosophy." He also credited James with pushing him toward social practice, turning him "back from the lovely but sterile land of philosophic speculation, to the social sciences as the field for gathering and interpreting that body of fact which would apply to my program for the Negro" (cited in West, 1989, p. 139). Posnock maintained that Du Bois' (1903) classic *Souls of Black Folk* and its attendant concept of *double consciousness* were statements of Jamesian pragmatism. To Posnock, Du Bois' work as editor of the NAACP journal, *The Crisis* (1910–1934), was pragmatist sociology. Overall, "Du Bois seems to have internalized pragmatism as a method and style of thinking . . . in good pragmatist fashion [interrogating] the limits of James's thought" (Posnock, 1998a, p. 114; see also Posnock, 1997, 1998b; Rath, 1997). Posnock also sees a pragmatist aesthetic in Du Bois' "Criteria of Negro Art" (1926/1996)—one that "prefigures Dewey's own project a few years later in *Art as Experience*" (1998a, p. 139; see also Hutchinson, 1995, pp. 42–50). Some scholars, however, have found little that is pragmatist in Du Bois' thought (e.g., Gooding-Williams, 1991; Zamir, 1995, pp. 11–16, 153–168).

Posnock and others have also drawn attention to Alain Locke (1886–1954), the African-American philosopher and aesthetician who was a key figure in the Harlem Renaissance of the 1920s and 1930s. Like Du Bois, Locke studied philosophy at Harvard. He was an undergraduate (1904–1907) when James taught there and a doctoral student a decade later. In 1925, Locke edited the important anthology of African-American writings, *The New Negro*, a work that consolidated a literary movement Locke dubbed "the Negro Renaissance." According to Shusterman (1999), the book articulated a historically informed, critically and socially engaged pragmatist aesthetic that "not only anteceded but probably also . . . influenced Dewey's" (p. 97). The anthology includes important essays on the popular arts (jazz, spirituals, drama, folk tales), humanistic community studies (of Harlem and Durham, NC), and cultural theory penned by Locke, Du Bois, and others. It is a rich intellectual and historical source for cultural studies of communication.

Locke's social theory has also been of interest. The political theorist Nancy Fraser (1998; see also Fraser, 1989), for instance, has argued that Locke's 1916 lectures, "Race Contacts and Interracial Relations," not only drew on pragmatism to reject racial essentialism, but also went further. They offered an alternative to "the overly integrative and idealist" social thought of the classical pragmatists. She sees in Locke resources for "an alternative multiculturalism that would integrate a nonessentialist cultural politics with an egalitarian social politics" (pp. 158, 159, 172; see also Harris, 1989). Posnock (1997) meanwhile has discussed Locke in comparison with another of William James' students, Horace Kallen, a friend of Locke's who coined the phrase *cultural pluralism* in his essay "Democracy Versus the Melting Pot" (1915/1996). In Posnock's view, Locke is the true inheritor of the Jamesian mantle, unlike Kallen willing to enter "into what is radical in James's pluralism—skepticism toward identity and the exclusionary bias of concepts" (p. 337).

Posnock's work on Du Bois and Locke are part of a broader excavation of Jamesian pragmatism and its literary influences. In good pluralist fashion, *The Trial of Curiosity* (1991) used the comparative method to discuss Henry James and his brother William, along with other intellectual figures, including George Santayana. In the process, Posnock argued that Henry James was not a fastidious and genteel elitist, but rather an "active, empirical, and pragmatic" thinker. Literary pragmatism is also part of the focus of Posnock's (1998a) *Color and Culture: Black Writers and the Making of the Modern Intellectual.* That book portrayed Du Bois and African-American novelists Zora Neale Hurston and Ralph Ellison as Jamesian pragmatists and deep pluralists who rejected appeals to identity as a grounding social and cultural category (chap. 6). Finally, Poirier (1992) argued that Gertrude Stein, Wallace Stevens, and Robert Frost (all students of James) gave the Jamesian legacy new literary and aesthetic dimensions.

Cambridge Reconsidered: Lippmann and Santayana

Walter Lippmann (1889–1974) also deserves recognition as part of the Jamesian lineage, something not typically done in communication studies. Lippmann is usually read via his differences with Dewey in the 1920s—an encounter sometimes made out to be a founding episode in media studies. Carey (1982) influentially made this argument. He championed Dewey as a democratic pragmatist and argued that Lippmann endorsed "a new priesthood" of experts and redefined "the problem of the press from one of morals and politics to one of epistemology" (pp. 78, 76). Peters (1989a) largely followed this characterization and claimed that Lippmann turned away from "the pragmatic insights available to him" and fell back on old dualisms of fact and fiction, objective and subjective, dualisms leading him to champion "a technocracy of experts" (pp. 208, 209). Without the same disdain for Lippmann, Schudson (1998) recently discussed the difference with Dewey similarly (pp. 211–219; see also Lasch, 1991).

Lippmann (like Schudson, as I argue in a moment) is recognizably pragmatist, and we should read his disagreements with Dewey as part of an ongoing intramural debate within the tradition. Lippmann studied with James at Harvard; the two met when James knocked on Lippmann's door impressed with an article the undergraduate had written in the college newspaper. When Lippmann left Harvard, he was among the first to go from the Ivy League to the rough world of journalism—like Du Bois, a public intellectual engaged in civic affairs. Diggins (1994) and Posnock (1997) demonstrated that Lippmann's first two books, *A Preface to Politics* (1913) and *Drift and Mastery* (1914/1961), maintained James' pragmatist legacy.

Public Opinion also bears clear pragmatist marks. Lippmann's valorization of expertise is simply one variation on the broader turn to science as metaphor or mode of inquiry, which characterized much of first-generation pragmatism, including Dewey's. One could read Lippmann's expertise as Deweyan experimental inquiry with finitude built in; he recognized that we might only practice disciplined investigation on a limited range of topics. Moreover, Lippmann's idea of *stereotypes*, ammunition for Carey's (1988) criticism of him, is recognizably informed by Jamesian psychology: that our stream of sensations are picked out selectively and framed by what we take to be meaningful categories of experience (e.g., James, 1891/1952, chap. 9). For Lippmann (1922/1997), stereotypes are simply the cultural forms that shape and prejudge direct experience—forms that we might modify through scientific discipline or by holding them loosely with tolerance for other competing stereotypes. In other words, stereotypes arguably fit in with a Jamesian pluralistic universe.

Lippmann also studied with George Santayana (1863–1952),[10] James' and Royce's colleague at Harvard and also the subject of revisionist scholarship on first-generation pragmatism. Santayana was a Spanish-born cultural Catholic and a closeted homosexual dandy. He quit his tenured Harvard professorship in 1912 and fled genteel, Calvinist New England to spend his remaining 40 years as a wandering expatriate in Europe (Posnock, 1995). Henry Levinson has shown Santayana's persistent pragmatism—from his five-volume *Life of Reason* (1905/1954), hailed at the time as the first comprehensive presentation of pragmatism, through his later work, explicitly critical of John Dewey and "the pragmatic school" (Levinson, 1992, pp. 3–19, 138–147, passim). Santayana offered a rich alternative vein of pragmatism. He blurred the lines between philosophy and literature and gave criticism and intellectual expression ironic and comic distance from social and civic realms (chaps. 6–7; see also Kuklick, 1977, chap. 19; Posnock, 1991, chap. 8).

Pragmatism and Sociology: Addams, Symbolic Interactionism, and Mills

Besides Cambridge-based pragmatism, the Chicago school has also been revisioned, and scholars have productively drawn attention to the women who helped shape it. Jane Addams (1860–1935) is the key figure. She and Dewey had contact even before he moved to Chicago, and—along with Mead—were involved together in the Settlement House movement. Life-long friends (Dewey dedicated his 1935 *Liberalism and Social Action* "To the Memory of Jane Addams"), they exercised mutually acknowledged intellectual influence on one another: Addams' social practice and thought

---

[10]In 1921, Lippmann wrote, "I love James more than any very great man I ever saw, but increasingly I find Santayana inescapable" (cited in Steel, 1980, p. 21).

helped focus Dewey's and Mead's philosophy (James was also appreciative); pragmatist philosophy came back to guide Hull House; and practice and theory alike influenced the new discipline of sociology (Deegan, 1988, pp. 118–121, 249–254; Mills, 1964, p. 307f; Seigfried 1996a, 1996b, pp. 44–45; 73–79). Like Addams, Charlotte Perkins Gilman has also been nominated as a pragmatist, although here it is less a matter of direct influences and more convergence of her own and Dewey's thought (Upin, 1993; see also Egan, 1989).

Pragmatism has had a varied career in U.S. sociology. Its early influence, especially on Chicago sociology, is clear. Like philosophy, however, by World War II, sociology was establishing new paradigms. Paul Lazarsfeld's more quantitative and behavioral work and Talcott Parsons' grand structural-functional theory took precedence over Chicago-school community studies. Still pragmatism retained a place in *symbolic interactionism*—a term Herbert Blumer invented in 1938 to describe a method indebted to his teacher, Mead (Joas, 1993, pp. 37–38; see also Blumer, 1969; Duncan, 1969; Meltzer, Petras, & Reynolds, 1975).

Moreover, as West (1989) has reminded us, C. Wright Mills maintained pragmatist sensibilities. Like Santayana, Mills was a cultural outsider, raised a Catholic in Baptist Texas, a Southerner on the faculty of Columbia University, a humanist sociologist equally critical of Lazarsfeld's *abstracted empiricism* and Parsons' grand theory (Mills, 1959; see also, Westbrook, 1995). Mills' 1941 dissertation, "A Sociological Account of Pragmatism" (published in 1964 with the misleading title *Sociology and Pragmatism*), examined "the pragmatic movement." It focused on the context of the social institutions where pragmatism flourished: from the Metaphysical Club to a professionalizing educational system to Hull House to the print-based publics for whom Dewey wrote (see also Mills, 1942/1963). This was a pragmatist approach to the sociology of knowledge—one Mills articulated in essays around 1940 (see 1964, pp. 423–468). In those, Mills drew on Mead, Dewey, Peirce, and Kenneth Burke to develop an alternative to Karl Mannheim and Marxian sociologies of knowledge. Mills worried that, because of what the Frankfurt School called the *culture industry*, "the means of effective communication are being expropriated from the intellectual worker"(1944/1963, p. 297). Still as a "neo-Deweyan radical social critic" (West, 1989), Mills found a way to be a pragmatist public intellectual in mid-century.

COMMUNICATION AND THE REVIVALISTS

Even more than the first generation, contemporary pragmatism speaks many dialects. Ray Carney (1994) drew on the doctrine to explore the experimental, independent films of director John Cassevetes, for instance, while Hans Joas (1996) put it in the service of a grand German sociological theory of action. The revival traverses many disciplines, primarily in the humanities. These include philosophy, history, literary theory and criticism, communication studies, political and legal theory, aesthetics, film studies, and religious studies.[11] Revivalists often draw on different first-generation thinkers, and one can usefully distinguish friends of James from friends of Peirce or Mead. Dewey has probably attracted the most attention, but his admirers often see different things in him. To modify a line from William James, there are a variety of Dewey experiences.

Like the first generation, however, contemporary pragmatism has been forged in deep contact with European thought. Instead of Hegel, Darwin, and Kant, this generation has confronted Nietzsche and his descendants, Martin Heidegger, Jacques Derrida, and Foucault (see e.g., Mouffe, 1996). This is especially true of Richard Rorty, who often read the Nietzscheans as halfway pragmatists (e.g., 1982, 1996). Marxian theory has also served as a resource and counterweight: Jurgen Habermas' launching pad was the Frankfurt School, whereas Cornel West's prophetic pragmatism warmly embraces Antonio Gramsci.

Moroever, like their predecessors, revivalists have often privileged tropes of communication. In so doing, they update the intellectual tradition of pragmatism and communication, calling out the names of the ancestors and adopting their dramatic personae in multiple and competing ways. From Habermas' communicatively grounded social and moral theories to Stanley Fish's interpretive communities and West's prophetic pragmatism, scholars from outside communication studies have developed pragmatism in communication-friendly directions. Meanwhile, within communication studies, Carey, Schudson, and Peters have reenacted the intellectual scripts of Dewey, Lippmann, and James.

Before (and Beyond) Rorty: Grand Philosophy and Antitheory

I resist the usual place to begin talking about the pragmatist revival, Richard Rorty's (1979) *Philosophy and the Mirror of Nature*. When he wrote that book, Rorty was just one of several powerful writers and intellects calling

---

[11]For useful, if sometimes selective, accounts of the revival, see Westbrook (1991, p. 537f), Bernstein (1992b), West (1993, chaps. 6, 9), Diggins (1994, chaps. 10–11), Goodman (1995, pp. 1–20), Hollinger and Depew (1995, pp. 227–237), Kloppenberg (1996), Menand (1997, pp. xxv–xxxiv), Dickstein (1998, pp. 1–17), and Cmiel (1999). The preface to Bernstein's (1983) *Beyond Objectivism and Relativism* offered a personal account of Bernstein's intellectual friendships with Rorty and Habermas as well as Hans-Georg Gadamer and Hannah Arendt. The varieties of pragmatism are displayed in three pragmatist collections: Goodman (1995), Menand (1997), and Dickstein (1998).

attention to first-generation pragmatism. *Mirror* was a big crossover hit, so its nomination of Dewey as one of "the three most important philosophers of our century" (p. 5) was significant. Dewey stock had fallen since the 1940s, and Rorty contributed to a Dewey revival that has continued into the present (see e.g., Hickman, 1998). Still Rorty's philosophical pragmatism was one among many in the late 1960s and 1970s.

One part of the revival was spoken with a distinctly German accent. In the 1960s, Karl-Otto Apel and Jurgen Habermas, colleagues at the University of Frankfurt, turned to Peirce and later Mead to aid their philosophical projects. Following a long and uneven history of German encounters with pragmatism (Joas, 1993, chaps. 3–4; see also Peters, 1994), Apel (1981) wrote long introductions to German translations of Peirce's work in 1967 and 1970. Apel was largely appreciative and saw Peirce as "the starting point for a new foundation of the human sciences and their method of 'understanding,' . . . conceiving them as sciences of communicative understanding" (p. 194). Habermas (1968/1971, chaps. 5–6) meanwhile featured Peirce in *Knowledge and Human Interests*.

Habermas has long put communication at the center of his thinking and felt affinities to pragmatism (see chap. 12, this volume). "Like Rorty," Habermas has written, "I have for a long time identified myself with that radical democratic mentality which is present in the best American traditions and articulated in American pragmatism" (cited in Bernstein, 1985, p. 198). His results have been very different from Rorty's, however. *Structural Transformation of the Public Sphere* (1962/1989) was a sociological history. It used Marxian concepts to investigate the question of the modern public so important to Lippmann and Dewey, although he did not explicitly draw on pragmatists. Habermas was writing about communicative action and drawing on Mead by *On the Logic of the Social Sciences* (1967/1988), work that culminated in *Theory of Communicative Action* (1981/1984), where Mead plays a key role (Section V; see also 1998). Habermas relies on Mead's accounts of intersubjectivity and the generalized other in his spin-off work on discourse ethics (e.g., 1990, 1993).

Richard Bernstein has been one of Habermas' most important North American philosophical dialogue partners. He has provided an important link between German encounters with pragmatism and Anglo-American varieties. Bernstein and Rorty studied together at the University of Chicago and Yale, and each has made important philosophical contributions to the Dewey revival. Bernstein's (1966) *John Dewey* began the reclamation project (before that he had edited a book of essays on Peirce). In later books (e.g., 1971) he went as far as anyone in putting pragmatist thought into dialogue with Continental theory. *Beyond Objectivism and Relativism* (1983) refracted pragmatism through hermeneutics (especially Hans-Georg Gadamer) and the Aristotelian-Marxian concepts of praxis (action) and phronesis (practical judgment). This social-democratic pragmatism featured metaphors of dialogue and conversation (an ideal the book followed in is tightly argued encounters with Gadamer, Arendt, Rorty, and Habermas). Like Dewey's pragmatism, it also yoked communication to the idea of democratic community (see also Bernstein, 1998).

Rorty's was then one of several significant interpretations of Dewey and first-generation pragmatism in the late 1960s and 1970s. His *Consequences of Pragmatism* (1982), a collection of essays from the 1970s, continued Rorty's canonization (some would say re-invention) of Dewey—one developed during the past two decades and distinct from the social-democratic pragmatism of Bernstein. Rorty instead used Dewey to defend "postmodernist bourgeois liberalism," a form of life marked by a dichotomy between public and private selves and the modes of communication characteristic to each. In private, individuals are ironists who invent themselves as *strong poets* and entertain doubts about their *final vocabularies* (the terms they use to explain the world). In public, however, they maintain communal ties of solidarity and shared commitment to reducing cruelty. This political project has no ultimate, universal theoretical justification, and philosophy in this world is akin to bourgeois literary conversation (see e.g., Rorty, 1989, chaps. 2–4; 1991, pp. 175–202). Ironist conversation differs from the more sincere dialogue that marks Bernstein's pragmatisms, where a more blurred line exists between private and public communication.

Stanley Fish is often associated with neopragmatism, and he offered another important account of communities and communication. His 1980 *Is There a Text in This Class?* introduced the idea of *interpretive communities* and spawned arguments against theory and for pragmatism in literary studies (e.g., Mailloux, 1995; Mitchell, 1985; see also Gunn, 1992). Fish's (1998) antitheory is linked to his notion of *interpretive communities*, local formations engaged in particular practices of rhetoric and persuasion and guided by *perspicuous meanings* that are "conveyed by public structures of language and image to which you and your peers can confidently point" (p. 419). Practice and interpretation are always local for Fish, and theory, which is general, can never guide it. Indeed, Fish (1998) insisted that "if pragmatism is true, it has nothing to say to us; no politics follows from it or is blocked by it; no morality attaches to it or is enjoined by it" (p. 419). From one angle, Fish's antitheory is a Jamesian defense of pragmata— things in their plurality expressed in the idiom of interpretive communities that resist being subsumed to any grander system of thought or practice.

West's *prophetic pragmatism*, in contrast, uses a religious trope of communication to name a doctrine with explicit public overtones and plenty to say to us politically. Instead of ironists or dialogians, West (1989) championed Gramscian intellectuals and called on critical individuals engaged in "practice that has some potency and effect or makes a difference in the world" (p. 232). West actively embraced religion and "the Jewish and Christian tradition of prophets who brought urgent and compassionate critique to bear on the evils of their day" (p. 233; see also West, 1993). Although West held up Dewey as the greatest figure of the tradition, he offered a pragmatism of prophecy, not conversation. An African-American public intellectual like Du Bois and Locke, West continues a tradition of pragmatism that directly confronts issues of race.

Carey, Schudson, and Peters

Like Bernstein and Rorty, Carey also wrote forcefully about Dewey in the 1970s. His 1975 "A Cultural Approach to Communication" (the lead article in his 1988 collection, *Communication as Culture*) put Dewey's *Experience and Nature* (1925/1981) and *Democracy and Education* (1916) in the service of Carey's classic distinction between communication as transmission and ritual. Dewey is mostly a jumping off point for a distinction that owes less to the pragmatist than to Harold Innis' theory of space- and time-binding media. Still the ritual view can be read as a Catholic extension of the largely Protestant tradition of American pragmatism. Like Bernstein and Rorty, Carey has also championed conversation as a communicative form (e.g., 1982, 1987, 1995) and tied it to Dewey's democratic theory.

Schudson (1997) rejected the *romance of conversation* (p. 307), and, in the process, played Lippmann to Carey's Dewey. At the end of *The Good Citizen*, Schudson (1998) defended the ideal of *monitorial citizens*—people with no single communicative role but rather engaged in a variety of roles. They scan the information environment and practice "environmental surveillance more than information-gathering"; occasionally they write letters or become involved, but "monitorial citizens tend to be defensive rather than proactive" (pp. 310, 311). Lippmann's (1922/1977) *Public Opinion* is often remembered as a technocratic argument for expertise, but he sketched a role for citizens similar to Schudson's: They look to newspapers to *signalize* events, concern themselves with the procedural fairness of public decision making, and occasionally go beyond that monitoring to join voluntary associations (pp. 226, 251–252). Public life involved individuals in a pluralistic array of roles, some of them relatively passive, others more organized and action-oriented, all of them part of a democratic life, like Schudson's, with no single communicative soul.

Joining Schudson and Carey in reviving dramatic personae of the first generation, John Peters recently weighed in as William James. *Speaking into the Air* (Peters, 1999b) is an intellectual history with Jamesian attention to the paranormal: attempted communication with the dead, animals, and extraterrestrial life, which for Peters are not categorically different from more ordinary communication. It also displays a 19th-century breadth of reading and historical imagination: from Jesus and Socrates to Heidegger, Peirce, and Emerson and many others. In Jamesian spirit, Peters (1999b) defended "a pragmatism open to both the uncanny and the practical," one with ample room for "the splendid weirdness of being" as well as "the curious fact of otherness" (pp. 19, 21, 22; see also Peters, 1999a). Dialogue is important, but it holds no privileged place, and what Emerson called *the condition of infinite remoteness* is central to the human condition. Communication does not name a way to eliminate that remoteness, but to live with it as bodily humans, the only way we could.

Pragmatism and the Canons of Communication Studies

If there is a canon in communication studies, it is one that is disputed, argued for, and periodically reinvented. The field is not a discipline in any narrow sense of the word, not one that is governed by common methods, common standards, common focus, or common knowledge. Nor should it be any of these things. The field is rather a set of questions pursued by a sometimes motley assortment of guerrilla bands that raid other disciplines for tools and texts. This pluralism and structural open-endedness are the strength of communication studies and offer it reservoirs for creativity. Unfortunately, these reservoirs are too seldom tapped.

The conditions of our intellectual production are partly established by the texts we read, teach, think with, and write about. The pragmatist revival gives us the opportunity to enrich our practices with a new collection of older texts and classic texts reinterpreted in new light. From the beginning, pragmatism has been about communication, although what *communication* and *pragmatism* mean have always been up for grabs. It is a variegated and rich intellectual tradition. If communication studies is a discipline, it should periodically discipline itself to visit old texts with new eyes, and pragmatism, expansively construed, is a good place to start.[12]

REFERENCES

Addams, J. (1911). *Twenty years at Hull-house, with autobiographical notes.* Chautauqua, NY: Chautauqua.
Apel, K.-O. (1981). *Charles S. Peirce: From pragmatism to pragmaticism* (J. M. Krois, Trans.). Amherst: University of Massachusetts Press. (Original work published 1967, 1970)
Bernstein, R. (1966). *John Dewey.* New York: Washington Square Press.

---

[12]The author would like to thank Marilyn Bordwell, Rob MacDougal, Pat Moynagh, John Peters, and Anne Rubenstein for commenting on earlier versions of this chapter.

Bernstein, R. (1983). *Beyond objectivism and relativism: Science, hermeneutics, and praxis.* Philadelphia: University of Pennsylvania Press.

Bernstein, R. (1985). *Habermas and modernity.* Cambridge, MA: MIT Press.

Bernstein, R. (1992b). The resurgence of pragmatism. *Social Research, 59*(4), 813–840.

Bernstein, R. (1998). Community in the pragmatic tradition. In M. Dickstein (Ed.), *The revival of pragmatism.* Durham, NC: Duke University Press.

Blumer, H. (1969). *Symbolic interactionism.* Englewood Cliffs, NJ: Prentice-Hall.

Brent, J. (1993). *Charles Sanders Peirce: A life.* Bloomington: Indiana University Press.

Brint, M., & Weaver, W. (Eds.). (1991). *Pragmatism in law and society.* Boulder, CO: Westview.

Carey, J. (1982). Mass media: The critical view. In *Communication Yearbook V* (pp. 18–33). Beverly Hills, CA: Sage.

Carey, J. (1987). The press and public discourse. *The Center Magazine, 20*(2), 4–32.

Carey, J. (1988). *Communication as culture: Essays on media and society.* Boston: Unwin Hyman.

Carey, J. (1995). The press, public opinion, and public discourse. In T. Glasser & C. Salmon (Eds.), *Public opinion and the communication of consent* (pp. 373–402). New York: Guilford.

Carney, R. (1994). *The films of John Cassavetes: Pragmatism, modernism, and the movies.* Cambridge, England: Cambridge University Press.

Cavell, S. (1998). What's the use of calling Emerson a pragmatist? In M. Dickstein (Ed.), *The revival of pragmatism* (pp. 72–80). Durham, NC: Duke University Press.

Cmiel, K. (1999). Talking it over. *Reviews in American History, 29,* 156–162.

Commager, H. S. (1950). *The American mind.* New Haven, CT: Yale University Press.

Conant, J. (1997). The James/Royce dispute and the development of James's "solution." In R. A. Putnam (Ed.), *The Cambridge companion to William James* (pp. 186–213). Cambridge: Cambridge University Press.

Cook, G. A. (1991). The development of G. H. Mead's social psychology. In M. Aboulafia (Ed.), *Philosophy, social theory, and the thought of George Herbert Mead* (pp. 89–107). Albany: State University of New York Press.

Cook, G. A. (1993). *George Herbert Mead: The making of a social pragmatist.* Urbana: University of Illinois Press.

Cotkin, G. (1994). Middle-ground pragmatists: The popularization of philosophy in American culture. *Journal of the History of Ideas, 55*(2), 283–302.

Coughlan, N. (1973). *Young John Dewey.* Chicago: University of Chicago Press.

Czitrom, D. (1982). *Media and the American mind: From Morse to McLuhan.* Chapel Hill: University of North Carolina Press.

Czitrom, D. (1990). Communication studies as American studies. *American Quarterly, 42*(4), 678–683.

Deegan, M. J. (1988). *Jane Addams and the men of the Chicago School, 1892–1918.* New Brunswick, NJ: Transaction Books.

Dewey, J. (1935). *Liberalism and social action.* New York: Putnam.

Dewey, J. (1948). *Reconstruction in philosophy.* Boston: Beacon Press. (Original work published 1920)

Dewey, J. (1962). From absolutism to experimentalism. In G. P. Adams & W. P. Montague (Eds.), *Contemporary American philosophy* (Vol. 2, pp. 13–27). New York: Russell & Russell. (Original work published 1930)

Dewey, J. (1972). Plan of organization of the university primary school. In *The early works of John Dewey* (Vol. 5, pp. 224–243). Carbondale: Southern Illinois University Press. (Original work published 1895)

Dewey, J. (1976). *The school and society.* In *The middle works of John Dewey* (Vol. 1, pp. 1–109). Carbondale: Southern Illinois University Press. (Original work published 1899)

Dewey, J. (1980). *Democracy and education. The middle works of John Dewey* (Vol. 9). Carbondale: Southern Illinois University Press. (Original work published 1916)

Dewey, J. (1981). *Experience and nature*. In *The later works of John Dewey* (Vol. 1). Carbondale: Southern Illinois University Press. (Original work published 1925)

Dewey, J. (1983). Pragmatic America. In *The middle works of John Dewey* (Vol. 13, pp. 306–310). Carbondale: Southern Illinois University Press. (Original work published 1922)

Dewey, J. (1984). *The public and its problems*. In *The later works of John Dewey* (Vol. 2, pp. 235–372). Carbondale: Southern Illinois University Press. (Original work published 1927)

Dewey, J. (1986). *Logic: The theory of inquiry*. In *The later works of John Dewey* (Vol. 12). Carbondale: Southern Illinois University Press. (Original work published 1938)

Dewey, J. (1987). *Art as experience. The later works of John Dewey* (Vol. 10). Carbondale: Southern Illinois University Press. (Original work published 1934)

Dickstein, M. (Ed.). (1998). *The revival of pragmatism: New essays in social thought, law, and culture*. Durham and London: Duke University Press.

Diggins, J. P. (1994). *The promise of pragmatism: Modernism and the crisis of knowledge and authority*. Chicago: University of Chicago Press.

Du Bois, W. E. B. (1903). *The souls of black folk*. Chicago: A. C. McClurg.

Du Bois, W. E. B. (1996). Criteria of Negro art. In E. J. Sundquist (Ed.), *The Oxford W. E. B. Du Bois reader* (pp. 303–343). New York: Henry Holt. (Original work published 1926)

Duncan, H. D. (1969). *Symbols and social theory*. New York: Oxford University Press.

Eco, U. (1995). Unlimited semeiosis and drift: Pragmaticism vs. "pragmatism." In K. L. Ketner (Ed.), *Peirce and contemporary thought* (pp. 205–221). New York: Fordham University Press.

Egan, M. (1989). Evolutionary theory in the social philosophy of Charlotte Perkins Gilman. *Hypatia, 4*(1), 102–119.

Fish, S. (1980). *Is there a text in this class? The authority of interpretive communities*. Cambridge: Harvard University Press.

Fish, S. (1989). *Doing what comes naturally: Change, rhetoric, and the practice of theory in literary and legal studies*. Durham: Duke University Press.

Fish, S. (1998). Truth and toilets: Pragmatism and the practices of life. In M. Dickstein (Ed.), *The revival of pragmatism* (pp. 418–433). Durham, NC: Duke University Press.

Fraser, N. (1989). *Unruly practices: Power, discourse and gender in contemporary social theory*. Minneapolis: University of Minnesota Press.

Fraser, N. (1998). Another pragmatism: Alain Locke, Critical "Race" Theory, and the politics of culture. In M. Dickstein (Ed.), *The revival of pragmatism* (pp. 157–175). Durham, NC: Duke University Press.

Gooding-Williams, R. (1991). Evading narrative myth, evading prophetic pragmatism: Cornel West's The American evasion of philosophy. *Massachusetts Review*, pp. 517–542.

Goodman, R. B. (1995). *Pragmatism: A contemporary reader*. New York: Routledge.

Grey, T. C. (1989). Holmes and legal pragmatism. *Stanford Law Review, 41*(4), 787–970.

Gunn, G. (1992). *Thinking across the American grain: Ideology, intellect, and the new pragmatism*. Chicago: University of Chicago Press.

Haack, S. (1997). "We Pragmatists . . .": Peirce and Rorty in conversation. *Partisan Review 1*(Winter), 91–107.

Habermas, J. (1971). *Knowledge and human interests*. Boston: Beacon Press. (Original German work published 1968)

Habermas, J. (1984). *Theory of communicative action*. Boston: Beacon Press. (Original German work published 1981)

Habermas, J. (1988). *On the logic of the social sciences*. Cambridge: MIT Press. (Original German work published 1967)

Habermas, J. (1989). *The structural transformation of the public sphere: An inquiry into a category of bourgeois society*. Cambridge: MIT Press. (Original German work published 1962)

Habermas, J. (1990). *Moral consciousness and communicative action*. Cambridge, MA: MIT Press.

Habermas, J. (1993). *Justification and application: Remarks on discourse ethics*. Cambridge: MIT Press.

Habermas, J. (1995). Peirce and communication. In K. L. Ketner (Ed.), *Peirce and contemporary thought* (pp. 243–266). New York: Fordham University Press.

Habermas, J. (1998). *On the pragmatics of communication*. Cambridge, MA: MIT Press.

Hardt, H. (1992). *Critical communication studies: Communication, history, and theory in America*. London and New York: Routledge.

Harris, L. (Ed.). (1989). *The philosophy of Alain Locke: Harlem Renaissance and beyond*. Philadelphia: Temple University Press.

Hickman, L. A. (1998). *Reading Dewey: Interpretations for a postmodern generation*. Bloomington: Indiana University Press.

Hollinger, D. (1980). The problem of pragmatism in American history. *Journal of American History, 67*(1), 88–107.

Hollinger, D. (1995). The problem of pragmatism in American history: A look back and a look ahead. In R. Hollinger & D. Depew (Eds.), *Pragmatism: From progressivism to postmodernism* (pp. 19–37). Westport, CT: Praeger.

Hollinger, R., & Depew, D. (1995). *Pragmatism: From progressivism to postmodernism*. Westport, CT: Praeger.

Hookway, C. (1985). *Peirce*. London and New York: Routledge.

Hookway, C. (1997). Logical principles and philosophical attitudes: Peirce's response to James's pragmatism. In R. A. Putnam (Ed.), *The Cambridge companion to William James* (pp. 145–165). Cambridge: Cambridge University Press.

Hoopes, J. (1991). *Peirce on signs: Writings on semiotic by Charles Sanders Peirce*. Chapel Hill: University of North Carolina Press.

Hutchinson, G. (1995). *The Harlem Renaissance in black and white*. Cambridge, MA: Harvard University Press.

James, W. (1952). *The principles of psychology*. Chicago: Encylopedia Brittanica. (Original work published 1891)

James, W. (1981). *Pragmatism*. Indianapolis: Hackett. (Original work published 1907)

James, W. (1987). The Ph.D. Octopus. In *Writings 1902–1910* (pp. 1111–1118). New York: Library of America. (Original work published 1903)

James, W. (1987). The pragmatist account of truth and its misunderstandings. In B. Kuklick (Ed.), *Writings 1902–1910* (pp. 918–936). New York: Library of America. (Original work published 1908)

James, W. (1890). *The principles of psychology*. Chicago: Encyclopedia Britannica.

James, W. (1992). Philosophical conceptions and practical results. In *Writings 1878–1899* (pp. 1077–1097). New York: Library of America. (Original work published 1898)

Jensen, J. (1995). Questioning the social powers of art: Toward a pragmatic aesthetics. *Critical Studies in Mass Communication, 12*(4), 365–379.

Joas, H. (1985). *G. H. Mead: A contemporary re-examination of his thought*. Cambridge, MA: MIT Press.

Joas, H. (1991). Mead's position in intellectual history and his early philosophical writings. In M. Aboulafia (Ed.), *Philosophy, social theory, and the thought of George Herbert Mead* (pp. 57–86). Albany: State University of New York Press.

Joas, H. (1993). *Pragmatism and social theory*. Chicago: University of Chicago Press.

Joas, H. (1996). *The creativity of action*. Chicago: University of Chicago Press.

Kallen, H. (1996). Democracy versus the melting-pot: A study of American nationality. In W. Sollors (Ed.), *Theories of ethnicity: A classical reader* (pp. 67–92). New York: New York University Press.

Kloppenberg, J. (1994). Democracy and disenchantment: From Weber and Dewey to Habermas and Rorty. In D. Ross (Ed.), *Modernist impulses in the social sciences, 1870–1930* (pp. 69–90). Baltimore: Johns Hopkins University Press.

Kloppenberg, J. (1996). Pragmatism: An old name for some new ways of thinking? *Journal of American History, 83*(1), 100–138.

Kuklick, B. (1977). *The rise of American philosophy: Cambridge, Massachusetts, 1860–1930.* New Haven: Yale University Press.

Kuklick, B. (1985). *Churchmen and philosophers: From Jonathan Edwards to John Dewey.* New Haven, CT: Yale University Press.

Langsdorf, L., & Smith, A. (Eds.). (1995). *Recovering pragmatism's voice: The classical tradition, Rorty, and the philosophy of communication.* Albany: State University of New York Press.

Lasch, C. (1991). *The true and only heaven: Progress and its critics.* New York: Norton.

Levinson, H. (1992). *Santayana, pragmatism, and the spiritual life.* Chapel Hill: University of North Carolina Press.

Leys, R. (1994). Mead's voices: Imitation as foundation; or, the struggle against mimesis. In D. Ross (Ed.), *Modernist impulses in the human sciences, 1870–1930* (pp. 210–235). Baltimore: Johns Hopkins University Press.

Lippmann, W. (1913). *A preface to politics.* New York: M. Kennerly.

Lippmann, W. (1961). *Drift and mastery: An attempt to diagnose the current unrest.* Englewood Cliffs, NJ: Prentice-Hall. (Original work published 1914)

Lippmann, W. (1997). *Public opinion.* New York: The Free Press. (Original work published 1922)

Liszka, J. J. (1996). *A general introduction to the semeiotic of Charles Sanders Peirce.* Bloomington: University of Indiana Press.

Locke, A. (1925). *The new negro: An interpretation.* New York: Albert & Charles Boni.

Lovejoy, A. O. (1908). The thirteen pragmatisms. *Journal of Philosophy, V,* 1–12, 29–39.

Lyne, J. (1980). Rhetoric and semiotic in C. S. Peirce. *Quarterly Journal of Speech, 66,* 155–168.

Mailloux, S. (Ed.). (1995). *Rhetoric, sophistry, pragmatism.* Cambridge: Cambridge University Press.

Maines, D. R., & Couch, C. J. (1988). *Communication and social structure.* Springfield, IL: Charles Thomas.

McDermott, J. J. (1986). The promethean self and community in the philosophy of William James. In *Streams of experience: Reflections on the history and philosophy of American culture* (pp. 44–58). Amherst: University of Massachusetts Press.

Mead, G. H. (1962). *Mind, self, and society.* Chicago: University of Chicago Press. (Original work published 1934)

Mead, G. H. (1964). Social psychology as counterpart to physiological psychology. In *Selected writings* (pp. 94–104). New York: Bobbs Merrill. (Original work published 1909)

Mead, G. H. (1964). The social self. In *Selected writings* (pp. 142–149). New York: Bobbs Merrill. (Original work published 1913)

Mead, G. H. (1964). A behavioristic account of the significant symbol. In *Selected writings* (pp. 240–247). New York: Bobbs Merrill. (Original work published 1922)

Mead, G. H. (1964). The objective reality of perspectives. In *Selected writings* (pp. 306–319). New York: Bobbs Merrill. (Original work published 1927)

Mead, G. H. (1964). The philosophies of Royce, James, and Dewey in their American setting. In *Selected writings* (pp. 371–391). New York: Bobbs Merrill. (Original work published 1930)

Meltzer, B. N., Petras, J. W., & Reynolds, L. T. (1975). *Symbolic interactionism: Genesis, varieties, and criticism.* London: Routledge & Kegan Paul.

Menand, L. (1997). *Pragmatism: A reader.* New York: Vintage.

Mills, C. W. (1959). *The sociological imagination.* London: Oxford University Press.

Mills, C. W. (1963). Pragmatism, politics, and religion. In *Power, politics, and people* (pp. 159–169). New York: Oxford University Press. (Original work published 1942)

Mills, C. W. (1963). The social role of the intellectual. In *Power, politics, and people* (pp. 292–304). New York: Oxford University Press. (Original work published 1944)

Mills, C. W. (1964). *Sociology and pragmatism: The higher learning in America*. New York: Oxford University Press.

Mitchell, W. J. T. (Ed.). (1985). *Against theory: Literary studies and the new pragmatism*. Chicago: University of Chicago Press.

Mouffe, C. (Ed.). (1996). *Deconstruction and pragmatism*. London: Routledge.

Peirce, C. S. (1906). Pragmatism in retrospect:•\ last formulation. In J. Buchler (Ed.), *Philosophical writings of Peirce* (pp. 269–289). New York: Dover.

Peirce, C. S. (1955). Some consequences of four incapacities. In J. Buchler (Ed.), *Philosophical writings of Peirce* (pp. 228–250). New York: Dover. (Original work published 1868)

Peirce, C. S. (1955a). How to make our ideas clear. In J. Buchler (Ed.), *Philosophical writings of Peirce* (pp. 23–41). New York: Dover. (Original work published 1878)

Peirce, C. S. (1955b). The doctrine of chances. In J. Buchler (Ed.), *Philosophical writings of Peirce* (pp. 157–164). New York: Dover. (Original work published 1878)

Peirce, C. S. (1955). Evolutionary love. In J. Buchler (Ed.), *Philosophical writings of Peirce* (pp. 361–374). New York: Dover. (Original work published 1893)

Peirce, C. S. (1955). Logic as semiotic: The theory of signs. In J. Buchler (Ed.), *Philosophical writings of Peirce* (pp. 98–119). New York: Dover. (Original work published 1897)

Peirce, C. S. (1991). On the nature of signs. In J. Hoopes (Ed.), *Peirce on signs* (pp. 141–143). Chapel Hill: University of North Carolina Press. (Original work published 1873)

Peters, J. D. (1989a). Democracy and mass communication theory: Dewey, Lippmann, Lazarsfeld. *Communication, 11*, 199–220.

Peters, J. D. (1989b). Satan and savior: Mass communication in progressive thought. *Critical Studies in Mass Communication, 6*, 247–263.

Peters, J. D. (1994). The curious reception of pragmatism examined—and exemplified. *Reviews in American History, 22*, 679–684.

Peters, J. D. (1999a). Exile, nomadism, and diaspora: The stakes of mobility in the western canon. In Hamid Naficy (Ed.), *Home, exile, homeland: Film, media, and the politics of place* (pp. 17–41). New York: Routledge.

Peters, J. D. (1999b). *Speaking into the air: A history of the idea of communication*. Chicago: University of Chicago Press.

Poirier, R. (1992). *Poetry and pragmatism*. Cambridge, MA: Harvard University Press.

Posner, R. (Ed.). (1992). *The essential Holmes*. Chicago: University of Chicago Press.

Posnock, R. (1991). *The trial of curiosity: Henry James, William James, and the challenge of modernity*. New York: Oxford University Press.

Posnock, R. (1995). George Santayana. In R. W. Fox & J. Kloppenberg (Eds.), *A companion to American thought* (pp. 611–612). Cambridge, MA: Blackwell.

Posnock, R. (1997). The influence of William James on American culture. In R. A. Putnam (Ed.), *The Cambridge companion to William James* (pp. 322–342). Cambridge: Cambridge University Press.

Posnock, R. (1998a). *Color and culture: Black writers and the making of the modern intellectual*. Cambridge, MA: Harvard University Press.

Posnock, R. (1998b). Going astray, going forward: Du Boisian pragmatism and its lineage. In M. Dickstein (Ed.), *The revival of pragmatism* (pp. 176–189). Durham, NC: Duke University Press.

Rath, R. C. (1997). Echo and Narcissus: The afrocentric pragmatism of W. E. B. DuBois. *Journal of American History, 84*(2), 461–495.

Rockefeller, S. (1991). *John Dewey: Religious faith and democratic humanism*. New York: Columbia University Press.

Rockefeller, S. (1998). Dewey's philosophy of religious experience. In L. A. Hickman (Ed.), *Reading Dewey: Interpretations for a postmodern generation* (pp. 124–148). Bloomington: University of Indiana Press.

Rorty, R. (1979). *Philosophy and the mirror of nature*. Princeton: Princeton University Press.

Rorty, R. (1982). *Consequences of pragmatism*. Minneapolis: University of Minnesota Press.

Rorty, R. (1989). *Contingency, irony, and solidarity*. Cambridge: Cambridge University Press.

Rorty, R. (1991). *Objectivity, relativism, and truth*. Cambridge: Cambridge University Press.

Rorty, R. (1996). *Truth and progress: Philosophical papers, Volume 3*. Cambridge: Cambridge University Press.

Royce, J. (1968). *The problem of Christianity*. Chicago: University of Chicago Press. (Original work published 1918)

Ryan, A. (1995). *John Dewey and the high tide of American liberalism*. New York: Norton.

Santayana, G. (1954). *The life of reason; the phases of human progress*. New York: Scribner. (Original work published 1905)

Schudson, M. (1997). Why conversation is not the soul of democracy. *Critical Studies in Mass Communication, 14*, 297–309.

Schudson, M. (1998). *The good citizen: A history of American civic life*. New York: The Free Press.

Seigfried, C. H. (Ed.). (1996a). Feminism and pragmatism special issue. *Hypatia, 8*(2).

Seigfried, C. H. (1996b). *Pragmatism and feminism: Reweaving the social fabric*. Chicago: University of Chicago Press.

Shalin, D. N. (1991). G. H. Mead, socialism, and the progressive agenda. In M. Aboulafia (Ed.), *Philosophy, social theory, and the thought of George Herbert Mead* (pp. 21–56). Albany: State University of New York Press.

Shusterman, R. (1999). Pragmatist aesthetics: Roots and radicalism. In L. Harris (Ed.), *The critical pragmatism of Alain Locke* (pp. 97–110). New York: Rowman & Littlefield.

Simonson, P. (1996). Dreams of democratic togetherness: Communication hope from Cooley to Katz. *Critical Studies in Mass Communication, 13*, 324–342.

Sprigge, T. L. S. (1997). Logical principles and philosophical attitudes: Peirce's response to James' pragmatism. In R. A. Putnam (Ed.), *The Cambridge companion to William James* (pp. 125–144). Cambridge: Cambridge University Press.

Steel, R. (1980). *Walter Lippmann and the American century*. Boston: Little, Brown.

Upin, J. (1993). Charlotte Perkins Gilman: Instrumentalism beyond Dewey. *Hypatia, 8*(2), 38–63.

West, C. (1989). *The American evasion of philosophy: A genealogy of pragmatism*. Madison: University of Wisconsin Press.

West, C. (1993). *Keeping faith: Philosophy and race in America*. New York: Routledge.

Westbrook, R. B. (1991). *John Dewey and American democracy*. Ithaca: Cornell University Press.

Westbrook, R. B. (1995). C. Wright Mills. In R. W. Fox & J. Kloppenberg (Eds.), *A companion to American thought* (pp. 458–460). Cambridge, MA: Blackwell.

Westbrook, R. B. (1998). Pragmatism and democracy: Reconstructing the logic of John Dewey's faith. In M. Dickstein (Ed.), *The revival of pragmatism* (pp. 128–140). Durham: Duke University Press.

Wiener, P. (1949). *Evolution and the founders of pragmatism*. Cambridge: Harvard University Press.

Wolfe, A. (1998). The missing pragmatic revival in American social science. In M. Dickstein (Ed.), *The revival of pragmatism* (pp. 199–206). Durham: Duke University Press.

Zamir, S. (1995). *Dark voices: W. E. B. Du Bois and American thought, 1888–1903*. Chicago: University of Chicago Press.

Chapter 2

Pragmatism as a Way of Inquiring With Special Reference to a Theory of Communication and the General Form of Pragmatic Social Theory

Vernon E. Cronen
John Chetro-Szivos
Fitchburg State College

Pragmatism places communication at the center of human concerns. In 1916, John Dewey wrote, "Society not only continues to exist by transmission, by communication, but may be fairly said to exist in transmission, in communication" (1916/1944, p. 4). This chapter concerns inquiry and, for pragmatism, human inquiry is a communication process. It also discusses the ways that pragmatist ideas about inquiry can inform communication research, theory, and practice. Because of our long involvement with the tradition of pragmatism, we cannot easily sort out its most important aspects for us. We are reminded of a story set in the mythical town of Chelm, where all inhabitants are either crazy or fools.

> Early one morning a resident of Chelm frantically knocked at the door of the rabbi's house. "Rabbi, you must help me!" The rabbi, half-asleep, let the man in. "Rabbi! My house has caught fire! Everything I own is in there, money, furniture, food for the winter, clothing, everything! What should I do?" Groggy with sleep, the rabbi said: "Hmmm, a fire? Let me remember what to do. Ah, take a stick and draw a circle around your house. Pace off four paces beyond that and draw another circle around the first." "Yes rabbi, what else?" "Next," said the rabbi, "Stand outside the outer circle looking toward Jerusalem and pray." "Thank you rabbi," said the man as he rushed out. The rabbi, now more awake, opened the door of his house and shouted to the man, "Wait! I think there is one more thing. What was it? Oh, yes, water! That's what I forgot! Before you draw the circles and pray, put lots and lots of water on the fire until it goes out!

What follows is our effort to remember the water as we consider what aspects of American pragmatic thought have most importantly informed our work. That work goes under the title of Coordinated Management of Meaning (CMM), a theory of communication (Cronen, 1994, 1995a; Cronen, Pearce, & Xi, 1989/1990; Pearce, 1989; Pearce & Cronen, 1980). In this chapter, we use this theory to illustrate how ideas from the tradition of American pragmatism were given form in theoretical and practical work.

We do not claim that CMM is the only theory of communication that could be developed in the tradition of pragmatism. Certainly that tradition informs other work in communication, as shown in this volume. We focus on CMM for two reasons. First, we illustrate how ideas from the pragmatic tradition can take specific form in a theory of communication. Second, we offer, for those already familiar with CMM, a more complete account of its theoretical background. Readers can examine our account of pragmatism and inquiry for its own sake, however, without concern for CMM.

Although no consensus exists concerning which authors to include in the tradition of philosophical pragmatism, those with the most importance for us include Charles Sanders Peirce, William James, John Dewey, and George Herbert Mead.[1] In this chapter, we draw primarily from their writings. Even within this limited set of contributors, the reader with a background in pragmatism can infer from what we have said here that we agree with Dewey, who described pragmatism primarily as a view of inquiry rather than as a theory of truth.

The chapter features three parts. In the first, we develop claims about the natural and social world into which we inquire. There we emphasize pragmatism's deep debt to evolutionary biology. In the second part, we discuss pragmatism's naturalized view of inquiry and the position of the inquirer in the process of inquiry. Finally, we extend the pragmatic tradition with our notion of Practical Social Theory.

THE NATURAL AND THE SOCIAL WORLD

In an exchange, Dewey (1939, 1941) rejected Russell's (1939, 1940) demand that he provide an account of the world prior to inquiry. Russell insisted that Dewey offer a metaphysical argument as a foundation for the

---

[1]Gunn (1987), for example, includes Kenneth Burke in the pragmatist pantheon, although Burke did not claim to be a pragmatist, to our knowledge. Self-proclaimed pragmatist Richard Rorty, although clearly in the tradition as a critic of foundationalist/structuralist philosophy, has little in common with Dewey's development of intellectual tools for inquiry. Thus, we think of his contributions as related but not central to the tradition. See especially his *Contingency, Irony and Solidarity* (1989).

ideas about inquiry developed in Dewey's (1938) *Logic: The Theory of Inquiry*. Dewey refused, saying that it is absurd to demand an account of reality prior to inquiry into it. As Burke (1994) said, however, Dewey did provide important statements about the world prior to any particular episode of inquiry. That account was not metaphysical, however. Instead his naturalized description rejected a firm line between philosophy and science.[2] Before discussing Dewey's ideas about formal processes of inquiry, we need to make some points about the natural and social world into which a communication researcher or practitioner inquires.

Realism and Social Construction

The inquirer in the pragmatic tradition is a realist but not an objectivist. Dewey (1922) said that philosophy and psychology too often treat social creations as natural objects. For example, he criticized the treatment of women and mental illness in Freudian psychology this way:

> . . . it flagrantly exhibits both the consequences of artificial simplification and the transformation of social results into psychic causes. Writers, usually male, hold forth on the psychology of woman, as if they were dealing with a Platonic universal entity, although they habitually treat men as individuals. . . . They treat phenomena that are peculiarly symptoms of the West at the present time as if they were the necessary effects of fixed native impulses of human nature. Romantic love as it exists today, with all the varying perturbations it occasions, is definitely a sign of specific historic conditions as are big battle ships with turbines, internal combustion engines, and electrically driven machines. (p. 153)

In the same book, however, Dewey acknowledged that impulses possessed by all persons enter into social creations. Without human physiology, including our hormonal systems, there would be no romantic love,

---

[2]Although Santayana (1925) correctly described naturalistic metaphysics as a contradiction in terms, Dewey's position makes sense. Dewey (1920/1948) described metaphysics as a mistaken path in Western philosophy. In the context of his debate with Santayana, he used naturalistic metaphysics to say that the only terms concerning human action that can ever act as foundational will emerge from inquiry into the existence of any cross-cultural, transhistorical features of embodied human life in this world. For example, it may be claimed that certain conditions of suffering—such as the experience of pain or the sadness over losing a loved one—have some common features across culture and time, although culture and institutions mark these experiences. Dewey said that a quest for fundamentals in experience should not be a matter of reasoning out universal terms needed for a complete, coherent account of the world, but rather an investigation. It would examine the "large and constant features of human sufferings, enjoyments, trials, failures and successes together with the institutions of art, science, technology, politics, and religion which mark them, communicate genuine features of the world within which man lives" (Dewey, 1927/1988, p. 75).

courtly love, impulsive love, Korean forms of marital bonding after marriage, or any other kind. Our physiology does not determine the kinds of love we may create, but we cannot account for love without it.

The inquirer with a pragmatist orientation to communication can neither ignore the physicality of the world nor reduce social phenomena to physical or psychical causes. In CMM theory, we do not follow extreme social constructionism and treat cancer, for example, as an action chosen to create particular relationships in a family.[3] Nor do we follow Kenneth Gergen's idea that the effects of modern medicine are just a set of stories no better than faith healing. We do explore the stories that can be constructed about disease and treatment. In Dewey's (1938) conception of inquiry, a researcher creates a fact during inquiry. However, he (1910) clearly said that facts are neither wholly objective, untouched by human minds, nor entirely a matter of linguistic creation outside our connections to the material world (pp. 10–13).

Continuity and the Rejection of Dualism

In evolutionary–biological terms, the distinction between one species of living things and another is a branching process. Thus, all forms of life possess commonality as well as difference. Advances in contemporary evolutionary biology have shown that life is not a substance that differs from the other materials of the world. Rather, it resulted from chemical combinations that occurred when the earth's atmosphere was different than now. Margulis (1998) closed the gap between bacterial and nucleated forms of life, showing nucleated cells to be an outcome of parasitic relationships among the former. Darwin argued that morality—a natural possibility created when creatures that survive by cooperation evolve a sufficiently complex brain—is continuous with evolution.

Like James before him, Dewey saw clearly the implications of moving from duality to continuity as a way of understanding. Earlier we discussed Dewey's position that experience is neither a purely psychical matter nor the simple recording of brute nature on the mind. Dewey recognized that this original Cartesian dualism of outer objects of knowledge and inner thought entailed a whole range of other dualisms. These include pitting theory against practice, individuality against sociality, researcher against practitioner, intellect against emotion, and the artistic against the instrumental.

Replacing dualistic thinking with an evolutionary–pragmatic sensibility takes us to a different way of making distinctions. The latter has several

---

[3]We have heard therapists do this. Nonetheless, systemic therapists have largely moved away from this extreme position. In one case some years ago, a client said: "I see. I got cancer so that I could reduce the dependence of my family on me."

important features. First, it recognizes that a distinction arises from the intersection of the researcher's or practitioner's experience, methods, and the phenomena studied. No distinction is wholly objective or entirely psychical. Second, it considers both continuities and differences in any act of distinguishing. For example, one can distinguish a chimp and a human, but we do have 98% of our DNA in common. Similarly, we can distinguish one person's conversational comments from those of another. We need not lose sight, however, of how one utterance contributes to the formation of the next utterance. If one makes evolutionary–pragmatic distinctions, one never neglects the temporal dimension of actions. Indeed, it is intrinsic to any distinction made. An event is not simply located at a static point along a ribbon of time, nor are temporal continuities limited to how the past creates the present. A distinguished event or object projects into the future, opening and closing possibilities for both the observer and the observed (James, 1912/1996).

Rejection of dualism is highly important to CMM because it opens a number of new ways to understand and act into social activity. For example, we do not separate the artistic and instrumental dimensions of social life into different domains. Instead, following Dewey (1934a), we look for the aesthetic dimension of everyday life. When our work focuses on a personal relationship, we are concerned with the ability of the couple to create beautiful moments together (Cronen, 1995a). In an organization, for example, we examine the opportunities that employees have to co-construct moments of excitement during work and moments when outcomes and joint actions attain an aesthetic fit. Dewey (1938) aptly identified the humdrum, rather than the aesthetic, as the enemy of science.

Persons, Selves, and Communication

Modern philosophical dualism originated in Descartes' notion that mind and body consist of different substances. Pragmatists reject this explicitly. They offer no place for mind, except as a summary term for what human brains do. Pragmatism also rejects the separation of thinking and acting. Instead, thinking is an aspect of action. In solitude, it amounts to a kind of action. We do not think and then do. After thinking in solitude, we then may engage in another action in which thinking is continuous with various body movements.

Humans are special kinds of creatures in many ways. Like certain other species, we depend on cooperation for survival. We do not exist as individual beings and then try to figure out how to communicate. The species would not have survived that way (Dewey, 1925/1958). We survive by interacting, and we have a special way of doing that using language. Thus, we can form distinctive kinds of association called *community*.

As humans, our specific kind of embodiment provides certain possibilities and closes off others under particular circumstances. Embodiment, however, does not determine the kinds of social selves we will be. That, Dewey (1916/1944, 1922, 1925/1958, 1934b) argued, emerges from communication. Individuality is never ignored; it is recognized as a wonderful social achievement. Dewey (1934b) worried that participation in particular kinds of institutional life can result in uniformity and a reduced range of interests and sympathies.

Mead's (1934) best known work—*Mind, Self, and Society*—extended the pragmatist point of view. He gave more explicit emphasis to the detailed, temporal process of gesture exchange from which selfhood continually forms. His "I" and "me" distinction avoided the paradox of self-consciousness created by what Wittgenstein might call the *language game* of individual psychology. If we think of consciousness in traditional ways, we encounter a problem. How can the self know the self if the self that knows is the same self as the object of knowing? Mead's differentiation of the "I" and "me" comes from the view that knowing is a kind of acting. To say "I know x" is not to posit an internal eye that must examine itself. Rather, in Mead's work, the pronoun "I" refers to an embodied being actively doing something. "I know" is an avowal, not a report (Harré, 1984). That "I" uses past experience in the creation of new experience with others. The new experience is formed not only by past experience, but also by the conditions created by the other. Thus, "I" can tell about the adventures, successes, desires, and sorrows that are "me" stories. This move wonderfully demystifies the process. To tell a story about ourselves is very much like telling a story about anything else. From our experience in the world, we learn how to tell such stories and use this ability in communication.

Cronen and Pearce (1989/1990) further explained the use CMM makes of Mead's ideas about the self. CMM provides a way to examine the communication patterns in which selfhood is formed. This takes us away form essentializing individuality. It also opens a variety of cultural questions about communication patterns, especially with children who are learning how to tell identity stories. The contributions of Dewey and Mead also lead us to think about the importance of institutional life for the existence of individuality. Differences between persons will always exist because no two persons, even identical twins, occupy the same temporal and physical place in patterns of conversation (Cronen, 1995a). Various kinds of differences have to be selected for attention and fostered. If we prize individuality, we cannot take it as something natural. Instead, we must look carefully at the vitality of the processes in which it develops.

CMM extends Mead's work by developing the idea that selfhood stories can be understood by how they are organized as part of one's grammatical ability for a particular moment of action. The authors' recent work for a police department provides one example. Data suggest that supervising officers organized autobiographical stories in important ways around common understandings about authority, honor, respect, and hierarchy. When used at work, these stories of selfhood depended on higher order stories about respect in the department and how top management shows respect. CMM also develops Mead's ideas by providing some detailed ways of examining episodes of what we call *situated identifying*. These express selfhood stories for the self and/or others in real material circumstances (Cronen & Pearce, 1989/1990).

The Connection of Things Natural and Social

In a living system, the logic of functioning evolves with the emergence of new forms of life. That process is coherent but not neatly predictable. Consider the logic by which flowering plants evolved. The dinosaurs that liked certain plants created an opportunity for the evolution of flowers (Gould, 1989). The logic of these developments was created inside the process of evolution. No prior determinant logic led to our rich array of flowering plant, and neither nature nor dinosaurs had any desire to produce them.

Evolutionary biology contributed greatly to pragmatism by introducing the idea of coherence made from within a process—coherence that is neither formal nor deterministic. No truth table can assess the formal acceptability of moves within the evolutionary logic. This understanding enriches the study of communication, moving it away from Aristotle's idea that coherence in human affairs (contingent subject matter) approximates formal logic. CMM theory extends this same idea by treating the logic of action as created in the course of conjoint action. Formal logics can be useful tools for some kinds of inquiry. However, the choice of one or another formal system cannot be justified by a higher order formal procedure, only by the success of its use in action. CMM's heuristic models direct the inquirer to consider moral operators such as *obligatory, legitimate, caused*, and *prohibited* as ways to describe the experience of actors at particular moments of communication. For example, a manager's stories about the performance of a subordinate and her own responsibilities could lead her to treat micromanaging as not merely legitimate, but obligatory. Of course, we are also interested in how the conjoint actions of manager and subordinate reflexively reproduce both the manager's and subordinate's stories.

The Social World as Continuous With the Natural World.   Distinctively human abilities and achievements such as language and culture are not set in opposition to the physical world, but are treated as evolutionary extensions of it. Language and the forms of art and culture that humans can achieve with it require a human brain and the rest of human physiology. *In Democracy and Education*, Dewey (1916/1944) offered an account of human development illustrating how biological inheritance is socially fashioned into ways of living. The social fashioning is not *added on*. We live by means of constructing social ways of living together. Our rational operations are not prewired like those of an insect, nor even so strongly informed by genetics as those of a dog or cat. Our rational abilities, made possible by our brains, grow out of our human activities (Dewey, 1938). It would thus be inconsistent with pragmatism and evolutionary biology to think this justifies biological determinism. To think that way assumes that earlier events fully determine future ones. That is not how evolution works. Past events create future possibilities. Dewey (1910) explicitly rejected what is now called *biological determinism*. The principles needed to explain life processes in a simple organism like a sponge, for example, obviously will not explain how nutrition works in a mammal.

The Coherence of Social Action: Forming Coordinations.   Dewey (1896) introduced the idea of *forming coordination* to replace the reflex-arc. Later Dewey (1922) used the term *habit* to indicate the creation of coherent connections in action. He chose it because habits, unlike instincts, are socially created. These habits need not persist in time, however. Forming coordinations integrate habits. Habits, like Wittgenstein's (1953) *rules*, function normatively, but they can form in one moment of social action and be changed or eliminated in the next. In CMM, we use Wittgenstein's term *rule* because we think tools for analysis that are associated with that term extend Dewey's ideas in useful ways. These ideas all depict rationality as an emergent, unfinished achievement within the process of communication.

In light of what a lioness does when she hunts, consider Dewey's talk about forming coordinations and the *continuity* of action. Imagine that she first observed the prey, then observed the position of the other lionesses, then selected a moment to move, and then responded to each of the prey's moves one by one. If so, she, her cubs, and the rest of the pride would starve. The lioness' way of observing is an aspect of an integrated pattern of coordinations. She observes the way she does because she runs and leaps the way she does. She anticipates how the prey will move and acts in response to the anticipations. As Mead (1938/1972) said, "A perception has in it, therefore, all the elements of an act—the stimulation, the response represented by an attitude, the ultimate experience which flows upon the reaction, represented by the imagery arising out of past reactions" (p. 1). If a perception contains the elements of an act, what can we make of the notion *cause*? Dewey earlier observed that *cause* does not describe a separate event different in quality from an effect. Rather, it is a temporal term useful for describing moments in integrated sequences (Dewey, 1910).[4]

These ideas contain many important implications for communication theory. First, consider the importance of treating the coherence of life as made in communication practices. One way to use this idea is to think about inquiry in social life as connecting with the grammar[5] (Dewey would say *organized habits*) of the participants. By that we mean finding a way to interview and observe that will allow us to find out how those we study construct coherence in action (Cronen & Lang, 1994).[6]

Let us apply this way of thinking to a communication event. When a father responds to his daughter's failure to eat her food, he is creating forming coordinations for dinner table talk with her and other family members. We use the analytic models of CMM to express forming coordinations (see Fig. 2.1). Perhaps this father has a story about his daughter and the possibility that she has an eating disorder. He may also have a story about his obligations as a father. He observes and feels the way he does in the context of these stories. The father also has a pattern of recall focused on what she has eaten in the past. All this relates to how he next speaks to her and what he expects and desires in response.

A forming coordination also guides the daughter. It may include her careful avoidance of eye contact and her anticipation of what will happen next, as well as stories about weight, attractiveness, and her relationship to her father. Together father and daughter constitute each other's ways of feeling, recalling, observing, and responding. The CMM analytic models uniquely work out Dewey's idea of forming coordinations. These coordinations are forming in conjoint action, not static. CMM models refer the researcher not only to the prefigurative and practical force of factors informing an act, but also to the reflexive needs and effects of action on those contextual factors, as shown in Fig. 2.2.

A practitioner using CMM or related systemic ideas does not refer to a universal account of the *mental disease* anorexia in a case like the foregoing. The therapist's goal is to find ways to enter into the grammars of action in ways that allow the family to discover new ways to live. Thus, anorexia is not taken as simply a disease. It does have a general cultural stability, but it must be learned and created in concrete situations. Anorexia is a way of living that is created in action.

---

[4]The reader familiar with family systems will notice how well this idea fits with Bateson's (1972) notion of *punctuation*.

[5]Here we use the term *grammar* as Wittgenstein (1953) did. It is a collective term for the rules persons use to coordinate language games. The rules are not limited to matters of language and include the organization of movement, feeling, and so on.

[6]The reader interested in how interviews are used to enter into the grammar of others guided by CMM should consult Cronen and Lang (1994).

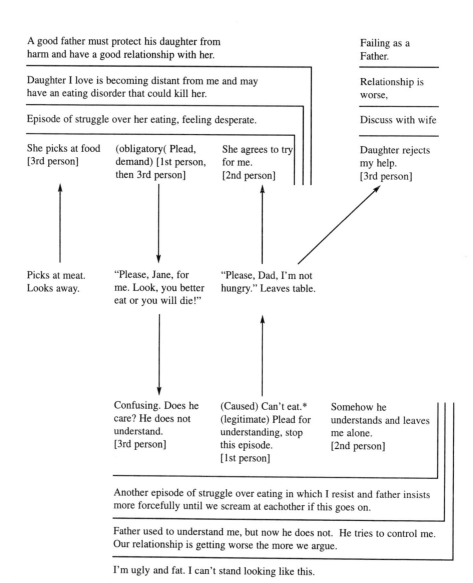

* The moral operator "caused" as used here does not mean daughter's behavior is physiologically determined. It is only reflects her past reports that it is beyond her control.

FIG. 2.1.   Sample CMM heuristic model.

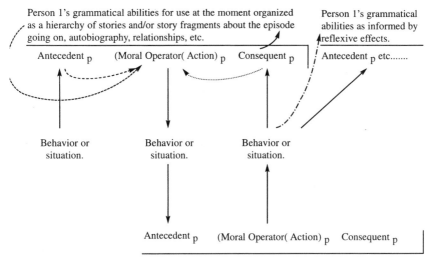

Person 1's grammatical abilities for use at the moment organized as a hierarchy of stories and/or story fragments about the episode going on, autobiography, relationships, etc.

Person 1's grammatical abilities as informed by reflexive effects.

Antecedent ₚ   (Moral Operator(Action) ₚ   Consequent ₚ   Antecedent ₚ etc.......

Behavior or   Behavior or   Behavior or
situation.   situation.   situation.

Antecedent ₚ   (Moral Operator(Action) ₚ   Consequent ₚ

Person 2's grammatical abilities for use at the moment organized as a hierarchy of stories and/or story fragments about the episode going on, autobiography, relationships, etc.

Where:

Antecedent	= Person's account of an event/utterance
p	= Position from which person acts or observes such as 1st person directly engage, 3rd person detached, or 3rd person conduit from another source.
⌐	= Indicates levels of context
Moral Operator	= Indicates person's felt logical force upon own action. In CMM these are: Legitimate, Obligatory, Prohibited, Unknown, Caused, Probable, Blocked, and Random.
Action	= Person's account of what they are doing.
Consequent	= Expected and/or desired response from the other.
----------------	= Prefigurative force. The influence of antecedent and other levels of context on person's actions.
....	= Practical force. The articulation of a person's action to a desired response.
————————	= Reflexive needs. How much a person feels the need for a certain response to change or sustain a contextual story.
—·—·—·—·—	= Reflexive effects. The effects of responses one gets on contextual stories.

FIG. 2.2.   Fundamental features of CMM heuristic models.

The pragmatist orientation to time and the relatedness of events has important implications for interventions into communicative action.[7] CMM's analytic models incorporate a triad of antecedent conditions, action, and consequent as shown in Fig. 2.2. These direct the consultant or therapist to the temporal details of action and to the way one action

---

[7]The kind of interviewing used with CMM is an adaptation of "circular questions." See Tomm (1985) and Cronen and Lang (1995).

informs another. A client typically reports events in this form: "If 'x' happens, then I can/must/must not do 'y.' If I do 'y,' then I expect or desire 'z' to occur." We do not theoretically think of the events x, y, and z as discrete, however.[8] What the client does ("y") evolved along with a way of observing that constitutes "x." Actions and anticipated consequents develop together not as wholly distinct units. Thus, we may recommend interviewing in a way that opens new possibilities by altering the temporal sequence. For example, we might suggest asking, "If you were the sort of father who did not comment about his daughter's eating [action], what would a father like that notice about his daughter's actions at the table [antecedent]?" In an organization, we might ask, "If a manager was not concerned with getting his employee to respond by agreeing immediately [consequent], what would that manager notice about the employee's comments [antecedent]?"[9]

Language as Action, Meaning as Use.   Dewey's ideas about language and meaning developed from those of Peirce and James. Early in the century, Peirce (1905; cited in Burke, 1994) argued that all description is action. He contributed one sort of dynamism to understanding language by offering a semiotic that emphasized how a sign mediates between the interpretant and its object. Peirce's development of a semiotic is more dynamic than Saussure's (1969). For Peirce, *mediation* consisted of a mutually informing relationship in that the sign is not simply understood by an interpretant, but also develops the abilities of that interpreter (Hookway, 1985). James' treatment of language introduced a more strongly temporal dynamic. James (1912/1996) observed that an utterance always points into the future, thus giving all language (indeed, all action) an intentional quality. Further development of meaning as action pointing into the future came with Dewey's treatments of thinking and communication. Dewey's (1911/1933) book, *How We Think*, included his first assertion that meaning is use. He agreed with James about the temporality of meaning. As Dewey said, "meanings are self-moving into new cases" (p. 188). His description of meaning as use in context extended James' position, however. Dewey (1925/1958) explained the implications of his idea that meaning is use in contrast to dualistic ideas. Speech is not the outer expression of an inner state (p. 169). Instead, any inner world of experience must depend on language—a social product (p. 173). Language becomes meaningful

---

[8]CMM heuristic models employ an "if . . . then . . ." symbol as a shorthand for what is thought to be implied in a conversant's report.

[9]In CMM-oriented interviews, we ask "circular questions." For a description, see Tomm (1985) and Cronen and Lang (1995). We want to recognize the influence of the Kensington Consultation Centre, London, and especially Peter Lang, Susan Lang, and Elspeth McAdam for illuminating for us the importance of future-oriented questions. For the use of future-oriented questions in brief therapy, see DeShazer (1985).

when a child and adult use it in conjoint action. Thus, "meaning is not, indeed, a psychic existence; it is primarily a property of experience and secondarily a property of objects" (p. 179).[10]

Treating human association as critical and distinctive, Dewey (1925/1958, pp. 178–179) discussed meaning as dependent on coordinated interaction in a temporal sequence. To fail to understand, he said, is to "fail to come into agreement in action; to misunderstand is to set up action at cross purposes" (p. 179).[11] The ability to engage in such coordination did not result from some miracle of language. It is the evolutionary development of interactive abilities (p. 176).

Dewey (1925/1958) developed the idea that intelligence and intention are created via communication. Rationality is tested and created within interaction processes (p. 188).[12] He observed the way that Person A requests Person B to bring something (e.g., a flower), to which A points (p. 178). B learns a coordinated action—to follow A's gaze and to coordinate with A. The responsive action makes intelligent meaning, not simply the other way around. Here we also see more fully Dewey's rejection of dualism. Language is not a self-contained system of signs distinct from other features of lived experience. Not only are gaze, movement, intention, anticipation, and recall aspects of meaningful action, but so also are feelings and aesthetic consummations. Dewey (1925/1958, 1934a) depicted speech as consummatory as well as instrumental. Mystery and poetry are achievements in the course of interaction, achievements without which human life would have little value.

The pragmatic view of language, meaning, and intelligence makes a dramatic difference in the way we look at communication. We ignore the pseudoproblem of how one mind can know another. Instead we look at the patterns of interaction in front of us to see how meanings are made and remade. All of this is consistent with Wittgenstein's later philosophy. However, Wittgenstein (1953) avoided detailed talk about any aspects of the communication process that are not immediately available for inspection. CMM follows Dewey's (1925/1958) and Mead's (1934) positions. It provides a way to inquire into the organization of persons' abilities as emergent contextualizing stories. Feeling, movement, and recollection are organized in and by these stories.

---

[10]Cognitivists should come to terms with these arguments rather than assuming cognition obviously is something internal. Davidson (1974/1984) argued Dewey's position, which rejects all such ideas as internal mental states and cognitive schemas, more recently and in more detail, but without any significant difference from Dewey's position.

[11]Many readers will at once notice the similarity of this to Wittgenstein's (1953) notion of language games and nonsense.

[12]Wittgenstein came to the same position independently a little less than three decades later. But then, who reads American philosophy?

Communication as a Special Kind of Interaction. For Dewey (1925/ 1958), "everything that exists in as far as it is known and knowable is in interaction with other things" (p. 175). Nonetheless, all interaction is not communication (Dewey, 1934a). Dewey located the difference in the distinctiveness of human discourse. He (1925/1958) first considered language. Of course, he did not make language disjunct from either behavior or thought. Language, however, permits various distinctively human forms of thoughtful action.

Language allows for multiple ways of acting that are more "amenable to management, more permanent, and more accommodating, than events in their first estate" (Dewey, 1925/1958, p. 167). It makes possible reflective thought, in which new ways of understanding and acting can be considered. Even the *dumb pang of an ache* can become an object of contemplation. Although reflective intelligence is important, Dewey warned that "the soliloquy is the product and reflection of converse with others. If we had not talked with others, we should never talk to or with ourselves" (p. 170). Thus, Dewey cautioned against the modern tendency to describe the world on the model of personal soliloquizing.

Dewey's emphasis on language should not deceive us into thinking that communication is limited to language. Dewey believed that communication has two dimensions—one instrumental and the other artistic. Artistic expressions are distinctively human forms of communication because they also provide flexibility in experience, opening new ways to act into the future (Dewey, 1934a).[13] Just as all meaningful language is "self moving into the future" (Dewey, 1925/1958, p. 188), art gives us a "quickened expansion of experience." Art "departs from what is understood and ends in wonder" (Dewey, 1934a, p. 270). Art becomes religion, Dewey (1934a) said, when consummatory experience has far-reaching consequences for our orientation to the world.

The Mosaic View of Connections and Punctuated Equilibria

We have sketched a view of the world as a system in which natural persons create a coherence inside communication processes. Now we need to distinguish this evolutionary view from a holistic one. A distinction is important because much talk describes systemic thinking as holistic. That is problematic. Russell (1939) missed the distinction in his critique of Dewey's (1938) work on inquiry. Russell argued that Dewey's view, based on evolutionary biology, logically required that nothing can change be-

---

[13]The reader interested in the art of emotional creativity should consult the work of Averill and Nunley (1992).

cause every element was held in place by every other element. If change did somehow occur, any small change must affect every other element in the system. Moreover, to understand any aspect would require the analysis of every element of the system. Russell had in mind something akin to Hegelian or Marxist holism. Both differ from Dewey's mature view (Burke, 1994; Westbrook, 1991).[14]

Dewey's ideas about change relied on a principle of biology we today call *mosaic evolution*. According to the mosaic principle, one element of a system may change without seriously affecting other elements for periods of time.[15] Elements are related so that the relatively stable condition of some facilitates variation in another (Gould, 1989). Consider, for example, the earth's atmosphere after the rapid spread of plants. It became a relatively stable aspect of the context in which multiple forms of animal life then evolved. The evolution of oxygen-breathing animals living interdependently with carbon dioxide-breathing plants, each relying on what the other exhales, created the environment our planet had, at least until the industrial age. We do not claim that evolution of new forms of animal life did not affect the atmosphere. Rather, dramatically greater changes occurred in species than in the atmosphere.

The importance of the mosaic principle is better understood in light of another principle, *punctuated equilibria*. According to it, evolutionary change is not constant. Periods of relative equilibrium occur, punctuated by rapid changes. Rapid change seems to happen either when environmental conditions drastically change and/or when members of some species are cut off from their usual contacts. The isolated species move to the periphery. Change there can take place quite rapidly (see Gould, 1989).

Consider what practitioners in the systemic tradition do by moving naturally interacting groups to the periphery of everyday activities and working with them in workshop or clinical setting. This may help open new ways of interacting, whereas the rest of the system the clients belong to remains relatively stable. Afterward the clients will have to create further connections between what they learn with the professional and aspects of everyday life when they are not working in the clinical periphery. That is why systemic professionals, including those who use CMM, do not see a family or individual three or four times a week as a Freudian does. The clients need to find ways to live the changes in the larger world of experience—in the activities of everyday family, organization, or community life.

---

[14]We are much indebted to Burke's treatment of the distinction between holism and Dewey's naturalistic view. The interested reader should consult it.

[15]Dewey (1938) used the term *situation* in a specialized way for those elements of a system that came into a problematic relationship. Other elements in the system made possible that problematic relationship, but those other elements did not determine the situation and did not require change to fix the problem.

They may find that some of their new learning is useful. Inevitably, they will extend and adapt learning in ways that the professional did not anticipate. New learning must be woven into other evolving patterns of new practice.

AN ORIENTATION TO INQUIRY

Dewey (1938) said that formal inquiry is an extension of the natural process of living. In Dewey's view, a garden flower engages in inquiry, which is primarily a matter of achieving the mutual accommodations and adaptations that make life possible. In the morning, the flower still faces west, as it did at sundown. When the sun appears on the horizon, the flower must move to put itself into a better relationship to sunlight. Its roots grow to better link with water and nutrients in the soil. The flower also drops leaves and changes the soil. It emits oxygen, maintaining the atmosphere and thus its sunlight filter. Inquiry, then, involves adjusting the relationships between or among organisms and between organisms and their environment. When a communication scholar inquires into social practices, he or she attempts to attain a better relationship of persons to each other and to their world. In the natural world, the possibilities for adaptation and accommodation are always influenced by evolutionary history. The flower cannot develop feet and accommodate to dry conditions by walking away to a different garden. Human social adaptation can be more rapid, but it too is influenced by the history of developed abilities with which people confront new circumstances.

Dewey's Definition of Inquiry

We inquire into situations. For Dewey, a *situation* involves a breakdown or disturbance in the functioning of certain related elements of a system as it operates in time and space. Because of mosaic organization, disintegration or dysfunction does not necessarily affect all related elements of a living system (Burke, 1994). This well fits CMM and any systemic approach in which an inquirer must decide empirically what persons and episodes to include. Once made, such decisions are not fixed or final. An inquirer may revise them as work proceeds.

Formal theoretical background provides an evolving guide to how we might usefully proceed when inquiring into a situation. It informs our abilities without exhausting them. Some learning occurs tacitly and is not neatly reducible to language. Indeed, Dewey (1938) recognized that human learning extends the nonlinguistic learning abilities of other animals. Theory guides our ability to decide what to call things as well as where and how to look for relationships. For example, an interviewer using CMM hears some responses and thinks, "This may be part of an important auto-biographical story." Later the interviewer thinks: "This bit is the client's story about how problematic episodes progress. I wonder how the autobiographical story is related to the story of the episode?" Here, in Dewey's terms, the controlled process of interviewing or observing is making an indeterminate situation determinate. It becomes determinate for both the consultant and the clients.[16] Assume that the interviewer asks, "Can you tell me a little more about what happens when you talk with your manager?" or "What happens that first gives you the idea that the talk has turned into an argument?" The client is hereby focused on making conversation determinate in a particular way, organizing conversation by episodes, and looking at temporal details. Part of the determination is the conjoint exploration and creation of coherence in the inquiry process.

CMM resembles other systemic orientations because it treats interviewing as a process of making connections.[17] As the interviewer proceeds, she or he begins to ask questions. One might be, "Is it typically after one of your subordinates is allowed to go over your head directly to upper management that you have coffee with other supervisors and talk about the 'old days' of dignity and respect?" Here the interviewer forms connections between an autobiographical story of threatened dignity or lost respect and stories about the organization's past. The interviewer also in so doing identifies particular events that seem to threaten dignity and thereby threaten glorification of the past. The interviewer does this because CMM's heuristic models direct him or her to sort out stories that conversants might use to formulate coherent utterances. They also direct the interviewer to find out how episodes are organized temporally.

In all of these activities, the inquirer weaves elements into a unified view. That matches Dewey's (1938) formal definition of *inquiry*: "Inquiry is the controlled or directed transformation of an indeterminate situation into one that is so determinate in its constituent distinctions and relations as to convert the elements of the original situation into a unified whole" (pp. 104–105). Next we look more closely at the determination process and the place of the inquirer in it.

The Position of the Inquirer

The idea of inquiry as a universal, natural process helps us situate the inquirer as engaged in processes of social life that concern him or her.

---

[16]This is a point that Dewey does not stress because his examples come largely from the physical sciences, but we find it quite consistent with Dewey's orientation because participants are inquirers too.

[17]This also holds for work on texts. The inquirer is making connections to find connections in the text.

Inside the Process With an "Attitude." If we take seriously the analogy of the inquirer to that of a flower attempting to attain a better relationship to other features of the world, then we understand the impossibility of a fully objective orientation. As systemic therapists put it, we cannot be outside the system. Dewey (1922) argued that the worst thing that happened in Western philosophy was the quest for certainty. Socrates and Plato started it in response to Athenian political failures. Descartes continued it with his effort to put knowledge on a foundation beyond doubt. From a pragmatic point of view, the inquirer is always part of the world of phenomena. Thus, human intelligence touches all knowledge. For this reason, just as no knowledge is objective, none is subjective either. That is because, as discussed earlier, intelligence is formed in the process of interaction/communication with others and with things in the world.

Although Dewey argued against the quest for certainty, he strongly endorsed what he called the *experimental attitude*. Dewey did not try to do social inquiry in the laboratory, although he did want science classes to spend more time in laboratories and less memorizing texts. By the *experimental attitude*, he meant the willingness to act in the world so as to make a difference and to take into account the effects our actions have. A communication consultant who derives principles from lived practice as well as from personal experience and academic sources, and who assesses those principles, modifying them as needed, exemplifies the experimental attitude. A consultant who takes a standard road show from one organization or community to another without engaging the details of participants' lived experience does not have such an attitude.

Avoiding the Psychology Fallacy. Social processes are always in motion. That does not mean ignoring ritualized activities. It means that persons must work to maintain stabilities. Sometimes the stories we have about the stability of practices do not reflect the change that must occur with new conditions and with the experience of having done the same thing before. These stories about stability do influence change, however. They may, for example, highlight continuity over creativity. They could then inform the practice of disattending to novel actions and of telling stories about what is repeated.

Although all life is in process, when we use reflective intelligence to examine any activity, we must in some way hold some aspect of it before us. That need not mean committing what James (1890/1950) called the "psychologist's fallacy" (p. 196). James' point was that psychologists tend to err by thinking that principles adequate to describe a finished product can explain satisfactorily the processes that led to its creation. For example, when studying a family, one could look at its communication pattern and report finding a coalition between father and son and another between mother and daughter. Perhaps one could say that the coalitions conflict. From this could come principles familiar to structural analysis, such as, "Cross-generational coalitions based on gender endanger the husband–wife relationship."

Now consider what the foregoing analysis misses: What was happening when the coalitions began to form? When were the coalitions enacted? In what kind of episodes? How is the action within an episode of coalition enactment done? What forms of action maintain the coalitions within and across episodes? Who feels most secure[18] when the coalition activity is enacted? When in the course of the action does someone begin to feel protected or threatened?[19] These questions help us and the clients understand how the logic of family practice was created in action. They also help the family see that other forms of coherence were and are possible.

Understanding the Inquiry Process as Action in the World

For traditionalists, Dewey (1938) seemed to invert most notions of logic and inquiry in an almost perverse way. The title of his book, *Logic: The Theory of Inquiry*, seems wrongheaded. Is not logic a self-contained subject of philosophy? Dewey said no. Action is the orienting conception, and logic is a tool integral to other aspects of inquiry. The logic of inquiry is an emergent creation in inquiry. One cannot separate it from how we attend, perceive, name, recall, state propositions, and act. If action is primary, then inquiry concerns the consequences that our judgments have. Inquiry is not only about supporting propositions. That is one possible activity in the inquiry process. Inquiry is about getting things done.

A person or persons identify elements of imbalance or discord in experience. The part of experience judged to be involved in the discord is studied so that the inquirer understands it in a particular way. Thus, in light of the inquirer's relationship to it, it becomes a *determinate situation*. The inquirer attempts to make (predicate) a *judgment* about that whole situation. That judgment implicates concrete lines of action with observable consequences, which should improve the situation.

The inquirer attempts to warrant the assertion of judgments. Doing so requires specifying features of the situation, ways of acting in it, and the consequents of action. These are not objectively given as this or that. No

---

[18]This kind of question comes from the idea that so long as the system exists at all, some features of it will serve to maintain it.

[19]A structural therapist with a systemic orientation might very well investigate some or all of these matters. Unlike a systemic therapist, however, the kind of change he or she would attempt to produce would be in the service of creating structure that conforms to universal structural principles.

observation is simply objective or subjective. They are created at the intersection of persons and phenomena. Picking out this or that as a relevant feature in inquiry is a matter of forming percepts in the course of engagement. Percepts can be temporarily stabilized for specific purposes as determinate objects of inquiry. In this process of making determinations, formulating propositions can be helpful. Propositions do many things. They can consist of hypotheses, the tests of which guide us toward warranted judgments. They can be theoretical descriptions that help us form percepts and objects. They organize relationships among objects. They add specificity of a kind to the consequences putting judgments into action.

This process is not linear. Emerging percepts influence the propositions that can be formed, just as propositions guide the formation of percepts as stable objects. Propositions as hypotheses emerge from observations, and they direct us to observe in certain ways. The consequences of our actions guided by these propositions can influence the way a situation is later specified, leading to new propositions, tests, and judgments. In other words, inquiry is a continual spiraling process of adaptation–adjustment. Our effort to *unpack* aspects of the foregoing sketch follows.

Determination of a Situation as the "Subject" of Inquiry. Someone engages in a process of inquiry to improve a situation. To do so, she or he acts to make the flow of raw sensory data determinate for her or his purposes. All living creatures do this all the time. When we identify a situation as needing improvement, we select and relate particular features of experience. It becomes, in Dewey's terminology, the *subject* of inquiry. Based on the mosaic principle of organizations, the inquirer need not study everything. Instead he or she must consider what features need to be included as part of the determinate situation. The subject of inquiry may evolve as it proceeds. To make a situation determinate, the inquirer constitutes particular phenomena as worthy of attention, as this or that feature of the subject.

The Limitations of Concepts and Variables in Making Determinations. Early in this century, James (1909/1996) called for *thick description* to replace the *thinness* of *concepts*. *Concepts*, he argued, are glosses that ignore the rich detail of life as lived. Just because you call someone an equestrian, James said, does not mean that person never walks. This reduction to concepts partly explains James' anger at *vicious intellectualism* in philosophy. Critical Cultural Studies of the Marxist sort well exemplifies just how reduction to concepts can reduce social analysis first to formula and category and then to impersonal hatred. Sets of people are often categorized as *working class* or *bourgeois* on the basis of their relationship to the means of production. In some perturbations, they may be categorized by their *identity* as gay or straight, male or female, colonized or colonialist. The details of family traditions and practices, personal talents, loves, hates, triumphs, cruelties, kindnesses, tragedies, accomplishments, and the like disappear. James (1909/1996) observed that this is how we set group against group.[20]

The critique of concepts leads directly to a critique of variable analysis. A *variable* is typically defined as a concept that can take different values. If the researcher recognizes what he or she is doing, there is nothing, in principle, wrong with using the logic of variable analysis for some aspects of inquiry. Quantitative work can be an excellent way to identify areas of inquiry. For example, quantitative findings about family violence not only focused qualitative inquiry on the problem, but also directed it away from the assumption that such violence is largely confined to the working class and undereducated people.

From a pragmatist's perspective, the tools of variable analysis can provide only a starting place for a detailed understanding of social action. First, this is because variables as concepts provide thin description. In addition, the assumptions of variable analysis do not closely match the ideas about language, coherence, and social order advanced by pragmatism's biological–evolutionary ideas. The logic of variable analysis requires each observation to be independent of others. In contrast, elements of a system do not just affect other elements. They are part of the formation of other elements.

Consider how, using CMM, we attempt to understand a man's statement that he must fight when someone insults a female family member or acquaintance. Quantitative research showing a probability beyond chance for a fight to occur following such an insult in a particular cultural setting may have sparked our interest. To understand these events, we would find out how stories of responsibility, responding to insult, family obligations, and so on integrally form the story of being a respected man. The fight response to insult is not a correlate of manhood. In some cultures, it is integral to the story of being a man.

"Percepts" and Definitions.   How can we get along without concepts and variables? Don't we have to define matters such as a cultural view of manhood? Isn't definition a matter of connecting here the concept *man* to concepts such as *protector*? Peirce (1905; cited in Burke, 1994) proposed the idea of *percepts* to replace or augment definitions. Although that term

---

[20]Nothing in pragmatism obviates considering matters such as modes of production, gender, colonialism, and so on. Indeed, Dewey wrote strong criticisms of capitalism, sexism, and colonialism. He did not, however, simply categorize persons or traditions without examination of the details of a person's practice or reduce social processes a priori to simple conflicts of the progressive elements and enemies of the people.

has lost currency, it can provide a richer way to think about elements in a statement.

Identifying something must include sensations, which are meaningless in isolation. They become meaningful when contingent on our actions and when they point us toward future actions. Sensations are only important as consequences of actions performed (Dewey, 1929/1960). Peirce regarded all inquiry as action. Dewey (1938, 1939) followed Peirce's revolutionary ideas about definitions that come from that insight.

Peirce used lithium to explain his *percept* notion. A textbook definition will give its atomic weight. An experienced scientist will tell you that, to find it among other elements, you must look for those with various properties. Peirce then offered examples of results expected from a number of scientific procedures using lithium. According to Peirce (1902):

> The peculiarity of this definition—or rather this precept that is more serviceable than a definition—is that it tells you what the word lithium denotes by prescribing what you are to do in order to gain a perceptual acquaintance with the object of the word. (cited in Burke, 1994, p.11)

All living creatures (within the scope of their neurophysiological possibilities) make identifications like this—they form percepts useful in action. In this way, raw sensory data are made determinate. In human inquiry, the process of making objects determinate often employs language. Notice that this Peirce–Dewey view differs from simple operationalism. The latter uses measurement operations to define objects for a particular study. In the pragmatic tradition, percepts continue to evolve in the course of experience. Indeed, our *feel for how to go on* (Wittgenstein's phrase) with a percept must go beyond what we can put into words. Polanyi (1958) called this *feel* the tacit dimension of inquiry.

The idea of *percepts* is equally useful when considering theoretical statements. Notice what happens to the relationship between a written definition of a term such as *context* that we use in CMM and the percept of context that inquirers develop employing CMM. We do not feel obliged finally to reduce the percept to a fixed definition of context. In a pragmatist way of working, inquiry consists of open-ended, continuous action in a changing world. The definitions we offer should help inquirers further develop their percepts and reflect on what they are doing at moments when this seems useful. If the theoretical line of work is useful, it will lead to successive enrichments and modifications of definitions.

CMM has been criticized for definitional imprecision. It does not have the clean, unchanging operational definitions found in theories with a different philosophical heritage (Griffin, 1999). Guilty as charged. CMM relies on case reports as well as descriptions and definitions to show how ideas such as context are used in this and that situation. As work develops, the descriptions of our terms should evolve in richness and become more useful tools.

Determining "Objects" That Point into the Future.
Evolving percepts lead to the forming of determinant objects at moments in the process of inquiry. We say, for example, "What we have just heard is an effort to terminate the episode." We have expressed it in language to facilitate reflection at a particular phase of inquiry. In that way, we have constituted it as a determinate object. The objects of inquiry are not given in nature and discovered by inquiry (Dewey, 1929/1960, 1938, 1941). As we work, percepts and their partial objectifications can change. A determination can never exhaust the percept that gives rise to it. We may usefully point to a constructed object such as *an episode termination move*, and we may have a definition for such observations. However, our percept includes the feel we have for the variety of such behaviors, their multiple possibilities, our way of listening for them, and much more.

Dewey used the term *object* to include a physical thing such as a table or bottle as well as an abstraction such as *context, act,* or *logical operator.* Dewey's concern with objects as they function to create a particular process of inquiry permits this expansion of usage. When we constitute objects, we create a way to continue working with them. They point us into the future. When a high school student asks a friend, "Want to get a Coke?", a can of soda may be constituted as a feature used in a pattern of social interaction. If a pragmatism-informed inquirer studied this interaction, the Coke would be constituted as a complex object. The inquirer would not ignore its relationship to capital and production, but she or he would not assume those relationships are the most important. Instead, the Coke would be constituted as an object within the details of the lives lived by the persons involved: Did they have a Coke together when they met? What are they feeling when drinking it? How do they communicate with the Coke in hand? How does the Coke relate them to other teenagers? As we study the place of Coke in various forms of interaction, we are continually forming a percept of Coke that we can treat as a particular stable object at a moment of inquiry.

Consider a different kind of object, such as the way a manager addresses subordinates. Using CMM, we constitute the manager's talk as a different object of study than would a traditional psychologist. We would constitute the talk as the conjoint action of the manager and her underlings. A traditional psychologist might constitute it as a symptom of a mental state. How the talk is constituted as an object of inquiry has obvious consequences for how inquiry is conducted. Notice also that theoretical objects such as contexts, conjoint action, and the like are also determinate for particular purposes. Of course, a reflexive relationship exists between the way objects in the situation and those in the theory are determined.

Propositions as Tools, Hypotheses as Kinds of Propositions. We now turn attention to the propositional statements in which objects are related.[21] This is not the place for a detailed reexamination of Dewey's view of propositions. It is crucial to observe that Dewey was interested in the functional value of propositions, however. They serve as instrumentalities—tools—in the process of moving toward judgments.

In Dewey's philosophy, propositions of different kinds perform a wide range of functions. Dewey treated all descriptions, synthetic statements, definitions, and hypotheses as various kinds of propositions. The most important thing about a proposition is whether it effectively moves inquiry toward sound judgment. Dewey (1938) used the example of this valid syllogism that relates two propositions and deduces a third:

(Major premise) All celestial objects are made of cheese.

(Minor premise) The moon is a celestial object.

(Conclusion) Therefore, the moon is made of cheese.

For Dewey, the most important problem with the major premise of this valid syllogism is not its falsity, in the abstract. The problem is that if we use the propositions constituting the major premise and conclusion as scientific tools, we do very badly in future scientific work.

So why bother with propositions at all? Propositions can serve as useful tools in organizing our ideas about the objects of inquiry by describing their relationships linguistically or with another formal systems. We should not be deceived, however, into thinking that the world somehow conforms to propositional forms or that our goal is to confirm propositions. Propositions are provisional and instrumental (Dewey, 1938, p. 283). They aid reflection, allowing us to hold ideas before us and consider them (Burke, 1994, p. 162). For example, in the course of extended inquiry, we might formulate some alternative systemic hypotheses—a set of statements providing different provisional accounts of how features of a situation work as a system. Dewey would consider them propositions. A simplified example, typical of situations many consultants have encountered, follows.

When working with members of an organization, suppose we are told that they are in crisis. We are also informed that everything will be fine because they know they are in a crisis. Members want to save the organiza-

[21]Dewey's approach to propositions is set out in two major works—the already cited *Logic* and in "Propositions, Warranted Assertability, and Truth" (1941).

tion because it is such a creative workplace. Here is one provisional systemic hypothesis that could integrate that and other information obtained:

> When the members of this organization determine their situation to be a crisis, they pull together. They tell stories about how, by pulling together, they can and have gotten out of crises. They also report the story that when there is no crisis, they should work independently, unconstrained by others. Finally, they acknowledge that without the constraint of coordinating, they produce crises. This loop is held together by the larger context of a shared story that creativity is an individual matter and is inhibited if constrained by others' activities. The pattern of repeated crisis proves their commitment to creativity, while their willingness to endure the crises proves commitment to the organization. (See Fig. 2.3.)

The foregoing is called a *strange loop* in CMM (Cronen et al., 1982). The highest context story of creativity is crucial. Without that, it would not be necessarily coherent to act without coordination until another crisis appears or to continue working in a situation of repeated crises. This hy-

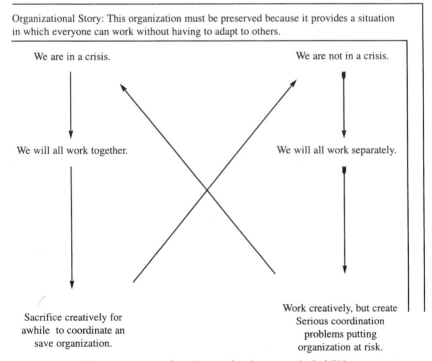

Creative Story: Creativity is of the highest value and it is an individual matter. Adapting to others restricts it.

Organizational Story: This organization must be preserved because it provides a situation in which everyone can work without having to adapt to others.

We are in a crisis.   We are not in a crisis.

We will all work together.   We will all work separately.

Sacrifice creatively for awhile to coordinate an save organization.

Work creatively, but create Serious coordination problems putting organization at risk.

FIG. 2.3. Strange loop in members' grammatical abilities.

pothesis guides work with the organization as we seek to act in ways leading to observations that we find consistent or inconsistent with it. Support for it is compared to that of other hypotheses. Typically we develop new hypotheses, modifying and discarding old ones in our ongoing work. This is consistent with most systemic practice and is not limited to CMM.

Judgments. According to Dewey (1938, 1941), we do not form judgments about propositions. We make judgments about the subject of inquiry. In the prior example, a belief that the systemic hypothesis stated earlier is better supported than are others would lead us to a judgment. The judgment might be, "The organization is caught in a strange loop of repeated crises from which it can't presently escape without change in its actions and stories." Such a judgment, according to Dewey, is the attribution of a determinate predicate to a determinate subject. That seems like traditional analytic logic talk, attributing predicates to subjects. However, *subject* has Dewey's specialized meaning here (a situation made determinate), and *predicate*, Dewey said, implies action. Judgment directs that a course of action should be predicated of the subject.

Why is predication fundamentally action? To understand, we need to return to pragmatist ideas about language. Dewey (1911/1933) argued that the verbal sounds around a child become meaningful in the contexts of activity, in patterns including objects and acts. "A child associates hat with putting something on the head when going out doors" (p. 144). The word *hat* attains meaning by its use in similar contexts. If we think about this activity in the abstract in philosophical terms, we can say that the action "putting-on-the-head" is the predicate of hat. Thus, predications are originally actions because meaning is use.

Actions and Consequences. Judgments such as the previous one imply material actions. In the foregoing example, a consultant might act in various ways. For example, he or she might lead organization members to explore the higher order creativity story. A reformulated story might not require the absence of any coordination. Another course of action might be to explore ways other than cycles of crisis production by which members show commitment to creativity and the organization. Many other possibilities exist. The inquirer must then look at the consequences of such actions. In other words, how has the problematic situation changed? Of course, consequences are percepts. Such percepts may need to be made determinate objects to facilitate reflection on the work.

If the inquirer is doing critical or interpretive rather than interventive work, a similar process occurs. Now the situation consists of an interpreter in a problematic condition with respect to understanding the text. Working with the text, the same hypothesis and others could be formulated. The hypotheses now guide the interrogation of the text. The judgment would be an overall account of the text that makes it a determinate whole. The resulting action implied is that it is useful to go on using CMM or other means in the critical enterprise, and that the ideas developing with the guidance of the theory facilitate carrying the work forward.

Warranted Assertability and Consequences

Warranted assertability replaces truth in Dewey's mature philosophy (Tiles, 1988; Westbrook, 1991). The support obtained for determinations—including theoretical objects, objects in the situation, and hypotheses—warrant a judgment. Most important, however, are the consequences obtained by actions stemming from a judgment. Judgments involve the connections between means and consequents (Dewey, 1938).

Dewey (1938) described his work on inquiry as a correspondence theory, but not correspondence between a propositional map and reality. Correspondence for him occurs between actions (means) based on judgments and the consequences brought about by those actions. What, then, makes for a powerful warrant? The answer is useful consequents of our judgments. Warranted assertability is not simply a claim by a particular inquirer. Dewey was very much aware of the role played by the community of inquirers in reaching agreement on ways to constitute objects, state propositions, and assess consequences. In this, he predated Kuhn (1962) by almost 25 years. In our organizational–crisis cycles example, the warranting of judgment occurs in several ways. First, it is done by showing how we established objects of inquiry, such as the story of creativity. It also occurs by appeal to the viability of the theoretical statements that guided us in our inquiry, including any modifications that took place as we proceeded. We appeal to the coherence of our chosen actions with the judgment. Finally, we examine the changes that occurred in the organization and the evidence that the changes had something to do with the details of our practice. For example, we diagram the strange loop hypothesis and also begin exploring new ways to be creative in a workshop or interview setting. Suppose weeks later we hear the report that when persons have not talked together about their work in several days, one person says to another, "Haven't heard from you, are you going strange 'loopy' on us?" This would be an unusually clear, but not unprecedented, indication of connections among judgments, means, and consequences.[22]

---

[22]Usually the support is less obvious. Nonetheless, The Kensington Consultation Centre, London, reports a case of a quarreling couple that asked to take a diagram of a strange loop home with them. They put it up in their bathroom. At their next session, when they began to repeat their old pattern, one of them said, "It's the loop in the loo again." Both laughed and the pattern stopped. They said that this has happened several times at home and it stopped the pattern every time.

Dewey's idea of consequences needs further elaboration. When Charles Sanders Peirce was asked why he did not call his theory *practicalism*, he responded that such a name implied a narrow, shortsighted view of consequence (Hookway, 1985). Dewey criticized James' (1897/1956) famous book *The Will to Believe* because he thought it amounted to saying that a belief that makes an individual feel good is thereby justified (Westbrook, 1991). Dewey (1922) based his view of consequences on his evolutionary–biological understanding. He argued that no action exists in isolation. It will connect with many other acts and thus will have multiple consequences. Establishing means–consequence relationships therefore requires a careful examination of those consequences. Indeed, they very well could extend beyond the original determination of the situation. In our organizational example, we must not only assess whether crises produce less stress, but also should examine whether creative work continues. If not, members no longer may value the organization. In an inquiry concerning labor–management problems, the inquirer might want to assess consequences in terms of the long-term welfare of workers and not just whether reduced conflict occurs.

The Evolving Ends of Inquiry.   In our example above, we found that assessing the consequences of action, like other moves in the inquiry process, can lead to a redefinition of the situation and thus to a different idea about the ends of our inquiry. For Dewey, (1925/1958) ends are always *ends in view*. They are constituted in the process of action. Research that claims to be practical but limits its scope to observing the way participants pursue preestablished goals, such as how a group solves a problem given to it, is not fully relevant to the world of experience.

TAKING DEWEY'S UNDERSTANDING OF INQUIRY SERIOUSLY: ADVANTAGES, LIMITATIONS, AND EXTENSIONS

A strange disjunction of emphasis appears in Dewey's work on inquiry. Dewey was heavily involved in social issues including women's rights, minority rights, the rights of working people, limiting the power of capital, educational reform, fostering grass roots democracy, and the proper treatment of China (Westbrook, 1991). However, in his discussion of inquiry, he mostly examined physical and natural sciences. Science works by careful observation, manipulation, and assessment of consequences. In so doing, it attained much more success than philosophy and social disciplines. Dewey thought the latter overemphasized detached speculation, instead of treating ideas as part of action in the world. Science presents a good model for the social disciplines if we consider the way scientists really work, as opposed to scientists' reconstructed reports (Dewey, 1938). Nonetheless, Dewey (1938) recognized that the world of human action is not amenable to the controlled studies of laboratory science. We think it is useful to reconsider Dewey's contributions from a more contemporary perspective. His naturalized view of inquiry offers the promise of enriching the way we do social inquiry with qualitative methods. In much of what follows, we are guided by the present work of systemic therapists and consultants.

New Forms of Research Reports

Making the account of inquiry closer to lived practice has the advantage of focusing the inquirer and the teacher of inquiry on crucial features that research reports typically treat as background and fail to discuss explicitly. A research report following Dewey's account would specifically include determination of the situation. To do this, a researcher should respect Dewey's understanding of the inquirer as an engaged participant. This would guide researchers in clarifying their relationship to what they study. They would have to go beyond identifying a topic and more specifically identify what is studied. For example, when working with a text,[23] the situation is not the conditions that the text describes. The inquirer can only work with, but cannot change, the text. The *situation* refers to a relationship between the text and the inquirer in which the inquirer needs a richer or more coherent understanding of the materials. In interventive work, *situation* (or some more felicitous term) refers to the relationships among the persons desiring consultation and their association with the inquirer.

The idea of the researcher as engaged participant leads to posing research questions, hypotheses, and other instrumentalities in view of the evolving relationship between the inquirer and participants or texts. If we follow Dewey, the literature review would conclude with research questions. However, a researcher typically would mark stated hypotheses as *provisional hypotheses*. The methods section would remain traditional, but a researcher might divide it into *initial methods* and *evolved methods*. This would clarify the choices a scholar made at the start of inquiry and what additional methods might be added as work progressed. On Dewey's model, the introduction of additional methods may accompany formulation of new hypotheses as tools if these methods remain consistent with other features of practice.

---

[23]We are using *texts* here broadly to refer to any fabrications such as transcripts, video tapes, and so on.

The report of data and interpretation would appear sequentially. It would include the creation of successive hypotheses and new descriptions, as well as the evolution of percepts and objects.[24] For example, in a study of a multicultural organization, Chong (1998) relied on excerpts from various interviews. These showed how she developed her own percept of what American salesmen considered "Korean Management Style" to be and how the salesmen developed their percept across very different contexts. This is much more useful than simply stating a definition. From her work, we share a bit of the feel for the percept as an emergent factor.

In CMM research, interpretation can include the role of the inquirer in the process of interactions with others. In some clinical studies, hypotheses about the relationship of the therapist to the client at a particular moment are crucial. That relationship can be part of the intervention (see Cronen, Pearce, & Tomm, 1985). In a nonclinical study, Marsh, Rosser, and Harré (1978) formulated hypotheses about how participants in disorder at English football games successively would adjust their accounts in light of their relationship to establishment professors. As new understanding of a situation emerges, and as the situation changes during inquiry, practitioners would report why new hypotheses are formulated and how those guided work.

A section entitled "Judgment and Consequences" would follow the discussion of findings and interpretations. This is more than a cosmetic move. It would refer to the overall impact of the work on the situation, much as a "Discussion" section does now. Labeling the section this way, however, alerts the reader and author(s) to the fact that judgments possess moral dimensions. Making a judgment about a situation involves more than weaving data and interpretations together. Use of the concept of judgment occurs because a claim is being made about how a current or changed situation contributes to a good life. Last would be a section entitled "Implications for Future Action" rather than "Conclusion." Here the author(s) discusses the implications for inquiry much as is done today. The fact that Deweyan inquirers view new principles as instrumentalities, not as maps of an underlying essence, suggests the need for the different label. Regarding the results of inquiry this way, however, requires a different view of generality.

Generality Based on the Case Law Analogue

Qualitative researchers in the tradition of pragmatism often are questioned about the generalizability of their work. If understandings are par-

---

[24]An excellent example of this kind of research report is Hernandez' (1999) dissertation study of the consequences of displacement due to political violence in Colombia.

ticular to situated interaction and are not considered representations of an unchanging foundational reality, what are they worth?[25] Dewey's contention that all propositions are instrumentalities to be used and modified in the process of inquiring implies the answer. Kvale (1996) discussed a form of generalization drawn from case law based on ideas first presented by Kennedy (1979). A new principle of law is derived from a specific case. One assesses its applicability to a future case by examining evidence and developing arguments for its applicability. In communication research, we can employ an additional kind of rigor as we investigate how well the principles developed in prior research guide us in new work.[26] As in case law, we would not expect the principle typically to be affirmed or rejected in whole, although that could happen. More frequently, it would develop as it is used in new cases.

Restricting the Term *Proposition* and Recognizing Other Forms

Much philosophical criticism claims that Dewey's ideas about propositions are not developed sufficiently (Burke, 1994). We think that he used the term too broadly. He obscured the distinctive functions of instrumentalities that are not propositional in form. Dewey treated descriptions, case references, and models as fundamentally propositions. We find it more useful to think of descriptions, extended case examples, and models as distinctive instrumentalities. For example, qualitative inquirers who study situated communication, particularly those who are practitioners, often appeal to prior cases. These references are very helpful for developing percepts because they deal with similar phenomena in various contexts while retaining the details of those contexts. In a similar way, prior case references guide the formation of hypotheses. Descriptions complement formal definitions because they are more open ended. They can be enriched and extended. Sometimes definitions mislead because they are thin. These do lend themselves to reflection and recall so long as we recognize their limits. They serve a useful, but different, function. In the pragmatist view of language, different function amounts to different meaning as discussed earlier in this chapter.

Models allow the inquirer to relate aspects of theory in ways other than the deductive form for which propositions are well suited (Harré, 1970).

---

[25]This argument that an unchanging reality must exist for knowledge to be possible started with Parmenides in the 6th century B.C.E. Dewey's response to it has much in common with Aristotle's account of the arts of *prasis* in his *Nichomachean Ethics*.

[26]When legal principles evolve in a way that seem to have bad social consequences, legislative action is required to change the direction in which case law is developing.

The relationships in Fig. 2.1 do not guide the inquirer through a series of deductions. We could restate Fig. 2.1 as a set of propositions, but that would obscure the way it guides inquiry by displaying multiple, changeable relationships. In this way, it encourages an inquirer to consider possible connections among phenomena to explore. Baker and Hacker (1984) have shown that forcing other kinds of statements into propositional form does not extract a propositional core; it changes the meaning.

Using propositions to cover many kind of instrumentalities also obscures the important role of analogues in the development of theory. Harré (1986) described how theory families develop using analytic analogues and source analogues. An analytic analogue provides guidance for where and how to look at the world. Darwin's work is one of Harré's crucial examples. Darwin seems to have looked at nature with "the eye of a country gentleman . . . seeing lines of descent, blood ties, etc., where another observer (Captain Fitzroy, for instance) might see the manifestation of God's munificence" (Harré, 1986, p. 202). Darwin's work in the natural world informed Dewey about how to look at the social world. CMM, in turn, uses Darwin's work for its analytic analogue. We consider social phenomena to be aspects of systems coevolving in situated action as described in the first part of this chapter. For example, persons' autobiographical stories are explored with a view to how they may be coevolving with stories about relationships and stories about particular episodes of action (Harré, 1986).

Source analogues provide ways to think about how one act, such as an expression of love, is consequential for a responsive act, and how those acts inform and are informed by stories of relationships and episodes. In CMM, we do not reduce social coherence to Darwinian causal principles. Evolution has produced distinctive ways of making social coherence. The CMM uses as its source analogue an encounter that Barnett Pearce had years ago. In that encounter, he and a passerby cobbled together a conversation about motorcycles that was useful in multiple ways, although they brought to the conversation very different cultural background, education, and communication styles (personal communication, 1976). In such encounters, persons cocreate what Dewey called *habits* and Wittgenstein called *rules*. This source analogue orients us to a dynamic conception of rules and away from treating formalized episodes as paradigmatic.

Going Beyond Homeostatic Explanations of Change

Our most serious criticism of Dewey's work is that it is far too homeostatic for a contemporary understanding of systems. He limited inquiry to situations of disequilibrium and breakdown. This is too constrained an understanding of evolution. Evolution does not merely respond to unfavorable conditions. If it did, how could we explain the human ability to sing opera (Gould, 1980)? Every evolutionary move opens new future possibilities. In institutional practice, those informed by ideas such as Senge's (1990) notion of the *learning organization* recognize this. Increasingly, consultants are being asked not only to help deal with problems, but also to inquire into organizational processes to improve their ability to act into the future. Another limitation occurs when some situations are problematic exactly because they *are* determinate for the participants, not because they are confusing. These may be so structured that they trap participants in unwanted, repeated patterns that they know and can describe very well (Bateson, 1972). Thus, a productive intervention may involve making the situation less determinate for the participants and creating new evolutionary possibilities.

A Revised Definition of **Inquiry.**   A two-sided view of inquiry for the social disciplines is called for if we abandon a strictly homeostatic orientation and recognize, with Dewey, that all involved are inquirers. The term *two-sided* refers to the perspective of the professional inquirer and to that of the other participants, who also are inquirers. We propose the following definition specific to social inquiry:

> Social inquiry is a process in which: (1) The practical specialist, using controlled investigation, engages with others making his or her relationship to a situation determinate for the purpose of facilitating new and productive affordances and constraints in future conjoint action. (2) Other participants in the situation engage to change the situation, making it less determinate and/or making new determinations, for the purpose of creating new and productive affordances and constraints in future conjoint action.

An Expanded View of Change in Human Systems.   Dewey's homeostatic view led him to the idea that major changes in human affairs occur because of discontinuity between native impulses and social obligations.[27] This is even a limited a view of homeostasis. Although we do not doubt that conflicts of native impulse and social expectations sometimes are constructed, we do not think they are the primary engines of major social change. All sorts of socially constructed ways of living can become problematic for reasons other than imbalance between impulse and social expectation.

---

[27]This sounds quite Freudian, but Dewey was not following Freud on this point. Freud thought that such conflict of social expectation and impulse was the constant and natural condition of human life. Dewey believed that discontinuity was the unusual result of social action.

Responding to the Danger of Self-Sealing Warrantability

Dewey was well aware that the consequences crucial to warranting a judgment must be understood in terms of the procedures used to determine them. This problem is not limited to Dewey's pragmatism and is as old as Plato's *Meno* dialogue. We think that pragmatist philosophy has more resources for responding to it than Dewey spelled out, however. At least three answers exist to the charge of solipsism intrinsic to pragmatism.

The first answer is that avoiding solipsism in this kind of work depends on the ability of a theory and those who use it to generate a number of alternative hypotheses. It also relies on their ability to reformulate hypotheses as percepts evolve through detailed engagement. This avoids a premature rush to interjudge consensus. The second answer is that a social theory should be learned in a wide educational context. We find it consistent with Dewey's ideas to observe that the value of a theory cannot be independent of the larger cultural and institutional practices in which it is embedded. If we want inquirers who can decide whether consequences fail to support their judgments and whether instrumentalities of their theory helpfully inform judgments, they need exposure to alternative ways of understanding not bound by one theory. That does not mean every program that provides training must train in alternative theories. Typically graduate students come to systemic programs with prior training in other kinds of work and a good liberal education.

The third answer is based on realism. Although reality does not mandate fully how we determine objects, propositions, or consequences, it plays a role. The character Linus from the comic strip "Peanuts" says, "No matter how hard you try, you cannot bounce a potato chip." We can ensure that the social world can speak to us if we develop theory based in large measure on data coming from inquirers' engagement with the complex lives of real persons who do things together. The third response to the prospect of solipsism leads us to the final topic in this chapter.

IMPLICATIONS FOR A DISTINCTIVE PRAGMATIST DEFINITION OF THEORY

We think the pragmatist understanding of inquiry suggests a distinctive kind of communication theory. CMM is one exemplar of what Cronen (1995b) identified as *practical theory* as distinct from *applied theory*. Applied theory retains the dichotomy of theory and practice. It simply means that theory, of whatever sort and however developed, can be applied in the world. Practical theory specifically rejects the distinction between theory and practice.

Dewey (1929/1960) strongly opposed the theory–practice dualism. Consistent with his view, practitioners who do interventive research and others who engage with the complexities of persons' lived experience become central to the inquiry process. By contrast, experimental laboratory research, with its emphasis on variable analysis and control, loses ecological validity for complex social systems that construct their own ends in view. As we have observed, distinctions emergent in natural and social evolution are not a good match for variable analysis. Moreover, the control of extraneous variables by random assignment of subjects typically used in that approach precludes investigating what in the system changes when an interventive move is made.

Historical, critical, and interpretive research can avoid those problems and make very important contributions. Interpretive and critical research that is based on bounded texts redefines the situation as a relationship between materials and the inquirer, however. This limits the positions from which inquiry can be conducted. Interventive research mandates acting so as to change the situation. This is Cronen's (1998, 2000) definition of *practical theory*: "A Practical Theory informs a coherent grammar, consistent with data, that facilitates professionals' ability to join with others in the co-creation of new affordances and constraints in social action." This definition does not map a newly discovered category *out there* in reality. It is an instrument intended to point inquiry in particular directions. The term *grammar* here refers to an inquirer's understanding of the communication process (theory) that guides engagement in the process of inquiry. A grammar consists of a set of abilities for responding to others that makes sense rather than nonsense, integrating the actions of observing, understanding, recalling speaking, manipulating, and moving. A practical theory provides a set of formal instrumentalities that inform the rules that inquirers use when joining with others. Of course, more than just theory informs a practitioner's grammar of practices. The past experiences of inquirers, their unique abilities, the conjoint action within a particular episode of inquiry, the specific methods used, and other factors also condition it. Consistent with what has been said, the data supporting a practical theory must come in important measure from the detailed engagement of practice. A consequence of immersion in practice is that practical theory principles evolve as they are used in new contexts of inquiry.

A practical theory is overtly a heuristic device rather than a map to be proved true. In CMM, for example, our main emphasis is not whether it is true that some stories provide context for others, although we do possess some traditional evidence for that. The most important evidence for that theoretical description is its instrumental value in working with particular situations. We might ask roommates from different countries, "How would things be different between you and your roommate if he did not cook unusual food in the room?" Here we would explore the relationship between stories about cooking episodes and stories about the relationship. Are the episodes about cooking the higher order ones within which the relationship story is forming? Is it the other way around? This has been a productive kind of question, and the consequences of its use support that aspect of the theory.

The definition of *practical theory* also directs attention to the way learning depends on the patterns that communication professionals and others conjointly produce. Change in patterns of communication is a co-construction, so the assessment of practical theories should include consequences for the professional as well as other participants. Work should show the continuing enrichment of principles and the development of tacit knowledge for all concerned. Professional inquirers should find that, by using a particular practical theory, they are developing a feel for how to act, just as a client should get a better feel for how to work with others.

Practical theories are not confined in their application to interventive work. The grammars they offer can be and are useful in doing interpretive and critical work. Critical and interpretive work can inform interventive practice reciprocally. Doing something that changes a situation is the fundamental form of inquiry for all life, however.

A FINAL NOTE

We offer the foregoing not as a final statement on what pragmatist inquiry really is, but as our way to engage the reader in thinking about how pragmatist ideas can be used to develop communication theory and research. For many years, communication has been treated as a questionable addition to the family of liberal arts disciplines. After all, its very name invites a grammar of action that culture and philosophy traditionally have set against a grammar of reflection. We do not say we have spent the last hour *psychologizing* or *anthropoligizing*. That sounds like nonsense. However, to say we have been communicating makes sense. Here we see Wittgenstein's point about a cloud of philosophy in a pinch of sentence-level grammar. Pragmatic tradition radically objects to the reflection–action duality. For a pragmatist, a grammar of action provides a sensible, naturalistic context within which features of inquiry may be understood. In pragmatism, communication is just the right sort of name for a discipline. It embraces the coherent continuity, the value of incompleteness, the spiraling quality of change and discovery, and the art and mystery in all human action.

We also offer the ideas developed herein with the hope that the reader will consider how this naturalistic understanding of inquiry might change the way we think about a number of important matters. These include the generality of findings, the criteria for evaluating theories, the role of definitions, the assessment of research outcomes, and the way scholars present research reports. In other words, we hope that, for our readers' ends in view, that we have not forgotten the water.

REFERENCES

Averill, J. R., & Nunley, E. P. (1992). *Voyages of the heart: Living an emotionally creative life*. New York: The Free Press.

Baker, G. P., & Hacker, P. M. S. (1984). *Language, sense & nonsense*. Oxford: Basil Blackwell.

Bateson, G. (1972). *Steps to an ecology of mind*. New York: Balantine.

Burke, T. (1994). *Dewey's new logic: A reply to Russell*. Chicago: University of Chicago Press.

Chong, H. (1998). Rethinking the role of a bicultural person in a multicultural organization. *Human Systems, 9*, 239–252.

Cronen, V. (1994). Coordinated management of meaning: Practical theory for the complexities and contradictions of everyday life. In J. Siegfried (Ed.), *The status of common sense in psychology* (pp. 183–207). Norwood, NJ: Ablex.

Cronen, V. (1995a). Coordinated management of meaning: The consequentiality of communication and the recapturing of experience. In S. Sigman (Ed.), *The consequentiality of communication* (pp. 17–65). Hillsdale, NJ: Lawrence Erlbaum Associates.

Cronen, V. (1995b). Practical theory and the tasks ahead for social approaches to communication. In L. Leeds-Hurwitz (Ed.), *Social approaches to communication* (pp. 217–242). New York: Guilford.

Cronen, V. (1998). Communication theory for the twenty-first century: Cleaning up the wreckager of the psychology project. In J. Trent (Ed.), *Communication: Views from the helm for the 21st century* (pp. 18–38). Needham Heights, MA: Allyn & Bacon.

Cronen, V. (2000, January). *Practical theory and a naturalistic account of inquiry*. Unpublished paper presented at the conference on Practical Theory, Public Participation, and Community, Baylor University, Waco, TX.

Cronen, V., Johnson, K., & Lannamann, J. (1982). Paradoxes, double binds and reflexive loops: An alternative theoretical perspective. *Family Process, 20*, 91–112.

Cronen, V., & Lang, P. (1994). Language and action: Wittgenstein and Dewey in the practice of therapy and consultation. *Human Systems, 5*, 5–43.

Cronen, V., Pearce, W., & Tomm, K. (1985). A dialectical view of personal change. In K. Gergen & K. Davis (Eds.), *The social construction of the person* (pp. 203–224). New York: Springer-Verlag.

Cronen, V., Pearce, W., & Xi, C. (1989/1990). The meaning of "meaning" in the CMM analysis of communication: A comparison of two traditions. *Research on Language and Social Interaction, 23*, 1–40.

Davidson, D. (1984). On the very idea of a conceptual scheme. In D. Davidson (Ed.), *Inquiries into truth and interpretation* (pp. 183–198). Oxford: Clarendon.

DeShazer, S. (1985). *Keys to solution in brief therapy*. New York: W. W. Norton.

Dewey, J. (1896). The reflex arc concept in psychology. *Psychological Review, 3*, 357–370.

Dewey, J. (1910). *The influence of Darwin on philosophy, and other essays in contemporary thought*. New York: Henry Holt.

Dewey, J. (1922). *Human nature and conduct*. New York: Henry Holt.

Dewey, J. (1933). *How we think* (rev. ed.). Chicago: Henry Regnery. (Original work published 1911)

Dewey, J. (1934a). *Art as experience*. New York: Minton, Balch.

Dewey, J. (1934b). *A common faith*. New Haven, CT: Yale University Press.

Dewey, J. (1938). *Logic: The theory of inquiry*. New York: Henry Holt.

Dewey, J. (1939). Experience, knowledge and value: A rejoinder. In P. A. Schilpp (Ed.), *The philosophy of John Dewey* (pp. 517–608). New York: Tudor.

Dewey, J. (1941). Propositions, warranted assertability, and truth. *Journal of Philosophy, 38,* 169–186.

Dewey, J. (1944). *Democracy and education.* New York: The Free Press. (Original work published 1916)

Dewey, J. (1948). *Reconstruction in philosophy* (enlarged ed.). New York: Beacon. (Original work published 1920)

Dewey, J. (1958). *Experience and nature.* New York: Dover. (Original work published 1925)

Dewey, J. (1960). *The quest for certainty.* New York: Capricorn Books. (Original work published 1929)

Dewey, J. (1988). Half-hearted naturalism. In J. A. Boydston (Ed.), *John Dewey: The later works* (Vol. 3, pp. 73–81). Carbondale, IL: Southern Illinois University Press. (Original work published 1927)

Gould, S. (1980). *The panda's thumb.* New York: W. W. Norton.

Gould, S. (1989). *Wonderful life: The Burgess shale and the nature of history.* New York: W. W. Norton.

Griffin, E. (1999). *A first look at communication theory.* New York: McGraw-Hill.

Gunn, G. (1987). *The culture of criticism and the criticism of culture.* Oxford: Oxford University Press.

Harré, R. (1970). *The principles of scientific thinking.* Chicago: University of Chicago Press.

Harré, R. (1984). *Personal being.* Cambridge, MA: Harvard University Press.

Harré, R. (1986). *Varieties of realism.* Oxford: Basil Blackwell.

Hernandez, M. P. (1999). *A personal dimension of human rights activism: Narratives of Trauman, resilience, and solidarity.* Unpublished doctoral dissertation, University of Massachusetts, Amherst, MA.

Hookway, C. (1985). *Peirce.* London: Routledge & Kegan Paul.

James, W. (1950). *Principles of psychology* (Vol. 1). New York: Dover. (Original work published 1890)

James, W. (1956). *The will to believe.* New York: Dover. (Original work published 1897)

James, W. (1996). *A pluralistic universe.* Lincoln, NE: University of Nebraska Press. (Original work published 1909)

James, W. (1996). *Essays in radical empiricism.* Lincoln, NE: University of Nebraska Press. (Original work published 1912)

Kennedy, M. (1979). Generalizing from single case studies. *Evaluation Quarterly, 3,* 661–678.

Kuhn, T. (1962). *The structure of scientific revolutions.* Chicago: University of Chicago Press.

Kvale, S. (1996). *Interviews: An introduction to qualitative research interviewing.* Thousand Oaks, CA: Sage.

Margulis, L. (1998). *Symbiotic planet.* New York: Basic Books.

Marsh, P., Rosser, E., & Harré, R. (1978). *The rules of disorder.* Boston: Routledge & Kegan Paul.

Mead, G. H. (1934). *Mind, self and society* (edited by C. W. Morris). Chicago: University of Chicago Press.

Mead, G. H. (1972). *The philosophy of the act* (edited with Introduction by C. W. Morris). Chicago: University of Chicago Press. (Original work published 1938)

Pearce, W. B. (1989). *Communication and the human condition.* Carbondale, IL: University of Southern Illinois Press.

Pearce, W. B., & Cronen, V. (1980). *Communication, action, and meaning: The creation of social realities.* New York: Praeger.

Polanyi, M. (1958). *Personal knowledge: Towards a post-critical philosophy.* Chicago: University of Chicago Press.

Rorty, R. (1989). *Contingency, irony, and solidarity.* Cambridge: Cambridge University Press.

Russell, B. (1939). Dewey's new logic. In P. A. Schilpp (Ed.), *The philosophy of John Dewey* (pp. 135–156). New York: Tudor.

Russell, B. (1940). *An inquiry into meaning and truth*. New York: George Allan & Unwin.

Santayana, G. (1925). Dewey's naturalistic metaphysics. *Journal of Philosophy, 22,* 673–688.

Saussure, F. (1969). *Course in general linguistics*. New York: McGraw-Hill. (Original work published 1916)

Senge, P. (1990). *The fifth discipline*. New York: Doubleday.

Tiles, J. E. (1988). *Dewey*. New York: Routledge & Kegan Paul.

Tomm, K. (1985). Circular interviewing: A multifaceted clinical tool. In D. Campbell & R. Draper (Eds.), *Applications of systemic family therapy: The Milan approach* (pp. 33–46). London: Gruen & Straton.

Westbrook, R. B. (1991). *John Dewey and American democracy*. Ithaca, NY: Cornell University Press.

Wittgenstein, L. (1953). *Philosophical investigations* (G. E. M. Anscombe, Trans.). New York: Macmillan.

Chapter 3

Transactional Philosophy and Communication Studies

Wayne Woodward
The University of Michigan–Dearborn

The pragmatist conception of transaction that provides a point of departure for this volume is the axis of a distinctive, comprehensive approach to inquiry. It is one that "develops the widening phases of knowledge, the broadening of system within the limits of observation and report" (Dewey & Bentley, 1949, p. 122). John Dewey[1] offered a defining distinction between *interaction* and *transaction*. The former relies principally on "procedure such that its inter-acting constituents are set up in inquiry as separate 'facts,' each in independence of the presence of others" (p. 122). The more encompassing transactional approach takes a view of "Fact such that no one of its constituents can be adequately specified as fact apart from the specification of other constituents of the full subjectmatter [*sic*]" (p. 122). Holistic attention to context and the interrelations of its constituent elements is a general hallmark of the pragmatist, transactional approach. (Ed. Note: Earlier in his career, Dewey often used the concept of *interaction*. Ironically, he applied it not in the sense developed here, but to describe his transactional ideas. Readers therefore should interpret its use,

---

[1]Dewey and Bentley (1949) jointly wrote *Knowing and the Known*, from which many of the observations about the transactional approach included in this chapter are taken. Bentley was sole author of three chapters of the volume; Dewey was sole author of one chapter; and the remaining eight chapters were co-authored. The emphasis here on Dewey highlights his particular importance to a pragmatist transactional philosophy, which was developed in other works as well—notably, Dewey's (1938) *Logic*.

with reference to Dewey's work, in other chapters of this volume in the transactional sense.)

A new transactional contextualism (Bruner, 1990) is taking shape in the contemporary human sciences. Psychologist Bruner (1986) noted its influence, that "[i]f you engage for long in the study of how human beings relate to one another, especially through the use of language, you are bound to be struck by the importance of 'transactions' " (p. 57).

Transactionalism, in both its originating and current formulations, is integral to a qualitative theory of action (Taylor, 1985) that advocates "a basic reversal in the order of explanation from the philosophy that Cartesianism and empiricism bequeathed to us" (p. 89). A "double shift" (p. 88) is involved. Movement "from a psychology of immediate self-transparency to one of achieved interiority" focuses attention on "the life of a living being who thinks" and whose "thinking is essentially expression" (p. 88). A corollary "principle of embodiment" implies a transactional view of experience as "the result, the sign, and the reward of that interaction of organism and environment which, when it is carried to the full, is a transformation of interaction into participation and communication" (Dewey, 1958, p. 22; see also Woodward, 1996, p. 165). Embodiment means that "[g]rasping things through symbols, establishing and maintaining practices, are things we do, are to be understood as activities" (Taylor, 1985, p. 87). In this light, the transactional approach is a theory of inquiry as practice and practice as inquiry.

This chapter begins with a discussion of core conceptual issues connecting qualitative philosophy with the pragmatist transactional position. Transactional concerns and commitments are then examined in relation to the development of communication theory. A commitment to neofunctionalism (Joas, 1996; see also Thomas, 1989) is advocated as a way of making the underlying organicism, or naturalism, of the transactional position compatible with insights of poststructuralist social science (see Denzin, 1997). The chapter concludes with specific assessment of the implications of transactional thought for contemporary and future communication studies.

A QUALITATIVE PHILOSOPHY OF ACTION

Transactional thought originates in a qualitative view of human action that results from an "expressivist turn" (Taylor, 1989, pp. 368–390) that Western thinking took in the 18th century. Philosophers of this era became preoccupied with "finding the good in our inner motivations" (p. 368). One central concern was to link inner experience with outer events by demonstrating how expression of the good depends on the communicative ability to "make it manifest in a given medium" (p. 368). This "principle of embodiment" (Taylor, 1985, p. 85) is a legacy of the qualitative view that becomes central to transactional theory. The emphasis on how the human "subject and all his functions . . . are inescapably embodied" (p. 85) is part of a "reaction against dualism" (p. 80) and an effort toward "recovery of the subject" (p. 80) that characterize debates of the earlier era as well as our own.

A key commitment of qualitative philosophy is its understanding of action, which rejects how Cartesianism "explains action in terms of the supposedly more basic datum of the mental" and instead "accounts for the mental as a development out of our primitive capacity for action" (Taylor, 1985, p. 90). This qualitative view of the subject as an agent holds that agency is realized through actions as the agent's identity unfolds in the process. The specific role of knowledge is to complete what action begins. Accordingly, the qualitative emphasis on "agent's knowledge" (p. 80) contrasts with observer's knowledge where cognition would receive prior emphasis.

The qualitative injunction to "understand reality as activity" (p. 83) challenges an empiricist or "causal view" of reality as "external event" (p. 81)—an objectified state of affairs to be contemplated from "a separate domain of inner, mental space" (p. 81). The causal account views action as primarily instrumental. Acts are directed toward external elements on the basis of "privileged access" I have to the motivating inner bias of "my desire, or intention—the cause of my action" (p. 81). In contrast, agent's action is creative (see Joas, 1996, p. 132)—a claim that pragmatist thought takes up and elaborates.

> Dewey and other pragmatists were concerned not to interpret all action according to the model of instrumental action, but, on the contrary, to offer a critique of the overly narrow "practical" orientation of American life. Thus, to regard action as the dimension on which all else rests precisely did not mean to conceive of the world as mere material for the intentions of actors. . . .
>
> These advances and modifications gave the pragmatist understanding of creativity clearer contours. It is indeed true that the pragmatists attempt to anchor creativity in the actions of human beings in their natural and social environment. (Joas, 1996, p. 132)

Qualitative, expressivist attention to action is advanced by pragmatist thinkers in the direction of a transactional theory of creative action. Particularly important from the standpoint of communication studies is the contributing notion of *situated creativity*, which is based on the premise that "[a]ll action is embedded in anthropological structures of communication" (p. 133). Sociologist Joas (1996) described the pragmatist view that "every situation contains a horizon of possibilities which in a crisis of action has to be rediscovered" (p. 133). It follows that,

> action consists not in the pursuit of clear-cut goals or in the application of norms, and creativity is not the overcoming of obstacles along these pre-scribed routes. Anchoring creativity in action allows pragmatists to conceive of creativity precisely as the liberation of the capacity for new actions. (p. 133)

This linkage of action and creativity within the context of anthropologi-cal structures of communication is a principal contribution of pragmatism to qualitative philosophy, particularly because such a philosophy provides direction for ethnographic examination of cultural and communicative practices. Joas (1996) asserted that "pragmatism is, put succinctly, a the-ory of situated creativity" (p. 133). This theory fundamentally challenges causal explanation, which is based on a "clear ontological separation be-tween outer event and inner background" (Taylor, 1985, p. 78). The prag-matist alternative holds that "action and purpose are ontologically insepa-rable" (p. 78) in that they are both grounded in situation.

Communication studies have been significantly shaped by the ways in which competing positions within the field "[draw] the boundaries quite differently, between 'inner' and 'outer' reality" (Taylor, 1985, p. 81). The divisions can be labeled in various ways,[2] but the basic issue is "an ontolog-ical one" (Stewart, 1996, p. 15), regardless of whether a paradigm upholds or challenges the presumption "that there is a fundamental distinction be-tween two realms or worlds, the world of the sign and the signified, symbol and symbolized, name and named . . ." (p. 15).

The pragmatist challenge to dualism draws its inspiration from the 18th-century debates and especially the expressivist anthropology that emerged. This culturally oriented view "differs radically from a rationalist definition of man as a rational being" (Joas, 1996, p. 79). The qualitative alternative "conceives of human reason not as a separate faculty which ex-erts a commanding influence on human sensuality, but rather as a specific way human beings have of interacting with themselves and the world" (p. 79). This position creates a fundamental linkage between identity and community, as Joas pointed out.

> Firstly, we form a clear picture of the meaningful substance of what we vaguely have in mind only through our efforts to express it; and secondly, in our efforts to express something, we always present that which is expressed

---

[2]The historically significant division between administrative and critical approaches is one example.

in such a way that other people can appreciate it. Our relationship to ourselves is therefore conveyed via a medium which we share with others. (p. 79)

The pragmatist position highlights these important consequences of the qualitative perspective: that it (a) foregrounds the study of communication as a focus for the human sciences, (b) predicates a transactional view of communication, and (c) links transactionalism with participation in community—ideally as dialogue.

To summarize these transactional commitments, first recall that communication becomes foundational as part of the qualitative challenge to Cartesianism. Assume that the observer's "self-transparency" (Taylor, 1985, p. 85) is not immediately and intuitively "constituted as data"—as empiricism predicates—but rather is "a goal we must work towards . . . something we have to achieve" (p. 85). Then qualitative attention turns inevitably to the question of how "self-understanding . . . is brought off in a medium, through symbols or concepts" (p. 85). Knowledge becomes "the fruit of an activity of formulating how things are with us, what we desire, feel, think, and so on" (p. 85). Accordingly, "formulating things in this medium"—arguably, the defining characteristic of communication—is established "as one of our fundamental activities" (p. 85).

Second, communication emerges as transactional when the human, as an expressive being, is defined as "a being whose thinking is always and necessarily in a medium" (Taylor, 1985, p. 85). This principle of embodiment is basic to the qualitative theory of the human, which regards "our primitive capacity for action" (p. 90) as the foundational precedent for experience. Certainly a basic attainment associated with human expression is to "become more knowledgeable about ourselves" (p. 91). This knowledge is achieved as part of a "long slow process which makes us able to get things in clearer focus, describe them more exactly" (p. 91). In short, expressive activities not only form the basis of personal identity, but they also "reveal things" (p. 91).

Finally, the norm of dialogue in community develops out of this process that brings the things of the human world into focus and relation by and with persons. Expressions are not solely mental or conceptual achievements. Instead they are, preeminently, bodily activities, of which it can be said that "their first uses are relatively unreflecting" (Taylor, 1985, p. 91). But not so their fuller development. An originating "aim to make plain in public space how we feel, or how we stand with each other, or where things stand for us" (p. 91) develops toward "a demand for reciprocal recognition, within the life of a community" (p. 88).

The principle of embodiment suggests that we transact our identities as we simultaneously transact our relations with others and as we transact patterns of exchange by means of the physical–artifactual substratum of human activity. Human action and communication are accordingly triadic (see Woodward, 1996). They entail transactions that complexly integrate the formation of (i) personal identities, (ii) social relations, and (iii) the physical–artifactual environments of human experience.

These transactional processes operate at the personal and collective—the "mutual-personal" (see Kirkpatrick, 1986, pp. 137–181; Woodward, 1996, 2000)—levels because the "true goal of the search for recognition remains community" (Taylor, 1985, p. 88). Communication as a form of participation establishes community and dialogue as normative-contextualist (Woodward, 1993) standards. Such standards are tied to "social meanings" (p. 166), which are "normative, while at the same time, they are also historically and culturally contingent." Philosopher Walzer (1983) explained this position—that although "[t]here is no single standard . . . there are standards (roughly knowable even when they are controversial) for every social good and every distributive sphere in every particular society" (p. 10). A situated or transactional approach to inquiry is required to understand social goods and distributions because "[m]en and women take on concrete identities because of the way they conceive and create and then possess and employ social goods" (p. 8). Walzer (1983) specified the transactional nature of the processes involved:

> In fact, people already stand in relation to a set of goods; they have a history of transactions, not only with one another but also with the moral and material world in which they live. Without such a history, which begins at birth, they wouldn't be men and women in any recognizable sense. (p. 8)

I have elsewhere labeled this a *transactional-participatory* (Woodward, 1996) approach as it applies to communication. I draw on this conception in returning to consideration of the pragmatist foundations of transactionalism established by Dewey.

TRANSACTIONAL INQUIRY

The defining themes and commitments of a qualitative philosophy of action are taken up by the pragmatist transactional approach. The holistic, integrative perspective requires

> insistence upon the right to proceed in freedom to select and view all subjectmatters [sic] in whatever way seems desirable under reasonable hypothesis, and regardless of ancient claims on behalf of either minds or material mechanisms, or any of the surrogates of either. (Dewey & Bentley, 1949, p. 124)

This methodological flexibility allows Dewey's transactional philosophy (Becker, 1964, p. 3, and passim; Eco, 1989, p. 27) to address dualist divisions of his own time between materialist and idealist positions. His formulation also anticipates aspects of subsequent debates that have opposed determinist views—materialist, behaviorist, structuralist (see Giddens & Turner, 1987, pp. 350–353, 58–81, 195–223)—to perspectives that uphold the shaping influence of human agency—dialogic, cultural, structurationist (see Buber, 1965; Carey, 1989; Giddens, 1984.). The integrative principle is "that 'thing' is in action, and 'action' is observable as a thing, while all the distinctions between things and actions are taken as marking provisional stages of subjectmatter to be established through further inquiry" (Dewey & Bentley, 1949, p. 123).

Communication is at the core of this transactional approach. Dewey (Dewey & Bentley, 1949) asserted that "[t]he transactional is in fact that point of view which systematically proceeds upon the ground that knowing is co-operative and as such is integral with communication" (p. vi). The relevant sense of communication is "the making of something common" (Dewey, 1938, p. 46). Williams (1976) characterized this usage as "the most general modern meaning" of the term—one that "has been in the language since C15 [15th century]" (p. 72). The transactional perspective unifies consideration of the physical and symbolic dimensions of communication. It does so by maintaining that "[l]anguage is made up of physical existences . . . [b]ut these do not *operate* or function as mere physical things when they are media of communication" (Dewey, 1938, p. 46). The appeal to "convention or common consent," which marks the communicative element of human experience, "is that of agreement in *action*; of shared modes of responsive behavior and participation in their consequences" (p. 46).

The transactional "operations" (Dewey, 1938, p. 14) that characterize action and participation "fall into two general types. There are operations that are performed upon and with existential material . . . [and] . . . operations performed with and upon symbols" (pp. 14–15). The integrative perspective of transactionalism holds that "symbols in the latter case stand for possible final existential conditions while the conclusion, when it is stated in symbols, is a pre-condition of further operations that deal with existence" (p. 15).[3]

By concentrating on the nexus of material/symbolic operations in communication, the transactional approach interrelates what academic study

---

[3]Carey (1989) presented this basic position succinctly with his formula that "[w]e first produce the world by symbolic work and then take up residence in the world we have produced" (p. 30). Carey concludes that "[a]ll human activity is such an exercise (can one resist the word 'ritual'?) in squaring the circle . . . Alas, there is magic in our self-deceptions" (p. 30).

in this field has traditionally separated into "communication . . . discourse as embodied language" and "communications . . . discourse in light of the context of its material embodiment" (see Heyer, 1988, p. 148). Consideration of the first dimension elicits the call for "an approach to the media which is fundamentally 'cultural' " and thus concerned "with the meaningful character of symbolic forms *and* with their social contextualization" (Thompson, 1995, p. 10). The study of communications conventionally implies a focus on the "technical medium" and "the material elements with which, and by means of which, information or symbolic content is fixed and transmitted from producer to receiver" (p. 18). The transactional approach challenges the historical tendency of communication studies to insert a fundamental division of labor between those investigating one or the other dimension of this supposed boundary.

Carey (1989) indicated the commitments associated with these divergent traditions. He contrasted a "transmission or transportation view of communication" (p. 42), which has characterized much of the development of American communication studies, with a "ritual view" (p. 43). The latter is Carey's preferred way of elucidating an alternative, culturally informed perspective. Although the first position considers communication "as a process of transmitting messages at a distance for the purpose of control" (p. 42), the latter perspective sees it as a "process through which a shared culture is created, modified, and transformed" (p. 43). The transmission view is based on interests that seek the "extension of messages across geography for purposes of control" (p. 43). It tends to establish communicative norms of "persuasion; attitude change; behavior modification; socialization through the transmission of information, influence, or conditioning or, alternatively, as a case of individual choice over what to read or view" (pp. 42–43). A ritual view "centers on the sacred ceremony that draws persons together in fellowship and commonality" (p. 43). It selects its archetypes or norms from "ritual and mythology for those who come at the problem from anthropology; art and literature for those who come at the problem from literary criticism and history" (p. 43).

Obviously, a contrast between a more instrumental and culturally attuned view of communication can be described in other terms than transmission versus ritual. From a transactional perspective, it is important to address a continuing tendency of American communication studies to segregate studies of the material and economic aspects of media and communication from sociocultural and symbolic analyses.

Thompson's (1995) social theory of the media illustrates a contemporary effort to combine insights concerning the interrelations of material and symbolic dimensions of communication. Thompson argued that an integrative understanding of discourse and its embodying "material substratum" (p. 18) should be organized around the postulate that "[t]ech-

nical media, and the information or symbolic content stored in them, can
. . . be used as a resource for the exercise of different forms of power" (p.
19). Furthermore, the dynamics of power are most appropriately examined from a view that regards technical media "as differing kinds of 'information storage mechanisms' which are able, to differing degrees, to
preserve information or symbolic content and make it available for subsequent use" (p. 19). Eisenstein's (1979) analysis of the "new process of data
collection" (p. 107) that emerged with the advent of print culture anticipated this information storage view of communication. Thompson's similar conclusions connect with an emphasis that cultural studies approaches,
including Eisenstein's, have placed on the political and cultural dimensions of communication:

> [T]he exercise of power by political and religious authorities has always been
> closely linked to the collation and control of information and communica-
> tion, as exemplified by the role of scribes in earlier centuries and the role of
> diverse agencies—from organizations compiling official statistics to public
> relations officers—in our societies today. (Thompson, 1995, pp. 19–20)

The transactional approach helps articulate and advance this information storage or data collection view of communication. The influence of
Carey's ritual emphasis on shared culture has solidified development of
an

> important movement in contemporary thought about communication . . . a
> view that concentrates on the construction of "symbolic universes" . . . how
> the elements that constitute a "common stock of information" . . . or "stock
> of knowledge" . . . within a community or culture are produced, reproduced,
> collected, stored, augmented, manipulated, and retrieved by members of
> that culture. (Woodward, 1996, p. 155)

Building on foundational "semiotic, sociological, and interactional" (p.
169) models of how "shared worlds" (p. 170) are constructed, a transactional perspective focuses on "three levels of structures—sign systems,
social relations, the physical/artifactual infrastructure" (p. 169) that provide the context for communication and action.

These three levels played a prominent part in Dewey's originating analysis of the "naming-named transaction as a single total event [that] is basic" (Dewey & Bentley, 1949, p. 137) to human experience. Dewey illustrated with the example of "a trade, or commercial transaction" (p. 270).
Attention to the semiotic level—the sign system in question—indicates
that what "determines one participant to be a buyer and the other a seller"
is that these social identities are "marked by the traits and properties
which are found in whatever is recognized to be a transaction" (p. 270).

Thus, a signifying system constitutes a first level at which "one exists as buyer or seller . . . *in and because of* a transaction in which each is engaged" (p. 270). A sociological level of analysis informs understanding of how the social identities in question are not only significations, but also " 'forms of sociation' that represent the multiple ways 'in which individuals grow together into units that satisfy their interests' " (Woodward, 1996, p. 159; cites Simmel, 1950, p. 41). Dewey observed of this second level that "because of the exchange or transfer, both parties (the idiomatic name for participants) undergo change" (Dewey & Bentley, 1949, p. 270) solely on account of "being a party in transactions in which cultural conditions partake" (pp. 270–271). The physical–artifactual substratum of action is observable when "specific things become goods or commodities because they are engaged in the transaction" (p. 270). This third level of analysis reveals how physical goods of exchange "undergo at the very least a change of locus by which they gain and lose certain connective relations or 'capacities' previously possessed" (p. 270).

Dewey recognized the triadic (see Woodward, 1996) elements of transactional analysis—signification, social relations, physical–artifactual substratum—in this example. In addition, he observed that the discussion remains only at the threshold of a fully transactional approach. However, until it is acknowledged how,

> no given transaction of trade stands alone. It is enmeshed in a body of . . . transactions that are neither industrial, commercial, nor financial; to which the name "intangible" is often given, but which can be more safely named by means of specifying rules and regulations that proceed from the system of customs in which other transactions exist and operate. (Dewey & Bentley, 1949, p. 271)

The importance of the underlying system of customs centers the transactional approach on cultural practices, highlighting the connection to Carey's and Thompson's ritual and social approaches to the study of communication. Dewey sought out more generalizable observations about the "conditions" of human experience that "have to do with those relatively invariant features of a process . . . [such as transactions] . . . that provide essential grounds for successfully realizing the aims of the process" (Woodward, 1993, p. 165).

> A trade is cited as a transaction in order to call attention to . . . the fact that human life itself, both severally and collectively, consists of transactions in which human beings partake together with non-human things of the milieu along with other human beings, so that without this togetherness of human and non-human partakers we could not even stay alive, to say nothing of accomplishing anything. (Dewey & Bentley, 1949, p. 271)

The culturally determined sense of transaction as an exchange centered on commercial or other forms of value (representing "the concerns, cares, affairs, etc., of common sense" [p. 285]) is accordingly extended toward a broader sense of transaction as "things done and to be done, facta and facienda, that . . . belong to and are possessed by the one final practical affair—the state and course of life as a body of transactions" (Dewey & Bentley, 1949, p. 285).

Dewey's transactionalism presses at the limits of a cultural analysis to seek out "protonorms" that "are of a universal order conceptually speaking; they reflect our common condition as a species" (Christians, 1997, p. 12). Consistent with the normative-contextualist position cited earlier, the notion of protonorms does not imply that "the forms of participation entailed should be considered as invariant across historical and cultural time and space" (Woodward, 1996, p. 169). Rather, "[a]ttention is directed toward comprehending how the norm of participation is sought out, achieved, and contested in diverse, historically concrete situations" (p. 169). Thus, a transactional approach can retain its commitment to situated analysis (see Joas, 1996, p. 160) while pressing toward norms that are grounded in "mutual humanity . . . the bondedness we share inescapably with others" (Christians, 1997, p. 12). Arguing that such norms "can only be recovered locally and inscribed culturally," Christians specified how "[l]anguage situates them in history . . . [and] . . . human beings enter them through the immediate reality of geography, ethnicity, and ideology" (p. 12). A "thicker view"—the "widening phases of knowledge . . . system . . . observation and report" (Dewey & Bentley, 1949, p. 122) that transactional inquiry requires—would suggest a standard that can "distinguish between the universal and the particular as with a windowpane, knowing there is a decisive break yet recognizing that the universal realm is only transparent in the local" (Christians, 1997, p. 12).

TRANSACTIONAL ANALYSIS IN COMMUNICATION THEORY

Consideration of how communication theory has incorporated elements of the transactional approach can take a number of paths. One approach is to concentrate on the "fresh perspective on communication" (Carey, 1989, p. 23) afforded by those cultural studies proponents who traced out alternative origins for the field. They have looked elsewhere than the empiricist's dominant paradigm (see Gerbner, 1983) for foundational concepts and orientations toward communicative processes. Carey (1989) specified that

> the resources were found by going back to the work of Weber, Durkheim, deTocqueville, and Huizinga, as well as by utilizing contemporaries such as

Kenneth Burke, Hugh Duncan, Adolph Portman, Thomas Kuhn, Peter Bur-
ger, and Clifford Geertz. Basically, however, the most viable though still inadequate tradition of social thought on communication comes from those
colleagues and descendants of Dewey in the Chicago School: from Mead and
Cooley through Robert Park and on to Erving Goffman. (p. 23)

Carey rightly observed that "[n]ames solve nothing" (p. 96). Nonetheless, the tradition they evoke provides alternative "concepts and notions
within which media studies might fruitfully circle" (p. 96). This tradition
situates the pragmatist transactional philosophy as the centerpiece of "a
theory of action and social order" (Joas, 1993, p. 17) focused on communicative processes. A direct intellectual lineage can be traced from these
founding figures of pragmatist and symbolic interactionist thought to contemporary scholars in the American cultural studies tradition (see Carey,
1997). This way of conceiving the development of transactional thought in
relation to communication theory seems to require no detour into "empirical media study" (see Czitrom, 1982, pp. 122–146) other than to note its
value as an antithesis against which to measure success in depicting cultural specificity.

An alternative approach highlights instances where transactional
thought appears as a contributing influence within empirical media studies. This avenue is preferable given several factors. Historically, empirical
research traditions developed alongside pragmatism, certainly in its later
manifestations as Chicago-school sociology and symbolic interactionism.
This "proximity . . . has provided a philosophical context for the celebration of instrumental value and the practicality of human action that reflects the utilitarian nature of liberal-pluralism" (Hardt, 1992, p. 5) in the
American context. In short, the pragmatist legacy retains important connections to empirical approaches to the study of communication and
other social phenomena. These need to be understood.

Assessing the Chicago-school tradition in terms of its relevance to contemporary sociology and social theory, Joas (1993) pronounced that "it
stands in the middle between the speculative evolutionist social philosophy of sociology's early years and empirical modern social science" (p. 26).
Hardt (1992) catalogued pragmatism's attributes more exhaustively, emphasizing proponents' interests in

reconciliation between morals and science . . . scientific practice based upon
the primacy of the community of inquirers . . . the importance of ethical
processes in the discussion of social interests . . . [and] understanding of the
practical character of thought and reality upon a behavioral interpretation
of the mind. (p. 34)

Hardt (1992) quoted Dewey (1931, p. 24) on the "fundamental difference" that distinguishes pragmatism from "historical empiricism," of

which it is an "extension": "that it does not insist upon antecedent phenomena but consequent phenomena; not upon the precedents but upon the possibilities of action" (Hardt, 1992, p. 34). Dewey concluded with the assessment that "this change in point of view is almost revolutionary in its consequences" (p. 34). Given these significant affinities, the effort to assess transactional thought in relation to empirical approaches to communication is worthwhile.

A second argument has to do with an increasing interest in research approaches that combine cultural studies with empirical research, often employing mainstream social science methods. Audience studies, in particular, have migrated toward such an integration (see Hay, Grossberg, & Wartella, 1996) that can readily be viewed as consistent with the methodological principles of transactionalism. Examples can also be cited from areas such as feminist theory, which has heard recent calls "to reconnect with more sociological and policy-relevant questions" to produce "a more applied feminist cultural studies armed with data and empirical facts" (Ferguson & Golding, 1997, p. xviii; see also McRobie, 1997). More generally, the prospect of a "new ethnography" (Morley, 1997, p. 121) capable of extending its alternative model of inquiry across media studies predicates a "return to the 'three Es': the empirical, the experiential and the ethnographic" (Ferguson & Golding, 1997, p. xviii). Again, the motivations to connect pragmatism with empirical traditions merit attention.

The empirical tradition is on the process side of a distinction between two main schools of communication study (Fiske, 1990). The process school is "concerned with how senders and receivers encode and decode, with how transmitters use the channels and media of communication . . . with matters like efficiency and accuracy" (p. 2). The "semiotics"[4] school is concerned with "production and exchange of meanings . . . the role of texts . . . signification . . . culture" (p. 2).

Two articles published in the 1950s represent the empirically oriented process school and introduce elements of a transactional perspective: the first, by psychologist Theodore M. Newcomb (1953), and the second, by communication scholars Bruce H. Westley and Malcolm S. MacLean Jr. (1957). These essays suggest the long-standing interest that certain empirical researchers have shown in integrating a more sociocultural view of communication as "communicative acts" with an empirical concern for measuring effects of the "transmission of information, consisting of discriminative stimuli" (Newcomb, 1953, p. 393).

---

[4]Stewart's (1995, 1996) critique of the semiotic model exemplifies an interest that contemporary transactionalism shares to transcend both the effects model and the symbol model by focusing attention on what Stewart labeled *articulate contact*—a notion that has much in common with transactional inquiry.

These articles share the premise that communication occurs as actions within a "life space" conceived as "the system of relations between two or more communicators and the objects of their communication" (Newcomb, 1953, p. 403). Additionally, communication is distinctively seen as the basis for creating "a more extended environment" (Westley & MacLean, 1957, p. 34), which it does "by means of symbols expressing shared meanings" (p. 34). Expression begins to be viewed here not solely according to a source-receiver view of message transmission. Rather, it becomes an attribute that characterizes "a person, or primary group, or a total social system" (p. 34). Such terms begin to suggest a cultural analysis that will take more definitive shape only a decade or more later (see Carey, 1989, 1997; Fergsuon & Golding, 1997; Hardt, 1992).

Newcomb (1953) introduced the notion of "co-orientation" (p. 393). It emphasizes how communication is "dependent upon a common environment" (p. 394). The "continued attachment" of communicators is seen as "contingent upon the discovery or development of common interests beyond themselves" (p. 394). Included here are "two considerations of complementary nature" (p. 394). The first is *environmental reference*—that the "more intense one person's concern for another the more sensitive he is likely to be to the other's orientations to objects in the environment" (p. 394). The second is *social reality*, in the sense that the "other's judgment provides a testing ground for social reality" (p. 395) or "what is true and valid" (p. 394). The integrative, transactional thrust of these observations is to suggest that "it is an almost constant human necessity to orient oneself toward objects in the environment and also toward other persons oriented toward those same objects" (p. 395). Furthermore, "[c]ommunication is the most common and usually the most effective means" (p. 395).

These foundational notions point toward a general theory that aims to be "sufficiently general to treat all kinds of human communication from two-person face-to-face interaction to intentional and intercultural communications" (Westley & MacLean, 1957, p. 38). This would include, of course, mass communications. "Advocacy roles" and "channel roles" for purposive and nonpurposive communicators would make up some of its elements. The parts would also include "behavioral system roles," meaning "a personality or social system requiring and using communications about the condition of its environment for the satisfaction of its needs and solution of its problems" (p. 38). This is often referred to as a receiver or public. In addition, the model includes the "totality of objects and events 'out there' " and "these objects and events as abstracted into transmissible form: 'messages' about . . . relationships" (p. 38). Expanded understandings of communication begin to suggest "[a] transactional approach [that] is seeing together what has been seen separately and held apart" (Steg & Schulman, 1979, p. 317).

These important additions to the paradigm of empirical, communication research nevertheless are limited by the narrow instrumentalism to which the authors often revert. The dynamics of the communication system are viewed primarily in terms of a message sender's possible solutions to communicative challenges, which are encountered in Newcomb's (1953) model:

> under conditions of demand for co-orientation . . . a problem which he can attempt to solve behaviorally (i.e., by communicative acts) and/or cognitively (i.e., by changing either his own orientations or his perception of . . . [another's] . . . orientations. (p. 401)

Consideration of mass communication contexts does not alter this behaviorist orientation. Although individual behavioral intentions may be more difficult to attribute, still this stage of development in process theory bases its analysis on the motivating factors of " 'need satisfactions' and 'problem solutions' " (Westley & MacLean, 1957, p. 36). Thus, the quality of analysis remains distantly removed from a view of transactionalism that emphasizes how "human action could not be fully or properly accounted for from the inside out—by reference only to intrapsychic dispositions, traits, learning capacities, motives, or whatever," but needed instead to be "situated . . . conceived of as continuous with a cultural world" (Bruner, 1990, p. 105).

The prospects for a transactional perspective to foster more productive dialogue between the traditions depend on recuperating functionalism. Functionalism is arguably a common reference point that empirical studies and the transactional perspective could mutually adopt and develop. The project must begin with reaffirmed rejection of any structural-functionalist paradigm that would attempt to establish sociocultural norms based on the ability of communication to successfully integrate diverse cultural interests under the banner of an attributed, shared worldview. A methodological bias toward "interpreting all ideas and practices as systemically normalizing" (Thomas, 1997, p. 83) renders this sort of functionalism largely incapable of explaining "evidence of unshared values or contradictory beliefs" (p. 82) when these emerge.

What is required, instead, is a functionalism attuned to communicative process in a manner that acknowledges how "[p]articular virtues perform certain functions, play certain roles in human life" (Wallace, 1978, p. 15). This approach starts out from the premise that "life is a normative concept that cannot be understood apart from the conception of a creature's good" (p. 16). It seeks to comprehend the culturally specific functioning of "[s]uch virtues as courage and restraint [that] enable individuals to govern themselves, to pursue plans, to act on principles, and to participate fully in a life structured by intelligence, institutions, and conventions" (p. 15). The underlying organicism of pragmatist transactional philosophy is developed in a critical spirit, avoiding two distortive extremes of relativism and ethnocentrism.

> A functionalism of this kind is critical relative to a broad conception of the proper activity of the organism and thus differs decisively from what might be called the *tout comprendre, tout pardonner* functionalism of cultural relativist anthropology. It is also different from Parsonian functionalism, which has dominated much of contemporary sociology and political science, since it begins with a set of provisional and corrigible claims about objective human needs and problems rather than with a list of the characteristic or necessary functions of social or political systems. (Salkever, 1983, p. 210)

This critical functionalism is designed to take on what Taylor (1989) considered to be "the greatest intellectual problem of human culture . . . distinguishing the human universals from the historical constellations and not eliding the second into the first so that our particular way seems somehow inescapable for humans as such . . ." (p. 112). Christians' (1997) advocacy of "a broadly based ethical theory of communication" approaches this challenge through a series of questions posed "at three different levels of abstraction" that contribute to a credible "normative vision" (p. ix).

> In foundational terms, what is the rationale for normativity in an age of normlessness? Within the domain of particular cultures, are there common values underlying them that are similar to those of other cultural traditions? And on the level of communication practice and policy, are there master norms that provide direction and boundaries for media morality? (p. ix)

Grounding the search for normativity in a critical functionalism may seem counterintuitive at first glance—an attempt to recommend functionalism to ethicists and cultural theorists whom we might expect to be its principal critics. For example, when Carey (1989) defined *communication* as "a symbolic process whereby reality is produced, maintained, repaired, and transformed" (p. 23), one is inclined to view this formulation in the light of Carey's accompanying critique of functionalism:

> Functional analysis, like causal analysis, goes directly from the source to the effect without ever seriously examining mass communication as a system of interacting symbols and interlocked meanings that somehow must be linked to the motivations and emotions for which they provide a symbolic outlet (p. 55).

Carey regarded functionalism as inevitably a species of causal explanation—a premise that anthropologist Rappaport (1979) questioned when he observed that "[w]e should beware of confusing explanation with informativeness or understanding" (p. 49). Rappaport's assessment of functional accounts was that

> whether or not they are "explanatory" (and if properly formulated and appropriately applied I take them to be), statements of "what it does" and "how it does it" may well be among the most informative, important, and interesting that may be made concerning an organ, an institution, or a convention. (pp. 49–50)

Rappaport moved into direct dialogue with Carey's position when he further observed that, "among the most informative things that can be said about structures or systems, be they organic, social, cultural, or ecological, are statements concerning how they maintain, order, reproduce, and transform themselves" (p. 50).

The tension between functional and cultural accounts begins to be resolved by the previously discussed distinction by Dewey between an empiricist concentration on "antecedent phenomena" and the "precedents of action," when compared with a pragmatist emphasis on "consequent phenomena" and the "possibilities of action." A neofunctionalism[5] attuned to creative possibilities aligns communication theory with "a social theory which is based on action theory, does not conflate functional analyses and causal explanations, yet contains the benefits of a controlled use of system models" (Joas, 1996, p. 222). Joas suggested that relevant approaches might be more appropriately conceived as "constitution theories" (p. 230)—a category elsewhere linked with the "normative-contextualist" thrust of transactionalism (see Woodward, 1993, p. 164). Regardless of the label one prefers, the key concern is to "make social processes intelligible in terms of the actions of the members of a society without assuming there to be some underlying transhistorical developmental trend" (Joas, 1996, p. 231).

TOWARD AN ECOLOGICAL TRANSACTIONALISM

The contemporary value of the transactional perspective to communication studies centers on the originating promise of pragmatist philosophy to uncover the "foundations of a theory of action and social order" and to develop "these fundamental ideas into concrete social scientific theory and empirical research" (Joas, 1993, p. 17). This suggests how the rele-

---

[5]Thomas (1989) presented the specific case for a revised and applied functionalism in communication studies in its broad implications.

vance of transactionalism extends beyond communication studies to the human sciences more generally. The integrative material/symbolic perspective of the transactional core philosophy responds to a general critique of social science that Bourdieu (1988) expressed. Bourdieu observed that it "oscillates between two seemingly incompatible points of view, two apparently irreconcilable perspectives: objectivism and subjectivism . . . physicalism or psychologism" (p. 14). He said that the social sciences tend either to "treat social facts as things" or "reduce the social world to the representations that agents have of it, the task of social science consisting then in producing an 'account of the accounts' produced by social subjects" (pp. 14–15). A transactional perspective envisions a remedy to this rupture by overcoming the "intellectual isolation . . . that separates studies of individual psychology from studies of the sociocultural environment in which individuals live" (Wertsch, 1985, p. 1). The appropriate interdisciplinary and integrative strategy characterizes pragmatist transactional philosophy.

Laboring to construct this transactional approach from his vantage point at mid-20th century, Dewey lacked essential critical insights and methodological resources to carry through on the envisioned program. Dewey's transactional philosophy sometimes evinced an "organic idealism" (see West, 1989, p. 95) that had essentialist, universalist tendencies. In addition, the notion of "organized intelligence" (see Schiller, 1996, p. 72, for a critique) extended the naturalism associated with the organismic metaphor, often uncritically, to the study of human activities and institutions. Its applications there must be carefully delimited. Treating "knowledge as itself inquiry—as a goal within inquiry, not as a terminus outside or beyond inquiry," the transactional perspective arguably embraces an antiessentialism that "excludes assertions of fixity and [all] attempts to impose them" (Dewey & Bentley, 1949, p. vi). At the same time, it develops its underlying organicism in ways that allow for normative statements to be generated based on "enriched descriptions of primary life processes in their environments and of the more complex behavioral processes in theirs" (p. 129).

Contemporary updating of the transactional model is made possible by what sociocultural researchers, as exemplified by Joas, have learned as a result of addressing the "crisis of representation in the human sciences" (Marcus & Fischer, 1986, p. 7). A "sixth moment" of interpretive and ethnographic sophistication—attuned to a "postcolonial world . . . defined by difference and disjuncture and shifting borders and borderlines" (Denzin, 1997, p. 265)—is called for as the progressive result of poststructuralist experimentation. Interactionist (see Denzin, 1989; Leeds-Hurwitz, 1995) and transactional models of sociocultural life are necessarily transformed in the process. Insights from contemporary cultural and interpretive theory—and particularly constructivist (see Pearce, 1995) views—can contribute to a more valid transactional synthesis of organismic with cultural perspectives (see Woodward, 2000).

One notable model for this integration is philosopher Jonas' (1974, p. xvii) long-term project to connect a "theory of organism" or "philosophical biology" (Jonas, 1966, p. 2) with "a reunion of ontology and ethics" (Vogel, 1996, p. 15). For Jonas (1974, p. xvii), the resultant "philosophical anthropology" or "philosophy of life" (Jonas, 1966, p. 282) pronounces in favor of an "intrinsic forward thrust of organic theory itself toward an ethical completion" (Jonas, 1974, p. xvii).

Jonas' (1984, p. 189) movement of thought is toward an ecological perspective (see Jagtenberg & McKie, 1997, for assessment of ecological approaches in communication studies), which is consistent with the overall trajectory of Dewey's transactional philosophy. Dewey referred specifically to the importance of the "descriptive spade-work of the ecologies" (Dewey & Bentley, 1949, p. 125). He considered ecological studies of his era to be "full of illustrations of the interactional . . . and . . . still fuller of the transactional . . . (where the observer . . . sees more sympathetically the full system of growth and change)" (p. 128). Thus, ecology was a likely source of "anticipated future development of transdermally transactional treatment" (p. 125) with its particular emphasis on "organism and environment" (p. 123). Penetrating beyond "current conventional distinctions between them" (i.e., organism and environment)—the transactional perspective "requires their primary acceptance in common system, with full freedom reserved for their developing examination" (p. 123). Nearly half a century later, Jonas (1984) invested primary importance in "the nascent science of ecology" (p. 6) as the source of relevant questions for ethical philosophers and sociocultural theorists of our time. It also is important as the impetus for the "interdisciplinary pooling and integration . . . [of] . . . the global environmental science that is needed" (p. 189) as a guide to his envisioned ethics of responsibility. On the basis of such connections among the past, present, and projected future of interdisciplinary research and activism, and notwithstanding important critical qualifications induced by historical perspective, Dewey's agenda usefully can inform a contemporary vision. The vision would focus on how critical inquiry should be carried out in a poststructuralist (see Best & Kellner, 1991, pp. 20–25; Giddens & Turner, 1987, pp. 195–223) or postsemiotic (see Stewart, 1996) spirit. This agenda can be aimed especially at understanding how language, action, and agency interrelate; how their dynamics influence the expression of social and personal identity; and the consequences this picture has for the symbolic and geophysical habitats of human action.[6]

---

[6]Jagtenberg and McKie (1997) indicated new maps of how postmodernist thought can combine with environmentalism to articulate norms of sustainability based on "ecological holism" (p. xii).

Dewey's orienting perspective on transactional analysis remains relevantly applicable to developing an antiessentialist, dialogic social constructivism (see Pearce, 1995) based in contemporary cultural studies and directed toward ecological holism. Advances in communication studies will prove central to its development. The transactional perspective contributes distinctively to communication studies by indicating how a culturally sophisticated ethnographic approach can address broad ecological concerns with an empirical rigor appropriate to its commitment to a "situated" (see Anderson, 1996, pp. 84–87) view of human action.

REFERENCES

Anderson, J. A. (1996). The pragmatics of audience in research and theory. In J. Hay, L. Grossberg, & E. Wartella (Eds.), *The audience and its landscape* (pp. 75–93). Boulder, CO: Westview.

Becker, E. (1964). *The revolution in psychiatry*. New York: The Free Press.

Best, S., & Kellner, D. (1991). *Postmodern theory*. New York: Guilford.

Bourdieu, P. (1988). Social space and symbolic power. *Sociological Theory*, 7(1), 14–25.

Bruner, J. (1986). *Actual minds, possible worlds*. Cambridge, MA: Harvard University Press.

Bruner, J. (1990). *Acts of meaning*. Cambridge, MA: Harvard University Press.

Buber, M. (1965). *Between man and man*. New York: Macmillan.

Carey, J. W. (1989). *Communication as culture*. Boston: Unwin Hyman.

Carey, J. W. (1997). Reflections on the project of (American) cultural studies. In M. Ferguson & P. Golding (Eds.), *Cultural studies in question* (pp. 1–24). Thousand Oaks, CA: Sage.

Christians, C. (1997). The ethics of being in a communications context. In C. Christians & M. Traber (Eds.), *Communication ethics and universal values* (pp. 3–23). Thousand Oaks, CA: Sage.

Czitrom, D. (1982). *Media and the American mind*. Chapel Hill, NC: University of North Carolina Press.

Denzin, N. (1989). *Interpretive interactionism*. Thousands Oaks, CA: Sage.

Denzin, N. (1997). *Interpretive ethnography*. Thousand Oaks, CA: Sage.

Dewey, J. (1931). *Philosophy and civilization*. New York: Minton, Balch.

Dewey, J. (1938). *Logic: The theory of inquiry*. New York: Henry Holt.

Dewey, J. (1958). *Art as experience*. New York: Capricorn.

Dewey, J., & Bentley, A. F. (1949). *Knowing and the known*. Boston: Beacon.

Eco, U. (1989). *The open work*. Cambridge, MA: Harvard University Press.

Eisenstein, E. (1979). *The printing press as an agent of change*. Cambridge: Cambridge University Press.

Ferguson, M., & Golding, P. (1997). *Cultural studies in question*. Thousand Oaks, CA: Sage.

Fiske, J. (1990). *Introduction to communication studies* (2nd ed.). New York: Routledge.

Giddens, A. (1984). *The constitution of society*. Berkeley, CA: University of California Press.

Giddens, A., & Turner, J. (1987). *Social theory today*. Stanford: Stanford University Press.

Gerbner, G. (1983). Ferment in the field (Special Issue). *Journal of Communication*, *33*(3).

Hardt, H. (1992). *Critical communication studies*. New York: Routledge.

Hay, J., Grossberg, L., & Wartella, E. (1996). *The audience and its landscape*. Boulder, CO: Westview.

Heyer, P. (1988). *Communications and history*. New York: Greenwood.

Jagtenberg, T., & McKie, D. (1997). *Eco-impacts and the greening of postmodernity*. Thousand Oaks, CA: Sage.

Joas, H. (1993). *Pragmatism and social theory*. Chicago: University of Chicago Press.

Joas, H. (1996). *The creativity of action*. Chicago: University of Chicago Press.

Jonas, H. (1966). *The phenomenon of life*. Chicago: University of Chicago Press.

Jonas, H. (1974). *Philosophical essays*. Chicago: University of Chicago Press.

Jonas, H. (1984). *The imperative of responsibility*. Chicago: University of Chicago Press.

Kirkpatrick, F. G. (1986). *Community: A trinity of models*. Washington, DC: Georgetown University Press.

Leeds-Hurwitz, W. (1995). Introducing social approaches. In W. Leeds-Hurwitz (Ed.), *Social approaches to communication* (pp. 3–23). New York: Guilford.

McRobie, A. (1997). The es and anti-es: New questions for feminism and cultural studies. In M. Ferguson & P. Golding (Eds.), *Cultural studies in question* (pp. 170–186). Thousand Oaks, CA: Sage.

Marcus, G. E., & Fischer, M. M. J. (1986). *Anthropology as cultural critique*. Chicago: University of Chicago Press.

Morley, D. (1997). Theoretical orthodoxies: Textualism, constructivism and the "new ethnography" in cultural studies. In M. Ferguson & P. Golding (Eds.), *Cultural studies in question* (pp. 121–137). Thousand Oaks, CA: Sage.

Newcomb, T. M. (1953). An approach to the study of communicative acts. *Psychological Review, 60*(6), 393–404.

Pearce, W. B. (1995). A sailing guide for social constructionists. In W. Leeds-Hurwitz (Ed.), *Social approaches to communication* (pp. 88–113). New York: Guilford.

Rappaport, R. (1979). *Ecology, meaning, and religion*. Berkeley, CA: North Atlantic Books.

Salkever, S. G. (1983). Beyond interpretation: Human agency and the slovenly wilderness. In N. Haan, R. Bellah, P. Rabinow, & W. M. Sullivan (Eds.), *Social science as moral inquiry* (pp. 195–217). New York: Columbia University Press.

Schiller, D. (1996). *Theorizing communication*. New York: Oxford University Press.

Simmel, G. (1950). *The sociology of Georg Simmel* (Kurt H. Woolf, Trans. and Ed.). New York: The Free Press.

Steg, D. R., & Schulman, R. (1979). Human transaction and adapting behavior. In K. Krippendorff (Ed.), *Communication and control in society* (pp. 317–340). New York: Gordon and Breach Science Publishers.

Stewart, J. (1995). *Language as articulate contact*. Albany: State University of New York Press.

Stewart, J. (1996). The symbol model vs. language as constitutive articulate contact. In J. Stewart (Ed.), *Beyond the symbol model* (pp. 9–63). Albany, NY: State University of New York Press.

Taylor, C. (1985). *Human agency and language. Philosophical papers I*. Cambridge: Cambridge University Press.

Taylor, C. (1989). *Sources of the self*. Cambridge, MA: Harvard University Press.

Thomas, S. (1989). Functionalism revised and applied to mass communication study. In B. Dervin, L. Grossberg, B. J. O'Keefe, & E. Wartella (Eds.), *Rethinking communication: Vol. 2. Paradigm exemplars* (pp. 376–396). Newbury Park, CA: Sage.

Thomas, S. (1997). Dominance and ideology in culture and cultural studies. In M. Ferguson & P. Golding (Eds.), *Cultural studies in question* (pp. 74–85). Thousand Oaks, CA: Sage.

Thompson, J. B. (1995). *Media and modernity*. Stanford: Stanford University Press.

Vogel, L. (1996). Hans' Jonas's exodus: From German existentialism to post-Holocaust theology. Editor's introduction to H. Jonas, *Mortality and morality* (pp. 1–40). Evanston, IL: Northwestern University Press.

Wallace, J. D. (1978). *Virtues and vices*. Ithaca, NY: Cornell University Press.

Walzer, M. (1983). *Spheres of justice*. New York: Basic Books.

Wertsch, J. (1985). *Vygotsky and the social formation of mind*. Cambridge, MA: Harvard University Press.

West, C. (1989). *The American evasion of philosophy*. Madison: University of Wisconsin Press.

Westley, B. H., & MacLean, M. S. (1957). A conceptual model for communications research. *Journalism Quarterly, 34*, 31–38.

Williams, R. (1976). *Keywords*. New York: Oxford University Press.

Woodward, W. (1993). Toward a normative-contextualist theory of technology. *Critical Studies in Mass Communication, 10*(2), 158–178.

Woodward, W. (1996). Triadic communication as transactional participation. *Critical Studies in Mass Communication, 13*, 155–174.

Woodward, W. (2000). Design/communication as mutual-personal creative action. In *Cultural studies: A review annual* (Vol. 5, pp. 307–332). Greenwich, CT: JAI Press.

Chapter 4

William James and the Uncertain Universe

William J. Leonhirth
Texas A&M University

Establishing the parentage of communication study in the United States has been an academic exercise for several decades. Various scholars have nominated Charles Horton Cooley, John Dewey, Carl Hovland, Harold Lasswell, Paul Lazarsfeld, Kurt Lewin, Walter Lippmann, George Herbert Mead, Robert Ezra Park, and Wilbur Schramm, among others, for at least a contributing role. The definitions of *communication*, what constitutes its study, and distinguishing the process of communication research from the academic disciplines whose members conduct such studies all have been at issue. The need for establishing its parentage may result from the relative youth of the field and its efforts to gain greater prestige in academia. Conflicts among its various schools of quantitative, qualitative, critical, and postmodern research also have contributed. Observers have viewed these contentions both as strengths and weaknesses. Their presence, however, also constitutes a reminder of ongoing philosophical debates about the natures of knowledge, perception, and reality. In such debates, the role of William James' ideas comes to mind.

Although parapsychologists, phenomenologists, philosophers, psychologists, and other scientists all have some claim on James, he contributed significantly to the study of communication and to an understanding of the role of communication in life. This chapter examines these contributions, but also tries to avoid the academic exercise of determining the parentage for communication research. James' influences on communication study include his influences on those that others have listed as founders of the field. To place James at the center of some historical structure of communication scholarship would counter his own views of natural order and relationships, however. The chapter briefly examines James' life, looks at the central tenets of his work that relate to communication studies, and discusses his influences on others who contributed to communication research. It also attempts to position James and his ideas in the rapidly changing communication environment of today. This atmosphere includes the challenges that digital, online communication is bringing to communication theories and to the definition of communication itself.

BACKGROUND

William James was a philosopher, physician, and psychologist. He brought broad experience to his work in all these fields. The James family also included his brother Henry, the author. It had the advantages of substantial wealth, social position, opportunities to travel and live in Europe, and relationships with the leading thinkers of the day. James' father, Henry, took a direct interest in the education of his children, but the priorities of that interest vacillated to the point that William sometimes questioned the adequacy of his primary education (Croce, 1995).

James attended schools in the United States and Europe and received home tutoring. After studying art for 1 year, James enrolled in the Lawrence Scientific School at Harvard University in 1861. He earned his M.D. in 1869 and received an appointment as a lecturer in physiology at Harvard in 1872. His interests turned to psychology. In 1890, he published the two-volume *Principles of Psychology*, which became the seminal work in the field at the time. *Principles* dealt with the philosophical as well as the physiological aspects of the mind and its functions (Myers, 1986). In it, James described the notions that man is more than a rational creature and that instinct and environment both affect human nature. Experience plays a role in mental processes and helps establish those processes. James (1890b) wrote:

> The connection of the reality of things with their effectiveness as motives is a tale that has never yet been fully told. The moral tragedy of human life comes almost wholly from the fact that the link is ruptured which normally should hold between vision of the truth and action, and that this pungent sense of effective reality will not attach to certain ideas. Men do not differ so much in their mere feelings and conceptions. Their notions of possibility and their ideals are not as far apart as might be argued from their different fates. (p. 547)

Soon after the publication of *Principles*, James began to write and lecture exclusively in philosophy and adopted the mantle of pragmatism. His published works include *A Pluralistic Universe* (1909/1977), *Pragmatism: A New Name for Some Old Ways of Thinking* (1907), *Some Problems of Philosophy* (1911), *The Varieties of Religious Experience* (1902), and *The Will To Believe* (1896). In the pragmatism volume, James (1907) clarified its advantages:

> Pragmatism represents a perfectly familiar attitude in philosophy, the empiricist attitude, but it represents it, as it seems to me, both in a more radical and in a less objectionable form than it has ever yet assumed. A pragmatist turns his back resolutely and once and for all upon a lot of inveterate habits dear to professional philosophers. He turns away from abstraction and insufficiency, from verbal solutions, from bad *a priori* reasons, fixed principles, closed systems, and pretended absolutes and origins. He turns towards concreteness and adequacy, towards facts, towards action and towards power. That means the empiricist temper regnant and the rationalist temper sincerely given up. It means the open air and possibilities of nature, as against dogma, artificiality, and the pretense of finality in truth. (p. 51)

James' pragmatism emerged at a time of great transition. Industrial expansion, labor unrest, political turmoil, and a growing presence of the United States in world affairs marked the 1890s. Social, political, economic, and even philosophical ideas battled for the attention of scholars and the public. Newspapers were at the peak of their *yellow journalism* frenzies that eventually culminated in promotion of the Spanish–American War (Hyde, 1991), which established the United States as a world power. The nation's material success brought calls for reorganization of the economy along socialist and communist designs (Jaher, 1964). It also led to questions about the social effects of industrialization and urbanization (Carey, 1989a) and efforts to provide a revolution in societal control (Beniger, 1986).

Reevaluations of economic forces, social order, and political organization resulted from social applications of Charles Darwin's theory (Collier, Minton, & Reynolds, 1991) and from Karl Marx's economic and social theories (West, 1989). These social and political movements brought challenges to traditional academic studies and methods at a time when the United States sought increased intellectual, political, and economic roles in the world (Collier et al., 1991). U.S. scholars would produce a "new psychology" (Wiener, 1971, p. 86), a "new philosophy" (James, 1907, p. 50), and a "new sociology" (Matthews, 1972, p. 2) while the nation trumpeted its technical achievements in industrial production, communication, and transportation (Beniger, 1986).

At the basis of most of the American academic initiatives were the pragmatic approaches of James and John Dewey (Myers, 1986). James tied pragmatism to empiricism and encouraged the study of the experience of humans rather than theoretical assumptions about the causes of their be-

havior (James, 1907). Nonetheless, James was not content with a mechanistic universe, and he contended that the senses have limitations in monitoring human experience. Although Ralph Waldo Emerson, Charles
Sanders Peirce, James, and Dewey all had ties to pragmatism, each took a
somewhat different route. James described his philosophy as *pragmatism* in
line with that of Peirce, but he generally seemed more comfortable with
the term *radical empiricism* as a description of his approach. Peirce eventually adopted the term *pragmaticism* (West, 1989, p. 56) for his philosophy
to show his displeasure with James' version.

James wrote exhaustively on a wide variety of topics. West (1989) described James not as a philosopher, but as "a cultural critic trained in medicine, fascinated with the arts, imbued with a scientific conscience, and
attracted to religion" (p. 54). James did not deal specifically with communication. He influenced the study of communication processes, however,
particularly with his analyses in *Principles*. Communication offers a means
to look at and know the world. It offers an exchange of information. Communication may even offer a negotiation of reality. James dealt with these
issues from several perspectives, including studies of perception, sensation, and information processing.

PROCESSES AND IDEAS

In *Principles*, James (1890b) addressed the perception of time, "things,"
space, and reality. *Perception* is the "consciousness of particular material
things present to sense" (p. 76). He immediately noted, however, that it
involves both direct sensations and "various remoter relations" (p. 76). In
addition, "the moment we get beyond the first crude sensation all our consciousness is a matter of suggestion, and the various suggestions shade
gradually into each other, being one and all products of the same psychological machinery of association" (p. 76).

According to James, "Perception thus differs from sensation by the consciousness of farther facts associated with the object of the sensation" (p.
77).

What is sensation? James wrote in *Principles* (1890a) that:

> The mental states usually distinguished as feelings are the emotions, and the
> sensations we get from skin, muscle, viscus, eyes, ears, nose, and palate. The
> "thoughts" as recognized in popular parlance, are the conceptions and judg-
> ments. When we treat these mental states in particular we have to say a word
> about the cognitive function and value of each. It may perhaps be well to no-
> tice how our senses only give us acquaintance with facts of body, and that of
> the mental states of other persons we only have conceptual knowledge. Of
> our own past states of mind we take cognizance in a particular way. They are

'objects of memory' and appear to us endowed with a sort of warmth and intimacy that makes the perception of them seem more like a process of sensation than like a thought. (pp. 222–223)

James also indicated that sensations are always new sensory impressions. "Pure sensations can only be realized in the earliest days of life" (James, 1890b, p. 7).

Although humans use senses to encounter the world, James was not content with the limits of empiricism. He wanted to counter the notions of idealism that held that ideas had existence outside of the human experience. However, his radical empiricism argued against the use of experience to establish any universal truth. James (1909/1977) contended that

radical empiricism allows that the absolute sum-total of things may never be actually experienced or realized in that shape at all, and that a disseminated, distributed, or incompletely unified appearance is the only form that reality may yet have achieved. (p. 44)

He opposed the notion of absolute or universal truth, which he termed *monism*. To James, even God is finite. James contended that pluralism is a more appropriate approach. Humans possess limited sensory capabilities to know their universe, and what humans learn from their experiences has a limited and relative value. James did not deny the existence of a fixed, objective universe. However, he did not find that humankind could actually *live* there.

James was a transcendentalist in his approach to knowledge of the universe and his philosophy. "Philosophy is essentially the vision of things from above," he observed (1909/1977, p. 277) in the lectures that became *A Pluralistic Universe*. James did not limit his inquiries to the roles of philosophy, psychology, or science. He wrote extensively on how to reconcile religious faith with secular philosophy and scientific theories. He did not discount any source of experience, including those that now would be described as paranormal or parapsychological. James served as president for the Society for Psychical Research in Cambridge.

He also advocated *fallibilism*, which takes the rather broad view that whatever a person believes actually may be wrong. James' critics, however, contended that his pluralistic views amounted to an "evasion of philosophy" (West, 1989, p. 5) or its abandonment. As Carey (1989b) noted, a rift exists between those who see science as a model for understanding of the universe and those who see science as merely one approach. In addition, "some such as William James, find the whole argument bootless, and just walk away from the discussion leaving nothing in its place" (p. 72). James and Carey, however, are not that distant in their views of the reflexive nature of reality. "The most important product of the mind is a produced and sustained reality," Carey noted (p. 74).

In his work, James established an intellectual foundation for the uncertainty that physical scientists would identify in their explorations of the subatomic world. Uncertainty, as James (1909/1977) contended, is not a pretty sight: "As compared with all these rationalizing pictures, the pluralistic empiricism, which I profess, offers but a sorry appearance. It is a turbid, muddled, gothic sort of affair, without a sweeping outline and with little pictorial nobility" (p. 45). Nor is it elegant. "The great 'claims' of the philosophy of the absolute is that the absolute is no hypothesis, but a presupposition implicated in all thinking, and needing only a little effort of analysis to be seen as a logical necessity" (p. 52).

INFLUENCES

James' writings both in psychology and philosophy affected those around him, who took an interest in the nature and processes of communication. His students at Harvard included Walter Lippmann and Robert Ezra Park. His works influenced Charles Horton Cooley, John Dewey, and Graham Wallas. Wallas in turn also influenced Lippmann. Dewey had viewed James' new psychology as his introduction to pragmatism, although the 1,400-page *Principles* did not specifically state pragmatist tenets (Dykhuizen, 1962). Dewey used James' work as a textbook for an advanced psychology course that he started teaching in 1891.

Few direct connections may link James with Schramm's (1997) so-called *founding fathers of communication studies*—Carl Hovland, Harold Lasswell, Paul Lazarsfeld, and Kurt Lewin. Nevertheless, one could note that Lasswell studied with Park and Wallas, Lewin was an experimental psychologist, and Hovland was a social psychologist. Schramm identified Cooley and Park as forefathers of communication research. He deigned not to give James that distinction, although Schramm noted the influence of James on both. In his genealogy of communication research, Carey (1989b) identified Cooley, Dewey, Park, and Mead as founders of communication studies (p. 143). Carey also described Lippmann's (1922/1949) *Public Opinion* as "the founding book in American media studies" (Carey, 1989b, p. 75). Schramm (1997) also testified to the value of *Public Opinion*:

> In our own century, after the World War of 1914-18 had introduced the great mass of people to propaganda, a few scholars such as Walter Lippmann, who was a practicing newsman, took the lead in introducing the mass audience to the importance of public communication. Lippmann's *Public Opinion* is still one of the most useful books that modern communication scholars have inherited from an earlier generation of scholars. (p. 8)

Schramm directed his attention to empirical foundations and Carey to cultural studies foundations. In addition, other schools of communication studies have some claim to James. Tuchman (1978) discussed the role of James' ideas in the work of Alfred Schutz and other phenomenologists. Rorty (1982) suggested that James is relevant to the work of postmodernists such as Gilles Deleuze and Michel Foucault. "On my view, James and Dewey were not only waiting at the end of the dialectical road which analytic philosophy traveled, but are waiting at the end of the road which, for example, Foucault and Deleuze are currently travelling" (p. xviii). Thus, Ford (1993) identified James as one of the "Founders of Constructive Postmodern Philosophy" (pp. 89–132).

Perhaps the only real gap exists with critical or Marxian scholarship. Nonetheless, Hardt (1989) contended that pragmatism may have provided the first critical analysis of communication in the United States through the work of James and Dewey. Although pragmatism and the Marxian notion of *praxis* would appear to have a direct relationship, Marxian scholars at times quickly discounted that view. They spoke of "a vulgar utilitarianism or pragmatism" (Howard, 1977, p. 86) and "an empty pragmatism." (p. 246). *Praxis* establishes a fundamental reality, according to these scholars, whereas pragmatism "is a fragmentary and piecemeal hypothesis that has to be applied to a particular experience" (Rotenstreich, 1965, p. 51).

Although James' writing often provides useful aphorisms for scholarly writing, his ideas also furnished a basis for some familiar communication theories. For example, James provided some early discussions of the notions of *public opinion* and *stereotypes*. Scholars have often quoted Lippmann's notion of "The Pictures in Our Heads," which is the title of the opening chapter of *Public Opinion*. Lippmann (1922/1949) wrote:

> Those features of the world outside which have to do with the behavior of other human beings, in so far as that behavior crosses ours, is dependent upon us, or is interesting to us, we call roughly public affairs. The pictures inside the heads of these human beings, the pictures of themselves, of others, of needs, purposes, and relationships, are their public opinions. Those pictures, which are acted upon by groups of people, or by individuals acting in the name of groups, are Public Opinion with capital letters. (p. 29)

In *The Great Society*, Wallas (1932) made similar observations about government officials in England who came to meetings with their "minds already saturated by those statements and arguments about the world beyond the reach of their senses, which reach them through newspapers and books" (p. 281).

Cooley (1909) wrote in *Social Organization*:

> There is no sharp line between the means of communication and the rest of the world. In a sense objects and actions are symbols of the mind, and nearly

anything may be used as a sign— as I may signify the moon or a squirrel to a child by merely pointing at it, or by imitating with the voice the chatter of one or drawing an outline of the other. But there is also, almost from the first, a conventional development of communication, springing out of spontaneous signs but soon losing evident connection with them, a system of standard symbols existing for the mere purpose of conveying thought; and it is this we have chiefly to consider. (pp. 61–62)

James (1890b) also discussed "pictures in the mind":

In other words, a blurred picture is just as much a single mental fact as a sharp picture is; and the use of either picture by the mind to symbolize a whole class of individuals is a new mental function, requiring some other modification of consciousness than the mere perception that the picture is distinct or not. (p. 43)

Despite his reservations about empiricism, James' writings on pragmatism provided support for a scientific and objective approach to social science, including communication studies. James (1907) wrote, "Against rationalism as pretension and a method pragmatism is fully armed and militant. But, at the outset, at least, it stands for no particular trends" (p. 54). His pragmatism "represented the attitude of looking away from first things, principles, 'categories,' supposed necessities; and looking towards last things, fruits, consequences, facts" (p. 55).

Sociologist Park (1950) said he went to Harvard and studied philosophy with James to gain insight into the

nature and function of the kind of knowledge we call news. Besides I wanted to gain a fundamental point of view from which I could describe the behavior of society, under the influence of news, in the precise and universal language of science. (p. vi)

Park brought a pragmatic and empirical approach into his direction of the sociological studies of students. Park's perspective of sociology as the "Big News" took his students out into the streets to have direct contact with the subjects of their studies—the immigrants, the hobos, and the prostitutes (Matthews, 1972). Park made the city his laboratory of sociology.

James had a direct influence on the work of Park. Park particularly recalled an essay, "A Certain Blindness in Human Beings," that James read to his class before its publication (Matthews, 1972, p. 32). James wrote:

The facts and works of life need many cognizers to take them in. There is no point of view absolutely public and universal. . . . The practical consequences of such a philosophy is the well-known democratic respect for the sacredness of individuality. (cited in Perry, 1935, p. 266)

Park also received support for empirical studies from James with the advice that "the most real thing is a thing that is most keenly felt rather than the thing that is mostly conceived" (Park, 1941, p. 39).

In his 1940 analysis of "News as a Form of Knowledge," Park (1967) also drew on James and the *Principles*. Park noted the observation of James and others of the two fundamental types of knowledge: *knowledge with* and *knowledge about* (p. 33). Park characterized *knowledge with* as knowledge "with use and wont rather than through any sort of formal investigation" (p. 34). *Knowledge about* is "formal knowledge; this to say, knowledge which has received some degree of exactness and precision by the substitution of ideas for concrete reality and the substitution of words for things" (p. 36). According to Park, news is somewhere on a continuum between *knowledge with* and *knowledge about*. Park also received some consideration as the originator of the cultural school of mass communication history with publication of "The Cultural History of the Newspaper" in 1925 (Sloan, 1991).

James also gave impetus to British political scientist Wallas' concept of *thought organization*. Lippmann's *Public Opinion* endorsed Wallas' notion of *thought organization*—the need to compensate for the impersonal communication that mass media had created (Wallas, 1932). Wallas compared the public opinion of the agricultural village on the day after each villager had discussed an important event with each other and the public opinion of a new suburb "where no one knows his neighbor and each season-ticket holder reads his newspaper in silence in the morning train" (p. 281). Wallas attributed his analysis to the psychological writings of James, with their notions of sensation and instinct and the idea that humanity sometimes acts in an irrational manner (Wiener, 1971).

Wallas saw the opportunity for application of James' new psychology in education and politics (Weiner, 1971, pp. 89–90). Wallas (1908) wrote *Human Nature in Politics* in an attempt to overcome the "tendency to exaggerate the intellectuality of mankind" (p. 45). *The Great Society* (1932) was the second book Wallas wrote to apply the new psychology to politics (Wiener, 1971, p. 104). Lippmann, who had studied with James and Wallas when he was a visiting lecturer at Harvard in 1910, was a popularizer for both of Wallas' books (Wright, 1973). Wallas dedicated *The Great Society* to Lippmann. Wallas (1932) wrote: "I send it to you in the hope that it may be of some help when you write this sequel to your *Preface to Policy* for which all your friends are looking" (p. v). Lippmann produced the sequel, *Drift and Mastery*, in 1914.

In *Public Opinion*, Lippmann (1922/1949) argued that representative government would not work unless an independent expert organization existed to make sense for decision makers "of the knowledge of the world beyond their reach" (p. 31). Lippmann also contended that the real environment is too complex for direct acquaintanceship. He envisioned a new role for political science:

The newspapers are regarded by democrats as a panacea for their own defects, whereas analysis of the nature of news and of the economic base of journalism seems to show that the newspapers necessarily and inevitably reflect, and therefore, in greater or less measure, intensify, the defective organization of public opinion. My conclusion is that public opinion must be organized for the press if they are to be sound, not be the press as is the case today. This organization I conceive to be in the first instance the task of a political science that has won its proper place as formulator, in advance of real decision, instead of apologist, critic, or reporter after the decision has been made. (p. 32)

In their reviews of *Public Opinion*, Park (1922) and Dewey (1922) criticized Lippmann's proposal for the development of thought organization to facilitate decision making in the government. Lippmann (1922/1949) called for the development of information bureaus in the federal cabinet offices and at other levels of government. Park and Dewey questioned Lippmann's (1922/1949) assumptions, particularly whether newspapers had failed to meet the communication needs of democracy. Park (1922) argued that the accuracy of news "depends upon the advancement of social science" (p. 234); in addition, to serve its role in democracy, news has to be intelligible and, in turn, interesting. "It is the task of the common school to make the facts about our common life intelligible to the ordinary man" (p. 234).

Dewey (1922) recalled the earlier view of sensational and wrote:

Mr. Lippmann seems to surrender the case for the press too readily and to assume too easily that what the press is it must continue to be. It is true that news must deal with events rather than events and forces. It is true that the latter taken by themselves, are too remote and abstract to make an appeal. Their record will be too dull and unsensational to reach the continuing study and record of underlying conditions. (p. 288)

Dewey also characterized *Public Opinion* as "perhaps the most effective indictment of democracy as currently conceived ever penned" (p. 286).

REALITY AND UNCERTAINTY

Whatever James' influences on early communication studies, he put himself at the center of debate about the nature of knowledge and reality. According to James (1909/1977), "Our thoughts determine our acts, and our acts redetermine the previous nature of the world" (p. 318). The debate about knowledge and reality continues today in communication schools, in the media, and even in the halls of Congress. What roles may science, religion, and communication media appropriately play as the 20th century ends and a new one begins? As new communication technologies develop and move into wide use, how will they affect social, economic, and political life? Differences of opinion on the roles of the mind and of ideas in human actions continue to divide those who investigate and analyze the human condition. James attempted to steer some course amid these divisions. Thus, he provides some counsel for current debates.

If one attempts to follow the historical and intellectual lines of such analysis of these divisions, they include the following:

—Through empirical means, observation, and experimentation, summary descriptions and explanations of the physical universe are possible and may have predictive capabilities. The physical universe constitutes reality. Ideas attain validity only to the extent that empirical evidence confirms or corroborates them. This essentially is the scientific or rational model that remains dominant in Western culture (Braybrooke, 1987; Little, 1991; Popper, 1959).

—The physical universe constitutes one component of a dual reality that also includes mental activity and its products—ideas. Ideas are at some level higher of intellectual importance than practical action (Nauen, 1971). Although this model generally represents idealism, postmodernism would also accept the detachment of the physical universe and ideas, if not the hierarchy (Lyotard, 1993).

—The physical universe constitutes reality, but each individual possesses a subjective reality because of the limitations of the senses and the ability of the mind to reconstruct physical reality through perception and cognitive processing. Due to these limitations, objective knowledge of the physical universe is not fully possible. This model describes phenomenology (Husserl, 1970; Schutz, 1967). At the extreme, phenomenology argues against even the existence of a physical universe. Such solipsism argues only for existence of the human self and its subjective reality.

—The physical universe exists and constitutes a reality, but the basis of human knowledge of reality is negotiation between or among the subjective realities of individuals (Blumer, 1969). This model includes symbolic interactionism and the theory of communicative action and is an outgrowth of phenomenology.

—The realities of the physical universe and of ideas exist on a dual basis, but ideas are the product of activities in the physical universe. Ideas have no foundations other than their physical origins. However, the physical, practical, or historical origins of ideas may not be clear to those, across generations who come in contact with the ideas. Foundations of this line include Marxism, pragmatism, and social construction theory. The Marxian line also provides that ideas or, more specifically, ideology mask the characteristics of domination and exploitation of social and political relationships (Thompson, 1990).

These historical thrusts represent the basis for methods and methodologies, political arguments, and worldviews. Adopting one such worldview may preclude acceptance of another, James argued. Even the existence of various worldviews provides realities in conflict.

These historical thrusts assume that humans exist, think, and interact. Any elaboration beyond such points generally requires some allegiance to a particular line of thought. Realism and idealism each provide an absolute. With realism, only a fixed reality is accessible. With idealism, in a postmodern sense, no fixed reality is available. Some bridge should exist between the world of substance and the world of illusion. Debates about methods and methodology have centered on the correlation between knowledge and reality. Science essentially is the testing of ideas through physical evidence obtained through sensory capacities. Vision, hearing, touching, and, to a lesser extent, smell, and taste provide the tools for validation. In their arguments against quantitative methods, critical and some qualitative researchers argue that the methods of science place too great a distance between the scientist and the reality of everyday life. Quantitative analysis transforms living beings into abstract numbers, and experiments study human behavior in an artificial environment. The issues of reflexivity and uncertainty are of equal concern. How can the subjective ideas and objective actions of the researcher not affect and help determine the outcome of their research?

Even for postmodern thinkers, however, physical reality provides a point of interest. Reality of an everyday world has even taken on some of the aggrandizement of the empathetic construction of the natural, premodern world. This is the often noted, but never located *village*, where humans lived in harmony, at least with themselves if not with their surroundings. Postmodern writings are replete with discussions of life world, real life, and everyday life (Bourdieu, 1994; Essed, 1991; Goffman, 1959; Habermas, 1981). Methodological problems exist in assessing or interacting with this everyday world without tarnishing real life with subjective ideas or objective action.

For modern and postmodern thinkers, interest in reality also seems to involve a premodern world or condition that shows no effects of science, society, culture, or mass media. Of keen interest has been natural man and woman stripped of all trappings of civilization and acculturation (Bourdieu, 1990). Alternative constructions have included the individual in the midst of basic survival and constantly on the verge of anarchy, except for social constraints in place, and the individual in the midst of some community of empathy until ambition, technology, or objectification disrupted the harmony.

At issue even have been the realities of the individual and society. Is the individual a product of society or is society a product of individual interaction? Mead (1934), for one, argued that the individual does not exist without a social context. Elster (1991) contended that only actions of individuals are possible, not actions of societies. The dominant view in the United States has depicted the rational individual who can collect and process the necessary information to make the best possible social, political, and economic decisions.

Physical reality may provide some standard against which to measure other realities, but in daily decision making that comparison may not be necessary or possible. Religion offers a case study for examination. People hold religious beliefs despite the lack of empirical evidence. Contradictory analyses exist for what empirical evidence may exist (e.g., in the Gospels). The argument against a measurable universe is that, at the quantum level, objective measurement has its limits. The argument against an empirical knowledge of the universe focuses on the notion that human senses cannot fully convey the reality of a physical universe.

These divisions again have become clear with the apparent transition from a modern to postmodern era in which ideas hold some primacy and some detachment from notions of a fixed, objective, physical reality. The primacy of ideas in a postmodern era requires a review of James' work, particularly in regard to his views of a pluralistic universe. In an age of ideas and information, communication may take on the central role in intellectual life that science has occupied in the modern era and that religion occupied in the premodern era.

Jamesian pragmatism, Marxism (Marx & Engels, 1964), and social construction theory (Berger & Luckmann, 1966; Searle, 1995) support the view that ideas result from human action. As he expanded the role of experience, James also made great effort to portray a discontinuous reality or multiple realities. Ideas at odds with this view include the scientism that reduced all human activity to the predictable patterns of the physical universe (Sorrell, 1991) and the idealism that established ideas as intellectual manifestations separate from human activity (Caldwell, 1913; Royce, 1919). James offered an intersection for idealism and scientism and the possibility of *competing realities*. Scientism argued for a fixed and objective reality, and phenomenology propounded the subjective reality of each individual. In contrast, James' course allows both for the intersubjectivity of scientism and the negotiation of reality of symbolic interaction (Blumer, 1969; Mead, 1934) or of communicative action (Habermas, 1981). This view does not preclude other realities—whether external from the physical universe or internal from the individual mind or body.

THREE PHASES

The nature of ideas and their relationship to the physical universe have long been the subjects of intellectual curiosity, analysis, and debate. Despite some aversion to linear time and processes, many scholarly analyses have dealt with three phases of human life. Scholars have termed the middle and baseline phase as the *modern phase*, the *industrial phase*, or the *scientific phase*. What preceded it? Characterizations have included the preindustrial phase and the premodern phase. What has succeeded it? Characterizations have included the postindustrial phase, the postmodern phase, and the poststructural phase. Although the latter two phases have succeeded the initial phase, some scholars have tried, in retrospect, to redefine the first phase in their own contexts or use the first phase to redefine their phases.

Other possible divisions for these phases—whose historical junctures remain a matter of contention—include the primary signifiers of nature, machine, and idea. Nature dominated the premodern era. Humans or their evolutionary predecessors simply were part of the physical universe. At some still unknown point, humans developed self-awareness. With that awareness came the capacity for objective action and subjective thought. Humans started to develop tools and social structures. The preindustrial phase included the natural years of hunting and gathering, agriculture, and processing of natural resources. Family-based or tribal social structures existed. Religion dominated such intellectual life as it existed. Political organization was family based, tribal, and religious. Barter, trade, and early mercantilism predated complex financial transactions. Individualism may have had some meaning in a limited context.

Machines have dominated the modern era. With combinations of tools and energy resources, machines literally began to command human life. That domination included not only the use of machines in the development of industry, but also the inculcation of the mechanical into explanations of nature and human interaction. The Newtonian view of the universe as a machine boosted science. Division of labor provided a mechanical means to organize human activities. Industry involved advances in processing of raw materials and manufacturing. Social and political organization expanded into the notions of society and the nation-state. Science flourished and supplanted religion in intellectual life. Rationalism neatly separated humans' minds from their physical condition and their physical universe. Mercantilism advanced and grew into finance and economics. Individualism flourished as libertarianism and supplanted theocracy and monarchy (Ellul, 1964; Ferre, 1988; Mumford, 1967).

Despite the dominance of mechanical thought, some modern thinkers attempted to provide a natural or biological explanation for human interaction. They relied on such notions as social organization and social Darwinism (Jones, 1980). The danger of the theory of evolution, for some, existed because it reinforced the notion of natural humanity (Hofstadter, 1945). Humans and their universe again were indistinct. Evolution, however, also contributed to the advancement of science as a linear process—particularly one of progress. At the end of a Darwinian evolution of natural selection would be the best and the brightest humans (Fine, 1979). At the end of a Marxist revolution would be the restored communism or community of humanity (Marx, 1964). Scholars of the postmodern phase have rebelled against the linear notion of rational thought that the theory of evolution helped to promote (Ani, 1994).

The postmodern era again has brought domination of the idea. Like the scientists before them, postmodern thinkers have tried to recast the natural universe. They have depicted it as a system of ideas, not as the scientists' machine, however. Ideas and their importance obviously did not begin in the postmodern era. The idealism of the modern era and its esoteric properties paled before the domination of science until the late 19th century. At this time, Marxism and pragmatism found a bridge between the physical universe and ideas. Also at this time, however, James and others explored the subjective universe of the individual mind and the limited capacity for the individual to know the physical reality of the universe. Science even added to the diminution of the mechanical universe in the early 20th century with the theory of relativity (Lorentz, Einstein, Minkowski, & Weyl, 1923) and the principle of uncertainty (Heisenberg, 1971). Measurement of objective reality had its subjective limits. The postmodern or postindustrial phase also represents the ascendancy of ideas in economic processes as information becomes a commodity. Social organization and political organization exist in a state of flux. Individualism remains in contention with collectivism despite the failure of Soviet communism. Science faces challenges from other idea-based systems, and communication, particularly the study of language, has gained intellectual prominence (Burke, 1966; Russell, 1990). Much postmodern thought has focused on language as the representation of reality (Chomsky, 1975; De Saussure, 1966). To some postmodern thinkers, language is reality such as it exists (Bourdieu, 1994).

A NEW COMMUNICATION MODEL

If the hallmark of intellectual life in the premodern phase was religion and the hallmark of intellectual life in the modern phase was science, then communication as the currency of ideas may be the hallmark of intellectual life in the postmodern phase. Communication serves as the medium for intellectual exchange and the site for the negotiation of reality. Explanations of communication have paralleled these characteristic phases of human life: nature, machine, and idea. The modern view of premodern communication has been that of a natural condition. Various modern thinkers including Ferdinand Tonnies, Max Weber, and Karl Marx have described a condition of empathy and unity, almost Edenic in nature. Those who criticize the excesses of the modern era depict premodern humans as living in total harmony with themselves and their universe (Marx, 1973; Tonnies, 1957). The modern view of communication has been mechanical (Shannon & Weaver, 1949). Communication is a process of transfer—either of individual messages or of culture. Communication and its content separate neatly.

In the postmodern phase, communication would serve as the site for the negotiation of reality amid competing constructions. Communication involves the construction and projection of messages and the perception and reconstruction of those messages on the basis of the recipient's acculturation and worldview. James (1890b) dealt with this process in his discussion of perception in *Principles*:

> Enough has now been said to prove the general law of perception, which is this, that whilst part of what we perceive comes through our senses from the object before us (and it may be the larger part) always comes (in Lazarus's phrase) out of our own head (p. 103)

As with perceptions and reconstructions of physical reality, a difference or gap exists between the constructed message and the recipient's reconstruction of that message due to sensory limitations and socially directed influences on reconstruction. The television news report or the newspaper article may elicit diverse reactions on the basis of the perspectives of individual audience members. Even individual words may result in varied and contradictory interpretations from audience members. Because of the gap between physical reality and its reconstruction or between construction and reconstruction of messages, ideas essentially may take on existences of their own. Similarly, objectification of these ideas further removes them from their physical foundations. Although a person may uncover the foundations of these ideas, such an exercise may not affect the relationship between idea and action because the actor may have no knowledge of the gap and the physical or social foundations of the ideas.

With his theory of communicative action, Habermas (1981) offered a bridge between modern and postmodern notions of communication. Communication remains a process in the theory of communicative action, but a process for the negotiation of reality between or among individuals with subjective realities. Postmodern critics of the theory of communicative action have disparaged its links to rationality, scientism, and the notion of a fixed, physical reality (Bernstein, 1985; Thompson & Held, 1982).

Why is reality so important? In the physical realm, reality may be a little easier to comprehend even if its measurement is now an issue of contention. Notions of uncertainty and relativity in qualifying the measurement of the physical universe have undermined fixed, objective reality. Uncertainty introduces subjectivity into the objective measurement of the physical universe, and relativity removes the fixed locus for the disinterested scientific observers. Deconstruction, from its foundations of literary analysis, similarly has separated texts from any historical or philosophical groundings (Silverman & Ihde, 1985). Phenomenology has located reality in every individual's mind. James (1890b) previewed his notion of a pluralistic universe of multiple realities in the *Principles*:

> The total world of which the philosophers must take account is thus composed of the realities plus the fancies and illusions. Two sub-universes, at least, connected by relations which philosophy tries to ascertain! Really there are more than two sub-universes of which we take account, some of us of this one, and others of that. (p. 291)

Is the modern word capable of dealing with multiple realities? In earlier eras, ideas may have been the province of the elite and the intelligentsia. As information becomes a commodity, persons on all socioeconomic levels will possess the opportunity to process and manipulate it. New technologies allow participation in *virtual reality*—a computer simulation of a reality. Will such experiences raise popular interest in the nature of the constructed realities in which individuals now live and act? Are individuals and existing social and political institutions ready to deal with multiple and competing realities? Challenges to assumptions about constructions of race, sex, sexual orientation, and class already exist alongside challenges to science and rationality. These are substantive and compelling challenges in the postmodern world. Does science—with its fixed, objective reality—provide the means to deal with these new challenges? Does idealism—in its postmodern formulation—even want to address them?

A fixed, objective reality of the physical universe may coexist with the multiple, subjective realities of individual minds, as James argued. In an information age, however, which realities will come into play for human action? Of central interest is the nature of reality and the reality of ideas. How do ideas arise? What is their relationship to physical reality? How do they affect action?

How effective is science in dealing with the products of the mind, which may not be rational or even in the same time frame as science? Despite the transition to a postmodern phase, the physical foundations of science continue to hold sway against an abstract swirl of ideas. In a practical and scientific world, ideas are only as good as the physical evidence to substantiate them. Pragmatism would seem best to address that concern with the contention that ideas have their foundations in practical action. Even if one argues for a fixed reality, the question arises about human perception and reconstruction. Is there a gap between physical reality and human knowledge of it? Putnam (1990) contended that philosophy in the 20th century deserves a respite from this question. Nonetheless, Putnam also defended the contention that "philosophy is construction and not description of things-in-themselves" (pp. 52–53).

In the postmodern world, ideas possess their own reality. An idea is real if it exists and has effects. No physical foundation is necessary. If the basis of human activity is the incomplete reconstruction of reality, then reality cannot serve as the basis of action. To follow James, reality, as perceived, is merely a stimulus or catalyst for mental impressions. The value of science, says Popper, exists not in its absolute depiction of reality, but rather in its relative value of intellectual constraints (Popper, 1990; see also Kuhn, 1970). Science provides safeguards for validity claims. Intersubjectivity, at least, allows some common understanding, some negotiation of assumptions. Replication and peer review of research exist as safeguards against fraud, as science provides a safeguard against superstition and irrationality (Babbie, 1992). Can science provide full analysis of mental or social constructions? Science is the study of the physical universe. What about the nonphysical universe? Does thought determine actions, behavior, and even somatic conditions?

THE POSTMODERN CHALLENGE

An uncertain universe poses more of a challenge than does a certain universe and a fixed reality. Without the guarantee of progress, there exists the possibility of creating a useful human experience if not a change in physical reality. One envisions somehing of a lifeboat or a desert island experiment. No guarantees of survival exist, but the lifeboat passengers or island survivors can work together to reach agreement to survive or perish. What is the larger challenge: to find order or create order? Such a challenge to create order requires negotiation, compromise, and consensus. These processes require communication.

Scientism offered the promise of the absolute even if humans do not have the capacity to perceive that absolute. Idealism offered a departure from reality, but one through which action may not be possible or desirable. Some middle course maintains hopes for the advancement of humanity and the means to achieve that advancement. At issue is how does one perceive, process, and communicate reality? Using the formulations of James, one can create a model of communication that presumes not a linear transfer of information or culture, but a disjunctive process of construction and projection and then perception and reconstruction. The disjunction prevents full correspondence between construction and reconstruction and allows negotiation as a basis of reconstruction. The model applies to perceptions and reconstructions of reality as well as to communication between humans. Such a model allows the existence of a physical, objective reality and the existence of individual, subjective realities. In the course of constructions and reconstructions, individuals use socially and culturally derived ideas. Construction and reconstruction are subjective processes. Means of projection and capabilities for perception also may alter the correspondence between construction and reconstruction. Such a model also provides for negotiation of reality because lack of correspondence may result in compensatory measures. Communication gains importance as the currency of ideas—the constructions and reconstructions of physical reality.

Postmodernism recognizes the inherent reality of ideas and gives primacy to ideas. The postmodern challenge is to give these ideas the attention that has gone to processes of energy and physical tools in affecting human action. The challenge of the postmodern era also includes developing the means for analysis and evaluation of the nonphysical universe of ideas. Science is self-limited in its analysis of mental constructions. All ideas are not rational or true criteria for science, and yet they affect the actions and reactions of people in the physical universe. Such a postmodern analysis does not deny science. In a pluralistic universe, such as James envisioned, room exists for physical, even objective, reality. Subjective reconstructions of reality conflict with physical reality and with each other.

The postmodern analysis also need not feature an abandonment of interest in or attention to the fate of individuals, their social structures, or their political organization. The analyses should acknowledge those interests and the inherent assumptions at the outset. Without such interests and assumptions, postmodern thought easily becomes a dismissal of the human condition and as irrelevant to that condition as its critics contend. For the human condition to move into some fourth phase, analysis of the currency of ideas is essential.

REFERENCES

Ani, M. (1994). *Yurugu: An African-centered critique of European cultural thought and behavior.* Trenton, NJ: Africa World Press.

Babbie, E. (1992). *The practice of social research* (6th ed.). Belmont, CA: Wadsworth.

Beniger, J. R. (1986). *The control revolution: Technological and economic origins of the information society.* Cambridge, MA: Harvard University Press.

Berger, P. L., & Luckmann, T. (1966). *The social construction of reality: A treatise in the sociology of knowledge.* New York: Anchor.

Bernstein, R. J. (1985). *Habermas and modernity.* Cambridge, MA: MIT Press.

Blumer, H. (1969). *Symbolic interactionism: Perspective and method.* Englewood Cliffs, NJ: Prentice-Hall.

Bourdieu, P. (1990). *The logic of practice* (R. Nice, Trans.). Cambridge, MA: Polity.

Bourdieu, P. (1994). *Language and symbolic power* (G. Raymond & M. Adamson, Trans.). Cambridge, MA: Harvard University Press.

Braybrooke, D. (1987). *Philosophy of social science.* Englewood Cliffs, NJ: Prentice-Hall.

Burke, K. (1966). *Language as symbolic action: Essays on life, literature, and method.* Berkeley, CA: University of California Press.

Caldwell, W. (1913). *Pragmatism and idealism.* London: Black.

Carey, J. W. (1989a). Communication and the progressives. *Critical Studies in Mass Communication, 6,* 270.

Carey, J. W. (1989b). *Communication as culture: Essays on media and society.* Boston: Unwin Hyman.

Chomsky, N. (1975). *Reflections on language.* New York: Pantheon.

Collier, G., Minton, H. L., & Reynolds, G. (1991). *Current thoughts in American social psychology.* New York: Oxford University Press.

Cooley, C. H. (1909). *Social organization.* New York: C. Scribner's Sons.

Croce, P. J. (1995). *Science and religion in the era of William James* (Vol. 1). Chapel Hill, NC: University of North Carolina Press.

De Saussure, F. (1966). *Course in general linguistics* (W. Baskin, Trans.). New York: McGraw-Hill.

Dewey, J. (1922). [Review of *Public opinion*]. *The New Republic, 3,* 286–288.

Dykhuizen, G. (1962). John Dewey and the University of Michigan. *Journal of the History of Ideas, 23,* 535–536.

Ellul, J. (1964). *The technological society* (J. Wilkinson, Trans.). New York: Knopf.

Elster, J. (1991). *The cement of society: The study of social order.* New York: Cambridge University Press.

Essed, P. (1991). *Understanding everyday racism: An interdisciplinary theory.* Newbury Park, CA: Sage.

Ferre, F. (1988). *Philosophy of technology.* Englewood Cliffs, NJ: Prentice-Hall.

Fine, W. F. (1979). *Progressive evolution and American sociology, 1890–1920.* Ann Arbor, MI: UMI Research.

Ford, M. P. (1993). William James. In D. Griffin (Ed.), *Founders of constructive postmodern philosophy* (pp. 89–132). Albany, NY: State University of New York Press.

Goffman, E. (1959). *The presentation of self in everyday life.* Garden City, NY: Doubleday.

Habermas, J. (1981). *The theory of communicative action* (T. McCarthy, Trans.). Boston: Bacon.

Hardt, H. (1989). The return of the "critical" and the challenger of radical dissent: Critical theory, cultural studies, and American mass communication research. *Communication Yearbook, 12,* 560.

Heisenberg, W. (1971). *Physics and beyond.* New York: Harper.

Hofstadter, R. (1945). *Social Darwinism in American thought, 1860–1915.* Philadelphia: University of Pennsylvania Press.

Howard, D. (1977). *The Marxian legacy.* New York: Urizen Books.

Husserl, E. (1970). *The crisis of European sciences and transcendental phenomenology: An introduction to phenomenological philosophy* (D. Carr, Trans.). Evanston, IL: Northwestern University Press.

Hyde, J. (1991). New Journalism 1883–1900: Social reform or professional progress? In W. D. Sloan (Ed.), *Perspectives on mass communication history* (pp. 199–212). Hillsdale, NJ: Lawrence Erlbaum Associates.

Jaher, F. C. (1964). *Doubters and dissenters; Cataclysmic thought in America, 1885–1918*. London: Free Press of Glencoe.

James, W. (1890a). *Principles of psychology* (Vol. 1). New York: Holt.

James, W. (1890b). *Principles of psychology* (Vol. 2). New York: Holt.

James. W. (1896). *The will to believe, and other essays in popular philosophy*. New York: Longmans, Green.

James, W. (1902). *The varieties of religious experience; A study in human nature*. New York: Longmans, Green.

James, W. (1907). *Pragmatism: A new name for some old ways of thinking*. New York: Longman.

James, W. (1911). *Some problems of philosophy: A beginning of an introduction to philosophy*. New York: Longmans, Green.

James, W. (1977). *A pluralistic universe*. Cambridge, MA: Harvard University Press. (Original work published 1909)

Jones, G. (1980). *Social Darwinism and English thought: The interaction between biological and social theory*. Sussex, England: Harvester Press.

Kuhn, T. (1970). *The structure of scientific revolution* (2nd ed.). Chicago: University of Chicago Press.

Lippmann, W. (1914). *Drift and mastery: An attempt to diagnose the current unrest*. New York: M. Kennerley.

Lippmann, W. (1949). *Public opinion*. New York: Macmillan. (Original work published 1922)

Little, D. (1991). *Varieties of social explanation: An introduction to the philosophy of social science*. Boulder, CO: Westview.

Lorentz, H. A., Einstein, A., Minkowski, H., & Weyl, H. (1923). *The principle of relativity: A collection of original memoirs on the special and general theory of relativity*. New York: Dover.

Lyotard, J. F. (1993). *The postmodern condition: A report on knowledge* (9th ed.; G. Bennington and B. Massumi, Trans.). Minneapolis, MN: University of Minnesota Press.

Marx, K. (1964). *Economic and philosophic manuscripts of 1844* (M. Milligan, Trans.). New York: International Publishers.

Marx, K. (1973). *Grundrisse: Foundations of the critique of political economy* (M. Nicolaus, Trans.). New York: Vintage.

Marx, K., & Engles, F. (1964). *The German ideology*. Moscow, USSR: Progress Publishers.

Matthews, F. H. (1972). *Quest for an American Sociology: Robert E. Park and the Chicago school*. Montreal, Canada: McGill-Queen's University Press.

Mead, G. H. (1934). *Mind, self and society from the standpoint of a social behaviorist*. Chicago: University of Chicago Press.

Mumford, L. (1967). *The myth of the machine: Technics and human development* (Vol. 1). New York: Harcourt.

Myers, G. E. (1986). *William James: His life and thought*. New Haven, CT: Yale University Press.

Nauen, F. G. (1971). *Revolution, idealism and human freedom: Schelling, Holderlin, and Hegel and the crisis of early German idealism*. The Hague, Netherlands: Martinus Nijhoff.

Park, R. E. (1922). [Review of *Public opinion*]. *American Journal of Sociology, 28*, 232–234.

Park, R. E. (1941). Methods of teaching: Impression and a verdict. *Social Forces, 20*, 39.

Park, R. E. (1950). *Race and culture*. Glencoe, IL: The Free Press.

Park, R. E. (1967). News as a form of knowledge. In R. H. Turner (Ed.), *On social control and collective behavior* (p. 33). Chicago: University of Chicago Press.

Perry, R. B. (1935). *The thought and character of William James* (Vol. 2). Boston: Little, Brown.

Popper, K. R. (1959). *The logic of scientific discovery*. London: Hutchinson.

Popper, K. R. (1990). *A world of propensities*. Bristol, England: Thoemmes.

Putnam, H. (1990). *Reality with a human face*. Cambridge, MA: Harvard University Press.

Rorty, R. (1982). *Consequences of pragmatism: Essays: 1972–1980*. Minneapolis, MN: University of Minnesota Press.

Rotenstreich, N. (1965). *Basic problems of Marx's philosophy*. Indianapolis, IN: Bobbs-Merrill.

Royce, J. (1919). *Lectures on modern idealism*. New Haven, CT: Yale University Press.

Russell, P. H. (1990). *Idealism and the emergence of analytic philosophy*. Oxford, England: Clarendon.

Schramm, W. (1997). *The beginnings of communication study in America: A personal memoir*. Thousand Oaks, CA: Sage.

Schutz, A. (1967). *The phenomenology of the social world*. Evanston, IL: Northwestern University Press.

Searle, J. R. (1995). *The construction of social reality*. New York: The Free Press.

Shannon, C. E., & Weaver, W. (1949). *The mathematical theory of communication*. Urbana, IL: University of Illinois Press.

Silverman, H. J., & Ihde, D. (Eds.). (1985). *Hermaneutics and deconstruction*. Albany, NY: SUNY Press.

Sloan, W. D. (Ed.). (1991). *Perspectives in mass communication history*. Hillsdale, NJ: Lawrence Erlbaum Associates.

Sorrell, R. (1991). *Scientism: Philosophy and the infatuation with science*. London: Routledge.

Thompson, J. B. (1990). *Ideology and modern culture: Critical social theory in the era of mass communication*. Cambridge: Polity.

Thompson, J. B., & Held, D. (Eds.). (1982). *Habermas: Critical debates*. Cambridge, MA: MIT Press.

Tonnies, F. (1957). *Community and society* (C. P. Loomis, Trans.). East Lansing, MI: Michigan State University Press.

Tuchman, G. (1978). *Making news: A study in the construction of reality*. New York: The Free Press.

Wallas, G. (1908). *Human nature in politics*. Lincoln, NE: University of Nebraska Press.

Wallas, G. (1932). *The great society: A psychological analysis*. New York: Macmillan.

West, C. (1989). *The American evasion of philosophy: A genealogy of pragmatism*. Madison, WI: University of Wisconsin Press.

Wiener, M. J. (1971). *Between two worlds: The political thought of Graham Wallas*. Oxford, England: Clarendon.

Wright, B. F. (1973). *Five public philosophies of Walter Lippmann*. Austin, TX: University of Texas Press.

Chapter 5

Art, the Public, and Deweyan Cultural Criticism

Joli Jensen
University of Tulsa

In American cultural criticism, the arts are imagined as an intervening variable that will transform the public. Critics presume that art possesses dramatic social power so that they and other intellectuals can keep their faith in the public even though they fear, and endlessly deplore, the cultural choices of actual people.[1]

Viewing the arts as social medicine is disrespectful, detrimental, and self-serving. It is disrespectful to members of the public because their cultural choices are being ridiculed and denigrated. It is detrimental because it directs resources toward an imaginary intervening variable—the arts—when we could be trying, directly, to improve social conditions. It is self-serving in that it presumes that the public would be improved, and democracy enhanced, if the public just had the sensibilities of intellectuals. It presumes that the public needs what professorial types approve of—"good culture"—for democracy to work.

In contemporary popular discourse, unfounded claims about the arts' manifold benefits for individuals and communities help justify support for the arts. In analyzing contemporary rhetorics of arts funding,[2] I have found a host of claims about the magical, medicinal power of the arts. Al-

---

[1] I base these claims in my analyses of arguments by Alexis de Tocqueville, Walt Whitman, and Lewis Mumford as well as groups of 20th-century intellectuals and social critics. Portions of this work appear in Jensen (1995) and in a book manuscript (*Imagining the Arts: High Culture and the Public*) currently under review.

[2] Using a Lexis/Nexis search, I examined more than 300 articles, selecting 85 for a rhetorical analysis of their arguments for public arts funding.

111

legedly, the arts can revive inner cities, increase brain power, improve prison life, and give unspecified aid and economic benefit to the young, the old, the marginalized, the criminal, and the disenfranchised. In the words of one campaign, "the arts enrich every aspect of civic life and contribute and enhance every citizen's ability to prosper and succeed, from cradle to grave" ("Campaign to Triple California Arts Funding," 1998).

Academic discourse has its own medicinal logic. We argue that the right kind of culture (be it labeled high, classical, avant-garde, popular, ethnic, subversive, or subaltern) benefits students and society, and we see the curriculum as the place to dispense it in the proper quantities. Whether we teach canonical or noncanonical work, we believe that we are offering good culture to those in need of its therapeutic effects.

Dewey's (1934) perspective on the arts offers us a valuable alternative conception of the arts, the public, and our social role. Dewey, like most American critics and arts commentators, cares deeply about the social good, and he values aesthetic experience. With them, he supports democratic possibility. Unlike them, Dewey does not imagine art as an outside force that can transform people into something more appealing. Thus, Dewey offers a way out of the most unsavory elements of our heritage of cultural criticism.

Dewey seeks to enhance people's inherent abilities for democratic life; his beliefs about the social role of the arts always connect with his faith in people's innate abilities. In contrast with most 20th-century social and cultural critics, Dewey does not presume that the people currently are deprived of intelligence and sensitivity and therefore need doses of art. He also does not presume that intellectuals possess special traits that the general populace lacks. This means he cannot presume that some distinct essence—art—can turn the populace into trustworthy citizens.

Virtually all the assumptions about the arts with which we are now familiar come unraveled once we deploy Dewey's more inclusive and egalitarian perspective. Dewey's perspective radically undermines—and can improve—our heritage of cultural thought. In this essay, I briefly critique dominant beliefs about arts and the public, contrast them with a Deweyan perspective, and argue for the benefits of adopting a Deweyan (1934) view of *art as experience*. I believe a Dewey-inspired pragmatic aesthetics offers us a way out of some of the most confining aspects of our current cultural criticism.

ART AND THE PUBLIC

Can the public be trusted? That central, obscured question shapes American cultural thought. It is central because a viable democracy requires a viable public—one that can be trusted to act wisely. It is obscured because

American social thought longs to be egalitarian and so can never explicitly mistrust the people.

The need to maintain faith in the people, despite their obvious flaws, explains the virulence of attacks on the media and the tenacity of belief in the redemptive power of the arts. American social thought develops and proceeds as a displaced discussion of what the people need to become to be trustworthy.

According to some critics, the people lack key ingredients—education, information, or sensitivity—necessary to become a true public. To others, outside forces—capitalism, industrialization, the media—have deformed the public, which must somehow be restored to virtue. For most, this combines into an assumption of delayed efflorescence—the ideal American public is waiting to be given the right stuff, at which point it will transform into what it once was or into what it should have become. The shared starting point is that the people, right here and right now, are not a true public.[3] They are inadequate and untrustworthy—an unstable collection of people in need of, or corrupted by, outside intervention. The critic knows what the people need or what it is that is ruining them.

Art—or good culture—offers one way for the critic to call for a salvational transformation. The right kind of culture will give or restore what the people need. By investing the arts with the power to make people wise, kind, sensitive, rational, balanced, humane, communal, energized, insightful, radical, conservative, traditional, rebellious, subversive, or whatever, the critic can keep faith with his or her vision of the public while disdaining the people who actually exist.

This is how and why art operates as such a powerful good in American cultural criticism. The critic operates in a terrain of imagined democracy that makes current conditions appear devastatingly bad. To keep faith with the future vision, in conjunction with such a distressing now, he or she must imagine a force that can create or restore the ideal America.

Cultural criticism, by its nature, involves the description of dangers and ills and the suggestion for their mitigation and cure. Dewey—like cultural critics including Walt Whitman, Lewis Mumford, Randolph Bourne, Mike Gold, Irving Babbit, Philip Rahv, Edward Shils, and Dwight Macdonald—writes to effect a cure for what ails the social body. The difference is that Dewey begins with the belief that American democracy is already operating with a relatively trustworthy public. Dewey finds evidence everywhere of people's intelligence, energies, interests, varieties, and potentials. His goal is to protect and enhance these traits. In contrast, most other critics want to save and/or change the public—turn them into something else.

---

[3]For an insightful analysis of the various ways the American public has been imagined and criticized, see Schudson (1998).

It is not that most other critics proceed with unmitigated (albeit deeply disguised) hatred of the public. A complex relationship exists between critics and the public, one that relies on faith in the abstract and founders on the traits of the concrete. American social critics love the idea of the public—the notion of the common man, the dream of democracy—but they almost always abhor people's actual habits, values, and practices. The disjuncture between the two visions, and the apparent impotence of criticism in the face of it, is extremely painful.

We see this most clearly in Whitman (1964), who is torn between his fascination with crowds and urban life and his sense that much of modern American life is gaud and fraud. His most clear-cut critique of American society was in his 1860s essay, "Democratic Vistas," where he struggles, with the reader, between "democracy's aspirations" and the dilemma of the people's "vices and caprices" (p. 364).

Whitman's essay can be read as an attempt to salvage faith in an America that has not embraced him as he embraces it. His ideal public—vital, adhesive, perfect men and women—offers a dispiriting contrast to the enervated, false, dyspeptic modern folk he sees around him. He imagines his public elsewhere (in the West!) amid the mechanics and woodsmen. He dreams of and writes for ways that they may be brought into existence. In the most widely known section of his essay, he imagines a salvational orbic literature created by a race of bards like him. He describes how this divine new form of literature will address, call forth, and bring into existence the here-to-fore obscured and deflected perfection of American men and women.

American cultural critics are more Whitmanian than they realize. Like Whitman, critics rage against the inadequacy of what they find and suffer because they cannot make the world into what they want it to be. They write in an attempt to transform the inadequate people into an ideal public, and yet they write to no visible effect. There is always frustration when the people do not heed the call, when they do not change, when instead they persist, stubbornly, in doing and being things that the critic finds destructive, unhappy, hollow, and foolish.

This dialectic of abstract faith and concrete disdain also defines Mumford's work. It began in the 1920s with great hope for social renewal and ended in the 1960s with despair over the unmitigated triumph of the mechanistic.[4] Like Whitman's public, Mumford's public is being deflected from and deformed by characteristics of modern life. Both presume a natural or harmonious mode of life, and both find in the arts expression of that mode. However, Mumford's critique relies on a historical analysis of the influence of technologies on values, habits, and social life.

---

[4]See Mumford (1979) for an overview and introduction to his impressive (and prescient) body of work.

Mumford presumes (like many contemporary critics) that the public is shaped by beliefs, habits, and forces of which it is not aware. A good life is a balanced life, where art and techne are in scale and in harmony. However, modern life is imbalanced, huge, and discordant in ways that we vaguely sense but do not understand. Mumford's public is being deformed, often unwittingly. The ease and efficiency of modern techniques fool and seduce it into living secondhand, hollow, desiccated lives. Redemption will come through a recognition of this, with the aid of art, which represents and contains much of what modern life destroys.

Mumford's early work involves viewing the arts as a source of social renewal, as did the 1920s Young American critics such as Waldo Frank, Randolph Bourne and Van Wyck Brooks. In their work on the magazine *Seven Arts*, as well as various books and essays, they argue that the public is not being given the new American art—energetic, original, spontaneous—that it needs to reenergize and recommit to the American dream. This slack, distracted, unaware public will become taut, focused, and fully alive under the influence of the right kind of new democratic culture. Like Whitman, Mumford assumes that art (therapeutically) can engage and release blocked or occluded characteristics of the public.

This is exactly what their contemporaries—New Humanists like Irving Babbit, Paul Elmer More, and Stuart Sherman—feared in the early 20th century. Their view of the public as needing the guidance of a special few, informed by the essential truths of art, is the least trusting and the most explicitly elitist. Yet a surprising egalitarian element exists in their assumptions of shared venality, and in their faith in the public's ability to respond to truth once it is made available to them.

The New Humanist presumes that we are all subject to passions and emotions, and so all (potentially) can become an unruly mob. We must study, learn, and expend effort to become true citizens and to create a true public. The truth and beauty found in the arts of the past—arts that distilled the wisdom of earlier civilizations—should guide this effort. Those who attempt to learn from and live by these truths are the best leaders. Others will recognize and can rely on their virtue. The New Humanists imagine a public that acknowledges the possibility of public restraint and civility through the edification of art as represented in the lives of the most educated and sensitive.

Marxist thought from the 1930s also presumes that some people can serve as a beacon for a less aware public. Its version of the public assumes false consciousness. The public is not simply unaware or misshapen; it is misinformed intentionally. It is the business of capitalism to lie; it is the responsibility of the radical to tell the truth. Truth can be told in art—faith in proletarian art amounted to a faith in the radical power of certain kinds of truth telling. Plays, novels, and paintings about poverty, oppression, or strikes all concerned the consequences of capitalism. The public could realize the lies it has lived by when faced with the truths it could trust. This public is a slumbering giant, lulled to sleep by false stories, ready to waken to the trumpet call of social reality.

However, as the New York Intellectuals of the 1930s, 1940s, and 1950s were forced to acknowledge, the public did not embrace much, if any, of the revolutionary culture proposed to save it. The mass public ignored each offered version—Whitman and the Young American's new democratic culture, the New Humanist's classic high culture, and the 1930s proletarian culture—in favor of burgeoning forms of commercial, mass-mediated culture. The public, ceaselessly worried over, spoken for, exhorted, and imagined, keeps turning down the opportunity for its salvation.

This is the conundrum of public taste. Throughout the 20th century, it became increasingly clear that the actual American public will not embrace easily or eagerly the cultural vehicles that intellectuals are sure will make it better. As a result, particularly unsavory strains in American criticism—disdain for the public and a vilification of the media as both causing and failing to cure the public's inadequacies—intensify.

All this brings us to the mass culture debate of the 1950s. Because American cultural criticism requires faith in the public, at least in the abstract, some blame has to be placed for the public's intransigence in the face of intellectuals' endless efforts at salvation. The media easily take the blame. They are seen as the prime purveyors of a mass culture that creates and sustains a mass society. The media hypnotize and dupe, narcotize and propagandize. The public now cannot respond to true art, timeless truths, revolutionary truths, or critical truths. Its members have fallen under a spell so severe, so total, that they cannot really be trusted or listened to. They are helpless pawns in some larger game of mediated modernity. They are not citizens, but consumers. As such, they will respond eagerly and foolishly to whatever blandishments the media disseminate.

This view of the mass public is the most hostile of the available models. Yet it continues today, in somewhat less virulent forms, in popular and some forms of scholarly discourse about media effects. This view relies on a long history of beliefs about the redemptive powers of art for the public in a democracy. If the arts are powerful, and the media are bad art, then the media are powerfully bad. In fact, they probably explain why the public is so very inadequate and America so very unsatisfying. The final proof is that people claim to actually *like* the trash that the media purvey—undeniable evidence that the media poison minds.

Belief in the salutary powers of art and in the destructive powers of the media[5] are closely linked and form an almost impregnable foundation for

---

[5]I have explored comparable beliefs about the detrimental effects of the media in Jensen (1990).

American cultural criticism. It is difficult to imagine how one can evaluate and comment on contemporary life without believing in art's ability to make people better and the media's role in making them worse.

One alternative possibility, a cheerful strain of media studies, simply inverts part of the argument—the media are in fact liberating, enlivening, enlarging, subversive. This move to valorize popular culture does not challenge the presumption that the arts have power; it simply gives to popular culture the powers that intellectuals have long ascribed to the noncommercial arts. Versions of media studies can explore television texts and find evidence of the discourses they hope to find there—disruptive discourses that challenge the dominant order.

Another possibility is to imagine contemporary life as engagingly postmodern—as fragmented and thus liberatory, as incoherent and thus playful and energizing. This positive postmodernism has been overshadowed by the more familiar, negative postmodernism—one that sounds almost exactly like the mass society of the mass culture debates. However, if we adopt positive postmodernism, we have not gotten far because we cannot get back to the questions that continue to bedevil cultural critics. The citizenry evaporates, the public sphere becomes the endless playground that mass culture critics so fear, and comparative valuation becomes the specious relativism that conservative commentators dread.

Yet viewing media texts as complex, contradictory, and liberating at least presumes that the audience can interpret, evaluate, and respond to complex and often contradictory meanings in texts. As such, this resembles the public Dewey sees and the ideal public for which critics long. This positive media studies view, associated with figures like John Fiske, is often dismissed as simplistic and optimistic, as failing to consider the forces that constrain understanding and that prevent the viewer from fully apprehending the social reality in which he or she operates. This is also, of course, a common critique of Dewey.

Can we construct a cultural criticism that takes seriously the ways in which our actions and beliefs are determined and yet holds out the prospect of popular democracy *without* the extraordinary intervention of high culture? A first step toward such a cultural criticism would be to question the necessity of extraordinary intervention.

ART AS EVERYDAY EXPERIENCE

What would cultural criticism look like if it cared about democratic possibilities, valued art, but did not presume that art can save or doom us? We can imagine such a criticism if we deploy Dewey's claims about the arts, public life, and democratic possibility. The result—pragmatic aesthetics—

challenges the ideology of redemptive art, presumes the media are pleasurable but not intensely powerful, and expects cultural critics to respect and respond to the aesthetic experiences of everyday people. In the end, pragmatic aesthetics fundamentally changes both the logic of American social criticism and the presumed responsibilities of intellectuals.[6]

Dewey's perspective on the arts is most directly developed in his 1934 book, *Art As Experience*. The book simultaneously critiqued mainstream aesthetic theory, articulated an alternative approach, and developed the central notion to Dewey's thought—experience. As Alexander (1987) noted, to understand how Dewey thinks about aesthetic experience illuminates the central themes of his whole philosophy.[7]

Dewey (1934) suggested that it is best to arrive at a new theory of art by way of a *detour*—a path away from artistic products and toward "ordinary forces and conditions of experience that we do not usually regard as aesthetic" (p. 4). Dewey contended that:

> The sources of art in human experience will be learned by him who sees how the tense grace of the ball-player infects the onlooking crowd; who notes the delight of the housewife in tending her plants, and the intent interest of her goodman in tending the patch of green in front of the house; the zest of the spectator in poking the wood burning on the hearth and in watching the darting flames and crumbling coals. (Dewey, 1934, p. 5)

Dewey wrote against an esoteric view that puts art on a pedestal, as something distinct from the everyday. He opposed theories that isolate and compartmentalize art—that " 'spiritualize' [art] out of connection with the objects of concrete experience." Dewey's (1934) goal was to "recover the continuity of esthetic experience with normal processes of living" (p. 10).

Why would Dewey want to do this? Of what value or purpose is it to consider works of art as something that "develop and accentuate what is characteristically valuable in things of everyday enjoyment" (Dewey, 1934, p. 11)? In reclaiming aesthetic experience as an aspect of everyday life, Dewey animated his philosophy of experience—giving it direction, purpose, and meaning. For Dewey, aesthetic experience is a clarified and

---

[6]I focus here on the consequences of Dewey's thought for social criticism writ large. For an interesting treatment of how Dewey connects to issues of philosophy and more traditional aesthetics and textual criticism, from rap to Rorty, see Shusterman (1992). For a personable discussion of how Dewey's notions on art can illuminate the nature and value of life, see Jackson (1998). Eldridge (1998) detailed Dewey's humanistic naturalism and the way that intelligence serves as the democracy-saving variable in Dewey's perspective. As Eldridge showed, thoughtful valuation is Dewey's instrument of social change, not art.

[7]Alexander (1987) effectively integrated Dewey's aesthetic thought with the basic themes and concerns that characterize Dewey's approach to experience; it is a valuable overview.

streamlined version of general experience—"freed from the forces that impede and confuse its development" (p. 274). It offers the philosopher a way to understand experience itself (p. 274), and it offers Dewey a way to argue for experience as organizing and animating action.

For Dewey (1934), "experience in the degree in which it is experience is heightened vitality" (p. 19). It is "active and alert commerce with the world; at its height it signifies complete interpenetration of self and the world of objects and events" (p. 19). Art/experience is the means by which individuals seek and maintain connections to the material world and to each other. It sustains the conjoint activity that is the ground and end of Dewey's philosophy.

Thus, consideration of how art operates as experience is Dewey's opportunity to explore how experience operates over all. Aesthetic experience becomes the particular case that illuminates the general condition—the organization of human energies. He argued that art operates by selecting "those potencies . . . by which an experience . . . has significance and value, . . . in art the forces that are congenial, that sustain not this or that special aim but the processes of enjoyed experience itself, are set free" (Dewey, 1934, p. 185).

Therefore, he finally considered the arts as a form of connection among people—a connection that encourages "the expansion of sympathies, imagination and sense" (Dewey, 1934, p. 332). The arts, as experience, are forms of communication, and communication is the vehicle for community. As he argued in *The Public and Its Problems* (1927), *community* is another term for democracy. Here the necessary connection for my argument is established—arts imagined as vehicles of democracy.

This is a difficult part of my argument—Dewey could seem, on a cursory reading, to make another version of the claim that "arts are what people need to be good citizens." However, Dewey is adamant that aesthetic experience is everyday experience, and that the arts are more intense, meaningful, revealing, and portable versions of things that happen each day. The arts offer people ways to connect with each other; they can also offer "a manifestation, a record and a celebration of the life of a civilization, a means of promoting its development, and . . . a judgment upon [its] quality" (Dewey, 1934, p. 326).

The arts operate in this way not because they have special powers, represent higher or better aspects of man, or contain essential wisdom. They do this because the arts *are* experience—they are the human practice of communication, and thus they exemplify valuable conjoint activity. The arts are widespread human actions, actions that become forms of recognizing, recording, celebrating, encouraging, and evaluating.

The arts are intrinsically ours—they are cultural and communal—and they are thereby valuable. Their everydayness makes them matter, and their inherent humanness makes them worthwhile. Dewey's perspective restores the arts to the concrete experience of all people and suggests that we sustain and develop them as the central mechanism of our common life.

ART, COMMUNICATION, AND DEMOCRACY

Dewey's philosophy connects communication with democracy most clearly in *The Public and Its Problems*. Here (Dewey, 1927) we can look for the implicit connections between his philosophy of art and his approach to democracy. The connecting term is *communication*, understood not as the transmission of ideas, but, as developed by Carey (1989), the creation and maintenance of common meanings.[8]

For Dewey, communication is the way that people come to share an understanding of the consequences of their combined actions; this understanding can "inform desire and effort and thereby direct action" (Dewey, 1927, p. 155). Free and unfettered communication is the way in which the public can become aware of itself and so can create and sustain a true community. Dewey believed "the clear consciousness of a communal life, in all its implications, constitutes the idea of a democracy" (p. 149).

Where does art fit in this connecting of communication and democracy? *The Public and Its Problems* contained Dewey's account of the problem of a democratic public. It appeared before he had fully developed an account of the ways in which art/experience operates. At this stage, he viewed art as a special form of social inquiry—a deeper and more compelling version of the knowledge that the public needs to become aware of itself.

Dewey wrote the book to suggest the conditions necessary to create an articulate, democratic public and thus the conditions needed to create and maintain fully democratic communities. It opposes all arguments, such as Lippmann's (1922), for the necessity of elite, expert, intellectual opinion. Lippmann's book represents the shadow opposition. In contrast, Dewey offered his notion of social inquiry—based in concrete experience, shared, circulated, made available for discussion and evaluation—as the necessary condition for democracy.

Art appears briefly, almost as an afterthought, as a potent disseminator of the full scope of social inquiry. Artists have always been the real purveyors of news, "for it is not the outward happening in itself which is new, but the kindling by it of emotion, perception and appreciation" (Dewey, 1927, p. 184). In this argument, art is the "art of full and moving communica-

---

[8]Carey (1989) developed this aspect of Dewey's thought more fully, tracing its implications for the study of communication. Carey's approach to communication has shaped several generations of students, including me.

tion" (p. 184). Because it touches the deeper levels of life, it can be combined with the explicitly analytic social inquiry. As Dewey argued, "the highest and most difficult kind of inquiry and a subtle, delicate, vivid and responsive art of communication" can breathe life into the machinery of the transmission and circulation of knowledge (p. 184). Democracy requires art because art is an enhancement of communication necessary for communion, community, and therefore democracy. In *Art as Experience*, he (1934) developed instead the notion of art as imaginative experience and gave it a role in the expansion and enhancement of human association.

It is this humane function of art that Dewey (1934) considered in his final chapter, "Art and Civilization." He explicitly contrasted his approach with those that presume "direct moral effect and intent to art" (p. 346). For Dewey, art operates "not directly, but by disclosure," and it offers a sense of unrealized possibilities and so makes us aware of "constrictions that hem us in and of burdens that oppress" (p. 346).

Dewey wrote that he agrees with Shelley—that imagination is the chief instrument of the good. For Dewey, imagination is the way in which individuals put themselves in other's places, the way that human loyalties operate, the way that thought and desire are commanded. Art "has been the means of keeping alive the sense of purposes that outrun evidence and of meanings that transcend indurated habit" (Dewey, 1934, p. 348).

So art becomes the way that modern America can be liberating and enlivening while offering connection in community. Dewey's vision of democracy, communication, and art is a simultaneous one—freedom in association, liberation in conjoint activity. Imaginative experience permits us both to free ourselves from that which constricts and binds and to connect ourselves with that which supports and sustains. Dewey (1934) argued that the liberating and uniting potentials of art proceed from imaginative experience, which is the heart of its moral potency (p. 349).

For Dewey, art is not in itself a power or force; it does not contain some substance that is transmitted from the mind of the artist to the waiting public. Instead, art is a form of imaginative kindling. It works against the local, provincial, and mistrustful toward a wider, more cosmopolitan, and empathetic understanding. It needs to be acknowledged as a central element in social relations, not "treated as the pleasure of an idle moment or as a means of ostentatious display" (Dewey, 1934, p. 348).

DEWEY, ART, AND INTELLECT

One of the things I like most about Dewey is that he presumes that everyday people are, in their way, artists and scientists—able to experience and explore, enjoy and explain. Some people possess gifts in aspects of these enterprises and receive the time and opportunity to develop and express those gifts more fully. However, all members of the public always engage in experience-based inquiry.

The experimental attitude—the approach to knowledge that Dewey believes is necessary for democracy to flourish—can and should be enhanced and developed. It represents an extension and refinement of the human desire and capacity for self-understanding, based in the evaluation of the consequences of everyday life. Education can be arranged to more fully develop and make use of these capacities. The media can fully report and circulate people's findings and experiences in modern life to improve everyone's ability to evaluate and choose actions. Dewey's goals are always socially inclusive, assuming that democracy needs more of what it already has—people's innate capacities for social intelligence.

The role of the intellectual in this process is not as a special class of people, whose education or aesthetic refinement makes them especially able to understand and evaluate the social world. This difference is obvious in Dewey's response to Lippmann's (1922) call for experts to guide the busy, distracted, and incompletely informed masses. Dewey assumes that the public consists of many publics that need to become more self-aware. Such awareness requires ongoing discussion and debate. It needs full and moving communication, which allows better solutions to be tried. Intellectuals are full participants in ongoing discussions with their fellow citizens, not philosopher kings to lead the rest of us toward better things.

This stance seems anti-intellectual, but it really is not. It is anti-elitist, but it is surely pro-intellect. Its critique of intellectuals applies only when intellectuals separate themselves from other people and concrete experience. According to a Deweyan perspective, such separation guarantees that social inquiry will not serve the needs of democracy.

In *Art as Experience*, Dewey (1934) developed this point in relation to criticism. He used a gentle but ultimately devastating analysis of how aesthetic and literary criticism (and philosophy) proceeds. He began, characteristically, by noting an aspect of human nature: "Desire for authority (and desire to be looked up to) animates the human breast" (p. 299). That desire means that much criticism acquits or condemns, via appeal to authority, rather than explicates. This explains the predominance of the judicial critic who "speaks as if he were the attorney for established principles having unquestionable sovereignty" (p. 299).

He continued:

> A judgement as an act of controlled inquiry demands a rich background and a disciplined insight. It is much easier to "tell" people what they should believe than to discriminate and unify. And an audience that is itself habituated to being told, rather than schooled in thoughtful inquiry, likes to be told. (Dewey, 1934, p. 300)

Such an approach is disconnected from the shared experience that must inform inquiry and from the world we inhabit together. Both the critic and the people suffer, Dewey implied, because each has been cut off from the concrete world and from the "emergence of experiences that have a distinctively new character" (Dewey, 1934, p. 304). Thus, Dewey concluded, the judicial critic succumbs to the temptation of authority and becomes a member of a self-enclosed, self-referential world. In short, the critic "erects the very things that are the dangers of his calling into a principle and norm" (p. 304). These words are still worth heeding.

Dewey (1934) also described these tendencies in the impressionistic critic who "goes off into irrelevancies and arbitrary dicta"; in formal critics who reduce art to particular categories; in psychoanalytic critics who use predefined factors to construct causal explanations; and in sociological critics who explain art solely by reference to historical and cultural and biographical information (pp. 314–318).

These critics (then and, I think, now) share a tendency to believe that their own theories and constructions are more valuable than the experience of the artist, performer, fan, and viewer.[9] Critics reduce the work of art to predetermined categories, which Dewey believes separate both critic and reader from the imaginative possibilities that art offers. This is the reductionist fallacy.

The other fallacy that concerns Dewey in this section is the confusion of categories. He believes that critics treat art as if it were "a reediting of values already current in other fields of experience" (Dewey, 1934, p. 318). Critics wrongly presume that artistic material is actually moral, philosophic, religious, or historical, rendered "more palatable by emotional seasoning and imaginative dressing" (p. 318). This approach then leads to criticism of the work of art in moral, philosophic, religious, or historical terms, rather than in relation to the aesthetic experience (pp. 317–319). This is, of course, a current claim in the so-called culture wars.

Dewey presumes a relationship among ideas, intellectuals, and the public that depends on mutual openness and responsiveness to common experience. By distrusting conceptual schemes, preconceived systems, explanation by reduction, and the theoretical apparatus in any version, Dewey assumes that all of us share the basic understandings needed to make good choices. The issue is not "Who has access to the right information, insights, theories?" Instead, we can ask, "How can we enhance our abilities to make, as a group, good choices?"

---

[9]Here Dewey's argument most directly reflects the beliefs of Albert Barnes, the eccentric art collector and philanthropist to whom Dewey dedicated *Art as Experience*. Barnes believed that the aesthetic experience must be kept distinct from the blandishments of critical systems, including museums. Barnes' relationship to Dewey is considered in Greenfield (1987).

In contrast to Lippmann (1922), the problem of the modern age (then and, I argue, now) is not found by asking, "Who has enough of the best information?" Instead we can ask, "How can we share the knowledge we gain from social inquiry?" This places the intellectual in a significantly different relationship to the public and to expertise. Intellectuals are expert only to the extent that they share in the world they seek to explain. They become valuable to the democratic process only to the extent that they belong to a community that is engaged in some common enterprise, in and through which intellectuals consider and explore. The intellectual's insights will be keenest, most useful, and most wise when they are most fully grounded in the concrete world of common experience. With every move away from that world—toward abstraction, authority, or theory—the intellectual loses the possibilities of his or her calling. He or she gives up the possibility of sharing in the social conversation.

We can, I hope, now see the contrast between the Deweyan perspective and the most common conceits of intellectuals and critics. It is easy to presume that cultural criticism represents the specialized practice of specialized people, gifted with intelligence and sophistication. Critics imagine themselves to have dramatic social responsibilities, especially in response to the tide of mediated mediocrity that seems to loom. Fear that the excellent and cultivated would be drowned out by the din of the brutal and vulgar animated 1950s critics as they participated in the mass culture debate; it is a fear rooted in their presumed difference from, and superiority to, the rest of the barbaric world.

Does this mean that Dewey is a precursor of postmodern populism—a celebrant of the common man who finds in mass, commercial culture all kinds of liberating and subversive possibilities? No. Dewey is not arguing that popular culture is full of wise and clever possibilities that insightful critics can decode and that readers (who need its liberatory potentials) can access. In addition, Dewey does not abandon judgments of differential quality, nor does he presume that all cultural expressions offer equal social benefit. He displays strong beliefs about what is better and worse in a society—he simply does not presume that art can purify and the media corrupt.

By focusing on art as experience, rather than art as artifact, Dewey can ask about the quality of the experience, rather than the quality of the artifact. This shift of attention represents the primary benefit of a Deweyan perspective on culture. It gets us out of the binds of high–low culture hierarchies without losing what matters most about making value distinctions—improving the quality of our common life. His concern is with what happens with art—with its consequences. The consequences he describes are imaginative ones—the broadening and deepening of experience by expanding the sympathies.

He writes to critique those theories that presume that art is something distinct and esoteric, outside of the realm of the every day. He noted the origins of theories of art, grammar, and rhetoric in the Alexandrian period and its loss of civic consciousness:

> Instead of connecting arts with an expression of the life of the community, the beauty of nature and art was regarded as an echo and reminder of some supernal reality that had its being outside social life, and indeed outside the cosmos itself—the ultimate source of all subsequent theories that treat art as something imported into experience from without. (Dewey, 1934, p. 328)

Dewey's purpose here is my purpose now—to critique the consequences of all theories that treat art as something that comes in from the outside to transform us. Such a perspective allows art to be imagined as a purifying force and the media to be imagined as a corrupting one. This supports a view of intellectuals as uncorrupted experts protected from the crude world by their association with aesthetic exquisiteness (and their disdain for popular culture). In the 1950s, it allowed intellectuals to write essays about levels of culture, the influence of mass culture on high culture, and the necessity for intellectuals to ignore the common life to protect intellectual things.

The mass culture debate remains so interesting because it addresses widespread and continuing fears about contemporary life. Lots of people assume, with the intellectuals of almost 40 years ago, that mediated and commercial art are ruining the people and that traditional or modern or community-based noncommercial art can improve them. Once one imagines art as an outside force, one can invoke it as a means to a desired end, as has occurred in recent calls for protecting or increasing public funding of the arts. The end that is desired, by this logic, is the saturation of the crude public in a refining bath of good art.

This logic leads to concerns about dilution: Does good art become lessened by being mixed in with the bad stuff—appearing in the media, being widely distributed, and being advertised and promoted? For some, good art must remain pure and inviolate, ignoring, of course, that the art world has been a commercial world since its inception. Others display a faith that if lots more good art is added to our lives, the level of culture will go up and people will become more rational and refined. In short, exposure to art will leave the public more like intellectuals presume themselves to be.

A Deweyan perspective cannot operate with such logic. It cannot imagine art as a force with both redemptive and corrupting powers. Art is experience; experience is saturated with art. The issue is the nature of the experience. Experiences of all kinds can be imaginative, enriching, and invigorating. Ultimately, for Dewey, the issue is the social efficacy of the ideas and beliefs that come from an experience—the imagination is always tested and developed against experiences.

So Dewey criticizes art that is shoddily made, dishonestly offered, and designed to pander. He presumes that it offers a degraded experience, with less potential for imaginative growth. It is not poison or corrupting. Instead, it represents a *missed opportunity*—a possibility deflected or denied. Dewey wants the public to make the most of the opportunities that modernity offers. These include the potentials of new devices of mass communication.

Art is a potent disseminator of the full scope of social inquiry. Artists have always been the real purveyors of news, Dewey (1927) said, "for it is not the outward happening in itself which is new, but the kindling by it of emotion, perception and appreciation" (p. 184). For him, art is both communication and experience at its most communicative and experiential. In an often quoted phrase, Dewey wrote, "Of all things, communication is the most wonderful" (cited in Carey, 1989, p. 13). He justifies that claim with his belief that communication is the human process of creating and sustaining a common world. Communication is democracy in that democracy is the co-creation of a social world in which to live—a creative process that engages us via experience. Our intellect, aesthetic desires, and imagination are all aspects of our engagement in communication and thus in our community.

This means that the mass media, as developed, can be criticized for how well they help us in our social inquiry. What are their consequences for our experience? Do they help us talk with each other, sharing our understandings and insights? Do they circulate the results of our social inquiry? Do they help us achieve full and rich understanding of our common possibilities? Do they help us, as members of a public, understand ourselves, our allegiances, our responsibilities, our potentials? The question is not, "How can we avoid, deflect, or mitigate the hypnotic power of the media?" Instead, we can ask, "How can the media help us do what we can to enhance democracy?"

DEWEY AND THE ROLE OF CULTURAL CRITICISM

These two questions can be posed about the media, but they can also be asked about cultural critics as well. From a mass culture perspective, one that continues in popular discourse, the question is how to either maintain or increase the presumably beneficial social power of art. This implicitly asks how to maintain or enhance the power of the intellectuals whose property art had become. Asked in this way, the answer involves insisting that the public be exposed to good art/good thought—usually via educative institutions such as museums and schools.

In this way, a stubborn public, as yet unable or unwilling to engage in good art and thought, can be uplifted. Belief in the social power of art comes from a belief that the public must be changed. It needs the salutary influence of some outside force such as art to do the difficult business of self-governance. Various institutions are proposed and supported in relation to their ability to transmit the agreed-on good stuff so that it can do its magic work on citizens. Schools are designed to turn the clay of children into the model citizens of tomorrow. Parks are developed to give unruly immigrants the experience of clipped and orderly promenades. Theaters and museums are designed to expose citizens to the healing powers of art. A system of cultural improvement is developed to transform an unsatisfactory public into something else.

Intellectuals draw from these currents a notion of their own importance in the process of public salvation. They come to see themselves as specially constituted for the task. Such people have found congenial homes in institutions dedicated to public uplift. They cherish the art forms they have come to define as those most likely to improve others. They teach the courses that they think are most necessary for transforming callow youth into desirable citizens. They write the indictments of current conditions that demonstrate the hollowness of contemporary experience and pierce the veil of deception covering the workings of contemporary culture. Intellectuals know more, and know better, than the public. The masses must learn how to see and respond to things as intellectuals do, and then democracy will be safe.

Dewey starts, and so ends up, in a very different place in relation to the public. His view of art, communication, and democracy ensures that he begins with the assumption that intellectuals are drawn to thinking about certain problems in certain ways. These ways may prove useful if they are grounded in and applied to common experience. Dewey argues adamantly that soliloquy is not communication. Thus, intellectuals matter only to the extent that they participate in a larger social conversation.

The public is muddled, confused, and inchoate to the extent that the means for such conversation have not kept up with the changes in pace and scale in modern life. *The problem is structural, not intellectual.* The public is not crude, vulgar, or stupid. It simply has less access to the means and modes of social inquiry than intellectuals have. Dewey attaches a common goal—to increase and enhance the public's engagement with its own problems—to education, intellectual activity, and mass communication. Schools should be remade to help students develop an experimental attitude—the ability to decipher and evaluate conditions and consequences. The media should serve the democratic function of communication within and across communities. They should offer experiences that enlarge the possibilities of face-to-face discussion. Both education and the media can offer liberation from the deadening and limiting influences of habit, tradition, inertia, and provincialism.

We intellectual types are fortunate in that we have had opportunities to experience afresh, imagine the new, and develop an experimental attitude. The democratic goal is to increase the opportunity for all citizens to develop those same capacities—capacities that too often remain stunted. It is not up to intellectuals to transmit truths to the lacking public, but to increase the chance for all members of the public to imagine, think, and decide wisely and effectively.

So the problem of cultural criticism and, I would argue, communication studies is the problem of democracy—how to increase the likelihood that the public can act prudently toward its own chosen ends. For Dewey, the answer lies in inclusion—including the public in the salutary processes of community via communication. Art is communication, for Dewey, and art offers a disclosure of possibilities and so can tell us of our constrictions. Dewey (1934) explained what art offers to democracy: "Art is the means of keeping alive the sense of purposes that outrun evidence and of meanings that transcend indurated habit" (p. 438). In contrast, "As long as art is the beauty parlor of civilization, neither art nor civilization is secure" (p. 344).

Art does not need to be kept pure and exalted; it is not an elixir that intellectuals can dispense, explain, or theorize. It does not contain wisdom and truth that must be inculcated into the masses. Instead, it is a means, as is all communication, by and through which the public can come to know and experience itself. We critics and scholars are socially valuable only to the extent that we actually participate in that process.

REFERENCES

Alexander, T. (1987). *John Dewey's theory of art, experience and nature: The horizons of feeling*. Albany, NY: State University of New York Press.
"Campaign to Triple California State Funding to the Arts" (June 1998), http://thecity.sfsu.edu/CALAA.
Carey, J. W. (1989). *Communication as culture: Essays on media and society*. Boston: Unwin Hyman.
Dewey, J. (1927). *The public and its problems*. New York: Henry Holt.
Dewey, J. (1934). *Art as experience*. New York: Capricorn Books.
Eldridge, M. (1998). *Transforming experience: John Dewey's cultural instrumentalism*. Nashville, TN: Vanderbilt University Press.
Greenfield, H. (1987). *The devil and Dr. Barnes*. New York: Viking.
Jackson, P. W. (1998). *John Dewey and the lessons of art*. New Haven, CT: Yale University Press.
Jensen, J. (1990). *Redeeming modernity: Contradictions in media criticism*. Newbury Park, CA: Sage.
Jensen, J. (1995). Questioning the social powers of art: Toward a pragmatic aesthetics. *Critical Studies in Mass Communication, 12*, 365–379.
Lippmann, W. (1922). *Public opinion*. New York: Macmillan.

Mumford, L. (1979). *Interpretations and forecasts: 1922–1972*. New York: Harcourt Brace Jovanovich.
Schudson, M. (1998). *The good citizen: A history of American civic life*. New York: Martin Kessler.
Shusterman, R. (1992). *Pragmatist aesthetics: Living beauty, rethinking art*. Cambridge, MA: Blackwell.
Whitman, W. (1964). Democratic vistas. In F. Stovall (Ed.), *Prose works 1892: Vol. II. Collect and other prose* (pp. 321–446). New York: New York University Press.

Chapter 6

Dewey and Gadamer on Practical Reflection: Toward a Methodology for the Practical Disciplines

Robert T. Craig
University of Colorado at Boulder

Communication studies can be thought of as a practical discipline—an organized effort to cultivate the social practice of communication through research, criticism, theory, and application.[1] Communication is not, of course, the only practical discipline. Many other fields of study, maybe even the human sciences in general, can usefully be thought of in this way. Professional fields like counseling, education, management, and planning are obvious candidates. Academic fields like modern languages, literature, history, and sociology are perhaps less obvious candidates. Nonetheless, each of theses disciplines can be thought of as an organized effort to cultivate its particular field of social practice (respectively, practices of language use, literacy and literary culture, collective memory, and social membership).

The implications of this perspective are not entirely clear. Practically speaking, what difference would it make to think of the human sciences as practical disciplines? If the practical disciplines were a distinct type of discipline, it seems that methodological principles appropriate to that type of discipline would need to be articulated, but this apparently has not yet been done. In this essay, I explore some possible foundations of a methodology for the practical disciplines.

---

[1] For the development of this idea and its theoretical and methodological implications, see Craig (1989, 1995, 1996a, 1996b, 1999) and Craig and Tracy (1995).

By *methodology*, I mean a second-order practical discipline that reflects on and guides the practices of first-order disciplines.[2] We tend to think of methodology exclusively in connection with empirical science, but any disciplined human activity has the potential to evolve its own specific methodology. Just as we now have a methodology for empirical science, if practical disciplines differ in certain important ways from scientific disciplines, then we can and probably should try to develop a methodology specifically for the practical disciplines.

That the practical disciplines constitute a distinct type of discipline is not a new idea. The roots of this concept are in a tradition of practical philosophy that originated with Aristotle's writings on ethics, politics, and rhetoric. Aristotle distinguished practical wisdom (*phronēsis*) from both theoretical knowledge (*epistēmē*) and technical skill (*technē*). For Aristotle, *epistēmē* is knowledge for its own sake that arises from the practice of philosophical speculation (*theōria*) on matters that can be known with certainty. *Technē* arises in productive art (*poiēsis*) as the ability to produce a definite product (like a boat, or a poem) as the outcome of a rational course of activity. *Phronēsis*, by contrast, is neither knowledge for its own sake nor knowledge for the sake of some specific product or outcome. Rather it arises in practical activity (*praxis*) as the ability to act wisely in the conditions of flux and uncertainty that characterize human affairs: to understand practical situations, deliberate rationally about what to do, and choose courses of action that aim truly for a vision of the good life. Practical philosophy, or speculative inquiry in fields of *praxis* (politics, ethics, etc.), is worthwhile, for Aristotle, only insofar as it potentially assists in the cultivation of *phronēsis*.[3]

Practical philosophy receded with the advance of modern science (which promised to transform both *praxis* and *poiēsis* within a newly enlightened *theōria*), but has regained prominence during the past century (Bernstein, 1971, 1983; Dunne, 1993; Toulmin, 1988, 1990). This revival of practical philosophy has taken several quite different forms within different philosophical schools of thought. However, all tend to reflect certain common impulses, especially a reaction against the modernist drive

---

[2]Compare Kaplan (1964). Communication studies, conceived as a practical discipline, constitutes a kind of methodology—a methodology for the practice of communication. All practical disciplines are methodologies in this sense. A methodology for the practical disciplines would therefore be a second-order methodology—that is, a methodology of methodologies (Craig, 1989, 1996; Craig & Tracy, 1995).

[3]See Aristotle (1941, Books I and IV). Other sources that have informed my understanding of praxis, *phronēsis*, and practical philosophy include: Bernstein (1971, 1983), Broadie (1991), Dunne (1993), Farrell (1993), Gadamer (1981), Hollinger (1985), Lobkowicz (1967, 1977), MacIntyre (1981), Reeve (1995), Toulmin (1988, 1990), Urmson (1988), and Warnick (1989).

to reduce moral and political questions to scientific and technological terms. This chapter pursues a comparative critique of two 20th-century formulations of practical philosophy: John Dewey's pragmatic theory of inquiry and Hans-Georg Gadamer's philosophical hermeneutics. I argue that a methodology for the practical disciplines, although it may be essentially a Deweyan pragmatist project, should also embrace Gadamer's corrective influence.

I focus on Dewey and Gadamer because they offer parallel and yet different theories of *practical reflection*—a concept fundamental to practical discipline as I understand it. In a practical discipline, theory and practice interact dialectically in a process of practical reflection that the organized discipline cultivates through critical inquiry (Craig, 1989, 1996a, 1996b; Craig & Tracy, 1995). Therefore, an essential task of a methodology for the practical disciplines is to give an adequate account of the reflective process that such disciplines are intended to cultivate. A comparative critique of Dewey and Gadamer brings us closer—although, I acknowledge, not quite all the way—to an adequate account of practical reflection.

DEWEY AND GADAMER

Dewey (1859–1952), a leading figure in American pragmatism, described himself as an instrumentalist and advocated the application of scientific methods to practical problems in everyday life. Gadamer (born in 1900), a student of Martin Heidegger, has pressed relentlessly against the encroaching dominance of technology, instrumental reason, and method in the human sciences and in social practice. At first glance, these two philosophies would appear so radically different that a comparison between them would not be fruitful; in fact, commentators on either philosopher have seldom found reason to mention the other.[4] The work of Richard Rorty (1979, 1982) has brought American pragmatism into closer contact with the hermeneutic phenomenology of Heidegger and, to some extent, Gadamer.[5] Despite his acknowledged influence on Rorty—and his important differences from Rorty—Dewey has remained in the background of this conversation, however. Nor has Gadamer himself, to my knowledge, until very recently ever explicitly commented on Dewey or suggested any relevance of Dewey's earlier work to Gadamer's own.

Gadamer's (1997) remarks on Dewey are in a brief reply to Alexander (1997). Addressing the problem of community, Alexander (1997) traced

---

[4]Alexander (1997), the only comparative essay on Dewey and Gadamer of which I am aware, is briefly discussed next.

[5]Also see Hollinger (1985) and Langsdorf and Smith (1995).

parallels between Dewey and Gadamer, suggested that pragmatism may offer hermeneutics "a robust philosophy of community" (p. 324), and found in Gadamer's hermeneutics "what might be called an aesthetic ontology of community" (p. 323) that complements Dewey's pragmatism. Gadamer (1997) generously described reading Alexander's essay as a "remarkable and profound experience" (p. 346) that discloses long-forgotten historical connections between American pragmatism and German phenomenology. Although he acknowledged that "the concurrences which Alexander notes are convincing as such" and that "some American readers of *Truth and Method* will be reminded of *Art as Experience*," he cautioned that "the path from Kant to Hegel makes itself felt in a very different way" in the two works (p. 347). Dewey, he noted, "cherished the optimistic expectation of his time" but history has taught us that "we cannot be too optimistic" (p. 347).

As we turn, then, to a comparative critique of Gadamer and Dewey on practical reflection, we must take care to note their important differences as well as their striking similarities. Nevertheless, we find that these two very different 20th-century versions of practical philosophy together can take us well along the way toward a methodology for the practical disciplines.

In addition to their common roots in Aristotle's practical philosophy (more explicitly acknowledged by Gadamer than by Dewey), the similarity of their accounts of practical reflection derives in large measure from ways in which each applies and transforms Hegel's philosophy of the dialectic.[6] Both Dewey and Gadamer, following Hegel, conceive of reflection as a process in which consciousness develops within an essentially negative form of experience, a disappointment of expectations, an encounter with contradiction that calls forth a new synthesis at a more encompassing level of understanding. Each departs, however, from Hegel's philosophy of history, which posited an inevitable, progressive evolution of consciousness toward an ultimate synthesis in absolute truth and self-awareness. Dewey and Gadamer envision no final escape from the contingencies of ongoing history, no truth not subject to revision in future experience, no finally formed, self-transparent consciousness. Although the growth of understanding faces no definite, predetermined limits, the highest form of consciousness for both Dewey and Gadamer is one that understands itself as limited and

---

[6]For Aristotle's influence on Dewey, see Tiles (1988, pp. 154–167). For Aristotle's influence on Gadamer, see Gadamer (1965/1984, pp. 278–289; 1981, pp. 88–112). For Hegel's influence on Dewey, see Bernstein (1971, pp. 165–173) and Dewey (1939/1989, pp. 544f). For Hegel's influence on Gadamer, see Gadamer (1965/1984, pp. 317–319; 1981, pp. 21–68). It is perhaps emblematic of their broader differences that Gadamer typically offers more, and more generous, comments than Dewey concerning the historical predecessors that have influenced him.

always anticipates that its understandings will be revised in future experience. For Gadamer (1965/1984), "The dialectic of experience has its own fulfillment not in definitive knowledge, but in that openness to experience that is encouraged by experience itself" (p. 319). For Dewey (1933/1989), inquiry leads to further inquiry and requires an attitude of "open-mindedness" (p. 136), "the habit of reasoning once instituted is capable of indefinite development on its own account" (Dewey, 1938, p. 57), and "*the* end [of self-development] is growth itself" (cited in Tiles, 1988, p. 227).

DEWEY'S PHILOSOPHY OF INQUIRY

Dewey's term for practical reflection is *inquiry*—a process that has emerged naturally in the evolution of organic life. Every organism lives only in, and by means of, an environment with which it is so fully integrated that "processes of living are enacted by the environment as truly as by the organism; for they *are* an integration" (Dewey, 1938, p. 25). Continually arising imbalances in organism–environment relations are counteracted by sequential adaptive processes that, in higher animals, produce changes both in the environment (e.g., through locomotion of the organism) and in the organism (through the formation of habits). These processes set the basic pattern of all inquiry: A disturbance arises not in the organism or the environment, but in the dynamic relation between them. It then leads to a temporal sequence of activities, including exploratory behavior, that produces reciprocal change in organism and environment and, finally, reintegration of the two.

In humans, the pattern of inquiry is complicated and extended by symbolic language. The environment of human action is largely determined by linguistically coded, culturally transmitted institutions, traditions, and beliefs that constitute distinctive forms of human interaction. The meaning of a linguistic expression is the anticipated consequences of its use within such a form of interaction.[7] With language emerges mind or conceptual thought—the symbolic projection and manipulation of forms and anticipated consequences of action, which now can occur in imagination detached from concrete action and experience of consequences. The linguistic abstraction and manipulation of forms of action "make[s] possible ordered discourse or reason" (Dewey, 1938, p. 52). The pattern of inquiry thus comes to include the symbolic projection and transformation of conditions, actions, and consequences in problematic situations, and inquiry can be brought under the control of "methods" or abstracted forms of reason.

---

[7]The similarity of this formulation to Wittgenstein's concepts of language game and form of life, which it anticipated by several decades, has been noted by Hickman (1990, p. 39).

"Inquiry is the directed or controlled transformation of an indeterminate situation into a determinately unified one" (Dewey, 1938, p. 117).[8] A situation is neither a subjective state of an organism nor an objective state external to the organism, but rather an evolving, organism–environment relation constituted in part by the organism's ongoing anticipation of actions and consequences. A situation is indeterminate when the organism anticipates indefinite or conflicting consequences to any projected action, so there is no determinate form according to which action can proceed. Dewey described this state of indeterminacy as "precognitive" (p. 107), meaning that the situation, including its mental aspect (projection of actions and consequences) is not yet objectified as such in consciousness.

It should be emphasized at this point that mind, for Dewey, is both largely unconscious and essentially social and historical in its constitution. "The greater part of mind," he wrote, "is only implicit in any conscious act or state; the field of mind—of operative meanings—is enormously wider than that of consciousness" (Dewey, 1929, p. 247). This field of operative meanings, like Hegel's objective spirit, is social, not individual, in origin. "[T]he mind that appears *in* individuals is not as such individual mind"; rather, mind comprises a field of symbolic forms "instituted under the influence of custom and tradition" (p. 180). Individual selfhood, subjectivity, and mental processes that creatively modify traditional forms are not constitutive of mind as such, but are "eventual functions" (p. 171) that develop through reflective processes. Mind, as social, is essentially historical in its constitution; it is "mindful of the past and the future"; it "cannot evolve except where there is an organized process in which the fulfillments of the past are conserved and employed" (p. 226). If language is "the tool of tools," this is not because it is an instrument completely objectified in consciousness; it can be "used as a means for consequences" only because it is "endowed with meaning" as "the cherishing mother of all significance" (p. 154). As Tiles (1988) summarized the point, we "cannot free ourselves wholesale from custom and tradition because we are not wholly individual minds capable of locating ourselves in a position of wholesale isolation from which to observe"; "we can only refine the habits and techniques [culturally transmitted, largely unconscious] which enable us to perceive" (p. 83; bracketed words added).

---

[8]Rhetoric is an art of inquiry in Dewey's sense—an art of discovering communicative means for the directed transformation of indeterminate social situations into determinately unified ones through the mediation of audiences (cf. Bitzer, 1968). This rhetorical art of inquiry calls for the creative invention of conceptual perspectives for understanding and changing problematic social situations (Hauser, 1986). Hence, although rhetorical invention relies heavily on traditional ideas, it engages a reflective capacity that, when properly cultivated as a social practice, can foster the growth of practical reflection in civic life (Farrell, 1993; Hauser, 1999).

Inquiry, then, for Dewey, does not occur apart from what Gadamer (1965/1984) called "hermeneutical experience" (pp. 300ff). Inquiry is practical reflection in which traditional meanings are adapted in being applied to reconstruct a present situation in which anticipation has been disappointed, interrupting action. This process emerges into conscious reflection, but is not brought about as a fully conscious act. "Consciousness," wrote Dewey (1929),

> is that phase of a system of meanings which at a given time is undergoing redirection, transitive transformations. . . . To treat consciousness as a power accomplishing the change, is but another instance of the common philosophic fallacy of converting an eventual function into an antecedent force or cause. Consciousness *is* the meaning of events in the course of remaking. (p. 251)

Within an indeterminate situation, the pattern of inquiry proceeds, according to Dewey (1938, pp. 101–119), first by noticing that the situation is problematic and then by determining provisionally what the problem is—formulating, so to speak, the *question* that the situation poses. This partly determines the solution to the problem just as every question partly determines an answer (Gadamer, 1965/1984, pp. 333ff). Possible courses of action are explored in imagination by reasoning to their anticipated consequences in conjunction with further observation and redefinition of the existing situation. This occurs much as Gadamer said a translator "will seek the best solution in the toing and froing of weighing up and considering possibilities" (p. 348).[9] The process terminates in the formation of a "practical judgment" (decision on a course of action) executed in "existential operations" to bring about "the re-ordering of environing conditions required to produce a settled and unified situation" (Dewey, 1938, p. 118).

Before turning to Gadamer, a further point concerning values and the relation of means to ends in Dewey's philosophy of inquiry should be touched on briefly. Inquiry, for Dewey, is not governed by a purely technical rationality that only seeks efficient means to achieve arbitrarily predetermined ends. In the course of inquiry, means and ends are determined reciprocally, "in *strict conjugate relation* to each other" (Dewey, 1938, p. 496; italics original). Tiles (1988) helpfully showed the kinship of Dewey's view to Aristotle's practical philosophy. Values (the aims or purposes governing action) become more concretely specified as possible courses of action are considered in reflection. "Ideally, Dewey thought, one should always be able to integrate whatever means one used in pursuit of some end

---

[9]"In reflective experience as such, in investigation called forth by problematic situations, there is a rhythm of seeking and finding, of reaching out for a tenable conclusion and coming to what is at least a tentative one" (Dewey, 1934/1958, p. 179).

into that end; so that 'instrumental' in the sense Dewey most favoured meant something like 'an organic constituent' " (p. 158; compare Gadamer, 1965/1984, pp. 286–287; 1981, pp. 81–82). Recall that the end of inquiry is not some predetermined outcome, but rather a *unified situation*. The instrumental reason that Gadamer always critiques and resists should not, then, be confused with Dewey's instrumentalism, which is quite different.

GADAMER'S PHILOSOPHICAL HERMENEUTICS

Parallels to Gadamer have been suggested throughout the discussion of Dewey's philosophy of inquiry, the presentation of which has highlighted aspects of Dewey's thought most relevant to the comparison. Gadamer's philosophical hermeneutics will now be further elucidated through a more explicit comparison with Dewey's pragmatism in regard to four themes: method, tradition, application, and theory.

Method

In traditional philology, hermeneutic methods of textual interpretation were thought necessary only when some obscurity in a text prevented understanding. Interpretation then required a back and forth movement between the particular details and the global meaning of the text, each reconsidered in light of the other until a unified understanding of the whole was achieved. In the 19th century, Dilthey posited this hermeneutic circle of understanding as a general method for the human sciences—a method that would produce objectively valid interpretive knowledge. The meanings of events and artifacts would be reconstructed in their historical contexts and made available to understanding within our present historical context.[10] Gadamer followed Heidegger in arguing that such an objectivist understanding of historical interpretation is untenable. Interpretation cannot objectively re-create the meaning of a historical text. The human sciences, and human experience generally, are hermeneutical in a more radical way. The hermeneutic circle possesses "an ontologically positive significance" (Gadamer, 1965/1984, p. 236); it involves the self of the interpreter and produces both new self-awareness as well as new meaning in the particular text and in the historical tradition to which both text and interpreter belong.

---

[10]Palmer (1969) gave a useful summary of Dilthey's hermeneutics and concluded that, by locating interpretation "within the horizon of historicality," he "renewed the project of a general hermeneutics and significantly advanced it" (p. 123).

Gadamer maintained that the "hermeneutical phenomenon is basically not a problem of method at all" (p. xi). It is an experience of truth that happens to us but that we cannot reliably bring about, nor scientifically validate, by any objectified technical procedure. As an experience that precedes science and makes possible all understanding, including scientific understanding, it belies "the universal claims of scientific method" (p. xii). Gadamer emphasized, in his Foreword to the second edition of *Truth and Method*, that his point is not to deny the usefulness of technologies in general or even the applicability of "the methods of modern natural science . . . to the social world" (p. xvii). His point is just that method is not the Royal Road to Truth in any field.

Dewey, like Gadamer, disclaimed any a priori universal method, conceived of objectified methods as extensions of mental processes that remain largely unconscious, and opposed unreflective technical rationality. The pattern of inquiry constitutes what Dewey called a *method*. By this he did not mean a fully objectified, normative procedure laid down a priori as the way to absolutely certain, objective knowledge—the sort of method to which Gadamer most fundamentally opposes the hermeneutical experience of truth. Methods (plural) for Dewey are instead procedural forms abstracted from past, successful practice and reflectively applied to govern subsequent practice, which thus becomes more self-aware. Dewey mentioned the example of common law, in which,

> formal conceptions arise out of the ordinary transactions; they are not imposed upon them from any external and a priori source. But when they are formed they are also *formative*; they regulate the proper conduct of the activities out of which they develop. (Dewey, 1938, p. 102; compare Gadamer, 1965/1984, pp. 289–305)

Logic, in Dewey's peculiar sense of it as the theory (or abstracted method) of inquiry, develops in this way from a general "inquiry into inquiry" (Dewey, 1938, p. 4). However, inquiry into inquiry is not conducted only at this general level because it also emerges independently within multiple fields. Inquiry "is the lifeblood of every science and is constantly engaged in every art, craft and profession" (p. 4). Thus, within its own inquiries, every self-aware practice develops special methods integral to its own special ends (see Dewey, 1933/1989, pp. 3–4).

Thus, although at a fundamental assumptive level there is much agreement between Gadamer's and Dewey's views of method, both of which can fairly be called postmodern (or antifoundationalist), it must still be acknowledged that their practical impulses push in quite opposite directions. Gadamer's project is always to resist and limit the encroaching claims of method and technique. For Dewey, in contrast, the solution to mindless technology is always more, and more mindful, technology (Hickman, 1990). As a matter of practical judgment, Dewey puts more faith and confidence than Gadamer in the efficacy of methods and the potential of a reflective technology that would integrate *technē* with *praxis*.

Tradition

Here again we find much implicit agreement and yet strongly opposed attitudes. For Dewey, no less than for Gadamer, the human environment, mind, and self are constituted historically and continually reconstructed in practical reflection. Neither view admits the possibility of an absolute objectivity that would escape the influence of tradition. Both anticipate that reflection, occasioned by the disappointment of expectations, will winnow and renew historically transmitted meanings. However, in attitude, Dewey is suspicious of tradition no less than Gadamer is of method. Dewey often uses the word *traditional* as a near synonym of *outdated*. Traditional beliefs and practices that do not continue to be useful are to be cast aside, without regret, in inquiry. Traditions as such possess no inherent authority for Dewey, no claim on us to keep and preserve them, but only consist of inherited meanings that either continue to be useful in experience or do not.[11]

Gadamer implicitly agrees with much of this. He, too, disclaims the sort of traditionalism that refuses to question or revise its prejudices; for him, too, the only valid truth we know is that disclosed in ongoing experience.

---

[11]This is perhaps overstated. Dewey asserted, in certain passages, a presumptively positive role for tradition, especially in *Art as Experience*, where he wrote that, for the artist it "is not enough to have direct contacts and observations [of nature], indispensable as these are. Even the work of an original temperament may be relatively thin, as well as tending to the bizarre, when it is not informed with a wide and varied experience of the traditions of the art in which the artist operates" (Dewey, 1934/1958, p. 265). He went on: "In this dependence on tradition there is nothing peculiar to art. The scientific inquirer, the philosopher, the technologist, also derive their substance from the stream of culture. This dependence is an essential factor in original vision and creative expression" (Dewey, 1934/1958, p. 265; also see p. 312 on the art critic's need for a wide knowledge of traditions). Characteristically, however, he concluded by warning against the tendency of "the academic imitator" to follow traditions on a superficial level, "as tricks of technique or as extraneous suggestions and conventions as to the proper thing to do" (Dewey, 1934/1958, p. 265). Tradition is valued primarily for its role in fostering creative adaptation to new circumstances. For Dewey, the artist is not essentially a medium for the transmission of tradition. "The function of art has always been to break through the crust of conventionalized and routine consciousness. . . . Artists have always been the real purveyors of news" (Dewey, 1927, pp. 183–184). In a still more cautious passage in *Experience and Nature*, Dewey (1929) wrote that "the products of the reflection of past generations and by-gone ages [i.e., traditions] . . . may become organs of enrichment if they are detected and reflected upon. If they are not detected, they often obfuscate and distort" (p. 34). A "special service" that philosophy may perform is thus to engage in this necessary "critique of prejudices" (Dewey, 1929, p. 34). Important similarities to Gadamer as well as strongly contrasting attitudes become evident in such passages.

However, Gadamer's attitude toward tradition can be described as *reverential*. One of the most striking aspects of Gadamer's philosophy is his argument that prejudice or prejudgment plays a necessary and even positively helpful role in interpretation. Prejudice is both unavoidable and potentially fruitful because it reflects the background of tradition without which it would be impossible for us to understand anything at all. If we approach hermeneutical experience with an attitude of openness, prejudice constitutes a horizon of meaning that is tested and revised as we move toward the other in a fusion of horizons between self and text. Tradition, as the necessary background of meaningful experience, for Gadamer holds a legitimate authority over us. "[O]ur finite historical being is marked by the fact that always the authority of what has been transmitted—and not only what is clearly grounded—has power over our attitudes and behavior" (Gadamer, 1965/1984, p. 249). All of the examined and unexamined beliefs and practices that make us who we are have been transmitted in tradition; so we tacitly accept the authority of tradition in our every act, and a developed historical consciousness must acknowledge this fact and understand its legitimacy. The office of the human sciences is to preserve, transmit, and renew tradition for the sake of the wisdom that it offers.

It is not unfair to conclude, then, that Gadamer, as a matter of practical judgment, puts more faith and confidence than Dewey in the efficacy of tradition and the potential of a nonauthoritarian, reflective traditionalism (see Hollinger, 1985, p. xv). Gadamer (1965/1984) admitted that his work has onesidedly "emphasized the element of the assimilation of what is past and handed down," but believed "that the onesidedness of hermeneutic universalism has the truth of a corrective" (p. xxv).[12]

Application

Dewey and Gadamer focus on rather different cases of practical reflection—a difference that both signifies and yet also may tend to exaggerate the larger differences between them. Dewey's exemplars of inquiry tend to be ordinary problem-solving situations in science or everyday life (a fallen tree has blocked the road and one must find a way to get on—such, for Dewey, would be a situation calling for inquiry). The hermeneutical experience for Gadamer is no less universal an aspect of human existence, but his examples are typically drawn from the more exalted realms of humanistic scholarship and high culture.[13] The exemplary situation of practical reflection in *Truth and Method* is most often that of a scholar interpreting a

---

[12]Alexander (1997) argued that Dewey's and Gadamer's views of tradition "are similar, but for the emphases due to temperament" (p. 340).

[13]Dewey, of course, also wrote about elite traditions, as in *Art as Experience* (1934/1958), but he always stressed the relevance of such traditions to quotidian experience.

canonical text, a historical document, or a work of art. Gadamer wishes to show that such a scholar is always engaged in practical reflection. This involves a dialogical encounter with the text in the medium of a common tradition, motivated by practical concerns, culminating in an experience of truth—a fusion of horizons between text and interpreter that necessarily involves some re-interpretation of tradition and of self.[14]

Interpretation, then, for Gadamer, always involves *application*, which "is neither a subsequent nor a merely occasional part of the phenomenon of understanding, but codetermines it as a whole from the beginning" (1965/1984, p. 289). Just as a judge can determine what the law precisely means only in applying it to each particular case, so the interpreter of any text can understand what the text *says*, "the meaning and importance of the text," only in applying it to his or her own particular situation. Because historical conditions (hence the practical interests that motivate interpretation) constantly change, "a text is understood only if it is understood in a different way every time" (p. 276).

All understanding is that of a historical consciousness orienting itself in relation to a past and future; so hermeneutical application involves projection. Hermeneutic experience has practical consequences for self-understanding, but does not necessarily require actually doing anything. Unlike Dewey's inquiry, hermeneutical experience for Gadamer does not explicitly terminate in "existential operations" bringing about "the re-ordering of environing conditions" (Dewey, 1939/1989, p. 118). In Dewey's instrumentalism, inquiry informs intelligent action, which is undertaken in view of its projected consequences—and evaluated in view of its actually experienced consequences. For Gadamer, understanding can be a more contemplative affair; it is an event we can hope to experience, but not an outcome we can bring about through instrumental action. An instrumentalist theory of action such as Dewey's is "voluntaristically distorted" and "can never do justice to the experience of history in which our plans tend to shatter and our actions and omissions tend to lead to unexpected consequences" (Gadamer, 1981, p. 46). As a matter of practical judgment, Dewey again puts more faith and confidence than Gadamer in the potential of what Dewey calls *inquiry* to bring the consequences of action under more intelligent control.[15]

---

[14]"To understand a text is to come to understand oneself in a kind of dialogue" (Gadamer, 1976, p. 57).

[15]Gadamer's textualism may also reflect an overly intellectualized approach to interpretation that underestimates the role of somatic experience, which for Dewey is essential. For an argument that "hermeneutic universalists" such as Gadamer fail to account adequately for somatic experience, see Shusterman (1992). In this regard, Dewey is closer to Heidegger's hermeneutic phenomenology than to Gadamer's philosophical hermeneutics. On parallels between Dewey and Heidegger, see Hollinger (1985) and Sukale (1976).

Theory

Gadamer (1981) wrote of his philosophical hermeneutics that "it is theory" and "has to do with a theoretical attitude toward the practice of interpretation." As theory, it is "not trying to resolve" any "practical situations of understanding," but "only makes us aware reflectively of what is performatively at play in the practical experience of understanding" (p. 112; also see Gadamer, 1965/1984, p. xiv). Although hermeneutical experience always involves application, hermeneutic philosophy is a theoretical project undertaken without any practical goals in mind. Yet Gadamer (1981) also wrote that it is "practical philosophy" (p. 111 et passim). Even Weinsheimer (1985), the most sympathetic of readers, characterized Gadamer's denial of practical intent in a similar passage as "extremely problematical" (p. 64).

Gadamer (1981) seemed to emphasize that philosophical hermeneutics is not, and cannot become, a method of interpretation, but "only describes what always happens" in hermeneutical experience (p. 111). This suggests that hermeneutic philosophy is *theōria*—an attempt to elucidate the universal features of hermeneutical experience. Yet in other passages, Gadamer (1981) suggested quite strongly that such a philosophy can have practical consequences and that it is undertaken with a broad practical intent, although without specific practical goals. On the model of Aristotle's ethics, practical philosophy involves a "mutual implication," a "reciprocity between theory and practice" (p. 111). Theory in practical philosophy is not the same thing as practical knowledge (*phronēsis*, the tacit knowledge of the practitioner) and can never replace it. Even so, it can be of some limited help to the practitioner. It "clarifies the good in sketchy universality," thus giving the practitioner a "target" to aim at (p. 134). It "can be a kind of assistance in the conscious avoidance of certain deviations . . . inasmuch as it aids in making present for rational consideration the ultimate purposes of one's actions" (p. 135). It "endeavors . . . to bring to our reflective awareness" those tacit "normative perspectives" that "shape" us but are not "fixed immutably" or "beyond criticism" (p. 135). Yet Gadamer resisted the conclusion that practical philosophy is undertaken at all for the sake of such consequences, although it cannot but anticipate them and even "endeavors" to help bring them about. On this point, there seems to be an unresolved tension in Gadamer's thought.[16]

Gadamer wants above all to avoid falling in with the voluntaristic and technologistic distortions of *praxis* that characterize modernist thought. He offers a version of practical philosophy that leans somewhat toward

---

[16]Sukale (1976, pp. 145–151) pointed out a similar gap in Heidegger's thought.

theōria—toward a *praxis* in which reflection deepens one's self-understanding but does not necessarily lead to action undertaken for the sake
of certain projected consequences in the world. Dewey, who wants above
all to avoid falling in with a purely contemplative, elitist tradition of
philosophy, offers a version of practical philosophy that leans somewhat
away from *theōria* and toward *poiēsis* or productive art. All practice for
Dewey, insofar as it has consequences, has a productive moment; it produces its consequences. Theory for Dewey is practice; as such, it is instrumental in the production of its consequences. Dewey consistently denies
any fundamental distinction between theory and practice. "Theory and
practice are in his view only different phases of a stretch of intelligent inquiry, theory being the 'ideal act' and practice the 'executed insight' "
(Hickman, 1990, p. 110). Theory is a conceptualized account of methods
abstracted from practice and tested in being applied reflectively to the rational governance of subsequent practice. Theory, for Dewey no less than
for Gadamer, serves to make practice more reflectively self-aware. However, for Dewey, the self-awareness that it produces should be intentionally productive of more intelligent (i.e., more satisfactorily productive)
practice.

CONCLUSION

In summary, we have seen that Gadamer's philosophy of practical reflection is compatible with Dewey's in many of its most basic tenets. Both hold
that consciousness is historically constituted and develops in dialectical
reflection under historically contingent circumstances. Both reject the
alienation of means from ends in technical rationality. Dewey makes no
absolutist claims for method while Gadamer denies neither the possibility nor the limited usefulness of methods. For both, theory produces
more self-aware practice. Their important differences can be summarized
in two connected points, both of which I have characterized as matters
of practical judgment—contingent matters about which it is possible to
disagree even in a context of broad agreement on many basic assumptions.
    First, Gadamer's approach to practical reflection emphasizes an aware-
ness of historical tradition as the ground of all meaning. He is confident
that deep reflection on materials handed down from the past will enrich
our self-understanding and cultivate practical wisdom in our *praxis*. Thus,
he acknowledges the authority of tradition as a source of normative ideas
derived through interpretation and applied in good hope to our present
situation. Dewey acknowledges the historical roots of meaning and iden-

tity, but his version of historical consciousness is oriented more to the future than to the past. Reconstruction and experimentation are more important for Dewey than preservation and interpretation. Tradition has the authority only of a hypothesis. The right balance between future and past in the constitution of historical consciousness is a matter of judgment. In my judgment, Dewey's perspective puts too little value on the rich heritage of meaning and wisdom that can be derived from an interpretive exploration of tradition, and it worries too little about the poverty of meaning produced by a shallow awareness of the past. Thus, Gadamer offers an important corrective in this dimension.

Second, Dewey's pragmatism is premised on the optimistic assumption that practical consequences can be brought under more intelligent control through inquiry. Gadamer questions this optimistic view. The potential for technological control of outcomes under historically contingent conditions is limited. Method is often ineffective: Our best laid plans fail, our actions lead to mostly unanticipated consequences. Moreover, the drive toward technological control, to the extent that it succeeds, is in danger of producing not the reflective *praxis* that Dewey hopes for and expects, but only an ever more mindless and ultimately destructive domination over nature and among human beings. For Gadamer, method is both too often ineffective and inherently dangerous, and therefore should be resisted. Gadamer's worries confront the practical disciplines with important caveats: How optimistic to be about the potential for methodological progress in the practical disciplines is a matter of judgment. Gadamer could turn out to be more right than Dewey about the actual consequences of methods. However, in this case, Dewey's path of inquiry would lead us finally to the same conclusion. Ironically, Dewey, not Gadamer, orients inquiry to the existential consequences of our actions and provides us with a positive account of instrumental reason, not as mindless technique but as a necessary moment within a reflective *praxis*. On this point, although Gadamer's doubts and warnings about method deserve serious consideration, in my judgment, it is Dewey who offers a corrective to Gadamer's excessively pessimistic turn.

My continuing project is to articulate a methodology for communication and the practical disciplines that builds on Dewey's pragmatism in a broad context of contemporary thought, including Gadamer's philosophical hermeneutics. Although some steps have been taken toward the elaboration of specific methods of inquiry for the practical disciplines (e.g., Craig & Tracy, 1995), much of this work remains to be done. Much also remains to be done before the underlying concept of practical reflection is fully worked out (Craig, 1996a, 1996b). As presented here, it does not yet adequately respond to the challenge of practical reflection as critique, especially in the critical theory of Habermas.[17] Nor does it adequately respond to challenges from postmodernist/poststructuralist theory to traditional notions of the autonomous subject or agent of practical reflection.[18] The present chapter, however, has taken us this far: It seems that if the practical disciplines are to have a methodology, they will find many of the basic materials out of which to construct one in Dewey. Gadamer's important contribution is that of a corrective—an alternative, antimethodological vision of the practical disciplines that alerts us to certain limitations and pitfalls that methodological reflection necessarily confronts and should not fail to address.

REFERENCES

Alexander, T. M. (1997). Eros and understanding: Gadamer's aesthetic ontology of the community. In L. E. Hahn (Ed.), *The philosophy of Hans-Georg Gadamer* (The Library of Living Philosophers, Vol. XXIII, pp. 323–345). LaSalle, IL: Open Court.

Aristotle. (1941). *Ethica nicomachea* (W. D. Ross, Trans.). In R. McKeon (Ed.), *The basic works of Aristotle* (pp. 927–1112). New York: Random House.

Bernstein, R. J. (1971). *Praxis and action: Contemporary philosophies of human activity*. Philadelphia, PA: University of Pennsylvania Press.

Bernstein, R. J. (1983). *Beyond objectivism and relativism: Science, hermeneutics, and praxis*. Philadelphia: University of Pennsylvania Press.

Bitzer, L. F. (1968). The rhetorical situation. *Philosophy and Rhetoric, 1*, 1–14.

Broadie, S. (1991). *Ethics with Aristotle*. New York: Oxford University Press.

Craig, R. T. (1989). Communication as a practical discipline. In B. Dervin, L. Grossberg, B. J. O'Keefe, & E. Wartella (Eds.), *Rethinking communication: Volume 1. Paradigm issues* (pp. 97–122). Newbury Park, CA: Sage.

Craig, R. T. (1995). Applied communication research in a practical discipline. In K. N. Cissna (Ed.), *Applied communication in the 21st century* (pp. 147–155). Mahwah, NJ: Lawrence Erlbaum Associates.

Craig, R. T. (1996a). Practical theory: A reply to Sandelands. *Journal for the Theory of Social Behaviour, 26*, 65–79.

Craig, R. T. (1996b). Practical-theoretical argumentation. *Argumentation, 10*, 461–474.

Craig, R. T. (1999). Communication theory as a field. *Communication Theory, 9*, 119–161.

Craig, R. T., & Tracy, K. (1995). Grounded practical theory: The case of intellectual discussion. *Communication Theory, 5*, 248–272.

Dewey, J. (1927). *The public and its problems*. Chicago, IL: Swallow.

Dewey, J. (1929). *Experience and nature* (2nd ed.). LaSalle, IL: Open Court.

Dewey, J. (1938). *Logic: The theory of inquiry*. New York: Henry Holt.

---

[17]Habermas' writings are voluminous, and the literature on Habermas is vast, but Habermas (1977) would be a good take-off point from the present chapter, and useful views on Habermas in the tradition of practical philosophy are offered by Bernstein (1983), Dunne (1993), and Farrell (1993). Also see Craig (1989).

[18]See Huspek and Radford (1997) for a recent anthology including some useful discussions and references. As noted earlier, Dewey and Gadamer can both be described as postmodern thinkers, so there is already much common ground from which to approach other postmodern views.

Dewey, J. (1958). *Art as experience*. New York: Capricorn Books. (Original work published 1934)

Dewey, J. (1989). Experience, knowledge and value: A rejoinder. In P. A. Schilpp & L. E. Hahn (Eds.), *The philosophy of John Dewey* (3rd ed., pp. 515–608). LaSalle, IL: Open Court. (Original work published 1939)

Dewey, J. (1989). *How we think* (rev. ed.). In J. A. Boydston (Ed.), *John Dewey: The later works, 1925–1953* (Vol. 8, pp. 105–352). Carbondale: Southern Illinois University Press. (Original work published 1933)

Dunne, J. (1993). *Back to the rough ground: "Phronesis" and "techne" in modern philosophy and in Aristotle*. Notre Dame, IN: University of Notre Dame Press.

Farrell, T. B. (1993). *Norms of rhetorical culture*. New Haven, CT: Yale University Press.

Gadamer, H.-G. (1976). *Philosophical hermeneutics* (D. E. Linge, Trans. & Ed.). Berkeley, CA: University of California Press.

Gadamer, H.-G. (1981). *Reason in the age of science* (F. G. Lawrence, Trans.). Cambridge, MA: MIT Press.

Gadamer, H.-G. (1984). *Truth and method* (G. Barden & J. Comming, Trans.). New York: Crossroad. (Original work published 1960; 2nd ed., 1965)

Gadamer, H.-G. (1997). Reply to Thomas M. Alexander. In L. E. Hahn (Ed.), *The philosophy of Hans-Georg Gadamer* (The Library of Living Philosophers, Vol. XXIII, pp. 346–347). LaSalle, IL: Open Court.

Habermas, J. (1977). A review of Gadamer's *Truth and Method*. In F. R. Dallmayr & T. A. McCarthy (Eds.), *Understanding and social inquiry* (pp. 335–363). Notre Dame, IN: University of Notre Dame Press.

Hauser, G. A. (1986). *An introduction to rhetorical theory*. New York: Harper & Row.

Hauser, G. A. (1999). *Vernacular voices: The rhetoric of publics and public spheres*. Columbia, SC: University of South Carolina Press.

Hickman, L. A. (1990). *John Dewey's pragmatic technology*. Bloomington, IN: Indiana University Press.

Hollinger, R. (Ed.). (1985). *Hermeneutics and praxis*. Notre Dame, IN: University of Notre Dame Press.

Huspek, M., & Radford, G. P. (Eds.). (1997). *Transgressing discourses: Communication and the voice of other*. Albany, NY: SUNY Press.

Kaplan, A. (1964). *The conduct of inquiry: Methodology for behavioral science*. San Francisco, CA: Chandler.

Langsdorf, L., & Smith, A. R. (Eds.). (1995). *Recovering pragmatism's voice: The classical tradition, Rorty, and the philosophy of communication*. Albany, NY: SUNY Press.

Lobkowicz, N. (1967). *Theory and practice: History of a concept from Aristotle to Marx*. Notre Dame, IN: University of Notre Dame Press.

Lobkowicz, N. (1977). On the history of theory and practice. In T. Ball (Ed.), *Political theory and praxis: New perspectives* (pp. 13–27). Minneapolis, MN: University of Minneapolis Press.

MacIntyre, A. (1981). *After virtue: A study in moral theory*. Notre Dame, IN: University of Notre Dame Press.

Palmer, R. E. (1969). *Hermeneutics*. Evanston, IL: Northwestern University Press.

Reeve, C. D. C. (1995). *Practices of reason: Aristotle's Nichomachean Ethics*. Oxford, England: Oxford University Press.

Rorty, R. (1979). *Philosophy and the mirror of nature*. Princeton, NJ: Princeton University Press.

Rorty, R. (1982). *Consequences of pragmatism*. Minneapolis, MN: University of Minnesota Press.

Shusterman, R. (1992). *Pragmatist aesthetics: Living beauty, rethinking art*. Cambridge, MA: Blackwell.

Sukale, M. (1976). *Comparative studies in phenomenology*. The Hague: Martinus Nijhoff.

Tiles, J. E. (1988). *Dewey*. London: Routledge.

Toulmin, S. (1988). The recovery of practical philosophy. *The American Scholar, 57*(3), 337–352.

Toulmin, S. (1990). *Cosmopolis: The hidden agenda of modernity*. New York: The Free Press.

Urmson, J. O. (1988). *Aristotle's ethics*. New York: Basil Blackwell.

Warnick, B. (1989). Judgment, probability, and Aristotle's rhetoric. *Quarterly Journal of Speech, 75*, 299–311.

Weinsheimer, J. C. (1985). *Gadamer's hermeneutics: A reading of* Truth and Method. New Haven, CT: Yale University Press.

Chapter 7

Truth or Consequences: Pragmatism, Relativism, and Ethics

Janet S. Horne
Salisbury State University

One cannot discuss the impact of Richard Rorty's work on the theory and practice of rhetoric without addressing the issue of relativism as it pertains to ethical questions. The topic has existed since Plato first denounced Gorgian rhetoric as mere cookery, compared with the noble aims of philosophy and science, and as a cosmetic rendering of appearance rather than a true philosophical search for reality. Furthermore, to argue with Rorty and the deconstructionists that we would be better off to accept the death of the correspondence theory of language is to propose removing our traditional source of judgment and validation of both the true and the good.

Removing consideration of the objectively true from judgment of the good also eliminates the foundations of the traditional dichotomies hierarchically separating rhetoric and philosophy throughout time. These include appearance versus reality, style versus substance, words versus deeds, and rhetoric versus action. Traditionally and popularly, rhetoric has always been linked with trickery, manipulation, seduction, and demagoguery—and with relativism rather than objective, durable methods of justification—when it has been disassociated from a philosophical notion of truth. Rorty's antifoundationalist pragmatism is also subject to such associations.

A well-noted link ties pragmatism to relativism and hence, at least potentially, with Machiavellianism. In surveying the classical pragmatists' positions on ethics or the "moral question," McDermott (1989) took pains to argue that "[a] pragmatic approach to philosophy is not a vulgar replay of British utilitarianism[, nor] . . . a gross manipulation of means for the sake of ends[, nor] . . . a caricature of a contemporary version of *realpolitik*" (p. 245).

Aristotle's assessment that men will naturally prefer the true, the good, and the just rather than the false, the bad, and the unjust is still rooted in two important themes. These are the need of the rhetor to be able to determine the true and the good and the need of the audience for enlightenment about the alternatives to be able to choose according to its nature. The classical Greek belief of the primacy of reason in human nature, however, provides the basis of Aristotle's view (Johanneson, 1990).[1]

Throughout questions of ethics and morality, this notion of the good hinging on the true nonetheless is pervasive. However, the pragmatist unhitches good from truth and attaches it to the assessment of results, outcomes, and consequences. As McDermott (1989) pointed out, "[the] fundamental point . . . reiterated constantly by James and Peirce, has to do with effects and consequences as the bottom line of worthiness of judgments, propositions, truth-claims, or decisions" (p. 246). Traditional, rationalist-based ethics relies on a priori criteria for decision making. These exist independently of the immediate situation. Thus, criteria precede events in time. In contrast, pragmatic ethics are based on temporally based judgments of the consequences or results of actions and decisions. Criteria are created in time. Analogously, social and moral theory can be seen traditionally to gain credence and legitimation based on their ability to ground social and moral practice (Condit, 1987).

Furthermore, the pragmatist disengagement of rules for action from a priori, rationalist-based truth claims renders ethical rather than epistemological questions central. The central question is not how to determine whether certain claims are true in a universal, ahistorical sense, or even accurate or correct in a more mundane sense. Rather, the central question becomes whether all possible views have been heard. Has the situation in question—the policy, the decision—been redescribed in as many available alternative vocabularies as possible (Rorty, 1989)?

Finally, a further consequence of the centrality of ethics to pragmatism emerges in Rorty's controversial division between public and private spheres of discourse, public rhetoric, and private self-creation (Rorty, 1989).[2] This consequence is proposed as supporting the view that commu-

---

[1]Johannesen (1990) noted Rowland and Womack's (1985) argument casting some doubt as to the validity of this received view of Aristotle's distinction between logical and emotional appeals.

[2]Private self-creation is emphasized in Rorty's (1991b) "Freud and Moral Reflection" (pp. 143–163) and in "Contingency, Irony, and Solidarity" (pp. 23–43) and "Private Irony and Liberal Hope" (pp. 73–95).

nication or rhetorical ethics form the wedge between public and private spheres, between private autonomy and self-creation and public commitment, community, and solidarity.

Three major factors relevant to questions of ethics emerge from Rorty's work and provide a structural framework for discussing its relevance here. These have to do with the relationship of ethics to truth, the relationship of ethics to the nature of human selfhood, and the distinction between public and private ethical demands. Discussion of the first factor focuses principally on relativism. The second revolves around Rorty's (1989) notion of the self as contingent and composed of a "web of beliefs and desires." The third highlights a Rortian view of communication ethics in terms of the public–private distinction.

Numerous related themes having to do with contemporary moral philosophy, particularly Rorty's moral philosophy in contrast with traditional and other contemporary frameworks, cluster around these major issues. Typically these Rortian topics tend to feature a vocabulary where issues of truth and selfhood might be discussed differently. These themes concern various issues or questions associated with ethical problems. They appear subsequently in this chapter. These include Rorty's distinction between public discourse and private self-creation and the family of terms and concepts (Rorty's and others') related to conversation, such as *free* and *open encounter*, *dialogue*, *ideal speech situation*, and the like. Other issues involve the primacy of freedom over truth, the relationship between contingency and responsibility, power relations, post-Enlightenment liberalism, and the ethics of criticism and critique.

RELATIVISM

The relationship of ethics to truth naturally brings to mind the issue of relativism. Relativism obviously has ethical as well as epistemological implications. Ethical relativism is often viewed as irresponsible, groundless, or opportunistic—along the lines of the Machiavellian utilitarianism that McDermott discussed. This view often relies on the assumption that if one professes no absolute standards for judging or deciding, then one must profess to have no standards. Rorty's (1982) response to this issue is characteristically to the point: " 'Relativism' is the view that every belief on a certain topic, or perhaps about *any* topic, is as good as every other. No one holds this view" (p. 166). This comment indeed recalls the dilemma of those Rorty called "wet liberals," who have discovered the ethnocentric bias of liberal society and realize that "We have become so open-minded that our brains have fallen out" (Rorty, 1991f, p. 203).

The point about this picture of relativism as a pseudoproblem is to support a commonsense view. According to it, even without claiming absolute standards for judgment, we rationally distinguish between better and worse cases every day of our lives. Following Sigmund Freud and Donald Davidson, we can do so because, contrary to Hume's notion of the mind as composed of discrete ideas and impressions, "[beliefs] and desires . . . come in packages" within which individual beliefs are "mostly true and mostly consistent" (Rorty, 1991b, p. 147).

Rorty (1982) derived his standards for evaluation conversationally. It goes without saying that communication and rhetoric scholars will be interested in ferreting out the full implications of such standards. Rorty made a couple of useful distinctions, for instance, between relativist and nonrelativist philosophers and between the importance of relativism for philosophical theories as opposed to real theories (Rorty, 1982). In the first instance, the nonrelativist or foundationalist philosophers call those philosophers " 'relativists' . . . who say that the grounds for choosing between [incompatible] opinions are less algorithmic than had been thought" (Rorty, 1982). These two banks of the philosophical stream consist of "those who think our culture, or purpose, or intuitions cannot be supported *except* conversationally, and people who still hope for other sorts of support" (p. 162; italics added).

Second, the charge of relativism derives from confusion about the pragmatists' distinction between philosophical theories and real theories, with reference to James and Dewey as, within certain limits, metaphilosophical relativists (Rorty, 1982). Philosophical theories are second-level abstractions of real theories or attempts to place real theories within an overall structural framework or worldview. Perhaps ironically, Rorty (1982) characterized these Platonic–Kantian philosophical theories as basically matters of taste and preference, rendering benign the relativism inherent in choosing among them: "Nobody really cares if there are incompatible alternative formulations of a categorical imperative, or incompatible sets of categories of the pure understanding" (p. 168). For Rorty (1982), relativism seems to matter to be "a disturbing view, worthy of being refuted, [only] if it concerns *real* theories, not just philosophical theories" (p. 168).[3] In the real world, individuals and groups daily make choices, which clearly indicate that one is not just as good as every other.

We do care, perhaps deeply, about concrete alternatives and proposals for social and political change: "When such an alternative is proposed, we debate it, not in terms of categories or principles but in terms of the various concrete advantages and disadvantages it has" (Rorty, 1982, p. 168). From a pragmatist perspective, the terms of these concrete advantages and disadvantages include considering the consequences of proposed

---

[3]In another essay, Rorty (1991h) referred to this distinction as the difference between trying to find a "skyhook" as opposed to a "toehold" while navigating through human activity (p. 9).

courses of action. Categories or principles might be seen as tests against which attractive proposals may be checked to examine their compatibility with our cultural vocabulary. Nonetheless, the pragmatist will not see them as grounds from which alternatives may be derived.

A serious contemporary example of a social, political, and ethical problem merits examination in terms of Rorty's suggestion for a conversationally based, contingent ethic. It illustrates the inadequacy of a priori, universalist principles. One typical universalist ethical principle is based on the a priori notion that immoral behavior will lead to retribution/punishment, such as getting AIDS. The original form of this principle was directed at homosexuals who *got what they deserved* for their sexual behavior. As the epidemic widened to include intravenous drug users, promiscuous heterosexuals, and other riffraff, it could still be blamed on immoral behavior. Hence, homosexuals, promiscuous heterosexuals, and drug abusers should have known that their behavior would eventually lead to ruin. It is a priori *reasonable* to predict such an outcome. The "innocent victims," however—the hemophiliacs, the health care workers, the Kimberly Bergalises—inject the role of pure chance and contingency into the scenario, whereby an a priori moral principle cannot explain the consequences. The sheer contingency of vulnerability to AIDS must rattle the cage of universalist certainty of religious fundamentalists, for instance. Plenty of evidence exists that the moral principles of the Reagan administration effectively blocked progress on AIDS research because the epidemic primarily and secondarily affected disenfranchised social groups. Hence, a universalist ethic of morality, preoccupied with assessing blame, blocked a pragmatic ethic of problem solving.

Ultimately, the issue of relativism should be set aside according to pragmatism (Rorty, 1979).[4] Rorty's (1991c) extensive commentary on Davidson rests on the latter's reinforcement of the notion that relativism is problematic only in terms of the "scheme/content" distinction, and the suggestion that the distinction be dropped (p. 9). Once we give up the notion of "transcultural . . . validity," the threat attached to relativism becomes minimized:

> Relativism seems a threat only to those who insist on quick fixes and knockdown arguments . . . [but even if] one drops the idea that there is a common ground called "the evidence," one is still far from saying that one person's web [of beliefs and desires] is as good as another. (Rorty, 1991g, pp. 66–67)

However, Rorty is not content with simply setting aside notions of scheme/content distinctions and transcultural validity. He also insists on

---

[4]Rorty (1979) denied that philosophers such as Wittgenstein, Heidegger, and Dewey proposed "alternative theories of knowledge or philosophies of mind. They set aside epistemology and metaphysics as possible disciplines" (p. 6).

undermining the basis for positive theory and foundational philosophy altogether. Rorty (1991h) warned that the realist is likely to interpret the pragmatist's position as "one more positive theory about the nature of truth [i.e., that "Truth is relative."] . . . a theory [which] would, of course, be self refuting":

> But the pragmatist does not have a theory of truth, much less a relativistic one. As a partisan of solidarity, his account of the value of cooperative human inquiry *has only an ethical base, not an epistemological or metaphysical one.* Not having *any* epistemology, *a fortiori* he does not have a relativistic one. (p. 24)

The distinction must be emphasized between Rorty's position and that of others who might argue from a relativist position. Rorty simply aims to render relativism meaningless—an irrelevant, nonuseful concept ready to be replaced. Rorty's (1991c) *antirepresentationalist* account should render other hierarchical distinctions irrelevant, such as the "Dilthey-like distinctions between explaining 'hard' phenomena and interpreting 'soft' ones" (p. 1). It should also make irrelevant the distinction between a feminine ethics of caring and connection and an absolutist masculine one of justice and rationality.[5]

THE SELF

Another major theme appearing throughout Rorty's works is central to a discussion of ethics. This is his highly controversial conception of human selfhood. It cuts to the heart of why many philosophers and other intellectuals find his work unpalatable.[6] Rorty presented us with a radical view of human nature comprising much of the first part of *Philosophy and the Mirror of Nature* and developed in several later essays. The title of Part One of *Mirror*, "Our Glassy Essence," reflects its theme: the impossibility of defining what one justifiably can call the universal "essence" of what it means to be human (Rorty, 1979, p. 6).

With respect to the self, Rorty's (1979) project attempted to overcome the temptation to ground human nature in a metaphysical or an onto-theological essence, in some essence that exists outside of individual human beings, in something extrahuman. The dominant question throughout Western history resulting from the metaphysical tradition has been: "Why is man unique?" (p. 41). The search for a metaphysical answer to that question has led to many philosophical problems and dualisms associated with the mind: mind–body, perception–reality, uncertainty–knowledge, particular–universal, and so forth. Rorty characterized philosophy's

---

[5]For instance, see Gilligan (1982) and Noddings (1984).
[6]See, for instance, Guignon and Hiley (1990).

failure in making us "more aware of our own nature" as a "moral failure" (p. 43).

Philosophers' dominant metaphysical answer to the uniqueness question, Rorty (1979) said, has been the definition of *humanness* as the capacity for contemplating universals. What Rorty (1991d) later came to conceptualize holistically with such terms as "non-reductive physicalism" (pp. 113–125), he introduced in *Mirror* (1979) as an attempt to overcome the dualism of mind and brain. "To suggest that there are no universals . . . is to endanger our uniqueness. To suggest that the mind is the brain is to suggest that we secrete theorems and symphonies as our spleen secretes dark humors" (pp. 43–44). In his fable of the Antipodeans, Rorty (1979) illustrated what beings would be like if they had never heard of the distinction between a metaphysical concept of mind and a physiological process called brain. This race of humans describes physical stimuli and emotional responses in terms of neural processes. In other words, if concepts such as the soul, mind, or universals did not exist, humans would have to invent them to provide an ethical foundation for otherwise purely amoral, physiological functions.

In later works, the nature of the self becomes a dominant theme. The two most important works are "Freud and Moral Reflection" (Rorty, 1991b, pp. 143–163) and *Contingency, Irony, and Solidarity* (Rorty, 1989, pp. 23–43). These provide the basis for Rorty's use of selfhood in other essays. We can initially summarize Rorty's reading of Freud as the position that, after Freud, human beings could no longer think of themselves as before. He offers a Baconian view of Freud and contrasts the impact of Freud's work on our concept of mind with the impact of Hume. The result confirms Freud's place among the ranks of revolutionary thinkers such as Copernicus and Darwin (Rorty, 1991b, p. 143).

In Rorty's view, Hume followed the Copernican and Newtonian mechanization of nature with principles for the mechanization of the mind. Such revolutionary processes lead to a kind of decentering: "Mechanization meant that the world in which human beings lived no longer taught them anything about how they should live" (Rorty, 1991b, p. 145). As if this were not traumatic enough, Hume's contribution "suggested that the mechanization of neither nature nor the mind mattered for purposes of finding a self-image" (p. 145). Hume brought the physical into the mental, but he did nothing to overcome the assumptions of metaphysics; the irrelevance of the physical to the moral still presupposes that moral reflection comes from somewhere else.[7]

----

[7]According to Rorty (1991b), this problem was solved by making "protopragmatists of most people. . . . They became accustomed to speaking one sort of language for Baconian purposes of prediction and control and another for purposes of moral reflection" (p. 146).

For Rorty (1991b), Freud's revolutionary contribution is his configuration of the mind as populated "not with analogues of Boylean corpuscles but with *analogues of persons*—internally coherent clusters of belief and desire" (p. 147; italics added). This move is radical because we begin to view the unconscious levels of the self as conversation partners rather than processes that we can safely ignore. "What is novel in Freud's view of the unconscious is his claim that our unconscious selves are not dumb, sullen, lurching brutes, but rather the intellectual peers of our conscious selves, possible conversational partners of those selves" (p. 149). What we previously might have seen as an interesting exercise becomes a "moral obligation" to get to know these partners more fully (p. 145).

We are obligated to discover not our common human essence, however, but rather "what divides us . . . our accidental idiosyncracies[,] . . . [the study of which] will let us enter into conversational relations with our unconscious and . . . let us break down the partitions" (Rorty, 1991b, pp. 148–149). The purpose of such introspection, however, is self-knowledge rather than self-purification, leading us from "an ethics of purity to one of self-enrichment" (p. 158). Rather than purging the brutal, irrational, and destructive unconscious, breaking down the partitions between the conscious and unconscious enlarges the self.

Furthermore, the "centerless web of beliefs and desires" paints an egalitarian rather than hierarchical view of the unconscious, privileging the superego no more than other parts of the psyche.[8] What is problematic is that if the self is centerless, then to what can we attribute ethical conduct? To our beliefs and desires, most of which are coherent and "reasonable," "What keeps one person's beliefs and desires from infringing on those of others?" the absolutist might ask. "Nothing," the pragmatist could answer. "Nothing absolute, nothing a priori, nothing essential, at any rate. Our only 'guarantee' is the propensity for enlarging our web to include others' beliefs and desires."

In Rorty's (1991b) post-Aristotlelian utopia, we not need discover our essence to consider ourselves moral beings (p. 160). Instead our morality depends on the "tissue of contingent relations" (Rorty, 1989, p. 41) between selves and societies. Self-creation and moral development consist of the enrichment of the "vocabulary of moral reflection at our disposal" (Rorty 1991b, p. 155). *Maturity* means developing an openness to "new redescriptions" of our individual histories, resulting in an "ironic" view of the self, rather than settling on a final "identity" (p. 155). Along these lines, in an enigmatic allusion concluding "Freud and Moral Reflection," Rorty implied a new interpretation of the need to lose one's soul to save it. That Biblical paradox can be paraphrased in terms of eschewing the

---

[8]Rorty (1991b) cited Rieff (1966) to support this view.

search for the center in favor of dispersing the self—in enlarging and extending it.

In "Freud," Rorty referred several times to the contingency of our personal histories—those "accidental idiosyncracies" that remain to be uncovered in the process of getting acquainted with our unconscious motivations. Rorty (1991b) agreed with Freud that chance is " 'not unworthy of determining our fate' " (p. 152). He concluded that we then have our specific motivations and emotions because of our past experiences, particularly from childhood and adolescence. One can view this fact of contingency from different perspectives, including determinism, nihilism, or existentialism. However, Rorty's pragmatic sense of the contingency of selfhood is distinct. It is the source of self-enlargement and self-creation. He emphasized how we play the hand dealt rather than the mechanism of chance that determined the cards we have.

In *Contingency, Irony, and Solidarity*, Rorty (1989) focused on the process of playing the hand. He examined the aesthetics of moral development that Freud and, to some extent, Friedrich Nietzsche opened up. These aesthetics of selfhood rest in the process of self-creation rather than in self-discovery. Rorty (1989) relied heavily on Harold Bloom's configuration of the "strong poet" who Bloom described as horrified " 'of finding himself to be only a copy or a replica' " of some earlier poet, as the exemplar of moral consciousness (p. 24).[9] In this essay, the emphasis in "Freud" on idiosyncratic residues within the unconscious is transformed to a stress on the distinctive shape of individual identity.

For Rorty, individuality, and therefore character, does not rest on discovering an essence—either common or distinctive—of humanity. Rather it consists of creating a distinctive and unique identity out of the raw material given to us by our contingent historical moment—a process of "acknowledging and appropriating contingency" rather than transcending it (Rorty, 1989, p. 28). For Rorty, contingency applies to every conceivable aspect of the time and situation in which we find ourselves. This includes our language, our parents, our culture, and even our morality. After Freud, we "see the moral consciousness as historically conditioned, a

---

[9]See *Contingency, Irony and Solidarity* (Rorty, 1989, p. 24). In this footnote, Rorty broadened Bloom's description of the poet to include such figures as important and revolutionary novelists, scientists, and edifying philosophers, "people [who] are also to be thought of as rebelling against 'death'—*that is, against the failure to have created*—more strongly than most of us." In my interpretation of this, Rorty took the description of the strong poet and democratized it, if you will, to include the creative potential in us all. Democratizing creativity is not to be identified with essentializing it, however; it is closer to the realization people are also capable of creating who never produce what are normally thought of as works of art, but who nevertheless live life creatively: "Anything . . . can, as Freud showed us, serve to dramatize and crystallize a human being's sense of self-identity" (Rorty, 1989, p. 37).

product as much of time and chance as . . . political or aesthetic consciousness" (p. 30).

This inevitable contingency presents us with our task, which implicitly
involves a choice. Not all of us can be "strong poets," of course, who domi-
nate a cultural generation or affect future generations. However, an aesthetic moral consciousness means that the line between the strong poet
and other humans has the moral significance that Plato and Christianity
attached to the distinction between the human and the animal. Although
strong poets are, like all other animals, causal products of natural forces,
they can tell the story of their own production in words never used before
(Rorty, 1989, p. 28).[10] Many of us cannot. Nonetheless, all of us—or at
least those who have language and even a small amount of leisure (pp.
35–36)—perhaps can be, to varying degrees, weak poets. Even the weak
poet can measure success in terms of "[escaping] inherited descriptions
. . . [and finding] new descriptions" (p. 29).

In its most radical sense, self-creation literally takes the contingent historical situation in which the human being finds itself and, in acknowledging and appropriating it, changes it:

> The fear in which Bloom's poets begin is the fear that one might end one's
> days in . . . a world one never made, an inherited world. The hope of such a
> poet is that what the past tried to do to her she will succeed in doing to the
> past: to make the past itself, including those very causal processes which
> blindly impressed all her own behavings, bear *her* impress. (Rorty, 1989, p.
> 29).[11]

If this sounds suspiciously like a Nietzschean "will to power," let me
suggest that the process of self-creation Rorty described here consists of
his redescription of Nietzsche's theme. However, it is the will to power
written for a humane liberal society. In an essay commenting on Michel
Foucault, Rorty (1991d) cited Vincent Descombes' distinction between the
"American Foucault" and the "French Foucault." The latter is the "fully
Nietzschean one" (p. 193). This Nietzschean Foucault's "project of autonomy" results in having "no 'worries about sharing our beliefs with our fellow citizens' " and a politics that is more anarchist than liberal (p. 193).

Consequently, and ironically, the most radical models of self-creation
we have—Nietzsche's will to power and Foucault's critique of power—
work best as models for private self-creation. Rorty (1991d) explicitly
warned against modeling culture and social order after them:

---

[10]Rorty acknowledged his debt to Nehamas' (1985) reading of Nietzsche.

[11]This concept bears a certain similarity to Heidegger's *thrownness*. An excellent analysis
appears in Guignon (1983).

We should not try to find a societal counterpart to the desire for autonomy. Trying to do so leads to Hitlerlike and Maolike fantasies about "creating a new kind of human being." Societies are not quasi-persons, they are (at their liberal, social democratic best) compromises between persons[, while making] it as easy as possible for people to achieve their . . . private ends without hurting each other. . . . In a liberal society, our public dealings with our fellow citizens are not *supposed* to be Romantic or inventive; they are supposed to have the routine intelligibility of the marketplace or the courtroom. (p. 186)

This position indeed is problematic for a rhetorical critic. The next section focuses on its significance.

First, we must turn to the topic of language before we can move from Rorty's treatment of the centerless self and its necessary interaction with other beings. Because language is a means of redescription rather than representation, and the *self* is defined as a "web of beliefs and desires," language becomes our means of reweaving the web. One major function of language remains essentially private. It constitutes a means of empowerment to self-creation. From this decidedly Nietzschean view, failure as a poet—the ideal human being—results from accepting "somebody else's description of oneself, . . . to write, at most, elegant variations on previously written poems" (Rorty, 1989, p. 28).

Language also has a clearly public, primary function. It is a tool of social interaction and communication. Even the strong poet needs to connect with others. Rorty (1989) presented Harold Bloom's work as a *needed corrective* to Nietzsche's divinization of the poet. The latter rests on the agreement that even if "languages are not media of representation or expression, they will remain media of communication, . . . ways of tying oneself up with other beings" (p. 41). The irony here consists of the essential conflict between the private project of developing one's own unique "metaphoric" self-description, which cannot avoid being "marginal [,] . . . parasitic," and useless (p. 41). The problem remains whether Rorty's pragmatism allows for the private, self-created, and potentially revolutionary individual to find a public voice.

The ironic self, however, knows that self-creation consists not of finding one's center, but of enlarging and reweaving the web of beliefs and desires that constitutes it. Therefore, in Rorty's terms, the nihilistic, Nietzschean, isolated, and useless aesthete becomes the contingent ironist. This ironist knows that language is contingent and constantly open to question (Rorty, 1989, pp. 3–22). The idea of contingency does not worry the ironist, but the fact of it causes her or him to worry "about the possibility that she has been initiated into the wrong tribe" (p. 75). Ironist self-creation may overcome self-deception.

PRIVATE SELF-CREATION AND PUBLIC DISCOURSE

In "Freud" and "The Contingency," Rorty's overt purpose is limited to an account of character. This particular account is problematic due to the Freudian (and, to some extent, the Davidsonian) redescription of the self as centerless, a "web of beliefs and desires," and because of the separation of the private from the public. In contrast to the goal of defining character in terms of finding one's center, the post-Freudian task becomes enlarging one's web—increasing the amount of territory one's imagination can traverse. Although Rorty (1989) maintained that he gave up "Plato's attempt to bring together the public and the private," enlarging one's web necessarily entails an encounter between something private and something public (i.e., outside of one's own web of beliefs and desires) during self-creation (p. 33). According to Rorty (1989), Freud's description of the self is consistent with the pragmatist's claim that there is "no bridge . . . provided by *universally* shared beliefs and desires" (p. 34; italics added). A harmonious, unproblematic encounter may occur between the "private ethic of self-creation and the public ethic of mutual accommodation" (p. 34). However, one may overpower the other, or the encounter may cause a clash of beliefs and desires that enlarges the scope of one's centerless self (p. 34).

Another possible consequence of such an encounter is revolutionary. A unique vision may emerge connects with a public cause, affecting it and transforming it into a social, scientific, cultural, political, or religious movement. In such cases,

> some private obsession produces a metaphor which we *can* find a use for, [and] we speak of genius rather than of eccentricity or perversity. The difference between genius and fantasy . . . is the difference between idiosyncracies which just happen to catch on with other people. . . . [Poetic], artistic, philosophical, scientific, or political progress results from the accidental coincidence of a private obsession with a public need. (Rorty, 1989, p. 37)

Thus, although Rorty does not explicitly develop the idea of communication as an interface between the private and the public, the implication clearly exists.

Furthermore, although the previous passage is couched in such positive terms as *genius* and *progress*, clearly it contains no hints of guarantees that a positive union will always occur between private obsession and public need. The pragmatist can offer no such guarantees. Persons who desire them are quite likely to be those who challenge the antifoundationalist philosopher to "answer Hitler."[12] The foundationalist cannot answer Hitler either. Knowledge claims are equally available to both the *bad guys* and the *good guys*. From a pragmatic perspective, the only guarantees we have against the bad guys' claims to truth—their messages—are other messages (Rorty, 1990, pp. 639–640).[13] Rorty called these other messages *redescriptions*. They are designed not to answer or refute the Nazi's claims, but to convert. An important passage deserves extensive quotation:

> If I were assigned the task not of refuting or answering but of *converting* a Nazi, . . . I would have some idea of how to set to work. I could show him how nice things can be in free societies, how horrible things are in the Nazi camps, how his Furher can plausibly be redescribed as an ignorant paranoid rather than as an inspired prophet, how the Treaty of Versailles can be redescribed as a reasonable compromise rather than as a vendetta, and so on. These tactics might or might not work, but at least they would not be an intellectual exercise in what [Karl Otto] Apel calls *Letzbegrundung*. They would be the sort of thing that sometimes actually changes people's minds. (Rorty, 1990, p. 637)

Exchanges in scholarly journals between Rorty and such critics as Thomas McCarthy and Richard Bernstein sharply define the issues surrounding Rorty's embrace of liberal democracy and his insistence on maintaining a distance between private and public selves. As we see, some of these criticisms are well taken, but others beg the question. I hope that looking at these disputes from the point of view of communication ethics will enable me to add my own assessments of Rorty's shortcomings and attempt to make Rorty safe for radicalized philosophers.[14]

To begin to examine Rorty's distinction between private self-creation and public discourse from a communication ethics perspective, I borrow from Arnett's review of the status of such scholarship and suggest that

---

[12]In a rather extensive passage here, Rorty (1990) maintained the impossibility of "answering" Hitler: "I have always . . . been puzzled about what was supposed to count as a knockdown answer to Hitler. Would it answer him to tell him that there was a God in Heaven who was on our side? How do we reply to him when he asks for evidence for this claim?" (p. 636).

[13]Similar themes are addressed in a recent column in the *New Yorker* about the Gennifer Flowers–Bill Clinton story: "Ironic detachment is the natural and not entirely unhealthy consequence of living in a media culture. When there are a thousand competing messages, it's not a bad idea to maintain a certain knowingness, a certain self-consciousness, about the process by which messages are put forward. But the danger of ironic detachment is that it easily becomes cynicism or, worse, uncritical passivity, in which we watch for the sake of watching, waiting for the next scene of a drama whose plot we already know" ("The Talk," 1992, p. 26).

[14]The commentary in the present essay is necessarily limited to the exchange with McCarthy.

three questions be of central concern.[15] What *can* be said? What *should* be said? What *must* be said?

Rorty's critics, especially McCarthy (1990a, 1990b), focus on three issues in their responses to his atheoretical liberalism. First is the inadequacy of critique without a theory, including the failure of pragmatism to give sufficient attention to the ills of capitalism in deference to his ideal of liberal democracy. Second is the alienation between private self-creation and public discourse. Third, given the weaknesses in pragmatism's position on the first two, is the resulting impotence of the intellectual at large and the philosopher in particular. Throughout the exchange, McCarthy claimed that Rorty's atheoretical pragmatism does not provide enough support for the kind of cultural critique demanded by critical theory. Rorty (1990) maintained that "we already have as much theory as we need" (p. 642). McCarthy wants to tie the concepts of *theory* and *critique* together, and Rorty separates them. His claim that we need "no fancier theoretical notions than 'greed,' 'selfishness,' and 'racial prejudice' " to explain American social inequities (p. 642) results from their separation.

This dispute clearly revolves around the question of what can be said within a particular framework or context of inquiry. Furthermore, McCarthy's position assumed that Rorty's distinction between private and public is manifest in alienation between the two realms. McCarthy's (1990a) emphasis on liberal ironism and self-creation as alienating and therefore powerless to effect change rested on two main points. First is Rorty's "failure to take seriously the fact that processes of individuation are interwoven with processes of socialization, . . . so that becoming who we are points in the opposite direction from improving our relations with others" (McCarthy, 1990a, p. 650). With these thoughts, we are moving from the process of asking what can be said to asking what should be said given our need to relate to others.[16]

Second, McCarthy's (1990a) claims that the "alienating thrust of ironist intellectual life *requires* that it be kept private" (p. 652; italics added). This more problematic argument suggests that the question is whether the lib-

---

[15]Arnett (1990) asserted that "[c]ommunication ethics assists us in combating the demagoguery of simply asking, 'Can it be done?' without the accompanying ethical question, 'Should it be done?' " I paraphrase Arnett's point and suggest that we ask a third question: "What *must* be done/said?" (p. 215).

[16]Consider the following passage in this context: "The strong poet's fear of death as the fear of incompletion is a function of the fact that no project of redescribing the world and the past, no project of self-creation through imposition of one's own idiosyncratic metaphoric, can avoid being marginal and parasitic. Metaphors are unfamiliar uses of old words, [but] . . . a language which was 'all metaphor' would be a language which had no use, hence not a language but just babble. *For even if we agree that languages are not media of representation or expression, they will remain media of communication, tools for social interaction, ways of tying oneself up with other human beings*" (Rorty, 1989, p. 41; italics added).

eral ironist vocabulary can engender critique because of its ironic alienation. On this point, Rorty appeared inconsistent.[17] Contrary examples exist to many of the claims McCarthy supported by quoting Rorty on the isolation and alienation of the self-created ironist, however. For instance, McCarthy maintained that public discourse must edify in the sense of calling forth the common tones of the prevailing civic virtues.[18] Yet Rorty consistently described philosophers such as Martin Heidegger, Nietzsche, and Jacques Derrida as edifiers. McCarthy claimed they did such a job on philosophy that even Rorty cannot answer them.

Second, if Rorty is a liberal ironist, then his own work contradicts McCarthy's question of whether the ironist can, should, or must publish.[19] In addition, if the ironist intellectual lacks power and is disenfranchised in liberal society—as Rorty claimed—then how does that shortcoming prevent us from asking why? If we do ask that question, we can immediately turn to Rorty's (1989) other claim that a liberal society is most likely to give the ironist a voice (p. 89). Fourth, McCarthy's focus on *Contingency, Irony, and Solidarity* (Rorty, 1989) neglected the power described in "Freud" of the private obsession that manages to meet a public need. Finally, perhaps more attention should be paid to the virtue of reading Rorty (as Barnett Pearce has suggested) on his own terms—that is, *ironically.*

I conclude from this ambiguity and confusion that the central question is not whether the liberal ironist vocabulary is useless for critiquing liberal culture because it lacks a theory, as McCarthy insisted. The question may not even be whether it is useless because it results from an inherently private process of self-creation. Perhaps the central question is how the liberal ironist vocabulary, which humiliates by pointing to the need to question final vocabularies in place, can survive the interface between the private and the public (Rorty, 1989, p. 90). On this point, Rorty appeared to waffle. As Pearce (1991) noted, however, "One must always be on guard when recounting what a self-proclaimed ironist has said. A prosaic reading clearly misses the spirit of [*Contingency, Irony, and Solidarity*], as does any attempt to summarize the 'propositions' it affirms" (p. 73).

---

[17]Compare, for instance, Rorty's relative optimism about the potential for private self-creation to exert public influence in "Freud and Moral Reflection," with the relative skepticism of "Private Irony and Liberal Hope," in *Contingeny, Irony, and Solidarity.*

[18]Further confusion results from Rorty's (1990) quotation of McCarthy's charge that pragmatism cannot support the goals of liberal society because it lacks claims of "transcultural validity," and thus is "unable to 'appeal to peer agreement, established norms, or anything of the sort' " (p. 637) Here McCarthy's argument seems to be far more vulnerable than Rorty's with respect to impotence for critique because McCarthy links critique to the ability to appeal to such *status quo* phenomena as "peer agreement" and "established norms" (Rorty, 1990, p. 361).

[19]McCarthy even seems to contradict his own accolades to Rorty in his original essay of this exchange, which placed him within the ranks of great public intellectuals of our century.

McCarthy (1990a) argued that, given the conversational rather than the epistemological context of inquiry, what one can or cannot say in any context reinforces the alienation between the private and the public. In other words, with merely conversational constraints, our cultural (i.e., political) context limits, even severely handicaps, what we can and should say. A Rortian might respond that sometimes it does; perhaps we have been initiated into the wrong tribe. However, sometimes our private obsessions can meet a public need to the point that they *catch on* as social and political movements. Real activists, however, often engage in powerful forms of redescription that fulfill the criteria of social and cultural critique. The example I discuss causes us to question who "we" are, thereby challenging us to enlarge our individual and collective identities in a radical way. It comes from a report of Jesse Jackson's 1988 presidential campaign:

> Eight years of Reagan and Bush, more millionaires on top but millions more in poverty, thirty-five million Americans with no health insurance. Something about that's not right. More working women in poverty, more children in poverty, expansion of hunger—something not *right* about that! Makes no difference whether you black, brown, or white, when your child's hungry, it hurts the same. When there's no heat in the house, we all cold. When they close down your factory or foreclose on your farm, and comes the time they pull the plug and the lights go out, we all—we *all*—look amazingly *similar* sitting there in the dark. Yet you hear folks who don't have dental care or health care, can't buy enough groceries or pay their 'lectric bill, hear 'em talking 'bout they somehow got something in common with Reagan and Bush. Say 'Me and Bush, we both for the flag, against crime, believe in prayer. Both us is *con-ser-va-tive*.' Naw. Naw—one of y'all is rich, and one of y'all is *po*'. (Frady, 1992, p. 51)

Among other things, Jackson illustrates the power of a private obsession with injustice to redescribe the injustice and remind us that this is not "us." Jackson seems to question McCarthy's (1990a) disquieting view that, according to Rorty, "what is objectionable about the hopelessness and misery of so many Americans, for example, is that they are 'fellow *Americans*,' and 'it is outrageous that an *American* should live without hope' " (p. 650; citing Rorty, 1989, p. 191). McCarthy apparently interpreted this point as viciously ethnocentric, whereas Jackson uses solidarity (Rorty, 1991h, pp. 21–34) to attack economic injustice.[20] The result is an attempt to make Americans see how this situation creates an incoherent collective social identity and diminishes the opportunity for self-creation for some citizens. It also encourages us to ask whether we might have been initiated into the wrong tribe.

---

[20]Rorty (1991f, pp. 203–210). By *vicious* ethnocentrists, Rorty seemed to mean "people who attempt to diminish [the] capacity" for tolerance of diversity.

Furthermore, Jackson's discourse illustrates the ability for metaphysical public discourse of flags, crime, and spiritual values to mask the pragmatic, economic needs of citizens (Rorty, 1989, p. 88). In 1988, the strategy clearly diverted attention from "what we need now . . .": "concrete utopias, and concrete proposals about how to get to those utopias from where we are now" (Rorty, 1990, p. 642). Ironically, Jackson implies the seductiveness of the metaphysical even for those most disadvantaged.[21]

Other examples also question the necessity for theoretically based critique. Consider the following passage from *Time*:

> In the late '80s, while American academics were emptily theorizing that language and the thinking subject were dead, the longing for freedom and humanistic culture was demolishing European tyranny. Of course, if the Chinese students had read their Foucault, they would have known that repression is inscribed in all language, their own included, and so they could have saved themselves the trouble of facing the tanks in Tiananmen Square. But did Vaclav Havel and his fellow playwrights free Czechoslovakia by quoting Derrida or Lyotard on the inscrutability of texts? Assuredly not: they did it by placing their faith in the transforming power of thought—by putting their shoulders to the immense wheel of the word. (Hughes, 1992, p. 46)[22]

Such descriptions illustrate the poverty of theory as a foundational, predictive, controlling force for critique.[23] I think we should emphasize and examine the absolutely clear and correct conclusion that we do not need theory for this. We can merely use words such as *greed, outrage, prejudice,* or *injustice* to discuss circumstances in our society that do not cohere with our self-image. Jesse Jackson does not need one; Vaclav Havel does not need one. Instead we need creative moral imagination to say what must be said.

---

[21]See Hughes (1992, p. 46). In this *Time* magazine cover story, Hughes suggested two meanings for the PC label: *politically correct* and *patriotically correct.*

[22]Hughes (p. 46). Similar sentiments are implicit in the report by Tom Mathews in *Newsweek* (December 30, 1991), which provides in engrossing narrative detail worldwide transforming events of the past decade. The report opens with the statement that "Democracy is in the details" (p. 32) and went on to claim that "individuals, not inexorable forces, shaped the Decade of Democracy" (p. 34). Mathews' description belies McCarthy's critical theorist's impatience with Rorty's approach to "*creating* human solidarity . . . detailed description by detailed description" (McCarthy, 1990a, p. 650).

[23]Here it is important to point out an area for further development; that is, to examine the claim that the reactive nature of pragmatism is one source of its weakness (Rorty, 1990, p. 184). There is some evidence presented in this essay that the usefulness of all social theory and theorizing is reactive despite any metaphysical claims to inexorableness of its tenets. Thus, once the useful parts of any theory have been ferreted out, they can explain events. However, there is no need for grand theory to attack real problems.

Other scholars also challenge McCarthy's position that liberalism cannot accommodate cultural, social, and political critique. In "The Theoretical Foundations of Liberalism," Waldron (1987) framed his discussion with the potential conflict between individual freedoms and social order. Although he couched his argument in a traditional rationalist, humanist vocabulary, Waldron's conclusions demonstrate considerable sympathy with Rorty's emphasis on the primacy of freedom and pull of solidarity. Waldron pointed out, for instance, the likelihood for the socialist, more than the conservative, to share the traditional liberal respect for rationalism and humanism: "Of course, [the socialist] will say, a good society is one that is penetrable and manipulable by the reason of free individuals acting in concert. But they share none of the liberals' optimism about *legitimating* existing societies in this way" (p. 149; italics added). In contrast to both the conservative and the socialist biases, Waldron concluded,

> [liberals] alone remain committed—ambiguously, uncertainly and precariously—to the prospect and possibility of freedom in the present, that is, individual freedom for people like us in the social world for which we are familiar. Neither burdened by a mystifying heritage of tradition nor bought off by the promise that freedom will come for all at its historically appointed time, the liberal individual confronts his social order *now*, demanding respect for the existing capacities of his autonomy, his reason and his agency. (p. 150)

A more inclusive examination does not confirm McCarthy's criticism of Rorty in terms of the impotence of the intellectual, that the ironist cannot "go public." Rorty's (1990) preoccupation with the modern novel as the preeminent source of critique is somewhat problematic on this score. Perhaps more emphasis on public rhetorical and political discourse from a global as well as a cultural perspective might alleviate the separation of private from public. It might also sharpen the focus on Rorty's ambivalent critical stance. For instance, Rorty's claim about the importance of ironist thinking vis-à-vis the higher degree of success of metaphysical structures of public discourse needs more examination. Jesse Jackson cannot win the presidency despite the power of his ability to question our national self-image. Jimmy Carter's appraisal of a national malaise cannot withstand the image of "morning in America." I am unconvinced that McCarthy's (1990a) view of "how Rorty's beloved liberal public sphere became the public-relations and public-entertainment monstrosity it is" (p. 653) totally explains such failures.

Although committed to the vocabulary of contemporary Marxist critique of ideology, McKerrow (1991) placed rhetoric (in its form as "critical rhetoric") within the maelstrom of the existing social order, "engaged" with it, but clearly engaged as a " 'transformative practice rather than as a method' of inquiry" (pp. 249–255). As such, rhetorical criticism is also transformed into cultural critique.[24] McKerrow (1991) also expanded the distinction between criticism and critique:

> The telos of criticism thus lies in the perpetuation of the ideals of "rational democracy," and the measurement of "reality" as it falls short of these ideals. The telos of critique has two potential objects. In terms of a critique of domination . . . the telos is that of emancipation. In terms of a critique of freedom, the telos is that of a never-ending self-reflexivity that does not privilege one form of "rationality" apart from others. . . . Criticism operates from an acceptance of the tenets of rational democracy, while critique offers the possibility of challenging those tenets. (p. 250)

First, McKerrow's analysis clearly placed the operation of critical rhetoric within the critical object (the political or cultural hegemony in place). In addition, to put the analysis in more Rortian terms, it presents the capability of the self-created individual to assert his or her vocabulary as a possible voice in the conversation of mankind. Consequently, social practice is continually open to challenge as being only one of many possible practices, for which no rationalist a priori standards exist to measure the challenges against.

But there are *ethical* criteria, and those criteria are based on solidarity:

> The best argument we partisans of solidarity have against the realistic partisans of objectivity is Nietzsche's argument that the traditional Western . . . way of firming up our habits simply isn't working anymore. . . . It has become as transparent a device as the postulation of dieties who turn out, by a happy coincidence, to have chosen *us* as their people. So the pragmatist suggestion that we substitute a 'merely' ethical foundation for our sense of community . . . is put forward on practical grounds. It is *not* put forward as a corollary of . . . an epistemological claim that we lack a faculty of moral sense. (Rorty, 1991h, p. 33)

As Rorty (1991a) concluded, pragmatism and critical theory share "our noncriterial conception of rationality." This leads both positions to decline defining irrationalism, "since for us 'rational' merely means 'persuasive,' 'irrational' can only mean 'invoking force' " (p. 220).

CONCLUSION

The significance of Rorty's pragmatic ethics for communication studies affects several areas and issues. It concerns communication/rhetoric at both

---

[24]McKerrow (1991) cited Benhabib's (1986) distinction, which rests on the rationalist, Platonic standards of universality and rationality to which criticism is inured, whereas "critique refuses to stand outside its object . . ." (p. 33).

the interpersonal and public levels in various contexts. Works such as those by Arnett (1990) and Johannesen (1990) illustrated these themes and contexts. In conclusion, I point out some preliminary distinctions and similarities between Rorty's pragmatism and the work of communication scholars. I indicate areas of further research and development for the topics discussed here.

Clearly Rorty's redescription of the self as a "centerless web of beliefs and desires" affects our understanding of both interpersonal interaction and the nature of character emphasized earlier. Analogous criticisms have appeared in the communication literature to those in the philosophy concerning this definition of selfhood. Rorty's centerless self reinforces the Hart et al. (1980) repertoire of selves outlined in work in rhetorical sensitivity. Guignon and Hiley (1990) and Fulkerson (1990) demonstrated that others find this problematic, however. They made strikingly similar arguments that Rorty's and the Hart et al. view of selfhood do not provide enough substance to enable a truly moral individual to make moral choices. Such critics maintain that the justification for moral choices still must come from somewhere outside the self.

Also needed is further examination of some of the similarities and differences between Rorty's pragmatic ethics and Deetz's (1990) discussion of interpersonal ethics. The latter is based on Hans-Georg Gadamer's ontology of understanding. I can only mention a few points for development here. Rorty and Deetz shared some sourcing of Gadamer's work. In *Philosophy and the Mirror of Nature*, Rorty (1979) built the entire concept of edifying philosophy on Gadamer's idea of education as self-formation. Deetz's work questions the efficacy of an ethics of human rights when one's interactants do not share such assumptions (p. 227). His effort to redefine effectiveness in terms of productiveness somewhat resembles a pragmatic point of view, as does the criterion of conversational blockage for evaluating discourse (pp. 230–233).

Finally, and similarly, examination of the interplay of messages—mentioned earlier as the only guarantees we have against deceptive and demagogic expression—are important to this line of development. Examining the issues of freedom of expression, deception, self-deception, and the possibility of critique may yield a significant integration of the philosophy of communication ethics based on the principles of pragmatism.

ACKNOWLEDGMENT

The author wishes to thank Raymie McKerrow of Ohio University for his comments and Lisa Clark of Salisbury State University for technical assistance on this manuscript.

REFERENCES

Arnett, R. C. (1990). The practical philosophy of communication ethics and free speech as the foundation for speech communication. *Communication Quarterly, 38*, 215.

Benhabib, S. (1986). *Norm, critique, and utopia: A study of the foundations of critical theory*. New York: Columbia University Press.

Condit, C. M. (1987). Crafting virtue: The rhetorical construction of public morality. *Quarterly Journal of Speech*, 79–97.

Deetz, S. (1990). Reclaiming the subject matter as a guide to mutual understanding: Effectiveness and ethics in interpersonal interaction. *Communication Quarterly, 38*, 226–243.

Frady, M. (1992, February 3). Outsider: I. The gift. *New Yorker*, p. 51.

Fulkerson, G. (1990). The ethics of interpersonal influence: A critique of the rhetorical sensitivity construct. *Journal of Communication and Religion, 13*, 1–14.

Gilligan, C. (1982). *In a different voice*. Cambridge, MA: Harvard University Press.

Guignon, C. B. (1983). *Heidegger and the problems of knowledge*. Indianapolis: Hackett.

Guignon, C. B., & Hiley, D. R. (1990). Biting the bullet: Rorty on private and public morality. In A. Malachowski (Ed.), *Reading Rorty* (pp. 339–364). Cambridge, MA: Basil Blackwell.

Hart, R. P., Carlson, R. E., & Eadie, W. F. (1980). Attitudes toward communication and sensitivity. *Communication Monographs*, 1–22.

Hughes, R. (1992, February 3). The fraying of America. *Time*, p. 46.

Johannesen, R. L. (1990). *Ethics in human communication*. Prospect Heights, IL: Waveland.

Mathews, T. (1991, December 30). Decade of democracy. *Newsweek*, pp. 32–42.

McCarthy, T. (1990a). Ironist theory as a vocation: A response to Rorty's reply. *Critical Inquiry, 16*, 644–655.

McCarthy, T. (1990b). Private irony and public decency: Richard Rorty's new pragmatism. *Critical Inquiry, 16*, 355–370.

McDermott, J. J. (1989). The pragmatists. In G. F. McLean (Ed.), *Reading philosophy for the XXIst century* (p. 245). Lanham, MD: University Press of America.

McKerrow, R. E. (1991). Critical rhetoric and propaganda studies. *Communication Yearbook, 14*, 249–255.

Nehamas, A. (1985). *Nietzsche: Life as literature*. Cambridge, MA: Harvard University Press.

Noddings, N. (1984). *Caring: A feminine approach to ethics and moral education*. Berkeley, CA: University of California Press.

Pearce, W. B. (1991). Review of *Contingency, Irony, and Solidarity. Communication Theory, 1*, 70–73.

Rieff, P. (1966). *The triumph of the therapeutic*. New York: Harper & Row.

Rorty, R. (1979). *Philosophy and the mirror of nature*. Princeton, NJ: Princeton University Press.

Rorty, R. (1982). Pragmatism, relativism, and irrationalism. In R. Rorty (Ed.), *Consequences of pragmatism* (p. 166). Minneapolis, MN: University of Minnesota Press.

Rorty, R. (1987). Thugs and theorists: A reply to Bernstein. *Political Theory, 15*, 564–580.

Rorty, R. (1989). *Contingency, irony, and solidarity*. New York: Cambridge University Press.

Rorty, R. (1990). Truth and freedom: A reply to Thomas McCarthy. *Critical Inquiry*, 639.

Rorty, R. (1991a). Cosmopolitanism without emancipation: A response to Jmean-Francois Lyotard. In *Objectivity, relativism, and truth* (Vol. 1, philosophical papers, pp. 21–34). New York: Cambridge University Press.

Rorty, R. (1991b). Freud and moral reflection. In *Essays on Heidegger and others* (Vol. 2, philosophical papers, pp. 143–163). New York: Cambridge University Press.

Rorty, R. (1991c). Introduction: Antirepresentationalism, ethnocentrism, and liberalism. In *Objectivity, relativism, and truth* (Vol. 1, philosophical papers, pp. 1–17). New York: Cambridge University Press.

Rorty, R. (1991d). Moral identity and private identity: The case of Foucault. In *Essays on Heidegger and others* (Vol. 2, philosophical papers, pp. 193–198). New York: Cambridge University Press.

Rorty, R. (1991e). Non-reductive physicalism. In *Objectivity, relativism, and truth* (Vol. 1, philosophical papers, pp. 211–222). New York: Cambridge University Press.

Rorty, R. (1991f). On ethnocentrism: A reply to Clifford Geetz. In *Objectivity, relativism, and truth* (Vol. 1, Philosophical Papers, pp. 203–210). New York: Cambridge University Press.

Rorty, R. (1991g). Pragmatism without method. In *Objectivity, relativism, and truth* (Vol. 1, Philosophical Papers, pp. 211–222). New York: Cambridge University Press.

Rorty, R. (1991h). Solidarity or objectivity? In *Objectivity, relativism, and truth* (Vol. 1, Philosophical Papers, pp. 21–34). New York: Cambridge University Press.

Rowland, R., & Womack, D. (1985). Aristotle's view of an ethical rhetoric. *Rhetoric Society Quarterly, 15,* 13–32.

The talk of the town. (1992, February 10, 1992). *The New Yorker,* p. 26.

Waldron, J. (1987). The theoretical foundations of liberalism. *Philosophical Quarterly, 37,* 128–150.

Chapter 8

Pragmatism and Mediated Communication

Timothy Meyer
University of Wisconsin–Green Bay

Pragmatism, as it applies to mediated communication, is best represented through a variety of perspectives (e.g., Rorty, 1982; Roth, 1993). One is symbolic interactionism. According to it, "the self and the social environment mutually define and shape each other through symbolic communication" (Lindlof, 1995, p. 40). Meaning for the individual in his or her environment comes from practical consequences (Blumer, 1969; Rock, 1979). Meaning is negotiated. When differences in meaning become apparent in certain situations, understanding is only achieved by recognizing that these result from different past experiences of the individuals involved. In turn, diverse experiences create varied expectations. Understanding expectations and anticipated consequences requires negotiation by participants.

Meanings are also dynamic. As events occur for individuals, meanings change as a result of interactions. When participants discern nonexistent or small differences, the change is akin to reinforcement of previous meanings. When they find more substantial differences, meanings can be altered in fundamental ways. As Shalin (1986) pointed out:

> Knowing does not exist for its own sake, but for the sake of doing. Whatever doubts the knower has about the nature of things, he alleviates practically, by manipulating his objects, putting them to different uses, literally forcing these objects to conform to this notion of them, and in the process of doing so establishing—in situ—whether a thing in question is what it is thought to be. (p. 11)

Anderson and Meyer (1988) described the pragmatics of communication in terms of performances:

> As a performance, sense making occurs in time and place as a scene unfolds in reference to the other and as a consequence of a particular actor. Each sense-making performance, then, has it own ends in the empowerment of the sense maker (interpretations make sense in—are appropriate to—the action-realm of the interpreter). Empowerment describes the method by which the premises of action are created and maintained. It is the method by which the pragmatics of communication are accomplished. These premises are the manner by which one understands the world or any part of it, and contain the alternatives of what can and cannot be done. (p. 28)

Anderson and Meyer maintained that interpretation results in meaning. Interpretation is governed by the individual interacting with the environment in a particular place at a particular time with particular participants. As a result, meanings are emergent, sometimes as the product of continuous negotiation. Meanings are also often prolific in that human beings will adjust and readjust meanings in different contexts or when called on or forced to create or move to a different level. Finally, meanings are *promiscuous*. This characteristic refers to the fact that meanings "are accomplished from a given perspective" (Anderson & Meyer, 1988, p. 32). Of course human beings can and do view things from various perspectives. When the perspective changes, so do the meanings that are attached and evoked.

The perspective developed by Anderson and Meyer is called *accommodation theory*. It posits that meaning is co-constructed by the self and others interacting in a particular environment—a social action perspective. Mediated content contributes directly or indirectly to individuals' environments and plays a role in negotiated, emergent meanings. Mediated content also enhances the range of meanings generated (prolificacy) and the interpretations of that content (promiscuity).

In this social action perspective, mediated content does not have meaning independent of an individual who uses some of the content elements to interpret and define his or her reality (see also Jensen, 1991). Content is produced and disseminated with the intention of audience attendance and receptivity. Negotiation of content meanings can occur for the individual acting alone or as a consequence of interactions with others where some content elements are part of this negotiation. In a simple example (at least on the surface), a movie character who shoots another character does not necessarily represent an incident of film violence. The context in which the shooting takes place and the context of reception for the viewer will interact with a given individual viewer and what he or she brings to the viewing situation. The shooting takes place as a mediated representation of a social context and event, and viewers in their respective social contexts perceive the content. Therefore, mediated content is used as raw material, parts of which the individual viewer accommodates, in much the same manner that other sources of meaning are accommodated by that same individual in the interpretation process. The text of media content is created jointly by the individual interpreting some of the elements of that content and with subsequent interactions with others in the social environment.

Both perspectives—symbolic interactionism and accommodation theory/social action—view human understanding and interactions with a high degree of similarity. Both are pragmatic in the sense that meanings are negotiated as a result of concrete situations, and that meanings are neither static nor universally held. Instead, negotiation is ongoing and the outcome of the specific individuals and contexts involved. In the section that follows, these common characteristics of the pragmatic perspectives are used to analyze some contemporary examples of different types of mediated communication. Some suggestions for a future research agenda with a pragmatic perspective at the core follow.

MAKING SENSE OF NEW FORMS OF MEDIATED COMMUNICATION INTERACTIONS

Interactive media have ushered in a new era that has brought and continues to bring about widespread changes in the patterns of daily human activity at home, at work, at play, and in between. In one sense, individuals no longer act as members of an audience when they shop electronically on a web site, any more than when they look through racks of clothing at a department store. Although marketers may classify these consumers as clothes shoppers, the label *audience* does not seem appropriate. An individual interacting with a video screen while processing information (whether to engage in commerce, learn new things, or simply enjoy what is found) is now acting in unique ways. One important question arises: In such individualized contexts, what meanings result or are assigned by individuals to what they are experiencing? Some overall perspective is helpful here.

Kammen (1999), a noted historian with an interest in popular culture, drew some meaningful distinctions between the terms *mass culture* and *popular culture*. Kammen argued that popular culture is characterized by an active audience that jointly participates in activities that are part of the culture, whereas in mass culture, activities are done mostly in private where others are unaware of those activities. The activities of audiences viewing television programs, for example, are indicators of popular culture. When an individual is watching "ER," an individual level of enjoyment operates simultaneously with an awareness that other people are also watching the same program on the same evening. Discussions with other family members, coworkers the next day, or casual conversations struck up with strangers might touch on that particular episode of "ER." When these types of activities take place, the meanings of the program's content are altered in some ways as these meanings are negotiated in conversation. Even superficial comments become part of the ongoing meaning negotiation.

In another sense, the viewing experience just described offers individual opportunities to evoke meanings that resulted from viewing in other ways. From the pragmatic perspective of social action, it is when the viewing experience is manifested as part of a future encounter that the meanings derived from that experience are evoked, presented, altered, and re-accommodated into the storehouse of past experience. Thus, it is the individual viewing experience that shapes meaning, as well as the act of viewing as a member of an audience that is shared with others who have seen the program. Even for those who did not watch the latest episode but have some familiarity with the program, social exchanges about that episode will affect held meanings.

Traditional audience uses of various forms of mediated communication seem to fall into Kammen's category of popular culture. Watching popular television programs (with ever-shrinking audiences), listening to a popular morning radio show or a nationally syndicated call-in radio program, reading the same morning newspaper as others you associate with, and so on are all examples of where popular culture persists.

Many other mediated communication activities, however, are being carried out, mostly in private, without any awareness that other people may be doing exactly the same thing. Although I may be alerted to how many *hits* have occurred on a web site I am using, when I use that site, I do not intend to participate as a member of the audience that shares a common interest in what that particular web site has to offer. My activities are particular to me and occur without regard to whether others have acted similarly. This type of activity would be labeled *mass culture* in Kammen's nomenclature. Some interesting examples apparently unique to the Internet help illustrate this point.

Land's End, a clothing business (that now sells much more than clothing) doing mostly mail-order business, was a pioneer in providing customers with an interactive shopping experience that overcomes many of the previously existing limitations problematic to selling clothing by catalog, mail order, or phone orders. The web site for Land's End allows a customer to enter in his or her sizes and then select various colors and patterns to see how various items either match or clash with one another. One also can see how the same item of clothing, which might look quite attractive in a much smaller size, actually looks quite awful in the large or extra-large sizes. For a customer who envisions him or herself as similar to the thin, attractive models wearing the clothing in the catalog, the reality of how items will look on someone with his or her body size can be quite revealing. The obvious business advantage is that it may stop the customer from ordering items that will almost surely be returned because they will look terrible when tried on. In addition, the customer saves some time and money in the process, which increases the odds that what the purchaser selects will closely resemble the image presented on the web site when the customer actually tries on the clothing.

This unique shopping experience presents other opportunities for the acquisition of meanings by the individual. The realization of one's actual body shape may have some important consequences. It may cause an out-of-shape individual to become depressed and not care about clothing. Another person similarly out of shape might have learned a valuable lesson in buying clothes that fit that person, rather than someone who has a body that the customer would like to have. Still another person may respond to this experience with some lifestyle changes—eating a healthier diet and exercising regularly. In this way, the Internet experience of shopping for clothes at Land's End or a similar site provides many opportunities for acquiring or modifying meanings in many different domains—self-image, healthy lifestyle, consumer behaviors, and so on.

Another unique Internet experience has occurred through the Internet web site for Victoria's Secret. It should surely come as no surprise to anyone that the overwhelming majority of the company's business comes from women. Getting men to purchase female lingerie and other intimate items has presented a huge obstacle for Victoria's Secret and its competitors. Until just recently.

Although many men have intimate knowledge of the Victoria's Secret catalog (after hours of intensive study), few have actually placed an order from it by mail. Even fewer males have actually set foot in a Victoria's Secret retail outlet or placed a phone order, facing the embarrassing prospect of having to give and request information from a female sales representative about intimate female apparel. From the retailer's point of view, selling lingerie as gifts for men to give to women is an appealing prospect. After all, men buy jewelry or perfume for women. Why not lingerie? Along comes the Internet as a solution to male embarrassment.

A customer can easily find the Victoria's Secret web site, scan the available items, and obtain advice on sizes, styles, colors, and so on without ever having to interact with a real-life female sales rep. The credit card transaction is easily made, and the item(s) are wrapped and shipped complete with enclosed gift card bearing the message of choice. All of this occurs with a few clicks of the mouse and some scrolling up and down of electronic pages (along with some selective downloading of images from the web site). Moreover, the company offers paid postage for items that need to be returned, eliminating some of the problems that arise when items are the wrong size (almost always too small). The web site offers a way through which male consumers can access a heretofore nearly exclusive female domain.

This type of transaction offers both commercial and individual advantages and consequences. Victoria's Secret gets an expanded market and increased revenue or profits. For male consumers, the consumption experience can produce changes in how these men think about what it means to purchase intimate items for a woman—the kind of purchase they might never have made without the web site. Males might also think differently about themselves and about those for whom the gifts were purchased. Women who receive the gifts will no doubt be affected by such an unexpected purchase and might evaluate their relationships and mates in different ways. Thus, the transaction and gift affect the individuals involved and their relationship. Again new meanings are acquired, previous meanings are modified, and future consumption behaviors result from the accommodation of these new and modified meanings.

Mass Culture, Popular Culture, or Some of Both?

Some audience activities involving mediated content seem to fall neatly into the mass or popular culture definition offered by Kammen. Most, I suspect, actually involve aspects of both forms of culture, however, operating for most individuals simultaneously. One key outcome is the ongoing negotiation and interpretations of meanings evoked by and derived from these experiences with mediated content and the technology.

When an individual repeatedly watches a favorite movie or videotaped program, the experience is mostly private. How these viewings will alter derived meanings obviously varies from individual to individual. Some manifestations of these viewing experiences would result in further alteration of meanings. The discovery that others may also view the same movie or program brings about an added dimension—that of joint participation in the social activity, popular culture. Until evoked in settings by others, the experience would be mostly mass culture.

A similar scenario would apply to couples watching a favorite movie or to a family getting together to watch a movie or videotape at regularly scheduled times, usually around major holidays. Many families talk about the annual holiday tradition of watching "National Lampoon's Christmas Vacation" and how it, like the popular films "A Christmas Story" or "It's a Wonderful Life," have become as much a part of the holiday season as decorating the Christmas tree or opening presents. Although the American

Film Institute's list of the all-time 100 best unjustly omitted "Christmas Vacation," the film nonetheless provides a regular opportunity for families to vicariously enjoy the trials, disasters, and triumphs of the Griswolds. At the same time, the family can analyze its experiences, relationships, and interactions surrounding the holiday. Some of the meanings derived will be individually situated, whereas a great many others will be further accommodated as the real-life holiday experiences play out for family members prior to, during, or after viewing the movie. In these situations, popular culture—interactive participation—would be the predominate use.

CHANGING FAMILIES, CHANGING TECHNOLOGIES, CHANGING EXPERIENCES

The settings in which mediated content is consumed have changed radically during the last 30 years. As U.S. households evolved from one to multiple television sets, from stereos to personal headsets, from a reliance on mainframe computers with boxes of punch cards to high-speed interconnections on the Internet, the family also underwent many profound changes. Recently released research from many different sources (e.g., Peterson, 1999) reveals the same conclusions. The U.S. family unit is now far removed from the traditional two parents, with only one working outside the home, and children (the once-famous average of 2.3 children per household). Today, many households contain only one parent or feature two parents who work outside the home. Children who are born and raised in a household with both parents from birth to adulthood are now in the minority, as the children of divorce, many of whom also have experienced failed marriages, raise children.

Paralleling these changes in family structure, information technologies have also undergone dramatic changes. Many children now find themselves in households that provide multiple channels that deliver information and entertainment and can be used in highly interactive ways, often without parental or adult knowledge or supervision (see Johnson, 1999). Consumption of mediated content is now done far more often on an individual basis with little time spent in a joint consumption activity. Children are often left on their own to peruse and consume various types of content. Even if one or more parents are in the household with them, they are often left unattended, quietly interacting with an outside world that offers a myriad of possibilities that grow exponentially on an almost daily basis. On the surface, such activities would appear to closely match Kammen's definition of *mass culture*—individualized and privatized. A closer examination, however, reveals a far more complex picture that actually shares attributes of both mass and popular culture. These experiences are unprecedented and still require a great deal of thought, attention, and research to seek out and identify the consequences, short and long term.

For many years, the media literacy movement (e.g., Potter, 1998) in the United States and in many other countries has emphasized the need for people to limit the amount of time spent in front of the television screen. First, it focused on the screen and presumed mostly passive viewers. Later this became the television screen as a computer monitor that was used for playing games or surfing the Internet. The main reason for limiting time spent with television was that excessive viewing is not healthy. If too much objectionable content were viewed, for example, then undesirable consequences would ensue (e.g., heavy viewers of televised violence would become desensitized to real-life violence or the probability of subsequent viewer aggression would be increased). Other unhealthy types of effects included the promotion of a sedentary lifestyle, devoid of physical or mental exercise and a diet replete with unhealthy junk food. Finally, and equally important, media literacy experts urged people, especially children and adolescents, to spend more time actually interacting with other people—social interactions so essential to the development of mentally healthy individuals. Social skills are best learned through interactions with other people and are not cultivated when so much time is spent with television and the pictures on it.

The Internet as a source of mediated content can no longer be treated as a noninteractive medium. In some ways, interaction among people is actually increased when the Internet is activated and used in certain ways. Internet interactions with other people differ from face-to-face interactions. They nonetheless are interactive and participatory. Many of these Internet uses exemplify new and exciting ways of people interacting with others—a far cry from the image of solitary individuals off in their own private worlds interacting with content presented on the television screen/ monitor. The Internet is potentially the richest source of human interaction in our history. The potential is there to link individuals who already share common interests, but are separated geographically, and for them to do so regularly and routinely. The potential is also there for individuals to cultivate new interests and connect with those who are more experienced. The potential also exists to find new, heretofore undiscovered sources of information that open up new avenues of thought and experience. For many people, of course, these potentials have already become reality and have been a reality for months or years. Consider the examples that follow, a mere sample of the vast resources available through the Internet.

Although a great deal of attention has been focused, appropriately, on e-commerce and the economics of supporting web sites and Internet services, many other sites regularly visited by millions of people (collectively speaking) have received only scant attention. These are the sites that provide individuals with the opportunity to interact and network with others who have similar interests. Several web sites are devoted to mothers and provide opportunities to discuss problems and concerns related to childrearing, juggling work outside the home with parental responsibilities, child care, spouse interactions, sexual feelings and behavior, and so on. Strategies for coping are shared among mothers, as are new products or services that can help with various facets of childrearing, or an opportunity is made available to vent one's feelings—these are just a few of the many types of activities and services provided. Years ago, this type of network would have been available to mothers who did not work outside the home and lived in a neighborhood where many others were in a similar position. Such opportunities basically have ceased to exist for most mothers. The stay-at-home mom often has no peers in her immediate neighborhood. This means she has no one to talk to or with whom she can sympathize, empathize, commiserate, help out, make suggestions, and so on. The web sites for mothers have created a network of peers in cyberspace such that, no matter what situation a specific mother finds herself in, she can communicate with others who are in the exact same situation. This *connection* provides a rich source of meanings that are accommodated, which in turn have consequences for a range of behaviors.

Women in the workplace—the U.S. norm—also have many web sites to turn to for help, guidance, advice, and so on. Again, widespread participation virtually guarantees that individuals can connect with others with identical situations. Some women will often comment that one of the biggest benefits of these web sites (the ones for mothers get a similar reaction) is the fact that, no matter how bad things are for them, some others seem to be in a much worse situation. Sometimes misery loves miserable company or the company of people who are even worse off.

Gays and lesbians have also found valuable support via the Internet (Cloud, 1997). Some younger males and females who have experienced shame and despair in the struggle to come to terms with being homosexual have also reported finding tremendously helpful web connections with others like themselves. Suicides have even been averted. The idea that one is not alone, and that similar others share one's concerns, is comforting and empowering.

Individuals who are affected by rare diseases and their families have also been able to connect and interact with those with similar afflictions. Here it is more than just the invaluable support and compassion that is vital. Shared information on the availability of new forms of treatment, drugs, therapies, experts to be contacted or avoided, how well certain therapies or treatments appear to be working, and so on also is important.

It would be nice to think that such information would be readily shared and available from those who provide and prescribe treatment in the medical community. Unfortunately, this is often not the case, especially with rarer diseases or afflictions. Victims of cancers that affect a great many people or various manifestations of coronary disease are much more likely to have many information and support groups available. When much smaller numbers come into play, the Internet provides an inexpensive and efficient means of connection. Again, these connections result in changes in meanings and behaviors as individual users of the system accommodate the content.

Access to pornographic materials presents an enormous range of possibilities for various Internet users. Policymakers, concerned citizens, legislators, and the courts all continue to struggle in their search for how to regulate and control what is out there and who is able to gain access to these materials. Anyone who has spent even a small amount of time sampling easily available porn sites quickly realizes that those who advocate any sort of regulation and control face an impossible situation. The recently publicized example of how a porn site had taken advantage of those seeking to access the White House by creating a porn web site at whitehouse.com is an excellent example (*the* White House is available at whitehouse.org). Some users expecting the president's site and getting pornographic images were shocked; some were confused; some were amused at the irony, given the sexual escapades that came to light during President Clinton's second term.

Although all porn sites require users to stipulate that they are either at least age 18 or 21, access to free sites remains only a deceitful click of the mouse away. Many of the really graphic sites require membership, proof of adult age, and credit card payments, but these are far from insurmountable obstacles for curious, excited minors. Who is better than young people at using the computer and finding ways to access desired sites? Beyond this, using a parent's credit card to access a site *for school research and stuff* is an effective ruse to gain admission. A parent sees an entry, without suggestive language, on a credit card bill that refers to an Internet company and thinks it is acceptable. In addition, that which is available free of charge is sufficiently graphic and detailed so that precious little is actually left to the imagination.

Young people with easy access to porn who spend major amounts of time by themselves or without a parent at home at all, or with a parent who is preoccupied with many other things to do, find themselves in historically unprecedented situations. The assumption has always been that young people need to learn about sex in an appropriately constructed and managed context. Images and words that portray only certain dimensions of sex and sexuality can easily lend themselves to misunderstandings, confusion, frustration, anxiety, and so on. Persons operating web sites devoted to porn maintain that they are clearly not directed at minors and that they make this clear when the web site is initially accessed. However, the explicit warning that a site contains graphic images of sexual acts may attract curious adolescents who are eager to see whatever it is they are not supposed to be seeing. In times past, adolescents could always seem to get their hands on an issue or two of some sexually explicit magazine or see some softcore R-rated videos (rented, purchased, or at a hotel on a family vacation). However, these images pale by comparison with those freely available on the Internet. How adolescents use this material, and how it affects them, is still largely unknown. Again the past may not be a good place to look for expectations or hypotheses. The situation is unprecedented, as are the meanings and interpretations derived from use and their short- and long-term consequences.

Other types of web sites that are matched up with users have proliferated on the Internet. These include sites devoted to sports, major or minor, national or international; hobbies—none is too obscure to not have a web site; shopping; banking, researching and buying stocks and bonds; travel; and other media (buying or viewing video materials, text stories, books, newspapers, etc.). All of these transactions and interactions present unique dimensions that produce or evoke new meanings that are and will continue to be accommodated by an increasing population of users of all ages and backgrounds.

In addition, typical Internet communication differs in important ways from normal face-to-face interactions. For example, personal e-mail correspondence usually is brief and asynchronous. Interactive responses may be separated by mere seconds, minutes, hours, days, or even months. It lacks visual cues, at least until such technology improves and proliferates. Personal e-mail is also limited in facilitating the expression of emotional states and usually does not concern lengthy, complex topics or positions. For interpersonal contact, e-mail is far better than nonexistent or intermittent contact, such as the long periods of time in between phone calls or even longer gaps separating letters or personal notes. It clearly is not equivalent to face-to-face communication, however.

Chat rooms and chat groups on the Internet also differ from a group of people discussing those same topics in face-to-face settings. In chat groups, a democratizing effect can more easily occur than in typical face-to-face encounters. In a work setting, for example, each individual's identity relative to one another is both known and important in affecting the nature of interactions. If your boss and your boss' boss are participating in a discussion about how to solve a particular problem, everyone participating knows the differences in status. What a boss thinks usually counts a lot more than what a subordinate thinks and says. In numerous ways, interaction may differ radically from what would occur in the absence of the boss and if no record was made of who said what. These features might involve the fear of disagreement, the desire to please the boss by verbally agreeing with or echoing the boss' position, or the fear of saying anything that could prove to be embarrassing, be perceived as stupid, or be an indication of a negative or hostile attitude.

In chat groups, participants usually only use first names or nicknames. Their status with fellow group participants is based on the essence of what each individual has to say and how each person reacts to what others are saying as the discussion unfolds. In this sense, who you are matters less than what you have to say. Positions are evaluated more on their actual merits than on the basis of the title or credentials of the person saying it. Such circumstances often facilitate a relatively uninhibited exchange of ideas and clash of opinions, free of reprisals and embarrassment, as each relatively anonymous participant is shielded from exposure. Such interactions present trade-offs. There are advantages and disadvantages.

Chat groups depend on the quality of the information presented. By omitting credentials, experience, and expertise of the participants, *leveling the playing field* to focus on the merits of what is said simultaneously presents an advantage and a disadvantage. In a context where going much beyond fairly superficial knowledge is difficult if not impossible, some people can make very little go a long way, greatly exaggerating their knowledge and expertise. Some who actually have a lot of expertise and experience to offer may become disenchanted and leave the group. Thus, those seeking to learn more and explore the topic in more depth or think about the topic in different ways from different perspectives will be limited to the experts who remain.

The absence of nonverbal cues, the limited feedback available, the absence of qualifying the expertise of individual participants, and the barriers to presenting complex, detailed information are all important differences between Internet chat groups and face-to-face discussions. Each form has its own advantages and disadvantages. Moreover, each form has its own unique consequences that require future research. A brief research agenda follows.

FUTURE RESEARCH

The preceding pages suggest several different avenues of future research in the pragmatics of mediated communication. Topics as well as proposed research methods are briefly described in the rest of this chapter.

Future research needs to examine mediated content attributes and features that incorporate important differences in the context of presentation of that content. For example, seeing an image on a web site is not the same as seeing that image in another medium. Reading a story from *Business Week* on the web site is not the same as reading the same article in the hard copy issue of the magazine that arrives in the mail. Identifying unique attributes and dimensions of mediated content that account for contextual nuances as well as obvious differences will be an essential building block for future research.

An examination of the many processes involved in individual uses of new forms of mediated content will also prove essential to our understanding. Researchers must study these with a variety of tools, including ethnographies, participant observation, case studies, surveys, experiments, and so on. Much can be learned from the identification of what the processes are, how they work, how they interrelate, and how they differ from those involved in mediated communication in our recent past.

Related to the study of process is the examination of how individuals choose where they go for information and how they move from one source to others. In this regard, it is worth noting how resources at an individual's disposal affect their choices. Resources would include available technology, user knowledge and skills, financial resources, available time, and others.

In terms of accommodation theory, future research will incorporate much of what is learned through research in the previously described areas in the search for consequences (e.g., Schoening & Anderson, 1995). The emphasis is on how individuals accommodate new forms of media and mediated content, how these accommodations have implications for subsequent behaviors and interactions with others, and how human beings evolve in their environments. This locus of study in turn leads us to the broader social implications as the culture is defined and redefined.

The research agenda presented in the study of the pragmatics of mediated communication is formidable and daunting. It requires an enormous amount of effort. In many respects, the field of communication is now much better prepared and willing to tackle such an ambitious and demanding agenda. In the last two decades, theoretical perspectives have expanded and the available arsenal of acceptable research methods has increased to the point that multiple perspectives and strategies are welcomed, as opposed to being barely tolerated or rejected as not being a part of traditional science (Anderson, 1996). This is perhaps the best sign of all—that researchers are up to the task of uncovering, discovering, and explaining what is going on around us in a much different world.

REFERENCES

Anderson, J. A. (1996). *Communication theory: Epistemological foundations.* New York: Guilford.

Anderson, J. A., & Meyer, T. P. (1988). *Mediated communication: A social action perspective.* Newbury Park, CA: Sage.

Blumer, H. (1969). *Symbolic interactionism: Perspective and method.* Englewood Cliffs, NJ: Prentice-Hall.

Cloud, J. (1997, December 8). Out, proud and very young. *Time,* p. 24.

Jensen, K. B. (1991). When is meaning? Communication theory, pragmatism, and mass media reception. In J. A. Anderson (Ed.), *Communication Yearbook 14* (pp. 3–32). Newbury Park, CA: Sage.

Johnson, P. (1999, November 18). TV grabs biggest share of kids' time. *USA Today,* p. 1D.

Kammen, M. (1999). *American culture, American taste: Social change and the 20th century.* New York: Knopf.

Lindlof, T. R. (1995). *Qualitative communication research methods.* Newbury Park, CA: Sage.

Peterson, K. (1999, November 24). Marriage losing key role in families. *USA Today,* p. 18D.

Potter, W. J. (1998). *Media literacy.* Newbury Park, CA: Sage.

Rock, P. (1979). *The making of symbolic interactionism.* Totowa, NJ: Rowman & Littlefield.

Rorty, R. (1982). *Consequences of pragmatism.* Minneapolis: University of Minnesota Press.

Roth, R. (1993). *British empiricism and American pragmatism: New directions and neglected arguments.* New York: Fordham University Press.

Schoening, G. T., & Anderson, J. A. (1995). Social action media studies: Foundational arguments and common premises. *Communication Theory, 5,* 93–116.

Shalin, D. N. (1986). Pragmatism and social interactionism. *American Sociological Review, 51,* 9–29.

Chapter 9

Shattering the Mirror:
Linking Media-Effects Research
and American Pragmatism

David K. Perry
The University of Alabama

Someone who examines the published literature concerning American pragmatism and media studies will find two recurrent views. Some scholars (Carter, 1989; Gonzalez, 1988; Perry, 1996b; Wenner, 1985) have argued that researchers who employ variable-analytic methods or who study media effects are often following the ideas of John Dewey and other pragmatists. After reading different sources (e.g., Carey, 1989; Peters, 1988), however, one might infer that pragmatist ideas in general, or those of Dewey in particular, could encourage the field to focus on more humanistic endeavors. For instance, Carey (1989) claimed that media-effects research has diverted energy from potentially more productive endeavors without producing much of scholarly merit. Beyond this, had it attained more success, its consequences would have been disastrous, he alleged. To Carey, identification of laws of human political behavior may contribute to external or technocratic, rather than participatory, political practices, for example. This sharply contrasts with the democratic ideals of many pragmatists.

This split is reminiscent of, if not always identical with, two contemporary conceptions of American pragmatism among philosophers. One, which postmodernists may find old fashioned, "attempts to relate inquiry to the objective and experimental methods of scientific intelligence" (Kurtz, 1992, p. 70). The other "maintains that this is not possible and that we need a holistic, poetic, and metaphorical approach to knowledge" (p. 70). The first form is found in the work of contemporary philosophers

185

such as Susan Haack and Paul Kurtz. The ideas of Richard Rorty exemplify the second form. Rorty (1983) dubbed these tendencies the "let's bring the scientific method to bear throughout culture" version and the "let's recognize a pre-existent continuity between science, art, politics, and religion" version (p. 260). Indeed, he found both evident in the writings of the major classical pragmatists—Dewey, William James, and Charles Peirce. Of course, advocates of the second form do not propound an end to all science. Instead, they often dispute the usefulness of essentialist concepts such as *objectivity* and *scientific method* as well as any idea that science is uniquely privileged.

In this piece, I propose a view of mass communication research that ultimately draws on what I consider the healthiest elements of each pragmatism. Thus, my arguments partly embody the traditional pragmatist aversion to sharp dualism. I perhaps remain a bit on the scientific side of the median in that I explicitly reserve a place for traditional empiricism. However, I embrace major aspects of the holism and continuity-of-science-with-art themes of the humanists. In doing this, this chapter endorses a number of the pragmatic ideas of philosopher W.V. Quine, but not certain beliefs of Rorty, his sometimes philosophically more radical influencee. Finally, I employ various metaphors, although readers may find my writing a bit more pedantic or prosaic than poetic.

In this way, I argue that pragmatist ideas can help mend some serious problems with, but need not cause researchers to end, contemporary media-effects research, to adopt a phrase from a notorious politician. Not entirely unlike Barone, Maddux, and Snyder (1997) in social psychology, I employ pragmatism in an effort to correct certain weaknesses linked to other philosophical influences. I maintain that viewing science holistically, and soberly recognizing its inherent limitations, should help clarify the lasting value of media-effects research. Beyond this, I suggest that scholars become public intellectuals and aim at the widest possible dissemination of knowledge. This could help nullify some of the potentially negative effects of knowledge and elevate the positive. Finally, I discuss some areas of pragmatist philosophy, especially of Dewey's work, that may not mesh well with contemporary media-effects research. In this chapter, I primarily focus on issues of public health, such as tobacco advertising and media violence. These are, in a sense, even more basic to human life than is politics. Some may find my interpretations a bit controversial. If so, I can only paraphrase the late Sidney Hook (1981). If you believe that I somehow misread Dewey, for example, take the results as my proposal to revise him.

I also combine two other versions of pragmatism. Philosophical (i.e., metaphysical) pragmatism appears in Dewey (1929a) and in Pepper's (1942) pragmatic contextualism world hypothesis. Pepper based contextualism on the root metaphor of the changing historic event. In this form, it denies the existence of permanent characteristics, such as Platonic forms or mechanistic space–time fields, in nature. Most of the details I associate with pragmatism appear in, or at least cohere with, such versions. These include an aversion to dualisms such as mind and body, individual and society, art and science, means and ends, facts and values, or analytic versus synthetic truth. Some of James' (1907) ideas exemplify what I call *methodical pragmatism*. He defined *pragmatism* as a method of settling philosophical disputes by examining observable consequences. In part, I discuss herein what difference it makes in the work of researchers whether ideas found within philosophical pragmatism, rather than from mechanism or Platonic realism, predominate. I also discuss what difference it makes if various versions of pragmatism prevail.

In making such points, this chapter rejects as impossible the separation between science and "meaningless" metaphysics that early logical empiricists attempted to draw. According to Quine (1951/1980), scientific sentences typically confront evidence collectively, rather than individually. Therefore, it becomes difficult to dismiss metaphysical ones for not being directly or individually verifiable. Empirically, it is infeasible to isolate, say, Pepper's (1942) world hypotheses from science. Historically, the two have often moved hand in hand. In addition to contextualism, Pepper (a pragmatist) located three highly adequate metaphysical world theories: Platonic or Aristotelian formism, the mechanism of scholars such as Descartes and Newton, and the organicism of Hegel and Royce. All such theories seek to explain the nature of reality and the structure of the world. They commonly condition both social scientific theories (Gillespie, 1992; Perry, 1996b) and research procedures (Georgoudi & Rosnow, 1985; Perry, 1988). Before developing the central points of this chapter, I need to introduce a few more interrelated philosophical themes.

THE FACT-VALUE DUALISM AND THE SPECTATOR THEORY OF KNOWLEDGE

Pragmatist philosopher Charles W. Morris (1946) found in Dewey's moral emphasis "a necessary corrective to the merely scientific study of communication, which because of its 'objectivity' has always the danger of loading the guns of persons who think of other persons merely as things to be 'manipulated' " (p. 283). As Morris well knew, however, Dewey did not want to subordinate science to morality. Instead, Dewey advocated precisely the opposite. He wanted to evaluate value judgments based on observable consequences. In Dewey's (1929b) famous words, "The problem of restoring integration and cooperation between man's beliefs about the world in which he lives and his beliefs about the values and purposes that should direct his conduct is the deepest problem of modern life" (p. 255).

Thus, Dewey rejected the sharp dualism between facts and values that much philosophy assumes. For example, logical empiricists (e.g., Ayer, 1936) sometimes denigrated values as mere emotions without scientific significance. Scholars sometimes see values as sources of bias that need to be excised from science. To many pragmatists (e.g., Kaplan, 1964; Toch & MacLean, 1962), values are intertwined with virtually every step of research processes. They influence selection of questions, evidentiary interpretation, and the judgments formed about implications for human life. In this light, values are not inherently biasing. What creates bias "is allowing them only a role that insulates them from the test of experience" (Kaplan, 1964, p. 396). Thus, by distinguishing the prized from the appraised, Dewey hoped to subject values to the same pattern of inquiry used in science. Dewey (1929b) defined them as "whatever is taken to have rightful authority in the direction of conduct" (p. 256). One might prize tobacco, which on appraisal, proves itself unworthy, for example. To me, this does not mean that one can deduce values from facts or that the two cannot be distinguished. Instead, if factual considerations inform values, the latter attain a kind of relative objectivity (Kurtz, 1990). One can use knowledge for contradictory purposes. For example, persuasion theory either may help sell tobacco or enhance the effectiveness of antismoking messages. In arguing for scientific evaluation, Kaplan (1964) said, "The product is always capable of a variety of uses, but this versatility does not imply that the appraisal of these uses therefore lies outside the process" (p. 400).

To a Deweyan pragmatist, means and ends codetermine each other, much as do facts and values. Something that is an end in one context becomes a means in another (Mounce, 1997). Recognizing this should encourage scholars not to regard research only as an end in itself. Instead, they can treat it as a means to other ends and study its practical, "real-world" effects. In turn, such knowledge may make feasible the control of these ends. A Deweyan argument "that wherever technological institutions fail to enhance desirable human goals there needs to be more, not less, technology" (Hickman, 1995, p. 86) follows. I use the term *technology* in a broad sense to include both research and education—a presumed source of research impact. In this way, pragmatism finds a place for both empirical and critical mass communication research. Television cultivation theorist Gerbner (1983) defined a *critical researcher* as one who is "prepared and free to scrutinize the ends as well as the means of any project" (pp. 355–356).

The legacy of the spectator theory of knowledge, however, also one of Dewey's favorite philosophical targets, may discourage researchers from concerning themselves with the "real-world" impact, or the lack thereof, from their work. It meshes with the traditional formist idea of truth as correspondence. The spectator theory is a lingering deposit of pre-Darwinian thought such as the formism of Plato and the mechanism of Descartes. Whether it technically fits into mechanistic worldviews, however, is a bit debatable (see Pepper, 1942). According to it, the purpose of human cognition (or of science, philosophy, or journalism) is merely to mirror, reproduce, or provide what philosopher Putnam (as cited in Rorty, 1990) called a "God's eye view" (p. 2) of the world. To Rorty, this is a view "irrelevant to our needs and practices" (p. 2) or that represents "things as they are in themselves" (p. 5). Such a view would be unaffected by human values, perceptual apparatus, or what not. Descartes' mind–body dualism lies behind many such conceptions. Descartes alleged that the human being consists of two, at least largely independent, substances: a mind that thinks and a body that occupies space. His spectator theory of knowledge (see Rorty, 1979) is sometimes presented as an ideal of basic research. Nonetheless, Dewey thought that modern science, with its active manipulation of subject matter, had undermined it. In its place, pragmatists often view cognition biologically as an evolved tool of survival.

THE QUINE–DUHEM AND UNDERDETERMINATION THESES: IMPLICATIONS FOR DISCUSSION OF THE MEDIA-VIOLENCE ISSUE

Perhaps one of the greatest barriers to the academic and public influence of media research is the seemingly endless disagreement among trained researchers about the answers to important research questions. In this section, I argue that a variety of interpretations of research evidence probably always will be possible. Therefore, something less than absolute certainty must serve as the criterion of judgment if one is to avoid the absolute skepticism some people express about social science. Such a criterion necessarily will involve values. It should rely, as far as can be, on ones that withstand empirical scrutiny.

Related to this, I argue that scholars should avoid treating media-effects questions in much the same way that philosophers at times have regarded logical principles—as immune to evidence. They also should admit the fallibility of their conclusions. To illustrate my points, I draw on the media-violence issue. Much of what I say could apply with all of science. I suspect, however, that potentially biasing values have influenced discussion here to a substantially greater degree than with many scientific issues. In particular, the effect of media on scholarly interpretation of research (Noelle-Neumann, 1983) may explain some existing problems. These effects are rooted in the links that academics have with industries that research may indict as sources of social problems. A perceived need to satisfy industrially oriented students, or the employers who hire them, may affect expressed judgments, for example. A desire to feel good about one's work may have similar effects. So may a wish to shield one's academic home from actual or potential trash-and-burn campaigns, in which universities close down entire departments.

Because of this, some might argue that for media researchers to become public intellectuals, as I argue later, would do as much harm as good. For instance, I sometimes hear scholars attempt to acquit media industries from well-documented (but fallible) effects allegations in much the same way that a defense attorney tries to shield a client. Occasionally such statements, made in classes and even in public forums, appear to betray an ignorance of widely recognized evidence. Such scholars, consciously or not, may promote their perceived self-interest in a way that could mislead the public. Of course, those accused of crime always deserve competent defenses. Scholars, however, really should concentrate on finding truth or, for the sake of skeptics, Dewey's (1938) fallibilist notion of *warranted assertion*. Media critics also make statements that sometimes betray an ignorance of research. In my experience, however, those that do so generally do not have academic titles or scholarly training to lend extra credence to such behavior.

Thus, I wrote the following section partially in hopes of mitigating unconscious bias among academics. My goal is to elevate rather than suppress discussion while recognizing that even defense attorneys every once in a while have truth on their side. As Diesing (1991) said, "The educators must first be educated" (p. 128). It focuses on the psychology of media inquiry and uses closely related ideas from pragmatic philosophy of science. An understanding of these points also might counter any influence, among the public or researchers, should scholars try to slant evidence. I presume that this will outweigh any help it provides to those who might do so. The latter may already understand these points, at least intuitively. My points mesh with a Deweyan hope that social inquiry can "help us to understand ourselves: how we think and inquire and why, when thinking and inquiry are successful, they are successful" (Manicus, 1998, p. 47). In so doing, this section may also clarify the lasting significance of effects research.

I rely heavily here on an extremely influential essay from the 1950s that helped resurrect pragmatism from near obscurity at the hands of logical empiricism. In it, Quine (1951/1980) condemned reductionism as dogmatic. The logical empiricists' verificationist theory of meaning relied on a reductionist assumption. In this sense, it is the notion that, in science, "each statement, taken in isolation from its fellows, can admit of confirmation or infirmation at all" (p. 41). Instead, Quine argued, the totality of human knowledge or belief, "from the most casual matters of geography and history to the profoundist laws of atomic physics or even of pure mathematics and logic, is a man-made fabric which impinges on experience only along the edges" (p. 42).

Conceivably, Quine's holistic notion could implicate all of science in any hypothesis test. More modestly, when a scientist tests a theory, he or she "is actually 'testing' a host of initial conditions, measuring instruments and auxiliary hypotheses that together form the *ceteris paribus* conditions" (Hunt, 1991, p. 356). In effect, individual hypotheses or scientific sentences become meaningful only when linked together. An exception might occur if a scientific sentence is lengthy enough to express a number of different hypotheses. Quine built on work by Duhem (1913/1990). Among philosophers of science, this Quine–Duhem thesis has generated some controversy and caricature (see Greenwood, 1990; Klee, 1992). Nevertheless, its influence remains great.

Therefore, if unexpected results occur, one will not know why. The theory, the deductive link between it and the hypothesis, the measuring instruments used, and so on could all be at fault. In short, a researcher has the ability to "adjust one strand of the fabric of science rather than another in accommodating some particular recalcitrant experience" (Quine, 1951/1980, p. 46). Related to this is the underdetermination contention, which claims that the same evidence can provide the basis for competing theories. Assume the evidence comes out as expected given one's theory. One can then invent a potentially infinite number of additional, logically inconsistent theories to account for the results. Thus, the evidence does not mandate one humanly invented interpretation. Instead, theories perhaps thrive or die in terms of their long-run, pragmatic consequences (Hesse, 1980; Mounce, 1997). These may include whether they enhance the prediction, explanation, and control of phenomena.

Until long-run consequences become evident, how can one choose among alternatives? Following Quine (1951/1980), pragmatic values such as simplicity or maintenance of earlier belief may be influential. Often a scientist may choose to retain as much as possible of what James called the *apperceptive mass*. This consists of "the assumptions, beliefs, tendencies one has acquired in the course of one's life" (Mounce, 1997, p. 76). Among scientists, it may contain a Kuhn (1970) paradigm. A paradigm includes the definition of the subject matter of the field, as well as identification of its important problems and methods that address these appropriately. It typically embodies a restricted version of a world hypothesis (Pepper, 1973/1982). Examples include the mechanism of Newtonian physics and Watsonian behaviorism in psychology. B. F. Skinner's psychological behaviorism (even if imperfectly) illustrates a pragmatic contextualist worldview (Hayes, Hayes, & Reese, 1988). Not coincidentally, Skinner and Quine often influenced each other as colleagues at Harvard University.

In fact, Quine's largely successful attack on reductionism was not entirely novel. Decades earlier, James developed similar ideas about the psychology of belief (Mounce, 1997; Nevo, 1995).[1]

> The process here is always the same. The individual has a stock of old opinions already, but he meets a new experience that puts them to a strain. Somebody contradicts them; or in a reflective moment he discovers that they contradict each other; or he hears of facts with which they are incompatible; or desires arise in him which they cease to satisfy. The result is an inward trouble to which his mind till then had been a stranger, and from which he seeks to escape by modifying his previous mass of opinions. He saves as much of it as he can, for in this matter of belief we are all extreme conservatives. So, he tries to change first this opinion, and then that (for they resist change very variously), until at last some new idea comes up which he can graft upon the ancient stock with a minimum of disturbance of the latter, some idea that mediates between the stock and the new experience and runs them into one another most felicitously and expediently. (James, 1907, pp. 59–60)

James described what he believed typical of human cognition. Similar or even derivative ideas (e.g., Festinger, 1957; Newcomb, 1953) underlie prominent psychological research concerning people's need for cognitive consistency. Regardless of the extent to which James' description applies to people in general, scientific training often encourages scholars to think in this way. Nonetheless, both fruitful and degenerate forms of such thought exist. Fruitful forms may combine novel facts with previously funded knowledge. In extreme cases, dysfunctional forms might involve selective attention, exposure, perception, or retention (see Perry, 1996b). For example, a scholar might simply maintain the coherence of his or her existing beliefs by forgetting or misinterpreting contradictory information. This clearly could hinder scientific work by separating a researcher from available evidence. In contrast, a sophisticated, but adamantly dogmatic, scientist need not descend anywhere near this far to protect especially cherished creeds.

This seems especially so to the extent that one follows Rortyan pragmatism, rather than its Quinean or (perhaps to a lesser degree) Jamesian variants. Unlike Rorty, James (1909) maintained a place for empiricism by applying the formist correspondence notion of truth distributively, rather than collectively (see Nevo, 1995). Individual ideas, such as those that impinge directly on experience, can copy reality, according to him. How-

---

[1]As Nevo (1995) pointed out, James' work preceded the 20th-century linguistic turn in philosophy, whereas Quine's did not. As a result, James tended to talk of ideas or experiences and Quine of sentences. Some discussion exists whether the linguistic turn hinders the evolutionary naturalism of traditional pragmatism (see Auxier, 1995; Donovan, 1995).

ever, the collective groups of ideas simultaneously implicated in research can only serve as instruments, rather than copies. Quine salvaged empiricism without relying on James' modest *mirror*. To do so, he introduced a postlinguistic-turn notion—the observation sentence. One example would be, "The thermometer reads 85 degrees Fahrenheit." People who speak an appropriate language can agree on these quite readily. Often this will include more or less everybody, but in some cases it will involve only members of a scientific community. As Gibson (1988) described such sentences: "The tug that tows the ship of theory is no more a mirror mirroring the shoreline than is the ship itself a mirror mirroring the shoreline. Rather, the tug is securely tethered to the shoreline via lines of conditioning" (p. 81). Thus, "verbal dispositions conditioned to stimuli" (p. 81) link theory to the world.

Such Skinnerian conceptions smack of nominalist mechanism (see Pepper, 1942), rather than any correspondence notion of truth. B. F. Skinner's psychology, however, adjudicated many mechanical ideas pragmatically by their workability (Hayes et al., 1988). Because of this, Quine's empiricism seems more adequate than James'. I wonder, however, whether Quine might profitably link his overall reconstruction of science to Dewey's social concept of intelligence. Instead of copying objects, intelligence takes account "of the ways in which more effective and more profitable relations with these objects may be established in the future" (Dewey, 1925/1973, p. 54). In any case, because of their underdetermination, the holistic clusters simultaneously implicated in tests of scientific theory differ from observation sentences.

In contrast, Rorty (1982) discarded traditional empiricism in favor of conversational guidance from other humans. Truth becomes a name for something one can defend against any comer. "In place of holism, we get a Nietzschean drama, a contest of elemental forces—the Apollonian versus the Dionysian" (Nevo, 1995, p. 164). Such neopragmatism may open the door to dogma, however. Quine's ideas suggest that one can virtually always defend conversationally any idea one wants, come what may. Absent some sense of empiricism, then all ideas may seem equally warranted (a point that Rorty surely would dispute). Quine's (1981) playfully approving description of the hypothetico-deductive method as "wishful thinking subject to correction" (p. 33) reduces to mere wishful thinking.

The Quine–Duhem and underdetermination theses are sometimes vague. This increases the underdetermination of my following application of them to the violence issue. Scientific research can be thought of as involving a kind of web (Quine & Ullian, 1970). At the periphery are the observation sentences. For example, among a group of schoolchildren, one purported measure of exposure to television violence may correlate, say, .3 with a presumed measure of aggressiveness. At the center of the web are principles used broadly (but usually implicitly) in science, such as the logical principle of the excluded middle. Near the middle is a set of abstract theoretical assumptions, such as those in social learning theory, relating to imitative behavior.

From these premises, a researcher deduces one or more hypotheses—say that exposure to television violence increases a child's aggression. The hypothesis lies closer than does the theory to the evidentiary periphery, and the evidence underdetermines it to a lesser degree. Of course, those familiar with issues of causation know that evidence never will uniquely mandate any single causal interpretation. This makes infallible conclusions about media violence elusive. Nonetheless, one can interpret observed correlations in only a small number of ways. One might consider reverse and third-variable causation, as well as the form predicted. For each such interpretation, researchers might invent an infinite number of theoretical explanations. Clearly, the mosaic metaphor used in James' (1912/1967) notion of experience applies. No cement in its bedding holds down its pieces, permitting one to rearrange them in various ways.

Thus, with theory,[2] conversational guidance from other humans becomes more important than with observational sentences or even hypotheses (see Nevo, 1995). In a sense, however, differences between observational and theoretical sentences are relative, not absolute. Quine (1981) maintained that researchers can reject observations rather than theory (e.g., by pleading hallucination). Such instances presumably occur rarely. Beyond this, they can even discard logical principles that earlier philosophers deemed self-evident and immune from evidence.

Let us consider two scholars who develop research-based opinions about the television violence issue. McA works for the research department of a television company and wants to make a positive contribution to society. The researcher has long been uncomfortable about some of the possible effects of television. Nevertheless, McA likes to think that the tube does more good than harm. To explain associations between viewing and aggression, McA prefers a predisposition theory. It holds that having an aggressive personality causes one to watch a lot of television violence (Fenigstein, 1979). Recent epidemiological research linking television and television violence to a doubling of the rates of U.S. homicide and other violent crimes during the 1960s (Centerwall, 1989, 1992)[3] draws an

---

[2]Quine changed his mind more than once about whether two logically inconsistent scientific, but empirically equivalent scientific theories are true. To my knowledge, his most recent answer is that only one of them can be true (see Gibson, 1988).

[3]Whether Centerwall's research, in which the independent variable is the timing of the introduction of television into a population, actually involves the effects of television violence has been the subject of some discussion (e.g., Medved, 1999). My view it that of course it does. In light of available evidence, it is simply difficult to believe that only nonviolent con-

especially sharp reaction from McA. Rates of U.S. homicide have recently declined substantially. No one has linked this to changes in television content or television exposure, McA alleges, which should discredit Centerwall's research. McA also cites evidence (e.g., McGuire, 1986) that exposure to television violence predicts only modest portions of the variation in audience aggressiveness.

MacB is a college professor who often teaches generic mass communication classes. Based on earlier research and certain interpretations of social learning theory, MacB vaguely suspected that the impact of television violence on audience behavior was real but rather modest. On reflection, however, Centerwall's research helped convinced him that a far greater problem exists. MacB believes television is responsible for perhaps 30% of homicide and other violent crime, rather than the 50% estimated in Centerwall's work. He believes Centerwall may have failed to control completely for factors such as the growth of the drug culture during the 1960s.[4] MacB also likes to describe as *moonshine* (a term he learned from James and Quine) conclusions that the low levels of explained variation cited by McA indicate television's unimportance in promoting violent crime. By this abuse of statistics, MacB points out, tobacco use would account for only perhaps 1% of lung cancer cases (J. Cohen & Cohen, 1983, p. 66; Perry, 1992). Instead, researchers link the majority of cases to it.

In classes and published work, MacB has often given qualified approval to Centerwall's work. This perhaps makes him want to explain the drops in violent crime in a way that coheres with it. By pointing to headlines proclaiming markedly declining homicide rates, McA possibly exaggerates the decline of violence. Recent sources (e.g., Grossman, 1998) have claimed that improving medical technology has reduced homicide rates uniquely, MacB discovers. He has his research assistant compile FBI crime data (USFBI, annual volumes). Sure enough, from 1991 to 1998, rates of

---

tent would have this effect. The pertinent question becomes whether other forms of television also contribute in ways other than, say, social learning to increased crime. Perhaps watching nonviolent television occupies time that a child might spend with activities that contribute to moral development.

[4]To my knowledge, Centerwall has never addressed the possible role of illegal drugs in explaining the growth of 1960s violent crime. Yet his work contains evidence that makes it seem unlikely that drugs were the primary culprit. After television appeared in the United States, urban rates of violent crime arrests began to increase disproportionately among youths ages 10 to 14 in about 1960 and only later among older age groups (Centerwall, 1989, pp. 41–43). I doubt that increased drug activity began first among those ages 10 to 14. One can speculate that even if drugs stimulated violence crime, television may have been an indirect cause. Perhaps the attention the medium focused on the counterculture contributed to drug use among its audiences. Beyond this, the introduction of television caused radio to shift its emphasis to popular music, which during the 1960s often featured lyrics that overtly, or in a thinly disguised way, glorified drug use.

murder and nonnegligent manslaughter (which FBI statistics combine) dropped substantially more than did overall violent crime. Both began declining after 1991. For each 100,000 people, the former rate fell by 35.7%, from 9.8 to 6.3, and the latter by 25.2%, from 758.1 to 566.4. The violent crime index includes aggravated assault, forcible rape, homicide, and robbery. This lends credence to the technology explanation, MacB believes. Presumably, such things as medical advances and 911 numbers have turned potential murders into lesser offenses. Meanwhile, the 1998 FBI violent crime index remained more than 3.5 times as high as in 1960, about the time Centerwall's postulated cohort effect of television began to show up. For 1960, the violence rate was 159 per 100,000. In developing this obviously post hoc argument, however, MacB has to rely less on the highly reliable homicide statistic (see Centerwall, 1989) and more on possibly less valid ones.

At this point, an extremely controversial and carelessly stated element of James' work arises. James (1907) equated truth, in the collective rather than distributive sense, with expedience. Some readers inferred that, in an underdetermined world, Jamesian truth may as well be whatever makes one feel good about oneself. In interpreting James, Nevo (1995) stated, "Theories mediate between new experiences and old beliefs, and their success in doing so is the measure of their truth" (p. 157). In addition, the "process of belief modification is the individual's way of escaping the 'inward trouble' generated in him by such contradictions" (p. 157). Why then cannot certain of the contradictory ideas of McA and MacB both be true if they form coherent webs and elevate the self-esteem of each? That is to say, cannot social learning from television both be and not be a substantial contributor to violent crime? In this way, Jamesian pragmatism collapses into a subjectivism not entirely unlike the one that critics (e.g., Kurtz, 1992) accuse Rorty of.

In all fairness, James at times more than encourages such interpretations. Yet certain of his qualifications cast doubt on the adequacy of these readings. For instance, he described truth as the expedient in *our* thinking "in the long run and on the whole" (James, 1907, p. 222). The collective pronoun suggests a communitarian reading (Murphy, 1990). It and the reference to long-run truth argue against a purely psychological interpretation. Similarly, Quine and Ullian (1970) prized consistency not because it feels good, but because it helps maintain previously warranted scientific statements.

In general, then, research interpretation involves values, although less so (some would argue not at all) with observation sentences and more so at the abstract reaches of theory (see Nevo, 1995). Which values we employ will depend on many factors. Some of them are relatively easy to ground objectively, such as consistency with previously funded knowledge or simplicity (see Quine & Ullian, 1970). Others may seem more individualistic or idiosyncratic. I am not arguing that psychological factors should not predispose researchers to adopt one position or another. Rather, more objectively grounded values should guide the ultimate choices. Clearly I think MacB (actually myself) makes a more compelling argument than McA (a partially fictionalized composite). Major reasons include a lack of self-interest and the clear preponderance of the available evidence (e.g., Paik & Comstock, 1994; Wood, Wong, & Chachere, 1991) linking the medium to aggression. From a scientific perspective, one key might be the appraised value of the apperceptive masses. Nonetheless, readers should form their own judgments.

Applying inherently fallible research will involve additional values. Parents who want to know whether to regulate a child's television-related behavior obviously should weigh the consequences of their decision. In doing so, they might rely on the preponderance of the evidence—the standard in civil court cases. Regulators who might act officially against media violence perhaps should wait until researchers establish guilt beyond and to the exclusion of every reasonable doubt—the stringent standard required in criminal cases. Even then, the degree of regulation may depend on how much of an effect occurs. As Hook (1980) put it, we can assume the desirability of protecting expression, but this presumption is refutable. I believe that evidence in the violence issue meets both standards. To my mind, the real lingering question concerns the extent of the effect. Others may disagree perhaps most often about the reasonable doubt criterion.

At bottom, given sufficient evidence, any serious scholar has to be willing, following careful appraisal, to abandon prized predispositions. Otherwise dogma blocks the road of inquiry, in Peirce's words. After all, ideas with wider scope eventually superseded even some extremely well-established Kuhnian paradigms, such as Newtonian mechanics. Many philosophers, including early logical empiricists, tried to maintain a sharp distinction between analytic sentences or statements and synthetic ones. Analytic statements are "grounded in meanings independently of matters of fact" (Quine, 1951/1980, p. 20). Synthetic ones are true because of the way the world is. Along with his argument against reductionism, Quine (1951/1980) claimed that philosophers have not adequately justified such a distinction. Typically, scholars have regarded logical principles as analytic and research hypotheses as synthetic. Given Quine's argument, even the latter can be seen as true (or false) regardless of evidence, however. A person only has to adjust his or her assumptive tapestry sufficiently. If experiments (see Paik & Comstock, 1994) suggest that violence exposure increases aggression, their artificiality renders them meaningless in describing the real world. If correlational and longitudinal work (e.g., Huesmann & Eron, 1986) implies such an effect, some unidentified third variable really is to blame. To so completely protect hypotheses from experience, however, at some point also renders them scientifically untestable. I suspect that this possibility has at times limited academic consensus on the television violence and other media issues. At worst, scholars may display dogmatic attitudes that might make them excellent advocates of scientific creationism.

In all likelihood, neither side of the media violence debate is entirely free of dogmatically shielding prized conclusions. Those who would acquit television sometimes may be especially susceptible, however, due to the massive preponderance of contrary evidence and their sometimes greater self-interest. In fact, rendering effects questions scientifically meaningless may fit in well with the apperceptive masses of some in the entertainment industry. Of course, such defensive attitudes are not limited to television people. They share them with producers and distributors of other attacked products such as automobiles, cigarettes, eggs, newspapers, and sugar.

Finally, the fairest argument that scholars could give parents might include the following. Substantial evidence exists that current exposure to television and television violence may increase the chance that children will commit violent crimes later in life. We cannot be entirely sure, however. Probably we never will be. Nor do we know exactly how much of an increase may occur. Nonetheless, imagine that you fed your child a dietary supplement that medical research suggests may affect the child's personality. This in turn may increase the chance that the child later will commit a homicide—say from 1:400 to 1:270. The supplement also may enhance the possibility that he or she will perpetrate far more common, but less serious, offenses. If so, would you continue the diet? Would you look for alternatives?

COMMUNICATION RESEARCH AND EDUCATIONAL PRACTICE

Once scholars reject the spectator theory, they can see themselves as participants in nature and culture. If so, they may feel encouraged to become public intellectuals and help others appraise forms of mass communication and the products peddled therein, which otherwise may be prized. The lives of scholars such as Dewey, Gerbner, Hook, Rorty, and Cornel West exemplify that of the *public intellectual* (Scott, 1994; Wartella, 1994). As adopted here, the term refers to scholars who move beyond traditional academic life toward various forms of engagement with the broader society (see Perry, 1996a). In this sense, a public intellectual is not satisfied solely to pursue specialized research, which appears in peer-reviewed journals. Rather, after such publication occurs, he or she may discuss the work with journalists, write articles for popular publications, and even appear on television or give speeches. In short, such scholars do not see themselves as mere ivory-tower bystanders.

By adopting this role, scholars can become research equivalents of public or civic journalists (Merritt, 1995; Rosen, 1994). Although precisely defining public journalism has proved somewhat elusive, its roots seem to lie in the Deweyan idea that the human mind is an active participant in nature, rather than a detached spectator. More specifically, as journalists who work for mainstream newspapers face increased competition from online services and other technological innovations, they may have to become more than detached spectators who observe and transmit information about news events. Instead they can become more active participants in their communities, helping to solve or at least providing a forum to address its problems. In short, certain of the problems of higher education, such as its lack of public support, may result from academics who attempt to work as detached onlookers.

It is the summer of 1998. I am sitting in my hotel room in Nuevo Casas Grandes, Mexico. The television is on. A cigarette ad appears. It depicts a handsome young fellow smoking a cigarette who socializes with various *senoritas bonitas*. Across the bottom of the screen appears a message in Spanish. It reads, "Smoking can cause cancer." I am struck by what I take to be the implicit message of the ad, meshing with the live-for-today culture of the country. "Live. Love. Smoke. Score. Enjoy the finer things of life. Sure, perhaps in some infinitely future decade your behavior will kill you. But, in the meantime, live," the commercial seems to scream. I am reminded of how many of the people I meet in Mexico smoke and of recent evidence (e.g., Pierce, Choi, Gilpin, Farkas, & Berry, 1998; Pierce & Gilpin, 1995) linking promotions to tobacco use among the young. Beyond this, I wonder whether psychological science, or just the shrewd intuition of its creator, is responsible for the ad's seemingly being as precisely adapted to its environment as are the creatures of the surrounding desert.

Surprisingly little is known about the effects of social research, whether for good or bad, on human well-being. Clearly the mirror metaphor may not encourage scholars to conduct this sort of needed work. One especially horrifying possibility is that, by making product promotions more efficient, applications of communication and psychological inquiries could contribute to widespread, needless human death. For example, they could help bring about the prediction that 300 million of the children and adolescents in the world today will die in adulthood from tobacco use (Deen, 1999). Funds spent on tobacco marketing apparently continue massively to outweigh those spent to unsell smoking (Elliott, 1999). Three hundred million deaths might well exceed, in a single generation, the number of deaths resulting from all 20th-century agents of mass murder (Hitler, Mao, Stalin, etc.) combined. For all I know, they also might surpass those caused by all wars in human history. Many of these are expected to occur in developing countries, which tobacco companies today are targeting (Deen, 1999).

Apparently with reference to similar cases, Dewey (1927/1946) wrote that the glorification of pure (as opposed to applied) science "is a rationalization of an escape; it marks a construction of an asylum of refuge, a shirking of responsibility" (p. 175). If scholars are merely mirroring an external world, rather than constructing instruments, how can a scientific field (much less an individual researcher) have any responsibility for what others do or fail to do with its work? To cite an extreme (and possibly real but perhaps fictional) example, this might help an academic who accepts a grant from a tobacco company to look at factors that impede or enhance product promotion feel more comfortable. Unless one's apperceptive mass embraces the spectator theory, however, such attitudes may seem akin to the "I was only following orders" defense at Nuremberg.

The problem, of course, perhaps is not with research that may identify circumstances in which persuasion is more or less effective. Instead it may lie with the social responsibility of scholars who fail to challenge an educational system that often primarily educates those who may use such research to manipulate others for pecuniary purposes. Doubtlessly, the mirror metaphor encourages scholarly disinterest here. Today the vast majority of higher education in mass communication focuses on training future producers of media messages. Theory and research courses tend to be subordinated to these goals, as when programs erect barriers to enrollment by nonmajors. Those of us who have taught undergraduate theory and effects courses know that the bulk of our students tend to major in subjects such as advertising and telecommunications. Many are looking for knowledge that will help them in their careers or for a class that will meet graduation requirements. Unfortunately, their careers may involve selling health-threatening products or attracting the young to media violence.

In contrast, Dewey and his followers often pointed out that a "community was not fully democratic until it had 'socialized intelligence' " (Westbrook, 1991, p. 436). Dewey (1930/1981) foresaw "a time when all individuals may share in the discoveries and thoughts of others, to the liberation and enrichment of their own experience" (p. 115). This emphasis on community coheres with his rejection of Descartes' individualism. Instead, Dewey defined the mind as an evolved ability to use language and other socially acquired symbols (see Morris, 1932). Thinking is a matter of talking with oneself. Thus, one's intellectual achievements depend on a cultural heritage from others, magnifying the duty to share. Along the lines of the work of psychologist Cialdini (1988), scholars could link old-fashioned propaganda analysis to the findings of persuasion research. The former documents the techniques employed in advertising and related fields. The latter can indicate how effective these are. Educational efforts then might focus on making people aware of the presumably often unconscious influence of ads on their behavior. This could mesh neatly with a Deweyan social science designed to help people attain self-understanding and "clear away misconceptions about ourselves and our arrangements and enpower us to reconstruct the social world more in accordance with our wants and aims" (Manicus, 1998, p. 47).

The issue in some ways reduces to whether we want to educate only persuasive communicators, perhaps hereby helping to promote relatively thoughtless and even lethal stimulus–response behavior among media audiences. Instead, perhaps we can help cultivate audience intelligence (see Dewey, 1922/1957; Westbrook, 1991). In all fairness, advertisers and marketers frequently seem uninterested in research, favoring instead a reliance on creativity and intuition. If so, their intuition about how to design messages sometimes seems amazingly accurate (see Cialdini, 1988). Even if our work is not even a bit player in tobacco-related extermination, we may commit sins of omission by failing to promote forms of education that could mitigate the situation. Some media programs have taken steps toward making parts of their curricula attractive and accessible to all university students. This is only a commendable first step. It falls well short of a Deweyan socialization of intelligence. A socialization of media literacy would likely involve including this topic in primary school curricula and making research accessible to everyone perhaps via the Internet. Along with courses to teach high school teachers how to teach journalism, for example, we might offer classes for media-literacy instructors.

In my opinion, the pragmatists' tendency (e.g., in Dewey, 1934/1958) to find continuity between science and art becomes especially valuable here. Dewey considered both science and educational practices, such as journalism and classroom teaching, as arts. He (1927/1946) liked to emphasize that "knowledge is communication as well as understanding" and that "a thing is fully known only when it is published, shared, socially accessible" (p. 176). The problem is not simply the antidemocratic consequences of isolating science from the communication of its findings. Nor is the field's evident satisfaction with something less than the widest possible distribution of its work just a matter of leaving something unfinished. It is no mere violation of Hegelian aesthetics, as some see a man who is without a woman (and vice versa or whatever). In the case of our field, the consequences for human life and well-being just might turn out to be substantial.

Thus, in Dewey's (1938) terms, my proposal could transform a troubled situation into one that is consummatory and accommodates apparently conflicting ideals. These include both audience well-being and the rights of marketers to advertise and apply existing research. Ultimately, however, evidence might justify comprehensive bans on promotions for products such as tobacco. European Commission nations are set to implement a broad advertising prohibition. Data from a variety of developed nations suggest that advertising increases, and only capacious proscriptions of promotional messages reduce (by perhaps at least 6% or 7%) tobacco consumption (Saffer & Chaloupka, 1999). A ban may especially be needed in societies such as Mexico, which lack adequate educational resources to counteract manipulative messages. Only its consequences can validate free speech. At some point, human life takes priority over commercialized near absolutes (see Hook, 1964). Perhaps socialized intelligence can only deal sufficiently with the psychological impact of promotions for less harmful products, such as fatty foods and speedy cars.

The barriers to my proposed reorientation of media education are clear. These days, U.S. public universities increasingly resemble public officials in Latin American. The latter often depend on *mordidas* and *propinas* (bites and tips) from private citizens for anything more than a bare existence. In our case, these often come from industrial interests that may hesitate to support critical education about their products. Educating the public about the findings of persuasion research may well lead to more thoughtful consumers and less profitability for some companies. The lingering cultural influence of mind–body dualism among the public may create another barrier, however. This may show up in the popular denigration of academic research as mere ivory-tower theory, which the academic's construction of Dewey's "asylum of refuge" also may encourage.

In any case, if we fail to reorient ourselves, as the casualties from tobacco and other products continue to mount, we could someday find ourselves on board (professionally if not physically) "The Last Train to Nuremberg," to borrow the title from a Pete Seeger song protesting the Vietnam War. Without evidence about the impact of our work on people's lives, we may continue to wonder whether we live in the belly of a (if not the) beast, to adapt a phrase used by an opprobrious Argentinean revolutionary. More modestly, we may at least miss a chance to recover some of the public support that higher education has squandered or otherwise lost during recent decades.

ADDITIONAL PRAGMATIST IMPLICATIONS

At this point, this chapter may leave readers with an excessively simplified impression. The ideas of pragmatist philosophers may seem to mesh neatly with contemporary media-effects research if scholars examine questions that some in the field might rather ignore and expand the scope of media education. The truth, however, is not quite so neat. I discuss the following ideas partly for completeness. Some recur among various pragmatists, whereas others appear in the work of a single figure such as Dewey. Scholars, of course, can accept some and reject others.

One purported problem can be handled rather easily. Because of Peirce's widely cited pragmatist maxim, some scholars (e.g., Abel, 1966–1967) have linked pragmatism with operationalism. As readers may recognize, versions of the maxim have been implicit in the arguments contained in portions of this chapter. As originally articulated in 1878, Peirce's maxim read: "Consider what effects, that might conceivably have practical bearings, we conceive the object of our conception to have. Then our conception of these effects is the whole of our conception of our object" (cited in Murphy, 1990, p. 27). This could only suggest that operational definitions specify meaning, rendering conceptual ones inapplicable. Of course, modern media research relies heavily on both (see Chaffee, 1991). A later version of Peirce's maxim, however, stated,

> In order to ascertain the meaning of an intellectual conception one should consider what practical consequences might conceivably result by necessity from the truth of that conception; and the sum of these consequences will constitute the entire meaning of the conception. (cited in Burks, 1951, p. 43)

Such a conception could range in length from a single word to an entire book or monograph (e.g., Shoemaker, 1991) or even more. Nothing here would treat conceptual definitions as inapplicable. Rather their meaning would arise from their implications for research practice or for other forms of action. In addition, drawing an absolute distinction between conceptual and operational definitions could involve exactly the kind of split that many pragmatists have always warned against accepting uncritically. Beyond this, Hayes et al. (1988) warned that use of nonfunctional (i.e., noncontextual) conceptualizations may inject mechanism into otherwise contextualist research, such as Skinner's. Even so, their use is at least consistent with methodical pragmatism. The emphasis on conceptual definition and explication is a consequence of philosophy's 20th-century linguistic turn (Quine, 1981) and the related ideal language school (see Diesing, 1991). The linguistic turn transferred criteria of meaning first from ideas to words and then from words to sentences. Finally, Quine (1981) advocated shifting meaning from sentences to series of sentences.

In communication research, pragmatism has often been associated with qualitative, instead of quantitative, methods. Despite this, nothing inherent in it suggests that a social scientist reject a priori controlled experimentation, causal analyses, or what not. Instead, pragmatists (e.g., Blumer, 1967; Kaplan, 1964) have repeatedly argued that scholars should be free to choose whatever methods prove fruitful in dealing with their subject matter. Philosophers, most obviously logical empiricists but (presumably) even pragmatists, should not dictate orders (Kaplan, 1964). Thus, communication researchers should not merely imitate what has worked in other sciences or what philosophers see as the essence of science. These may or may not be applicable with communication phenomena. One should judge methods instead by the consequences of their use.

Yet Dewey's psychological ideas were a bit more radical than this. Allport (1939/1968) noted his tendency to reject areas of psychology, such as the theory of fixed instincts, that seemed to Dewey undemocratic. Shockingly, Dewey did so on the basis of ideological affiliation alone, rather than evidence. This position clearly conflicts with Dewey's refusal to subordinate science to morality and his advocacy of the autonomy of inquiry (see his introduction to Dewey, 1927/1946). Therefore, to my mind, one need not take it seriously.

More significant, Dewey detected relics of dualism in the field, which traditionally has assumed a mind–body monism. This framed his extremely influential (1896) reflex-arc critique. The "older dualism of body and soul finds a distinct echo in the current dualism of stimulus and response," Dewey wrote (p. 358). Similar to the means–ends dualism, this is inappropriate in part because what a perceiver takes as a stimulus depends on prior response and his or her purposes. For instance, when a child sees a flame, it is "the movement of body, head and eye muscles determining what is experienced" (p. 358). It becomes a stimulus only when a child chooses to attend to it. Beyond this, stimulus–response psychology leads to a "patchwork of disjointed parts, a mechanical conception of unallied processes" (p. 358). Instead, stimulus and response serve as functional distinctions within a broader circuit of behavior, he maintained.

This could pose difficulties for effects research. Even so, Allport (1939/1968) overstated things: "Evolving circuits there may indeed be . . . but spiraling processes make orderly analysis in terms of separate variables impossible" (p. 349). According to Ryan (1995), Dewey merely wanted to see more subtle interpretations of laboratory learning experiments. Gifford and Hayes (1999) maintained that B. F. Skinner's functional distinction of stimulus and response echoes Dewey's 1896 argument. Other scholars (e.g., Mounce, 1997) disputed this. In any case, Wenner's (1985) transactional models of media uses and effects describe a way to at least begin to accommodate such ideas within variable-analytic frameworks. In my view, one implication of rejection of a dualism of stimulus and response should be an expectation that media effects will occur conditionally (McLeod & Reeves, 1980). Their nature and degree of presence will depend on how individuals interpret stimuli such as violence (Mounce,

1997). This implies that education could play a vital role in mitigating these effects among those exposed, as some research (see Rosenthal, 1986) has demonstrated.

A final objection might be that, by stressing the need to communicate knowledge as broadly as possible, Dewey's participatory pragmatism could undermine substantial portions of communication and psychological science. If everyone understood the factors that influence behavior, many of these might no longer apply (see Apel, 1977; Gergen, 1973). Scientific psychology, for instance, could cancel itself out. A consideration of real-world consequences yields my final response. At some point, one can only say, "I certainly would hope so."

REFERENCES

Abel, R. (1966–1967). Pragmatism and the outlook of modern science. *Philosophy and Phenomenological Research*, 27, 45–54.

Allport, G. (1968). Dewey's individual and social psychology. In G. Allport (Ed.), *The person in psychology* (pp. 326–354). Boston: Beacon. (Original work published 1939)

Apel, K. (1977). The a priori of communication and the foundation of the humanities. In F. R. Dallmayr & T. A. McCarthy (Eds.), *Understanding and social inquiry* (pp. 292–315). Notre Dame, IN: University of Notre Dame Press.

Auxier, R. (1995). The decline of evolutionary naturalism in later pragmatism. In R. Hollinger & D. Depew (Eds.), *Pragmatism: From progressivism to postmodernism* (pp. 180–207). Westport, CT: Praeger.

Ayer, A. J. (1936). *Language, truth, and logic.* New York: Oxford University Press.

Barone, D. F., Maddux, J. E., & Snyder, C. R. (1997). *Social cognitive psychology: History and current domains.* New York: Plenum.

Blumer, H. (1967). Threats from agency-determined research: The case of Camelot. In I. L. Horowitz (Ed.), *The rise and fall of Project Camelot: Studies in the relationship between social science and practical politics* (pp. 153–174). Cambridge, MA: MIT Press.

Burks, A. W. (1951). Charles Sanders Peirce: Introduction. In M. H. Fisch (Ed.), *Classic American philosophers* (pp. 41–53). New York: Appleton-Century-Crofts.

Carey, J. W. (1989). *Communication as culture: Essays on media and society.* Boston: Unwin Hyman.

Carter, R. F. (1989). On paradigmatic productivity. In B. Dervin, L. Grossberg, B. J. O'Keefe, & E. Wartella (Eds.), *Rethinking communication: Volume 1. Paradigm issues* (pp. 144–147). Newbury Park, CA: Sage.

Centerwall, B. S. (1989). Exposure to television as a cause of violence. In G. Comstock (Ed.), *Public communication and behavior* (Vol. 2, pp. 1–58). Orlando, FL: Academic Press.

Centerwall, B. S. (1992). Television and violence: The scale of the problem and where to go from here. *Journal of the American Medical Association*, 267, 3059–3063.

Chaffee, S. H. (1991). *Communication concepts 1: Explication.* Newbury Park, CA: Sage.

Cialdini, R. B. (1988). *Influence: Science and practice* (2nd ed.). New York: HarperCollins.

Cohen, J., & Cohen, P. (1983). *Applied multiple regression/correlation analysis for the behavioral sciences* (2nd ed.). Hillsdale, NJ: Lawrence Erlbaum Associates.

Deen, T. (1999, March 4). *U.N. health arm seeks global treaty against smoking.* Inter Press Service. Available: Lexis-Nexis, allnews files.

Dewey, J. (1896). The reflex arc concept in psychology. *The Psychological Review, 3*, 357–370.

Dewey, J. (1929a). *Experience and nature* (2nd ed.). LaSalle, IL: Open Court.

Dewey, J. (1929b). *The quest for certainty: A study of the relation of knowledge and action.* New York: Minton, Balch.

Dewey, J. (1938). *Logic: The theory of inquiry.* New York: Holt.

Dewey, J. (1946). *The public and its problems.* Chicago: Gateway. (Original work published 1927)

Dewey, J. (1957). *Human nature and conduct.* New York: The Modern Library. (Original work published 1922)

Dewey, J. (1958). *Art as experience.* New York: Capricorn Books. (Original work published 1934)

Dewey, J. (1973). The development of American pragmatism. In J. J. McDermott (Ed.), *The philosophy of John Dewey: Vol. 1. The structure of experience* (pp. 41–58). New York: Putnam Sons. (Original work published 1925)

Dewey, J. (1981). Individuality in our day. In J. A. Boydston (Ed.), *The later works, 1925–1953/ John Dewey* (Vol. 5, pp. 111–123). Carbondale, IL: Southern Illinois University Press. (Original work published 1930)

Diesing, P. (1991). *How does social science work? Reflections on practice.* Pittsburgh, PA: University of Pittsburgh Press.

Donovan, R. (1995). Rorty's pragmatism and the linguistic turn. In R. Hollinger & D. Depew (Eds.), *Pragmatism: From progressivism to postmodernism* (pp. 208–223). Westport, CT: Praeger.

Duhem, P. (1990). Logical examination of physical theory. *Synthese, 83,* 183–188. (Original work published 1913)

Elliott, S. (1999, August 2). Reversing the message, ad agencies switch sides. *The New York Times,* pp. C1, C13.

Fenigstein, A. (1979). Does aggression cause a preference for viewing media violence? *Journal of Personality and Social Psychology, 37,* 2307–2317.

Festinger, L. (1957). *A theory of cognitive dissonance.* Stanford, CA: Stanford University Press.

Georgoudi, M., & Rosnow, R. L. (1985). Notes toward a contextualist understanding of social psychology. *Personality and Social Psychology Bulletin, 11,* 5–22.

Gerbner, G. (1983). The importance of being critical—In one's own fashion. *Journal of Communication, 33*(3), 355–362.

Gergen, K. J. (1973). Social psychology as history. *Journal of Personality and Social Psychology, 26,* 309–320.

Gibson, R. F. (1988). *Enlightened empiricism: An examination of W. V. Quine's theory of knowledge.* Gainesville, FL: University Presses of South Florida.

Gifford, E. V., & Hayes, S. C. (1999). Functional contextualism: A pragmatic philosophy for behavioral science. In W. O'Donohue & R. Kitchener (Eds.), *Handbook of behaviorism* (pp. 285–327). San Diego, CA: Academic Press.

Gillespie, D. (1992). *The mind's we: Contextualism in cognitive psychology.* Carbondale, IL: Southern Illinois University Press.

Gonzalez, H. (1988). The evolution of communication as a field. *Communication Research, 15,* 302–308.

Greenwood, J. D. (1990). Two dogmas of neo-empiricism: The "theory-informity" of observation and the Quine-Duhem thesis. *Philosophy of Science, 57,* 553–574.

Grossman, D. (1998, August 10). Trained to kill. *Christianity Today,* pp. 1–8.

Hayes, S. C., Hayes, L. J., & Reese, H. W. (1988). Finding the philosophical core: A review of Stephen C. Pepper's *World hypotheses: A study in evidence. Journal of the Experimental Analysis of Behavior, 50,* 97–111.

Hesse, M. (1980). *Revolutions and reconstructions in the philosophy of science.* Bloomington, IN: Indiana University Press.

Hickman, L. A. (1995). Pragmatism, technology, and scientism: Are the methods of the sci-entific-technical disciplines relevant to social problems? In R. Hollinger & D. Depew (Eds.), *Pragmatism: From progressivism to postmodernism* (pp. 72–87). Westport, CT: Praeger.

Hook, S. (1964, April 12). Pornography and the censor. *The New York Times Book Review*, pp. 1, 38–39.

Hook, S. (1980). Are there limits to freedom of expression? In S. Hook (Ed.), *Philosophy and public policy* (pp. 124–129). Carbondale, IL: Southern Illinois University Press.

Hook, S. (1981). Introduction. In J. A. Boydston (Ed.), *The later works, 1925–1953/John Dewey* (Vol. 1, pp. vii–xxiii). Carbondale, IL: Southern Illinois University Press.

Huesmann, L. R., & Eron, L. D. (1986). *Television and the aggressive child: A cross-national com-parison.* Hillsdale, NJ: Lawrence Erlbaum Associates.

Hunt, S. D. (1991). *Modern marketing theory: Critical issues in the philosophy of marketing science.* Cincinnati, OH: South-Western.

James, W. (1907). *Pragmatism: A new name for some old ways of thinking.* New York: Longmans.

James, W. (1909). *The meaning of truth.* New York: Longmans.

James, W. (1967). A world of pure experience. In J. J. McDermott (Ed.), *The writings of Wil-liam James* (pp. 194–214). New York: Random House. (Original work published 1912)

Kaplan, A. (1964). *The conduct of inquiry.* San Francisco: Chandler.

Klee, R. (1992). In defense of the Quine–Duhem thesis: A reply to Greenwood. *Philosophy of Science, 59,* 487–491.

Kuhn, T. S. (1970). *The structure of scientific revolutions* (2nd ed.). Chicago: The University of Chicago Press.

Kurtz, P. (1990). *Philosophical essays in pragmatic naturalism.* Buffalo, NY: Prometheus.

Kurtz, P. (1992). *The new skepticism: Inquiry and reliable knowledge.* Buffalo, NY: Prometheus.

Manicus, P. T. (1998). John Dewey and American social science. In L. A. Hickman (Ed.), *Reading Dewey: Interpretations for a postmodern generation* (pp. 43–62). Bloomington, IN: In-diana University Press.

McGuire, W. J. (1986). The myth of massive media impact: Savagings and salvagings. In G. Comstock (Ed.), *Public communication and behavior* (Vol. 1, pp. 173–257). Orlando, FL: Ac-ademic Press.

McLeod, J. M., & Reeves, B. (1980). On the nature of mass media effects. In S. B. Withey & R. P. Abeles (Eds.), *Television and social behavior: Beyond violence and children* (pp. 17–54). Hillsdale, NJ: Lawrence Erlbaum Associates.

Medved, M. (1999, April 29). Nonstop kids' TV: It's time to face real media culprit. *USA To-day,* p. 15A.

Merritt, D. (1995). *Public journalism and public life: Why telling the news is not enough.* Hillsdale, NJ: Lawrence Erlbaum Associates.

Morris, C. W. (1932). *Six theories of mind.* Chicago: The University of Chicago Press.

Morris, C. W. (1946). *Signs, language, and behavior.* New York: Braziller.

Mounce, H. O. (1997). *The two pragmatisms: From Peirce to Rorty.* London: Routledge.

Murphy, J. P. (1990). *Pragmatism: From Peirce to Davidson.* Boulder, CO: Westview.

Nevo, I. (1995). James, Quine, and analytic pragmatism. In R. Hollinger & D. Depew (Eds.), *Pragmatism: From progressivism to postmodernism* (pp. 153–169). Westport, CT: Praeger.

Newcomb, T. M. (1953). An approach to the study of communicative acts. *Psychological Re-view, 60,* 393–404.

Noelle-Neumann, E. (1983). The effect of media on media effects research. *Journal of Com-munication, 33*(3), 157–165.

Paik, H., & Comstock, G. (1994). The effects of television violence on antisocial behavior: A meta-analysis. *Communication Research, 21,* 516–546.

Pepper, S. C. (1942). *World hypotheses.* Berkeley, CA: University of California Press.

Pepper, S. C. (1982). Metaphor in philosophy. *The Journal of Mind and Behavior, 3,* 197–206. (Original work published 1973)

Perry, D. K. (1988). Implications of a contextualist approach to media-effects research. *Communication Research, 15,* 246–264.

Perry, D. K. (1992). Assessing the import of media-related effects: Some contextualist considerations. *World Communication, 21,* 69–82.

Perry, D. K. (1996a). *Mass communication research, public intellectuals, and the theory of value in pragmatic naturalism: An integrative proposal.* Paper presented to the Mass Communication Division of the International Communication Association, ICA annual conference, Chicago.

Perry, D. K. (1996b). *Theory and research in mass communication: Contexts and consequences.* Mahwah, NJ: Lawrence Erlbaum Associates.

Peters, J. D. (1988). The need for theoretical foundations: Reply to Gonzalez. *Communication Research, 15,* 309–317.

Pierce, J. P., Choi, W. S., Gilpin, E. A., Farkas, A. J., & Berry, C. C. (1998). Tobacco industry promotion of cigarettes and adolescent smoking. *Journal of the American Medical Association, 279,* 511–515.

Pierce, J. P., & Gilpin, E. A. (1995). A historical analysis of tobacco marketing and the uptake of smoking by youth in the United States: 1890–1977. *Health Psychology, 14,* 500–508.

Quine, W. V. (1980). Two dogmas of empiricism. In W. V. Quine (Ed.), *From a logical point of view* (2nd ed., pp. 20–46). Cambridge, MA: Harvard University Press. (Original work published 1951)

Quine, W. V. (1981). The pragmatists' place in empiricism. In R. J. Mulvaney & P. M. Zeltner (Eds.), *Pragmatism: Its sources and prospects* (pp. 23–39). Columbia, SC: University of South Carolina Press.

Quine, W. V., & Ullian, J. S. (1970). *The web of belief.* New York: Random House.

Rorty, R. (1979). *Philosophy and the mirror of nature.* Princeton, NJ: Princeton University Press.

Rorty, R. (1982). *Consequences of pragmatism.* Minneapolis, MN: University of Minnesota Press.

Rorty, R. (1983). Pragmatism without method. In P. Kurtz (Ed.), *Sidney Hook: Philosopher of democracy and humanism* (pp. 259–273). Buffalo, NY: Prometheus.

Rorty, R. (1990). Introduction: Pragmatism as anti-representationalism. In J. P. Murphy, *Pragmatism: From Peirce to Davidson* (pp. 1–6). Boulder, CO: Westview.

Rosen, J. (1994). Making things more public: On the political responsibility of the media intellectual. *Critical Studies in Mass Communication, 11,* 363–388.

Rosenthal, R. (1986). Media violence, antisocial behavior, and the social consequences of small effects. *Journal of Social Issues, 42,* 141–154.

Ryan, A. (1995). *John Dewey and the high tide of American liberalism.* New York: Norton.

Saffer, H., & Chaloupka, F. (1999, February). *Tobacco advertising: Economic theory and international evidence* (Working paper No. 6958). Cambridge, MA: National Bureau of Economic Research.

Scott, J. (1994, August 9). Thinking out loud: The public intellectual is reborn. *The New York Times,* p. B1.

Shoemaker, P. J. (1991). *Communication concepts 3: Gatekeeping.* Newbury Park, CA: Sage.

Toch, H., & MacLean, M. S., Jr. (1962). Perception, communication and educational research: A transactional view. *Audio Visual Communication Review, 10*(5), 55–77.

U.S. Federal Bureau of Investigation (annual volumes). *Uniform crime reports for the United States.* Washington, DC: U.S. Government Printing Office.

Wartella, E. (1994). Challenge to the profession. *Communication Education, 43,* 54–62.

Wenner, L. A. (1985). Transaction and media gratifications research. In K. E. Rosengren, L. A. Wenner, & P. Palmgreen (Eds.), *Media gratifications research: Current perspectives* (pp. 73–94). Beverly Hills, CA: Sage.

Westbrook, R. B. (1991). *John Dewey and American democracy.* Ithaca, NY: Cornell University Press.

Wood, W., Wong, F. Y., & Chachere, J. S. (1991). Effects of media violence on viewers' aggression in unconstrained social interaction. *Psychological Bulletin, 109,* 371–383.

Chapter 10

Intersections of Feminism and Pragmatism: Possibilities for Communication Theory and Research

Sherianne Shuler
The University of Alabama

Melissa Tate
Samford University

Communication scholars (e.g., Cronen, 1995; Langsdorf & Smith, 1995; Shepherd & Rothenbuhler, in press) appear to show increased interest in incorporating pragmatist perspectives. In a much-cited essay, Craig (1989) argued for an acknowledgment of communication as a practical discipline and for a renewed commitment of scholars to praxis—a nurturing of the dialectic between theory and practice. Scholars should not view praxis as base utilitarianism, but rather as "a way of emphasizing this fuller practice of reflectively informed, morally accountable human action" (Craig & Tracy, 1995, p. 249). To embrace praxis is not simply to engage in amoral theorizing about communication so as to apply scholarly theories in the real world. Rather, we should see the wedding of conceptual thought and situated action as an ongoing, hermeneutic process. It is "a formal, scholarly enterprise that attempts to extend, facilitate, and inform this reflective cycle of thought and action by engaging in systematic, critical study and theoretical reconstruction of practices in society" (p. 252). A commitment to praxis shapes our theories, rather than simply guiding what happens to them later. Praxis encourages scholars to remain engaged in the world and to study people's real problems.

At this juncture, perhaps, pragmatism most naturally fits with feminist theory. As Deming (1989) observed, to the extent that the goal of praxis places lived experience as central, it is compatible with "feminism's first impulse [of the] recognition of difference between the world encountered by women and the world described and codified as human by the dominant paradigm" (p. 163). Indeed, the developing tradition of feminist praxis is influencing theory and methods both within and outside the communication discipline.

This focus on praxis coincides with theoretical claims of contemporary pragmatists from other fields (e.g., Rorty, 1989; West, 1993) about the centrality of communication in constructing the social world. These scholarly traditions seem well positioned for integration. Nonetheless, their mutual suitability is often overlooked (Seigfried, 1996). Before examining the contemporary compatibilites between pragmatism and feminism, this chapter explores their historical connections. We hope that the juxtaposition of pragmatism and feminism in both historical and contemporary scholarship will influence communication scholars to reclaim and revalue these rich traditions. Finally, the chapter offers a feminist pragmatist research exemplar to serve as a call for praxis in communication scholarship.

LIBERATORY IMPULSES IN EARLY PRAGMATISM

Seigfried's (1996) work provides a historical account of the early pragmatists' public and scholarly (if not personal) marginalization of women scholars' work. Her work furnishes the context to help explain why pragmatist scholarship has not often been viewed through a feminist lens, but also offers hope for the emergence of a new feminist pragmatism that responds to social advances. This chapter discusses some of the ideas of three early pragmatists: William James, John Dewey, and Charles S. Peirce. In particular, feminist scholars can see some of their views as both liberating and empowering. These include their focus on the social nature of truth, inquiry as grounded in experience, and science as a value-laden human creation. Reviewing some of their work with a feminist theoretical lens produces interesting, fitting compatibilities. We discuss Seigfried's work in the next section in detail.

According to James (1909/1977), pragmatism's notions about the nature of truth provide the key to understanding it:

> Pragmatism asks its usual question. "Grant an idea or belief to be true" it says, "what concrete difference will its being true make in any one's actual life? What experiences [may] be different from those which would obtain if the belief were false? How will the truth be realized? What, in short, is the truth's cash-value in experiential terms." (p. 311)

Further, he pointed out, "The truth of an idea is not a stagnant property inherent in it. Truth happens to an idea. It becomes true, is made true by events" (p. 312).

This understanding of truth as based in experience, rather than as absolute and universal, was a liberating idea in its time (and, indeed, is in ours). Instead of seeing truth as eternal, James (1907/1977) conceived of it as historically contingent:

> Our rights, wrongs, prohibitions, penalties, words, forms, idioms, beliefs, are so many new creations that add themselves as fast as history proceeds. Far from being antecedent principles that animate the process, law, language, truth are but abstract names for its results. (p. 450)

Although, as a pragmatist, James embraced the possibilities of science and the scientific method, many of his ideas more closely resemble those of the postmodern thinkers than those of modern-day positivists. The pragmatist method, James argued, is not the search for absolutes. Rather, it is "The attitude of looking away from first things, principles, 'categories,' supposed necessities; and of looking towards last things, fruits, consequences, facts" (1907/1977, p. 380). In addition, James' pragmatism recognized that science is a human activity. As such, science should not seek some kind of absolute truth outside of human activity and tradition. Such truth does not exist. Indeed, "the trail of the human serpent is thus over everything" (p. 384). Similarly, Peirce prized science and its method, but he saw pragmatism as a "cultural demystifying activity" (West, 1989, p. 44) that treated science as a value-laden human practice.

Likewise, Dewey (1989) was an avid proponent of the use of science to better society. He took care not to overstate its place, however. In contrast to the prevailing beliefs of his time (which remain today), Dewey asserted, "it is no longer possible to hold the simple faith of the Enlightenment that assured advance of science will produce free institutions by dispelling ignorance and superstition: the sources of human servitude and the pillars of oppressive government" (p. 102). Here, Dewey acknowledged that scientists cannot always be counted on to advance positive human realities with their knowledge, but he did not give up on the potential contributions of science either.

Dewey (1927/1991) also argued against seeing science as something that stands outside or above other discourse. All belief should be thought of as experimental and subject to revision in the face of new evidence. Putnam (1995) called this the ideal of "democratically conducted inquiry" (p. 74). This, he argued, was an important methodological commitment of the early pragmatists. To Putnam, democratically conducted inquiry is most valued "not because it is infallible, but because the way in which we will find out where and how our procedures need to be revised is through the process of inquiry itself" (pp. 74–75).

Like James, Dewey (1958) asserted that all intellectual activity, including science, is partial. To him,

man (sic) is within nature, not a little god outside, and is within as a mode of
energy inseparably connected with other modes, interaction is the one unes-
capable trait of every human concern; thinking, even philosophic thinking,
is not exempt. (p. 434)

Because all human activities exist within interaction, all intellectual discourse is subject to the bias, partialities, and values of its users. Recognizing this does not diminish the role of scholarship, but it disallows notions of pure research conducted by experts removed from practical
affairs. For Dewey (1927/1991), it also leads to a commitment to connect
theory with practice. This link means that the intellectual class' knowledge
will be useful to society only if subjected to broad public scrutiny and debate.

It is one-sided to describe Peirce only in terms of logic, rationalism, and
his technical approach to semiotics (West, 1989). As a devout Christian,
Peirce constantly sought to integrate his commitments to the advances of
science, to community, and to love. Peirce's efforts eventually took shape
in *agapism*. Agapism challenged Darwin by asserting that love, rather than
natural selection, powers evolution. West (1989) argued that Peirce developed this idea of evolutionary love to counter what he saw as an encour-
agement of selfish individualism, Darwin's own "gospel of greed," being
projected onto nature. Although James and Dewey made clear that truth
and science are inherently value laden, Peirce most clearly couched these
concepts in moral discourse.

As Seigfried (1996) pointed out, early pragmatism is amenable to feminism in many ways. Its "emphasis on the reciprocity of theory and praxis,
knowledge and action, facts and values follows from its post-Darwinian understanding of human experience, including cognition, as a developmental, historically contingent process" (p. 7). Why then did the writings of
Dewey, James, and Peirce not reflect this logical fit? Part of the answer lies
in the historical contingency of their work and the common, uncritical acceptance of patriarchical discourse. Despite the early pragmatists' disap-
pointing scholarly blindness, Seigfried (1996) noted that mentoring relationships with them empowered a number of woman scholars. We next
explore this paradox in detail.

FEMINISM AND PRAGMATISM: A LOST TRADITION

Although this book attempts to relocate and recover the tradition of
American pragmatism in communication theory and research, this chapter concerns the possibilities inherent in recognizing the mutual influ-

ences of pragmatism and feminism. Acknowledging the buried influence of feminism on early pragmatist thought makes moving forward to new scholarly possibilities more fruitful.

Seigfried's (1996) work both sympathizes with and criticizes early pragmatists in her fascinating account of the historical feminist–pragmatist connection. On the one hand, she cited many instances in which Dewey and James encouraged and supported women students; on the other hand, they remained silent about their mutual influence. Both James and Dewey advocated women's co-education and helped empower and encourage their female students to challenge the academic system in various ways. Unfortunately, due to their gender, several of James' students were not awarded Ph.D. degrees from Harvard despite completing degree requirements. Even if they obtained their degrees, women had limited professional opportunities (Seigfried, 1996). The early pragmatists' women students typically were barred from positions on academic faculties despite recommendations from their mentors. This limited their scholarly status and influence. Despite being supportive of women students, James (and, to a lesser extent, Dewey) uncritically accepted the naturalization of gender differences and perpetuated male-dominated views of the world (Seigfried, 1996).

The omission of feminism in Dewey's scholarship is particularly vexing. He was an outspoken public advocate of many feminist causes, such as women's rights to birth control, economic equality, and co-education. For example, Dewey wrote an article in support of co-education for the *Ladies Home Journal*. Nonetheless, he did not incorporate these profeminist ideals into his other philosophical writings. In addition, privately Dewey lavishly recognized the influences of women on his scholarship (Seigfried, 1996). Seigfried argued that Dewey maintained a very significant relationship with Jane Addams and many other female students, educators, and philosophers. Although he thanked these women scholars in dedications, acknowledgment pages, and personal correspondence, he failed to credit them within his scholarship. Unfortunately, this silence has been perpetuated over the years by many male philosophers' exclusion of women scholars from philosophical discussions and from collections of pragmatist work. Clearly an oppressive social system for women surrounded and constrained the early pragmatists, but they also perpetuated it.

Even so, Seigfried (1996) contended that the pluralistic ideals of pragmatism can help further feminist goals. At its heart, pragmatism is "founded on the centrality of praxis with its emancipatory goals" (p. 9). Combining this with the pragmatist focus on the centrality of communication makes both pragmatism and feminism very powerful for contemporary communication theory and research. We explore these connections next.

CONTEMPORARY INTERSECTIONS OF FEMINISM
AND PRAGMATISM

Several contemporary feminists and pragmatists see a historical, current, and potentially positive theoretical and methodological relationship between feminism and pragmatism. Rooney (1993) claimed that the pragmatism of Peirce, James, and Dewey and feminist epistemology share important characteristics and would benefit mutually from a critical dialectical relationship. She said, "Pragmatist reflections on the role of reason and philosophy in a changing world encourage us to see that philosophy's most creative and most responsible future must also be a feminist one" (p. 15). Both traditions link philosophy to new possibilities of action and power, and both resist the "inherited dichotomies, dualisms, and disjunctions," especially the separation of theory and praxis, of traditional philosophy (p. 16). Each, Rooney contended, is "perched between the past and the future, with a focus both on historical contexts and future relevance and responsibility" (p. 18). As Rooney pointed out, both embrace what is historically and contemptuously regarded as feminine epistemology. This includes the interrelationship between the knower and known; the moving nature of belief; the roles of action, body, and experience in "truth"; and the rejection of correspondence and foundationalism "under" truth. Rooney claimed that both traditions view knowledge as something that people learn to have and do socially, in context, through language and communication, with a strong affective, qualitative component.

Seigfried (1991) encouraged a "feminist revisioning of pragmatism and a pragmatist version of feminism" (p. 1). She contended that today's feminists would view as strengths characteristics of pragmatist philosophy that caused its marginalization after World War II. These include its antipositivist interpretation of science, its recognition of the value dimension of facts, and its location of aesthetics in everyday experience. Other reasons include the dominance of other discourse; its preference for social, cultural, and political issues rather than logical ones; its alignment of theory with praxis; and its emphasis on experience instead of epistemology.

Two aspects of pragmatism that likely led to its marginalization particularly appeal to feminism. These are pragmatists' position linking categorization with value judgments and the feminine nature of their philosophy. Seigfried contended that the philosophy of the early pragmatists (except Peirce) is stereotypically feminine in style, at least in terms of characteristics associated with women during the late 19th and early 20th centuries. These include a penchant for indirect, metaphorical discourse rather than a deductive and reductively symbolic one, the concreteness of pragmatist methodology, and their tendency to philosophize out of their own experience and everyday problems. Pragmatists' priority of human relations and actual experiences rather than abstract conceptual distinctions, their goal of shared understanding and communal problem solving rather than rationally forced conclusions from philosophical discourse, their valuing of inclusiveness and community instead of exaggerated claims of autonomy and detachment, and their developmental rather than rule-governed ethics represent other reasons. As Siegfried argued,

> When separation, generalization, sharp boundaries, and the drive to reduce the multiplicity of experience into as few categories as possible are categorized as masculine, then inclusiveness, concreteness, vagueness, tolerance of ambiguities, and pluralism are seen as feminine. But these latter traits are also characteristic of pragmatist thinking. (p. 12)

Harding (1986) did not discuss the feminine nature of pragmatism, and her understanding of the social nature of the categories of *male* and *female* certainly would not allow her to accept James' views about essential feminine nature. In contrast, Harding (1986) embraced feminist standpoint theory. This is premised on the recognition that women (and other marginalized groups) occupy social positions that allow them a less distorted understanding of the social world than those who inhabit more privileged positions.

Science, Harding argued, is not a sacred and objective activity that is removed from the world. Rather, it is fundamentally social. The early pragmatists would agree with this, but Harding also foregrounded the role of the social category of gender on the creation of scholarship. "Far from inhabiting a single society, women and men appear to live in different worlds. But it is only the men's world that social science takes to be the social world" (Harding, 1986, p. 89). Scientists who masquerade as objective often deride feminist scholarship as biased. Harding argued, however, that it is "only coercive values—racism, classism, sexism—that deteriorate objectivity; it is participatory values—antiracism, anticlassism, antisexism—that decrease the distortions and mystifications in our culture's explanations and understandings" (p. 249). The recognition that politics and dogmatism structure science, Harding (1986) contended, is the first step to creating more liberatory scholarship.

The interconnection of experience and scholarship in both theory and methods is key to distinguishing feminist scholarship. Although there is nothing inherently feminist or antifeminist about any research method, Harding (1987) argued that there are methodologies and epistemologies that are more or less feminist. Some shared commitments for the nature of good social research make feminist inquiry unique. These include a focus on women's experiences as valid and valuable resources, developing findings useful to women, and the location of the researcher on the same plane as research subjects or participants. As they attempt to connect the two traditions, contemporary feminist pragmatists such as Harding embrace these commitments.

Seigfried (1991) agreed that Harding's (1987) three commitments of feminist analysis correspond well with pragmatic inquiry. Further, Seigfried contended, pragmatism insists on the specific, the historical, the material, and the contextual. That context, she concluded, includes class, gender, race, and sexual preference. Schwandt (1994) claimed that feminist standpoint theories and pragmatism can work together because they use critical theories to analyze material conditions of women's lives. They share a postmodern concern for ethnography that opens to scrutiny the "inquirer's history, values, and assumptions," and they examine the social construction of the research process and its "continuous reflexivity" (p. 128). A feminist–pragmatist position means that we can respect informants' attempts to make sense of their lives. Scholars can conduct interpretive work that includes exchanging ideas and viewpoints with informants and judging them against the realities of their lives rather than against our standards, "without claiming that either inquirer or actor is the final arbiter of understanding" (p. 132).

In addition to shaping methodological commitments, feminist pragmatism may influence the purpose and goals of our scholarship. As Seigfried (1996) pointed out, a pragmatic approach often requires that we set aside pure theoretical beliefs to decide on actions. In addition, she argued that a goal of feminist pragmatism is to build temporary coalitions and seek possible political unities. It can do so by determining "what mechanisms—social, institutional, educational, political, and cultural—open possibilities of consensual decision making and revisioning in light of desired, eventual, concrete outcomes and which ones preclude or diminish it" (p. 275).

Building temporary coalitions is a goal of feminist pragmatism that neopragmatist Richard Rorty echoed. He called this the *construction of solidarities*. Rorty (1989) pictured utopia as populated by liberals who think "cruelty is the worst thing we do" (p. 85) and who are universally committed to ironism. Ironism recognizes the contingency of all beliefs and desires, even the most central ones. In the liberal ironist utopian society, making *them* part of *us* creates solidarity.

Rorty (1989) argued that feelings of solidarity depend on "which similarities and differences strike us as salient" (p. 192). Of course, these choices are also historically contingent. He argued that solidarity will not come from recognizing some essential human characteristics that everyone shares. Instead, it involves the ability to see "differences (of tribe, religion, race, customs, and the like) as unimportant when compared with similarities with respect to pain and humiliation—the ability to think of people wildly different from ourselves as included in the range of 'us.' " Rorty argued that these solidarities will not emerge naturally, but must be created. In fact, they should be sought. "We should stay on the lookout for marginalized people—people whom we still instinctively think of as 'they' rather than 'us' " (p. 196), and we should try to create solidarity with them. These solidarities can occur, according to Rorty, if we embrace the conception of contingent truth proposed by James and other early pragmatists.

Although Rorty (1989) acknowledged the external world, he contended that it does not make sense to call it true or false. Only sentences can be true or false. Because humans create false sentences, truths are also human creations. Part of the language game that we play is the constant creation of new language and, therefore, of new truth. This linguistically based pragmatism, Rorty (1991) argued, is a tool for feminists. To change the linguistic truth of gender oppression requires that the cultural discourse about women move toward "semantic realization" of what women are (p. 235). "Gays, blacks, and women will succeed in inventing moral identities when their language is spoken by everybody, when society comes to terms with something new" (p. 249). Eventually, he contended, changed language will appear in society at large, and opinions will change.

Rorty (1993) later suggested that forms of feminism are appropriate models of alternative social practices for modern intellectuals, and others may be less useful. For example, deconstruction may show that practices and objects, including masculine repression of the feminine, are social constructs. He disagreed with attempting to use deconstruction to reach the essence underneath ideology. No such thing exists, Rorty argued. Beyond demonstrating the social construction of gender (and other categories), deconstruction loses its usefulness, he argued. It cannot help us decide "which constructs to keep and which to replace, or in finding substitutes for the latter" (p. 99). What matters "is what we can do to persuade people to act differently than in the past" (p. 100).

Rorty (1993) argued that pragmatism is gender neutral, but can be an effective tool. It does not offer "deep secrets." Instead, it can provide:

> advice on how to reply when masculinists attempt to make present practices seem inevitable. Neither pragmatists nor deconstructionists can do more for feminism than help rebut attempts to ground these practices on something deeper than an contingent historical fact—the fact that the people with the

slightly larger muscles have been bullying the people with the slightly smaller muscles for a very long time. (p. 101)

One contemporary pragmatist, Cornel West (e.g., 1993), advocated a brand of pragmatism that is especially amenable to feminist pragmatist inquiry. His prophetic pragmatism builds on ideas of James and Dewey about the social nature of truth but goes further. West argued that "the condition of truth to emerge must be in tune with those who are undergoing social misery—socially induced forms of suffering" (p. 4). A sense of the tragic is a crucial element that pragmatists must hold in bringing about this alliance with those suffering. This sense results from acknowledging evil that propels us to seek justice with hope and a sense of the possibilities for righting social wrongs. A Christian theology that locates love in the center of human life influences West, much like it affected Peirce.

West is located politically within the disciplines of Religious Studies and African-American Studies. Nonetheless, like other pragmatists, he has much to say about the philosophy of communication. According to West (1993), "People don't live on arguments. They are influenced by arguments, we hope. But, they don't live on arguments. They live on love, care, respect, touch, and so forth" (p. 24). Taking such statements to support the cliche that "actions speak louder than words" mischaracterizes West's position, however. He also argued that "there is no such things as a purely intellectual form of assertion which has no element of action about it. An opinion is a deed. It is a deed intended to guide other deeds" (p. 38).

The juxtaposition of these arguments provides an excellent example of West's commitment to praxis, which he ultimately recognized as being in concert with feminist goals in theory and research. West (1993) discussed the practical feminist problem of how to reorganize the family to respond to the changing roles of women without leaving children behind. He argued, "it becomes incumbent upon those of us, the feminist movement and those who support them with goodwill, to come up with relations of nurturing that are de-patriarchalized" (p. 25). As Putnam (1995) argued, James was "concerned with real hungers, and whose thought, whatever its shortcomings, provides substantial food for thought—and not just for thought, but for life" (p. 23). Given his similar commitments and his Jamesian understanding of a *plastic* universe and truth that is still and always being made, West's prophetic pragmatism fits the feminist contention that all of our theorizing has both moral and practical consequences. Both feminist and pragmatist scholars seek to embrace this notion and use it to shape and inform their work. They do not try to avoid or deny the influence of their experience on science.

Some feminists understandably are cautious about the simplistic way that neopragmatists such as Rorty and West invoke feminism. Fraser (1989, 1991, 1995) responded skeptically to Rorty's call to use pragmatist tools to redescribe gender linguistically and create new vocabularies. The women's movement is too broad and heterogeneous to evoke a single linguistic redescription, she warned, and even in Rorty's pragmatist ideal of free and unfettered conversation, not everyone is heard equally. Fraser and other feminists (e.g., Harding, 1986) wonder who will be empowered to create the appropriate new descriptions of women that Rorty advocates. Indeed, although Harding (1986) called Rorty's (1979) earlier work *illuminating*, she also labeled it *nonfeminist* and casted doubt on women's inclusion in the conversation. Harding (1986) asked, "how can we have the 'conversation of Mankind' (sic) when those who conduct the heretofore politically powerful conversations have such limited tastes, indeed poor tastes, in conversational partners?" (p. 194).

Fraser (1995) suggested that feminist philosophers consider an "impure, eclectic, neopragmatic approach" that would "encompass the full range of processes by which the sociocultural meanings of gender are constructed and contested . . . [and] would maximize our ability to contest the current gender hegemony and to build a feminist counterhegemony" (p. 158). In addition to the gender struggle, she argued, other intersections of difference and power exist. These include class, race/ethnicity, sexuality, nationality, and age. The frameworks to study such structures must accommodate both small- and large-scale objects of inquiry, contextual and connective forms of inquiry, and inquiry that will allow fallible historical accounts as well as projections of emancipatory and utopian hopes and futures. Language, meaning, and signification need to be "socially and historically contextualized, situated in time and place, institutionally and structurally grounded," as well as "linked to other modes of critical theorizing," including "analyses of institutions and political economy" (p. 160) she claimed. According to Fraser, "We should adopt the pragmatic view that there are a plurality of different angles from which sociocultural phenomena can be understood. Which is best will depend on one's purposes" (p. 166). She admitted that we do not know precisely how an "eclectic, neopragmatist feminist theory will develop. That it should develop—and indeed is developing—seems clear. But its concrete elaboration is a collective task for a political and intellectual movement" (pp. 167–168).

One means of such concrete elaboration is the conduct of feminist pragmatist inquiry with emancipatory goals. The preceding review of contemporary feminist–pragmatist philosophy would fall short if it failed to provide examples of contemporary feminist–pragmatist communication research. Rather than briefly touching on several efforts, the final section of this chapter discusses one in detail. Tate (1999) provided a model of what feminist–pragmatist communication research might look like. Perhaps it will lead to more such ambitious efforts.

SEVENTEEN MAGAZINE AND ITS READERS: A FEMINIST–PRAGMATIST COMMUNICATION RESEARCH EXEMPLAR

A pragmatic–feminist standpoint enables us to move beyond theoretical differences to examine who benefits from controlling hegemonic gender discourse. Tate's (1999) recent study of teen girls' readings of *Seventeen* magazine provides a model of praxis in communication research. This study meets Harding's (1987) characteristics of feminist inquiry and Seigfried's (1991) contention that they correspond to pragmatic inquiry. Therefore, we argue that it serves as an exemplar. By examining the world of adolescent girls and seeing their experiences as worthy of research, Tate met the first criterion. Tate took the worlds of teenage girl seriously, rather than dismissing their popular reading material as trivial. Therefore, she overcame elitist and male-centered scholarly tendencies that plague all fields, including communication. Choosing to focus on teen girls and their reading of *Seventeen* met Harding's (1987) second criterion by responding to a problem that women face: Should we support our daughters' reading of *Seventeen*? The wedding of theory with practical problems is especially poignant here. At the theoretical level, she examined meaning, power, and agency in hegemonic texts and consuming audiences. At the practical level, she addressed scholarly and popular criticism of and concern with the consequences of a popular media text on adolescent females. Finally, Tate's use of multiple methods allowed for various perspectives and voices to appear in her text. Significantly, she positioned herself as a mother and an academic. With respect, she gave voice to the perspectives of the young women, whom she interviewed on their turf—their bedrooms.

Following a close analysis of the rhetoric of *Seventeen*, interviews with some of its teen readers, and observation and interrogation of the interpretive context of reading, Tate (1999) concluded that the magazines create a rhetorical vision. This involves an essential, natural, female, middle-class reality obtainable from self-help advice and through the purchase and use of commercial products. She further found wide variation in readers' interests, cognitions, and reactions. These related to ideological messages in the text, the disjunctures between their lives and those the magazine depicts, and the possibility of thinking and acting in opposition to the text. Finally, reading teen magazines involves a relaxing, unengaged visual search for identity models and the consumer products through which teen girls can explore those identity issues, she found.

Tate's (1999) pragmatic–feminist approach recognizes our inability to move outside of our political, linguistic, and performative reality to contest gender oppression. It also notes our ability to conduct resistance at all levels from where we already are. Tate contended that most adolescent and teenage girls are neither interested in nor capable of participation in collective opposition to either gender or economic oppression. Smaller, closer areas of gender resistance are open to them, however. In some cases, *Seventeen* helps them perform—perhaps even incites—those resistances. She found evidence of small personal and interpersonal resistance both within the text of *Seventeen* and in the negotiated readings and private and personal actions of the readers. These include changes in gender depictions that suggest gender parody (Butler, 1990) and the usage of magazines as tools of interpersonal bonding with one another and with their mothers. Finally, the magazine could help them escape from boredom, from their not-so-perfect lives, and from the forces and institutions that control them. These personal and small-group resistances change the reader. At some point, the cumulative effect of small, personal changes will be profound socially and culturally.

The practical question behind this study remains: How should we respond when our daughters bring home *Seventeen*? Although Tate acknowledged the feminist critique of women's magazines, she also admitted enjoying some of the materials in popular magazines and recognized that forbidden media can take on even more significance and appeal for adolescents. She suggested conditional acceptance. This follows Radway's (1991) call for tolerance from privileged, enlightened academic researchers toward readers and writers of what academics might consider *lower* literary forms, such as romance novels. Readers of such materials are "struggling with gender definitions and sexual politics on their own terms, and what they may need most from those of us struggling in other arenas is our support rather than our criticism or direction" (p. 18). Our conditional acceptance of the magazine validates the potential for gender resistance, which *Seventeen* reflects and even encourages. If the magazine helps young women find their voice for resistance and if an adult or parent can use the magazine as a catalyst for discussion, perhaps the gender resistances can be reinforced. Tate pointed out that adults should make alternative materials, including noncommercial and culturally inclusive teen magazines, available for the young reader. She warned that young women ultimately may find resistance to consumer ideology more difficult than opposition to gender ideology. Adults must model options and lives that resist both oppressive gender roles and consumer forces, and they should discuss these with young people (Tate, 1999).

CONCLUSION: THE COMMUNION OF FEMINISM
AND PRAGMATISM

The early pragmatists certainly had blindnesses with regard to feminism and, even more generally, in their treatment of women scholars. Nonetheless, this chapter has argued that the liberatory impulses of the theories of James, Dewey, and Peirce make pragmatism amenable to feminism. Pragmatist ideas about truth as socially produced and contingent, their belief in the importance of conducting inquiry grounded in practical experience, and their insistence that science is a value-laden human activity can be seen as both liberating and empowering to feminist scholars.

For the recent revisionings of the field of communication as a practical discipline (Craig, 1989; Craig & Tracy, 1995; Deming, 1989) to take root, theory must be wed to practice. A renewed commitment to feminist–pragmatist communication research holds great potential for our discipline. Although those outside the field (Rorty, 1989; West, 1993) pointed to the centrality of communication in human community, communication scholars only slowly have adopted this perspective in theory and research (for a recent exception, see Shepherd & Rothenbuhler, in press). The exemplar presented here (Tate, 1999) provides one model for the kinds of questions that feminist–pragmatist scholars should ask and the kind of commitments to method that should guide our inquiry. More such scholarship is needed from our ranks to help communication take its rightful place in the center of academic, civic, and practical discourses.

In addition to conducting research, feminist–pragmatist communication scholars would do well to bring our perspective to bear on issues of public interest and controversy. Dewey's *Ladies Home Journal* article advocating women's co-education provides an interesting example. Although engaging each other in scholarly debate is worthy, feminist–pragmatist communication scholars should not stop there. We should ask ourselves the questions about our scholarship that James asked of truth—What are its consequences?

One contemporary (if often tiresome) issue of public debate and interest that feminist–pragmatist communication scholars are poised to enter involves changing language. According to Rorty (1989), liberal society depends on open-mindedness, a lack of taboo discussions or words, and reliance on persuasion rather than on the use of force. Perhaps some progressive social movements, including many feminisms, have focused too much on the creation of taboo words. Possibly part of the backlash against *politically correct* language is due to the way that the attempts at change have been framed. Instead of presenting a list of prohibited words, feminist pragmatists should critique sexist language and discuss the consequences of its use. Rather than allowing those who would advocate the use of oppressive language to frame the debate in terms of censorship and policing, liberal ironists must reframe it in terms of solidarity and contingency. For example, a feminist pragmatist might argue:

> We do not say that you cannot use such and such a word, we only say that you must be aware that all language is historically and culturally contingent and constantly in process, and that in our current state of contingency, language that excludes women produces the opposite of solidarity in our community. You certainly have the autonomy and freedom to use "man," for example, when referring to all people, but in exercising your autonomy in this way, you are damaging the freedom of others and the sense of solidarity with others.

Members of the public who actively scoff at *political correctness* may find pragmatist feminists' ideas more compelling if we eliminate the focus on taboo words and sense of forced change and instead frame arguments in terms of critique and consequences.

If the fruit of our communion of feminism and pragmatism leads to participation in both academic and public discourse, and if these conversations create new truths that contribute to forming a more just, more empowering, and more liberating society, we shall say that we are succeeding.

REFERENCES

Butler, J. (1990). *Gender trouble: Feminism and the subversion of identity*. New York: Routledge.

Craig, R. T. (1989). Communication as a practical discipline. In B. Dervin, L. Grossberg, B. J. O'Keefe, & E. Wartella (Eds.), *Rethinking communication* (Vol. 2, pp. 97–122). Newbury Park, CA: Sage.

Craig, R. T., & Tracy, K. (1995). Grounded practical theory: The case of intellectual discussion. *Communication Theory, 5*, 248–272.

Cronen, V. E. (1995). Practical theory and the tasks ahead for social approaches to communication. In W. Leeds-Hurwitz (Ed.), *Social approaches to communication* (pp. 217–242). New York: Guilford.

Deming, C. (1989). Must gender paradigms shift for themselves? In B. Dervin, L. Grossberg, B. J. O'Keefe, & E. Wartella (Eds.), *Rethinking communication* (Vol. 1, pp. 162–165). Newbury Park, CA: Sage.

Dewey, J. (1927/1991). *The public and its problems*. Athens, OH: Swallow Press.

Dewey, J. (1958). *Experience and nature*. New York: Dover.

Dewey, J. (1989). *Freedom and culture*. Buffalo, NY: Prometheus.

Fraser, N. (1989). *Unruly practices: Power, discourse, and gender in contemporary social theory*. Minneapolis, MN: University of Minnesota Press.

Fraser, N. (1991). From irony to prophecy to politics: A response to Richard Rorty. *Michigan Quarterly Review, 3*, 259–267.

Fraser, N. (1995). Pragmatism, feminism, and the linguistic turn. In S. Benhabib, J. Butler, P. Cornell, & N. Fraser (Eds.), *Feminist contentions: A philosophical exchange* (pp. 157–171). Chicago, IL: University of Chicago Press.

Harding, S. (1986). *The science question in feminism*. Ithaca, NY: Cornell University Press.

Harding, S. (1987). Introduction: Is there a feminist method? In S. Harding (Ed.), *Feminism and methodology* (pp. 1–14). Bloomington, IN: Indiana University Press.

James, W. (1977). The meaning of truth. In J. J. McDermott (Ed.), *The writings of William James: A comprehensive edition* (pp. 311–317). Chicago, IL: University of Chicago Press. (Original work published 1909)

James, W. (1977). Pragmatism: A new name for some old ways of thinking. In J. J. McDermott (Ed.), *The writings of William James: A comprehensive edition* (pp. 376–390, 449–472). Chicago, IL: University of Chicago Press. (Original work published 1907)

Langsdorf, L., & Smith, A. R. (1995). *Recovering pragmatism's voice: The classical tradition, Rorty, and the philosophy of communication*. Albany, NY: SUNY Press.

Putnam, H. (1995). *Pragmatism*. Cambridge, MA: Blackwell Press.

Radway, J. (1991). *Reading the romance: Women, patriarchy, and popular literature*. Chapel Hill, NC: University of North Carolina Press.

Rooney, P. (1993). Feminist-pragmatist revisionings of reason, knowledge, and philosophy. *Hypatia, 8*(2), 15–37.

Rorty, R. (1979). *Philosophy and the mirror of nature*. Princeton, NJ: Princeton University Press.

Rorty, R. (1993). Feminism, ideology, and deconstruction: A pragmatist view. *Hypatia, 8*(2), 96–103.

Rorty, R. (1989). *Contingency, irony, and solidarity*. Cambridge, England: Cambridge University Press.

Rorty, R. (1991). Feminism and pragmatism. *Michigan Quarterly Review, 3*, 231–258.

Schwandt, T. (1994). Constructivist, interpretivist approaches to human inquiry. In H. Denzin & Y. Lincoln (Eds.), *Handbook of qualitative research* (pp. 118–137). Thousand Oaks, CA: Sage.

Seigfried, C. (1991). Where are all the pragmatist feminists? *Hypatia, 6*, 1–20.

Seigfried, C. H. (1996). *Pragmatism and feminism: Reweaving the social fabric*. Chicago: University of Chicago Press.

Shepherd, G. J., & Rothenbuhler, E. W. (in press). *Communication and community*. Mahwah, NJ: Lawrence Erlbaum Associates.

Tate, M. (1999). *The interpretive, performative relationship between* Seventeen *magazine and its readers* (Doctoral dissertation, University of Alabama, 1999). *Dissertation Abstracts International, 60–06A*, AA69935580.

West, C. (1989). *An American evasion of philosophy*. Madison, WI: University of Wisconsin Press.

West, C. (1993). *Prophetic thought in postmodern times*. Monroe, MA: Common Courage Press.

Chapter 11

Habermas, Dewey, and Pragmatism

Thomas L. Jacobson
State University of New York at Buffalo

Given his status as heir to the Frankfurt tradition of critical theory, it is not always recognized that Jurgen Habermas is deeply committed to pragmatist thought. George Herbert Mead's work figures centrally in his approach to social theory. His base propositions are empirically oriented. Habermas (1985) largely followed Charles S. Peirce's critique of foundationalist philosophy: "As a good pragmatist, I hold the view that a philosopher's capacity to create problems through intentionally inciting doubt is quite limited. I share Peirce's doubt about any type of Cartesian doubt" (p. 198).

In addition, Habermas' work shares much with John Dewey. The Frankfurt School is generally identified with a neo-Marxian orientation to critical theory. Although Habermas retains a substantial role for elements of Karl Marx's thought, he now uses Marx only as one among many substantive theorists to advance his own program. The spirit of Habermas' critique shares much with pragmatism. As Habermas (1985) put it, "I have for a long time identified myself with that radical democratic mentality which is present in the best American traditions and articulated in American pragmatism" (p. 198).

One can fairly argue that his major project—the theory of communicative action—is emblematic of pragmatism and represents a major contemporary expression of pragmatist social thought. As such, it is relevant to contemporary debates within pragmatism.

Pragmatism is experiencing a revival today, both within and outside the field of communication (Langsdorf & Smith, 1995). It is being pulled in many directions. Joas (1993) sees the essence of pragmatism as concerned with creative action. West (1989) draws on Emerson's contribution to argue for a prophetic pragmatism. Another draw on pragmatism's energies comes from a culturalistic approach enriched by postmodernism (Mouffe, 1996). Habermas' work weighs in on a tension evident in Dewey's work. Consider two different views of what pragmatism represents.

One view describes pragmatism as an empirical scientific alternative to the Cartesian philosophical framework. Peirce produced definitive critiques of Descartes. With his concept of *abduction*, he sought a better account of how inquiry actually operates within scientific communities. Dewey shared this program in a number of respects. In place of absolute truth claims, Dewey proposed *warranted assertability* as a criterion for scientific statements. His empirical theory of learning was justified on the basis of warranted assertions about the relation between experience and action. This theory was connected within an analysis of society in an attempt to explain democratic and moral impulses.

A second view of pragmatism is more culturalistic. As an alternative to the Cartesian framework, this pragmatism abandons questions of truth, of the means of finding this truth, and so on. For scholars such as Richard Rorty, philosophy must give way to literature and art as the means by which society reflects on its past and future. Justice and democracy are not implied by any philosophical theory of knowledge or any empirical theory of learning or experience.

There are two views. One represents a scientific approach that is also moral/practical. The other sees pragmatism mainly as a culture critique of foundational philosophy. Habermas' work can be placed in relation to this tension. His theory is more similar to the first view, both social scientific and moral/practical.

A significant difference within the framework of communication theory does exist between Habermas and the first view of pragmatism, however. Dewey prized communication, but for him the psychology of experience was more central. Habermas' work is based on communication theory rather than psychology. Nevertheless, both pursue their central aims in a manner that treats philosophical dilemmas in part with a scientific approach. Each would look to the results of science for at least some basis for moral political ideas.

This chapter explores the way in which the theory of communicative action pursues Dewey's own pragmatist ends by a different means. In so doing, it proposes that Habermas' work offers pragmatism an empirical, critical direction in which to develop. The argument proceeds in three parts. The first visits an essay of Rorty's. He argues that the tensions outlined

earlier exist in Dewey's own work, that late in life Dewey recognized the futility of his scientific program, and that this suggests the validity of the
culturalistic path for pragmatism. A second part discusses the theory of
communicative action. It touches on the work of pragmatists such as
Peirce and Mead, but focuses on parallels between Dewey and Habermas.
It highlights the more empirically oriented elements of Habermas' theory.
This part suggests viewing the theory of communicative action as an attempt to pursue Dewey's own aim of a scientific program, although of
course in an entirely different conceptual direction. The chapter concludes by suggesting two alternative ways to read the theory of communicative action as an update on the pragmatist tradition.

DEWEY'S PROJECT

Dewey and Peirce both abandoned the search for an ultimate grounding
for knowledge. Although Peirce focused on logical problems associated
with epistemology to supercede epistemology, Dewey analyzed experience
and sought to connect the results of his analysis to a wide range of topics.
These included democratic practice, social change, aesthetics, and his
widely acclaimed philosophy of education. Dewey began with an early interest in Hegel. He eventually gravitated to what became a life-long pursuit of a scientific approach to philosophy primarily based on a psychological account of experience.

Dewey thought that previous philosophies suffered from an impover-
ished conception of the manner in which learning of any kind results from
experience. His analysis started with the belief that the phenomenal world
is continuous—running from physical to biological to human processes.
Organisms of all kinds operate on the basis of interaction (or *transaction*—
a term he preferred late in life) with their environments. Higher organisms learn from it. This approach to analyzing experience gives it a realist
orientation in that interaction with the surrounding environment must
above all be successful. For humans, this interactive experience develops
cognitive as well as physical and emotional dimensions.

Human experience comprises far more than sensory observations of
the kind emphasized by British empiricists. Their idea—that sensory impressions are received raw—is untenable because an organism's evolution
has designed it to receive certain impressions useful for its survival. The
idea that these impressions are associated with one another through simple syllogisms, which then comprise the whole of experience, also makes
little sense. Even a casual reflection on experience reveals that behavior
leads to emotional as well as sensory data, which become part of the experiential mix. Moreover, humans pursue ends that are projected into the
future. Therefore, present experience in certain respects contains the fu-

ture. The notion that as organisms we start out with a tabula rasa is no more reasonable than the notion that a paramecium starts out with a table rasa. They and we evolved so as to interact with the world in certain ways, and certain goods are associated with the particularly human form of existence that become human ends and values.

With a biological element to his analysis of experience, Dewey engaged in a decades-long attempt to redefine philosophical inquiry generally on a psychological basis. This included a deep-seated distrust of philosophical dichotomies such as fact and value, individual and society, knowledge and aesthetics, philosophy and education, and so on. He viewed such dichotomies as fabrications that merely preoccupy philosophy, keeping it from addressing meaningful matters.

Of course, communication played an important role in Dewey's program. "Of all things, communication is the most wonderful" (Dewey, 1929, p. 126). On the one hand, communication in the form of language was for Dewey the medium through which humans apprehend processes in the world. Here he took what would later be called a *linguistic turn*. All such apprehension occurs within the context of a culture-bearing system of language. On the other hand, this language system circulates through social institutions, which are also cultural and linguistic constructions. Therefore, in addition to explaining something about the nature of basic perceptual apprehension, communication is central in comprising social subsystems. For this reason, communication, in the form of public discourse and the circulation of ideas through public media, is a key to democratic culture and society (Dewey, 1927).

Dewey's plan was ambitious because it sought a single explanatory framework for physical as well as social, moral processes. Thus, he described his attempt as an *empirical metaphysics*. In his metaphysics, he sought "a statement of the generic traits manifested by existences of all kinds without regard to their differentiation into physical and mental" (1929, p. 412).

Rorty clearly wants to rehabilitate Dewey. He believes Dewey is one of America's most important philosophers and should be read more widely. But he would have us read Dewey in a certain way. In an essay entitled "Dewey's Metaphysics," Rorty begins by characterizing the naturalistic/scientific element of Dewey's project as a failure (Rorty, 1982, pp. 72–89). To Rorty, the abandonment of philosophical foundationalism was well enough, but the attempt to substitute a scientifically grounded philosophy went only half the proper distance. It remained committed to a "permanent neutral matrix for future inquiry" (p. 80). For Rorty, this is as fruitless as a philosophical foundationalism.

Rorty (1982) argues that Dewey's metaphysics remained unclear: ". . . two generations of commentators have been puzzled to say what method might produce a 'statement of the generic traits manifested by existences of all kinds without regard to their differentiation into mental and physical' " (p. 73). This lack of clarity is not surprising because of the largely undeveloped, sought-after conceptual framework. Dewey's main conceptual strategy consisted of explaining the untenability of philosophical dichotomies, the partial nature of previous analyses of experience, and the need for a scientific rather than a philosophic approach. Dewey, however, never convincingly tied the scientific avenue he started down with his writings on the "reflex arc" concept in psychology (e.g., 1896) to the broader issues. Rorty (1982) recalls the charges of some of Dewey's sympathetic critics:

> These critics welcomed with enthusiasm Dewey's suggestions about the cause and cure of traditional empiricisms and rationalisms, but were unable to see much point in Dewey's own "constructive" attempts to produce a philosophical jargon that was dualism-free, nor in his claim to be more "empirical" in method than his opponents. (p. 80)

Rorty (1982) wants to emphasize a second Dewey—the culture critic:

> Dewey set out to show the harm which traditional philosophical dualisms were doing to our culture, and he thought that to do this job he needed a metaphysics—a description of the generic traits of existences that would solve (or dissolve) the traditional problems of philosophy. (p. 85)

Others, including pragmatists, had done this in part. Peirce and James sought to break down false Cartesian dichotomies. However, Rorty values Dewey because of the unique way that Dewey connected these philosophical observations with an analysis of contemporary public life—the way in which Dewey illustrated the presence and participation of philosophical dualisms in our social, educational, and political problems. These problems included a philosophy that was irrelevant to public affairs, a corrosive veneration for technology, sclerotic democratic institutions, and mind-numbing schools. Rorty appreciates the way Dewey argued that these philosophical constructions are cultural and that not only conceivable, but possible, alternatives can improve our state of affairs.

This in sum represents Rorty's treatment of the tension he sees in Dewey. Rorty argues that late in life Dewey saw the futility of his life-long attempt to develop an empirical metaphysics. Although this might seem somewhat tragic from Dewey's point of view, it is not at all so for philosophy. For Rorty, Dewey's mistake is trivial compared with what Dewey bequeathed by way of criticism. Rorty's position is predictable insofar as Rorty's program consists of advocating that philosophy can offer social reflection only criticism. For him, any guidelines for social or moral practice will be derived from art and literature, not from philosophy and certainly not from science. This is why Bernstein (1992) characterizes Rorty's as an "aesthetisized pragmatism" (p. 233). In any case, Rorty understandably interprets Dewey to suit his purposes.

There is much to recommend Rorty's view today. The social sciences have achieved relatively little scientific grounding for theories concerning broad sociological questions. In addition, postmodernism has hammered away with the argument that the social sciences have not even the slightest logical possibility of so doing. In this context, Rorty's insistence that vocabularies provide the only tools available for inquiry is alluring. If this suggests relativism, then so be it. If social science becomes simply an arena for debate, okay. Is relativism so bad?

Of course, Rorty's prescription may or may not represent Dewey's final view. If Dewey's metaphysics fails, then so does the compelling argument that his education and politics represent the outcome of scientific research. If Dewey's account of experience is nothing other than his account of experience, then so too are his accounts of sclerotic democracy, mind-numbing educational institutions, and corrosive technological fetishism just his views of contemporary society. If Dewey accepted this critique, he might well have continued in the role of a public-spirited and publicly engaged intellectual. However, he could not say that nature tells us anything about how we ought to proceed. Dewey could rely only on the hope and the values he had come to cherish by way of his upbringing. Would Dewey have accepted this result? Would he, given a hypothetical 30 years added onto his life, have sought another avenue for empirical exploration?

This avenue would again head in the direction of a scientific account of our social processes, problems, and prospects. It would abjure foundationalist epistemologies, recognize the role of values in inquiry, and nevertheless seek empirical corroboration of Dewey's claims. This avenue would indicate the untenability of the philosophical dichotomies Dewey abhorred and the artificiality of the strict partitioning of philosophy, science, aesthetics, and politics. It would also stress the human nature of our moral intuitions and the idea that democratic institutions reflect something deeper than preference.

THE THEORY OF COMMUNICATIVE ACTION

Habermas' (1984, 1987) theory of communicative action weighs in against Rorty's interpretivist pragmatism. It supports the prospect that results of scientific inquiry have something normative to tell us about social processes. Like Dewey, Habermas wants to commit social theory to a practical critique of society. With Dewey, he pursues his aim in the form of a scientific program of research. Like Dewey, he believes that preferences for democratic norms and institutions originate in something fundamentally human. His role is largely restricted to outlining this program rather than pursuing empirical investigation. However, the program is avowedly and clearly based on empirical questions.[1]

For Habermas, there is no way back to a philosophical account of reason of science or critical theory. Here Habermas finds in pragmatism a nonphilosophical avenue for analysis without following Dewey's approach. Dewey's failure, on Habermas' view, occurred because Dewey remained too closely tied to a philosophy of the subject. In viewing knowledge as culturally conditioned, Dewey took a step in the right direction. Yet this step merely collapsed, rather than properly conceptualized, relations between the subjective and objective worlds.

Instead, a more complete, empirical elaboration of the linguisticality of knowledge is needed. In this view, knowledge is not simply connected to or dependent on experience. Instead, it differentiates the linguisticality of experience in several specific ways. From this we learn that the only lawful uniformities bridging the objective, moral, and subjective worlds are the ways in which linguistic negotiation of objective, moral, and subjective concerns take place.

This is the chief purpose of Habermas' analysis of validity claims, ideal speech, and discourse. Communication in general relies on the reciprocal presumption of claims regarding the truth, rightness, and sincerity of expressions. Even attempts to deceive rely on these presumptions insofar as lies violate them.

These three kinds of claims represent the means by which behavior can be coordinated with regard to three different world relations. Truth claims coordinate behavior with respect to the objective world. Claims of rightness, or normative appropriateness, are the means by which behavior is coordinated with respect to the social world. Sincerity claims coordinate behavior with respect to subjective affairs.

When validity claims are questioned, discussion—with the aim of redeeming the claim—can address them. This discussion is discourse, and various kinds are employed with different sorts of validity claims. Theoretical discourse is used to negotiate truth claims. In scientific communication, a truth claim is a proposition backed up by evidence. The relevant community of competent researchers determines the acceptabilty of evidence. Here Habermas (1971, 1992) draws from Peirce's account of scientific inquiry. What counts as theory and data in science may be more highly formalized than in everyday settings, but the pragmatist criterion holds just the same. In this sense, theoretical discourse is empiricist and refers to the world outside, but does not search for foundational certainty.

---

[1]For applied and empirical studies based on Habermas' theory, see Chambers (1996), Jacobson and Kolluri (1999), Johnson (1993), Pusey (1991), and Scambler (1996).

Normative practical discourse negotiates claims regarding rightness or normative appropriateness. Truth claims cannot resolve normative questions. However, the force of the better argument can lead to assent in normative matters just as argument-backed assent settles truth. Therefore, normative matters have a claim to reason. Strictly speaking, sincerity claims are not susceptible to discourse. Only consistent behavior and a lack of contradiction over time can redeem their validity.

It is important to understand the status that Habermas attributes to this framework of validity claims. They are not the kind of claims always consciously recognized among parties, nor are they culturally variant language game rules that people need not recognize consciously to follow. Their existence is required for communication of any kind to occur. Superficially they might appear as transcendentally a priori conditions necessary for communicative reason. Some of Habermas' readers, including Rorty (1982), interpret him this way. However, this is a bad, or at least unfair, reading. The framework of validity claims, discourse, and ideal speech are an empirically oriented reconstruction of the conditions making communication possible. The presumptions represented by the framework have evolved as an outcome of the pragmatic conditions of human existence. Empirical corroboration is needed to determine their plausibility.

Referring back to Dewey, our interactions with the world as perceived within a cultural context can explain the sources of our experience. For Habermas, this experience is differentiated linguistically around spheres of validity reflecting three world relations. These include the world outside, the world of other people, and the subjective world. When validity claims with regard to any of these are contested, discourse can redeem or address them.

Of course, discourse is a complex behavior. The ideal speech situation represents Habermas' account of the required discursive behavior that makes redeeming validity claims possible. In a world brimming with difference, the idea that claims may be valid requires a means for addressing them that allows involved parties to resolve them satisfactorily. Certain rules are required. All parties in ideal speech interaction must have an equivalent chance to contribute to discourse. Power must take a back seat to the force of the better argument. The discourse must be oriented toward reaching understanding generally. As Habermas (1984) put it, "I shall speak of *communicative* action whenever the actions of the agents involved are coordinated not through egocentric calculations of success but through acts of reaching understanding" (pp. 285–286; italics original).

Thus, Habermas begins the empirical reconstructive study of communicative competence as the ability to employ speech to coordinate behavior. It serves as foreground in a theory that acknowledges the prevalence of strategic and manipulative action but focuses on communicative action as a universal pragmatic requirement of behavior. As reconstructive theory, it joins the theories of Noam Chomsky, Jean Piaget, Lawrence Kohlberg, Mead, and others. Many of Habermas' theoretical studies attempt to knit these theories together by providing each with a communicative dimension.

Piaget attempted to explain the acquisition of cognitive abilities within a program of developmental psychology. He characterized the acquisition process as proceeding through a series of stages. Early stages represent simpler cognitive abilities, which are required for the acquisition of subsequent abilities at a higher stage. In addition to purely cognitive abilities, Habermas proposes that children acquire social interaction skills in stages. These skills focus on requirements for the coordination of action through communication. A staged set of communicative interaction skills parallels, and interrelates with, Piaget's cognitive development stages (Habermas, 1979, 1984).

Another linkage occurs with Piaget's work as well. Habermas (1990) associated the ability to interact socially with the ability to reason ethically. He follows the research of Kohlberg and his associates into the staged acquisition of ethical reasoning, which is also based on Piaget's theory. Kohlberg's theory describes the acquisition of abstract reasoning capabilities as a prerequisite for autonomous ethical reasoning in which complex ethical contingencies can be weighed one against the other.

Kohlberg's work is attractive to Habermas because it illustrates that learning occurs with normative as well as instrumental cognitive skills. However, Kohlberg's account ties normative ethical reasoning too tightly to purely cognitive skills. The ability to analyze complex sets of contingencies in complicated ethical situations requires cognitive abilities. This alone, however, does not explain why difficult decisions should be made or why ethical considerations are bothered with at all. It is also necessary to account for the sources of insight into the ethical situations of others, the binding force of ethical norms, and so on.

In Habermas' view, abstract reasoning about ethical situations relies on concepts of the self, other, and the generalized other as analyzed by G. H. Mead. Habermas employs Mead in tying the processes through which cognitive, ethical, and social interaction skills are acquired to the development of individual identity. In fact, Mead's model of the acquisition of role expectations is central to Habermas' (1987) elaboration of language use.

For Mead, the self-concept emerges from an ability to see oneself hypothetically through the eyes of the other. Only participation in the medium of a culturally shared language makes this ability possible. Intersubjectivity consists in this language participation. Although validity claims are conceptualized categorically, they are employed behaviorally in an overlapping fashion and entirely within the horizons of a shared language. Reciprocal expectations of recognition between self and other, self and the generalized other, and so on accompany reciprocal expectations regarding validity claims. In this way, communicative action ties together much more than cognitive and ethical reasoning. It also connects these with individual identity and social-level meaning structures.[2]

The assertion that individual-level communication presumes the intent to reach understanding should not suggest that social conditions at the institutional level need to nurture this behavior in individuals. Ruling powers have not always prized the inherent inclination to communicate, which has only become so valued relatively recently in human history. For this reason, the relationship between micro- and macrolevel communication processes is not simple in the sense of one being a functionalist projection into the other. Instead, each must be seen as figuring into the other in a historically contingent manner. In analyzing these relationships, the theory of communicative action includes an account of social evolution, in addition to its psychological and social psychological elements.

In mythically oriented societies prior to the rise of civilization, human communication did include presumptions regarding validity. It also necessarily performed the functions of coordinating behavior with regard to the three worlds, but in an undifferentiated way. Early civilizations moved away from this undifferentiated social form. Role specializations began to emerge. With these, technical skills, social norms, and aesthetic expression began a structural differentiation so that practices within these spheres could be undertaken in semiautonomous ways. Social evolution can be seen as a process in which discourses for addressing these three worlds—or cultural-value spheres—become structurally differentiated from each other. From this perspective, modernity appeared in Europe as scientific thought, government, and art escaped from dictates of the church and from each other. Increasingly, government made fewer economic decisions. Scientific inquiry pursued its own ends. Each sphere began to evolve discourses tailored for action therein.

In addition to providing a communicative account of reason at the individual level, the theory of communicative action also advances a historical evolutionary account of the societal embodiment of communicative reason. As Habermas put it,

> The release of a potential for reason embedded in communicative action is a world-historical process; in the modern period it leads to a rationalization of life-worlds, to the differentiation of their symbolic structures, which is expressed above all in the increasing reflexivity of cultural traditions, in proc-

---

[2]Habermas' theory of communicative ethics is developed most extensively in *Moral Consciousness and Communicative Action* (1990) and *Justification and Application* (1993).

esses of individuation, in the generalization of values, in the increasing prevalence of more abstract and more universal norms, and so on. (cited in Dews,
1992, p. 180)

Habermas uses this historical account of social evolution to tie the cognitive elements of the theory of communicative action to the macrolevel
required to analyze contemporary society. Here he engages Emile Durkheim, Marx, Talcott Parsons, Max Weber, and others.[3] For example, to
explain changes in the nature of social norms across historical periods requires a theory. In viewing the origins of contemporary norms in systems
of sacred meaning that were dominant prior to the Enlightenment, Habermas uses Durkheim. Durkheim also helps him analyze the transformation of this meaning into secular forms.

A theory is also required to explain the differentiation of social roles.
Sociologists such as Durkheim, Georg Simmel, and Weber projected a
break into history. To them, modern societies differ from traditional ones
by virtue of different binding principles. Weber's analysis of rationalization in modern societies and the embodiment of this rationalization in
bureaucratic institutions, in particular, has influenced modern social
thought powerfully. This is for good reason, but Habermas sees it as one
sided. Bureaucracy has perhaps run wild, but the appearance of nontrivial
freedoms in the spheres of inquiry, government, and art also characterizes
modernity. A complete account of differentiation must discuss the institutions in which these freedoms are embodied. This cannot be done simply
in terms of a dichotomous conceptual scheme with binding principles.

In place of Weber's account, Habermas analyzes the emergence of modernity as the institutionalization of the three spheres of discourse found
in the three world relations. This framework makes it possible to see the
predominance of technical instrumental reason as a matter of imbalance.
The imbalance eclipses, but leaves as significant, normative and aesthetic
reason. The remaining presence of these forms of reason provides the
possibility of improvement in social conditions if they can gain an equal
footing with technical instrumental concerns.

Finally, theory is needed to identify and properly characterize the primary social problems of our time. Here, Habermas (1987) employs his
synthesis of the previously discussed theories to provide the foundation
for his diagnosis of high capitalism as suffering from "colonization of the
inner life world" (pp. 301–405).

Contemporary developed societies do not suffer from any ideological
malaise even if one extends the concept of ideology to include scientism,

---

[3]For his major reconstructions of macrosociological theories, see, primarily, *Legitimation
Crisis* (1975) and *Communication and the Evolution of Society* (1979), in addition to the *Theory of
Communicative Action* (1984, 1987).

techno fetishism, and so on. Yes, there is too much emphasis on instrumental reason—on administrative and market solutions. Questions that a normative or aesthetic basis could address appropriately are systematically distorted when routinely subjected instead to administrative and market solutions. However, no single story of modern life holds sway today. Rather, the opposite is true. Many stories—some provided by cadres of specialists who are insulated from broader social life worlds—compete. Given this cacophony, a reasonably coherent grasp of society is difficult to come by. Reason is eclipsed in the sense that ignoring normative and aesthetic concerns unbalances it. It is also fragmented, however. The subjective outcome must be outlined in terms of anomie, alienation, and cultural impoverishment.

The colonization thesis holds this fragmentation responsible for individuals' anomie and alienation. In turn, these translate into institutional problems. To the extent that the integration of individuals into adequately sustaining normative frameworks fails, modern administrative and governmental institutions will be overtaxed. These frameworks comprise the terms embodying the consent to be governed. The legitimacy of government is challenged and eventually withdrawn as the sense of meaningless spreads.

To reverse this erosion of legitimacy, the theory would suggest that the forces of social integration must be rebuilt in a highly pluralistic cultural matrix. No single cultural framework can be imposed on all others. Here the concepts of universal treatment before the law must be used to negotiate differences in a communicative manner. Public discourse is the most important tool for rebuilding legitimacy, and not because it represents some kind of natural right. Its importance occurs because it is the medium through which the individual finds self-recognition in collective processes.[4]

Finally, he holds this out as universalistic. Individual claims vary immeasurably in their cultural diversity, and they can only be validated with discourse. This is because the self can recognize itself in others and fully recognize otherness only through discourse. Communicative action is universalistic because everyone needs this validation for these reasons. The democratic impulse is an expression of a communicative ability that makes both individual and social life possible. Violations of this life-giving ability are not simply an abuse of someone's preferences.

This, then, provides a brief outline of the theory of communicative action. The framework of validity claims, discourse, and ideal speech come

---

[4]Habermas' most clearly political early work on the public sphere was *The Structural Transformation of the Public Sphere* (1989). For an update on this line of thought, including an analysis of contemporary conditions in industrial democracies, see *Between Facts and Norms* (1996).

under scrutiny often and for good reason because this framework is intended to provide a universalist grounding for the rest. Only if the reciprocal expectation of validity claims is universal can it be said that violations of the intent to reach understanding have any moral force beyond personal or cultural preference. Only if the reciprocal expectation of validity claims is universal can widespread historical growth in the frequency of struggles for democracy be explained as something other than a happy accident. Nevertheless, scholars often overlook the ties among the theory of ideal speech, individual level moral/cognitive development, social norms, and political institutions.

Of course, scholars have subjected Habermas' work to widespread debate. Several criticisms have appeared. The concept of reason is imperialistic—the latest export from Europe. The theory's concern with shared presumptions overlooks and downplays the importance of difference. It is just another form of philosophical foundationalism. The ideal speech situation is idealistic and aloof from the reality of pervasive power. Finally, the scientific status of his claims may be questionable. Habermas has taken these charges seriously and responded to them, revising or refining his theory along the way.[5] This chapter does not review the debates. Their review is not needed to compare Dewey with Habermas. It is not needed to make a claim on Dewey's legacy that counters Rorty's.

CONCLUSION: PRAGMATISM AS BOTH EMPIRICAL AND MORAL PRACTICAL

Dewey and Habermas share many assumptions about the nature of human inquiry, learning, identity, democratic society, moral intuition, and more. Both understand inquiry pragmatically. They view learning within normative contexts and treat democratic practice as a required medium for identity and culture to flourish. Neither treats morality as simply chosen. Moral intuitions have a basis in something deeply human, and this too is related to democratic practice.

Of course, their theoretical tools differ dramatically. Dewey's began with an analysis of experience in an effort to break down then-prevalent philosophical dualisms. With these down, relationships between inquiry and social values, the individual and society, and politics and morality could be explored. However, Habermas is heir to subsequent develop-

---

[5]Critical reviews of Habermas' work can be found in Calhoun (1992), d'Entreves and Benhabib (1997), Honneth, McCarthy, Offe, and Wellmer (1992), Kelly (1994), and White (1995). For recently translated essays on multiculturalism and otherness, see Cronin and De Greiff (1998).

ments in philosophy, empirical psychology, and sociology. He draws on a wide range of theories to examine a set of relationships that overlap considerably with those Dewey explored.

Most important for the purposes of this chapter, both attempt to ground their social, ethical, and moral analyses within a framework of scientific claims. Dewey hoped to find "a statement of the generic traits manifested by existences of all kinds without regard to their differentiation into physical and mental." For Habermas, the issue is not "traits" about which we can make statements, but rather the communicative process employed to coordinate behavior. In both cases, however, the basic theoretical propositions are intended to be empirical.

Habermas' work is deeply associated with pragmatism. This exists in his use of Peirce's account of scientific inquiry. It can be seen in the considerable significance he attributes to Mead's social psychology, to which I have barely pointed. These occur in addition to the parallels with Dewey.

As a result, Rorty offers pragmatism an aesthetic direction, whereas Habermas gives it a more empirical, critical one. Habermas' is empirical not only by virtue of the role of empirical theoretical proposals in the analysis of communicative action, but also because of the psychological and sociological studies contained in his theory. It is critical by the way communicative action represents a standard against which systematic distortions in communication can be measured today. The example of moral commitment evidenced in Habermas' own numerous and ongoing political debates also contributes to his critical direction (Holub, 1991).

Finally, Habermas' offers stand regardless of the scientific success of his program. As with Dewey, one can find two views on Habermas. One takes Habermas' program on its own terms. This reading provisionally accepts the possibility that the empirical propositions can and will be borne out. In this case, Habermas' analysis of communication, social evolution, and lifeworld colonization all have an anchor that secures them in something more firm than our own culturally determined preferences.

The other finds in Habermas a social theorist of remarkable insight and moral passion despite the possibility that his search for empirical grounding may come up empty. On this view, sufficient empirical evidence cannot be adduced to corroborate Habermas' theory scientifically. Even so, the theory of communicative action can be interpreted as something like a critical hermeneutic analysis, rather than as an empirical reconstruction (Bernstein, 1992; Bohman, 1999). As a project of critical hermeneutic analysis, it would not be universalistic but could still be valorized. Lifeworld colonization could not be judged negatively on the grounds that it violates deeply human predispositions. Nevertheless, Habermas' analysis of it would stand as a penetrating critical study of contemporary social conditions. Finally, morality could not be explained by the acquisition of ethical reasoning skills, but Habermas' communicative ethics would still represent an ingenious approach to analyzing relations between particular cultural forms and the global spread of human and political rights.

In other words, Habermas someday may be forced to give up on his attempt to ground critical theory empirically. He then would share even more with Dewey. Pragmatists could look back on them both as part of a tradition that is not satisfied with relativism. Whether one reads the theory of communicative action as an empirical reconstruction or a critical hermeneutic project, it remains pragmatist. It is pragmatist in its post-epistemological assumptions and in its Deweyan unhappiness with contemporary social conditions. Finally, it is pragmatist in its intellectual engagement on behalf of changing social institutions for the sake of social progress. Habermas' work and his personal example revive the first Dewey—the one Rorty rejected regardless of whether Habermas' scientific claims stand. This offers pragmatism the example of an empirical critical direction in which to pursue studies into the state of affairs in contemporary society.

REFERENCES

Bernstein, R. J. (1992). *The new constellation: The ethical-political horizons of modernity/post-modernity.* Cambridge, MA: MIT Press.

Bohman, J. (1999). Theories, practices and pluralism: A pragmatic interpretation of critical social science. *Philosophy of the Social Sciences, 29*(4), 459–480.

Calhoun, C. (Ed.). (1992). *Habermas and the public sphere.* Cambridge, MA: MIT Press.

Chambers, S. (1996). *Reasonable democracy: Jurgen Habermas and the politics of discourse.* Ithaca: Cornell University Press.

Cronin, C., & De Greiff, P. (Eds.). (1998). *The inclusion of the other/Jurgen Habermas.* Cambridge, MA: MIT Press.

d'Entreves, M. P., & Benhabib, S. (Eds.). (1997). *Habermas and the unfinished project of modernity.* Cambridge, MA: MIT Press.

Dewey, J. (1896). The reflex arc concept in psychology. *The Psychological Review, 3,* 357–370.

Dewey, J. (1927). *The public and its problems.* Athens: Ohio University Press.

Dewey, J. (1929). *Experience and nature.* New York: W. W. Norton.

Dews, P. (Ed.). (1992). *Autonomy and solidarity: Interviews with Jurgen Habermas.* New York: Verso.

Habermas, J. (1971). *Knowledge and human interests.* Boston: Beacon.

Habermas, J. (1975). *Legitimation crisis.* Boston: Beacon.

Habermas, J. (1979). *Communication and the evolution of society.* Boston: Beacon.

Habermas, J. (1984). *The theory of communicative action: Volume 1. Reason and the rationalization of society.* Boston: Beacon.

Habermas, J. (1985). Questions and counterquestions. In R. J. Bernstein (Ed.), *Habermas and modernity* (pp. 192–216). Cambridge, MA: MIT Press.

Habermas, J. (1987). *The theory of communicative action: Volume 2. A critique of functionalist reason.* Boston: Beacon.

Habermas, J. (1989). *The structural transformation of the public sphere: An inquiry into a category of bourgeois society*. Cambridge, MA: MIT Press.

Habermas, J. (1990). *Moral consciousness and communicative action*. Cambridge, MA: MIT Press.

Habermas, J. (1992). *Postmetaphysical thinking: Philosophical essays*. Cambridge, MA: MIT Press.

Habermas, J. (1993). *Justification and application: Remarks on discourse ethics*. Cambridge, MA: MIT Press.

Habermas, J. (1996). *Between facts and norms: Contributions to a discourse theory of law and democracy*. Cambridge, MA: MIT Press.

Holub, R. C. (1991). *Jurgen Habermas: Critic in the public sphere*. London: Routledge.

Honneth, A., McCarthy, T., Offe, C., & Wellmer, A. (Eds.). (1992). *Cultural-political interventions in the unfinished project of enlightenment*. Cambridge, MA: MIT Press.

Jacobson, T. L., & Kolluri, S. (1999). Participatory communication as communicative action. In T. L. Jacobson & J. Servaes (Eds.), *Theoretical approaches to participatory communication* (pp. 265–281). Creskill, NJ: Hampton.

Joas, H. (1993). *Pragmatism and social theory*. Chicago: University of Chicago Press.

Johnson, J. (1993). Is talk really cheap? Promoting conversation between critical theory and rational choice. *American Political Science Review, 87*, 74–86.

Kelly, M. (1994). *Critique and power: Recasting the Foucault/Habermas debate*. Cambridge, MA: MIT Press.

Langsdorf, L., & Smith, A. R. (Eds.). (1995). *Recovering pragmatism's voice: The classical tradition, Rorty, and the philosophy of communication*. Albany, NY: SUNY Press.

Mouffe, C. (Ed.). (1996). *Deconstructing pragmatism: Simon Critchley, Jacques Derrida, Ernesto Laclau & Richard Rorty*. London: Routledge.

Pusey, M. (1991). *Economic rationalism in Canberra: A nation-building state changes its mind*. Cambridge: Cambridge University Press.

Rorty, R. (1982). *The consequences of pragmatism*. Minneapolis: University of Minnesota Press.

Scambler, G. (1996). The "project of modernity" and the parameters for a critical sociology: An argument with illustrations from medical sociology. *The Journal of the British Sociological Association, 30*(3), 567–581.

West, C. (1989). *The American evasion of philosophy: A genealogy of pragmatism*. Madison, WI: The University of Wisconsin Press.

White, S. K. (Ed.). (1995). *The Cambridge companion to Habermas*. Cambridge: Cambridge University Press.

Chapter 12

Pragmatism and Tragedy, Communication and Hope: A Summary Story

Gregory J. Shepherd
University of Kansas

This chapter tells a certain story of American pragmatism and communication. It is one narrative among an infinite number that might be told (cf. Jacobson, chap. 11, this volume). To employ MacIntyre's (1977) wording, it is an "argumentative retelling" and, as such, "will itself be in conflict with other argumentative retellings" (p. 461). Thus, as Bernstein (1995) noted about his story of pragmatism, my story of pragmatism and communication might be judged as better or worse than other competing stories based on the story's usefulness (a self-evident point given the topic of the narrative). I try then to make this a useful argumentative retelling—one that might help make sense of where a tradition has been and where it might be headed. This chapter is neither as careful nor as sweeping as Simonson's smart opening chapter (chap. 1, this volume). Our tasks, I think, are different. As a conclusion, my chapter must circumscribe; as an introduction, Simonson's could not constrain. After all, introductions open, whereas conclusions close. Thus, I try to weave the other chapters in this volume into my story so that the narrative might also serve as an acceptable, if unconventional, summary chapter.

My story of pragmatism and communication relies heavily on a certain reading of William James' successful struggle against the pull of suicide. James' neurasthenic crisis occurs with the realization that our circumsolar journey is one around a very dark star; his recovery comes with the knowledge that active and collective resistance to its gravitational pull can change the universe. In other words, this is the story of pragmatism as a theorization of despair and communication as a justification for living against such hopelessness. I begin the story, then, with an account of James' struggle and move on to outline its conceptualization in his work. With help from the other chapters in this collection, I conclude by arguing that pragmatism made space for an ontology of communication.

WITH NEITHER OTHERS NOR CERTAINTY: JAMES' (POST)MODERN DESPAIR

In December 1869, William James was falling into a deep depression.[1] In his journal entry of December 21, he considered himself estranged from all others, unfit for and incapable of forming "any affectionate relations with others." He acknowledged, with despair, that he could never embrace others "as a whole or incorporate them with myself." This 27-year-old who had received his medical degree in June of that year realized, with devastating clarity, the doomed isolation of his own existence. He saw his own inability to do anything but watch others live from the position of an imprisoned self, just as others could only watch him from behind their own impenetrable individualities.

He suffered for weeks. Early in 1870, around the time of his 28th birthday (January 11), he experienced complete mental collapse. On February 1, James reached a moment of crisis. On that day, his journal entry recorded that he "about touched bottom," and he realized he faced a choice, whether to be or not, whether to exert himself or not, whether to live.

Sometime thereafter, James experienced a despair-induced hallucination, one many scholars take to be recounted two decades later in his sixth lecture on *The Varieties of Religious Experience* (1902/1985):

> Whilst in this state of philosophic pessimism and general depression of spirits about my prospects, I went one evening into a dressing-room in the twilight to procure some article that was there; when suddenly there fell upon me without warning, just as if it came out of the darkness a horrible fear of my own existence. Simultaneously there arose in my mind the image of an epileptic patient whom I had seen in the asylum, a black-haired youth with greenish skin, entirely idiotic, who used to sit all day on one of the benches, or rather shelves against the wall, with his knees drawn up against his chin, and the coarse gray undershirt, which was his only garment, drawn over

---

[1]Both Lewis (1991) and McDermott (1977) offered fairly detailed accounts of James' period of depression and recovery. I rely here especially on Lewis' Pulitzer prize-winning book, and his citations from *The Letters of William James*, edited by William's son, Henry James, 2 vols., the Houghton Library at Harvard University. All quotations from James' diary are taken from Lewis, pp. 201–205.

them inclosing his entire figure. He sat there like a sort of sculptured Egyptian cat or Peruvian mummy, moving nothing but his black eyes and looking absolutely non-human. This image and my fear entered into a species of combination with each other. That shape am I, I felt, potentially. Nothing that I possess can defend me against that fate, if the hour for it should strike for me as it struck for him. There was such a horror of him, and such a perception of my own merely momentary discrepancy from him, that it was as if something hitherto solid within my breast gave way entirely, and I became a mass of quivering fear. The universe was changed for me altogether. I awoke morning after morning with a horrible dread at the pit of my stomach, and with a sense of the insecurity of life that I never knew before, and that I have never felt since. It was like a revelation; and although the immediate feelings passed away, the experience has made me sympathetic with the morbid feelings of others ever since. It gradually faded, but for months I was unable to go into the dark alone. In general I dreaded to be left alone. I remember wondering how other people could live, how I myself had ever lived, so unconscious of the pit of insecurity beneath the surface of life. (pp. 160–161)

James' deep melancholy and fear consumed him for many more weeks. However, on April 29, a momentous realization occurred—one with great implications both for James' personal life and the tradition that was to become pragmatism and communication theory. Struck while reading an essay by Renouvier in which he discussed free will, James recorded these thoughts in his diary:

My first act of free will shall be to believe in free will. . . . Hitherto, when I have felt like taking a free initiative, like daring to act originally, without carefully waiting for contemplation of the external world to determine all for me, suicide seemed the most manly form to put my daring into; now I will go a step further with my will, not only act with it, but believe as well; believe in my individual reality and creative power. My belief, to be sure, can't be optimistic—but I will posit life (the real, the good) in the self-resistance of the ego to the world. Life shall [be built in] doing and suffering and creating.

Most of the story to be told about pragmatism and communication theory can be found in the foregoing account of James' period of depression and renewal in the winter and spring of 1869 to 1870. In that time, James realized the twin tragedies of life: Our utter isolation and the tenuousness of it all. He eventually countered those awful realities with hopefulness, but not optimism, in our power to create. This became pragmatism's sense of the tragic—embodied in Abraham Lincoln, poeticized by Walt Whitman, preached by Josiah Royce, articulated by Sidney Hook, and so well theorized by Cornel West (see e.g., West, 1993a). It also allowed for communication's sense of possibility, however, as witnessed by the authors of this volume's many chapters. These two senses unfold next.

A SENSE OF THE TRAGIC: FROM MODERN SELVES
TO POSTMODERN TRUTHS

The rise of modernity corresponds with the rise of the individual. The *Oxford English Dictionary* (1971) dated the earliest use of the term *individual* to refer to "a single human being, as opposed to society, the family, etc." (p. 1419) in 1626. The idea of the sovereign self had, of course, been percolating for more than a century. In theology, for example, the significance of privately held beliefs, personal faith, and individually forged covenants with God were central to the Protestant reformation of the early 16th century (Shepherd, in press). But only in the 17th century's dawning enlightenment did the idea of the individual take hold. MacIntyre's (1981) description of heroic society contrasted nicely with the modern society (and individuals) that James encountered with his depression. In heroic society, absent "a place in the social order, a man would not only be incapable of receiving recognition and response from others; not only would others not know, but he would not himself know who he was" (MacIntyre, 1981, p. 116). Any meaningful sense of self could only be held in a social sense—that is, in relation to others. In modern society, however, quite the opposite became true. Descartes' (1641/1960) famous dictum, *cogito ergo sum* made the individual mind the very determinant of being.

Two centuries later, James poured the effect of modernity's individualism into the diary entry that despaired over the impossibility of ever embracing another *as a whole* or incorporating another within himself. This realization eventually found theorization in his *Radical Empiricism*. James' belief in the primacy of experience (i.e., empiricism) was radical because of his insistence that experience was both foundational and plural. "To the very last, there are various 'points of view' which the philosopher must distinguish in discussing the world; and what is inwardly clear from one point remains a bare externality and datum to the other" (McDermott, 1977, p. 135).[2]

James' *Radical Empiricism* scoffed at the idea that science can somehow be objective: "The popular notion that 'science' is forced on the mind *ab extra*, and that our interests have nothing to do with its constructions, is utterly absurd" (p. 115). Underlying this skepticism was his appreciation for the radical, or plural, character of experience. After all, scientists tended to be empiricists. Nevertheless, science seemed to insist on the possibility of monistic experience—that with proper procedure, observational statements, measures, and all, experience could be universal (replicated and

---

[2]Unless otherwise noted, page numbers for all subsequent quotes attributed to James are from McDermott (1977).

shared). James' disdain for logical empiricism (or positivism) was often on display. He simply did not think that positivists (or ordinary, nonradical empiricists) thought very carefully about the metaphysical contradictions in their philosophy. How, in particular, could selves and individual thoughts be sovereign, but experience be made common?[3] Edie (1987) quoted from a letter that James "wrote to the positivist psychologist Ribot":

> Empirical facts without metaphysics will always make a confusion and a muddle. I'm sorry to hear you still disparage metaphysics so much, since rightly understood, the word means only the search for clearness where common people do not even suspect that there is any lack of it. The ordinary positivist has simply a bad and muddled metaphysics which he refuses to criticize or discuss. (p. ix)[4]

However, the metaphysic James has here discovered is not yet one that is very heartening. It seems, in fact, solipsistic—a point James recognized when he asked, "What can save us at all and prevent us from flying asunder into a chaos of mutually repellent solipsisms? Through what can our several minds commune?" as he wondered whether "it is indeed time to say with Thackeray, 'My friend, two different universes walk about under your hat and under mine' " (p. 150).

In short, if the measure of all is the individual, then the measure of all is small indeed. Ultimately, his radical empiricism, as an entelechial philosophy of modernity, directly suggests the contingent character of truth that is the hallmark of pragmatism and even what we come to call the *postmodern era*. That is, if the major lesson of modernity is that each one of us is all that there is, then James' despair is understandable. Yet how much deeper the depression when one realizes how accidental and momentary that makes us. James' anticorrespondence theory of truth is, perhaps, the most famous and lasting point of his pragmatism. However, his belief that "purely objective truth . . . is nowhere to be found" (p. 384) rests on a rather desperate realization that, to some considerable extent, "everything here is plastic" (p. 383). The plural character of experience creates, in turn, a plurality of truths. If truth is relative to experience, so is existence. What, then, can or does separate any one of us from James' "epilep-

---

[3]Some time later, something similar happens with a philosophy of communication that insists that "meanings are in people, not in words," yet wants to allow for the possibility of what it is theorizing—communication.

[4]James' belief in the importance of metaphysics is evidenced in various writings, although one might not know it from common current characterizations of pragmatism as antimetaphysical.

tic idiot?" Ironically, our ultimate isolation—our complete contingency—makes us only momentarily discrepant from the most unimaginable condition (or, alternatively, from whatever horror we can imagine—e.g., the horror of utter insignificance). It was James' look into the "pit of insecurity beneath the surface of life," that tragic realization, that gave him his pragmatic sense of truth.[5]

A SENSE OF HOPE: THE MELIORISTIC POWER OF COMMUNICATION

"Can only those hope who can talk?"—Ludwig Wittgenstein (1958)

The solipsism of modernity's sovereign self leads rather directly to the relativism of postmodernity's indeterminate truth. Realization of this might leave one feeling, as it did James, the hopelessness of nihility. Why resist the pull of darkness if nothing more than nothingness is all that is possible? That is the question James confronted. The answer is one displayed in Wittgenstein's rhetorical question and present in each one of the chapters in this collection: The promise of communication provides the hope necessary to an active resistance to a given universe.

As Simonson noted in chapter 1 of this volume, "pragmatism has been about communication since the beginning." That is an important sentence. It deserves repeating, with a touch of strategically placed emphasis: "Pragmatism has been *about* communication since the beginning." Pragmatism has always been all around communication, near to it, surrounding it, because "as a doctrine" it has always "held that the world is open-ended and in process" (Simonson, chap. 1, this volume). The idea of communication was,

---

[5]I have elsewhere written (in press) of the curious correspondence between James' theory of truth and Nietzsche's. So too have others (e.g., Seigfried, 1990). However, I know of no attempts to make sense of such similarities in terms of the two men's shared sense of tragedy. I would argue, however, that what each man does with this tragic realization is of greatest importance. There is a sense in which Nietzsche loses his struggle after having glanced into the pit, whereas James ultimately overcomes the despair of such a realization. James finds a way in his pragmatism (as discussed later) to find hope in the unfixed nature of all. To James and his followers, the contingent nature of truth means we have the power to define it as "a species of the good" (as do Dewey and West). Nietzsche, and many who follow him, seems to see the same contingency as suggesting only appropriation, injury, oppression, and exploitation (see Nietzsche, 1998, pp. 152–153). Perhaps this comparison echoes that made by Jensen (chap. 5, this volume) between positive and negative postmodernism. I have often, in my graduate seminars, called James and the American pragmatists *happy postmodernists* in contrast to Nietzsche and the more commonly identified postmodernists of continental philosophy.

from the beginning, implicated in James' resistance to the world. James knew that his existence depended on believing that this is an unfinished universe and that each of us can have a hand in its making. That knowledge is knowledge of the possibility of communication.

Meyer's characterization of meaning (Anderson & Meyer, 1988) as negotiated, dynamic, emergent, prolific, promiscuous, and co-constructed shows appreciation for James' pluralistic universe—that oxymoronic-sounding thing. Meaning is both many and one. Because it is dynamic, emergent, prolific, and promiscuous, it never seems fixed, it appears to be multiple, and it always suggests perspective. Yet meaning, as something negotiated and co-constructed, is also something accomplished—something social and whole. It is of individuals, but never individually made; it is collective, but never collectively determined. The idea that significance is something made, not found, something constantly constructed rather than forever forged, is a manifestation of James' resistance to a fixed universe. Each of us has a hand in the making of significance, in the construction of a universe of meaning. Here, then, is an idea of hope.

Woodward's characterization of communication as foundational is important in this regard. Communication can be thought of from this pragmatic perspective as a kind of antifoundational foundation. It is a ground whose only base is change, a generative mechanism that generates even itself, a given whose only universal is anti-essentialism. It is foundational in the way that Habermas (1979) characterized language as "what raises us out of nature [and] the only thing whose nature we can know" (p. xvii). Woodward (chap. 3, this volume) relied heavily on Carey's social constructivism as an aid in explaining the foundational character of communication. He quoted Carey (1989): "We first produce the world by symbolic work and then take up residence in the world we have produced" (p. 30). This is a very Jamesian notion: We build the world in which we live.

That this building project is a wholly symbolic one is acknowledged by James and made central in the chapter by Cronen and Chetro-Szivos (chap. 2, this volume). In *Pragmatism*, James argued that "All human thinking gets discursified; we exchange ideas; we lend and borrow verifications, get them from one another by means of social intercourse. All truth thus gets verbally built out, stored up, and made available for everyone" (1907/1991, p. 94). Citing Dewey, Cronen and Chetro-Szivos also argued the same point, noting how "past events create future possibilities." Truths may be constructed, but they are also contingent on prior truths (which is why it is not quite right to say that all truths are possible, but rather that conditions are already present for the creation of some possible truths). Cronen and Chetro-Szivos went on to write, "Just as no knowledge is 'objective,'" none is 'subjective' either. That is because . . . intelligence is formed in the process of interaction/communication with others and with things in the world."[6]

One can hear the postmodern sound of this argument. As Leonhirth (chap. 4, this volume) wrote, "If the hallmark of intellectual life in the premodern phase was religion and the hallmark of intellectual life in the modern phase was science, then communication as the currency of ideas may be the hallmark of intellectual life in the postmodern phase." Leonhirth clearly understands that the communication demanded by pragmatic postmodernism is not the mechanism of transfer familiar to modernity (see Shepherd, 1998). Rather, communication now presents the continual possibility of negotiating and renegotiating "reality under competing constructions." Communication, then, promises the power to construct. This hope provided by the idea of communication is our escape from the nihilism we associate with much of what we consider to be postmodern.

Of the many good ideas expressed in this volume, I am most taken by one from Jensen's chapter (chap. 5). When she, through her reading of Dewey, defined *art* as "full and moving communication," Jensen opened communication to potent interpretation. Suppose we think of communication as Jensen thinks of art (i.e., suppose we look at Jensen's equation running the other way—communication as full and moving art). If we re-defined *communication* into the enhanced version Jensen associated with art as experience (the one "necessary for communion, community, and therefore democracy"), we would have, I think, something much like what I have proposed elsewhere as a definition of communication needed at the end of modernity: "The simultaneous experience of self and other" (Shepherd, in press). This definition urges the same focus on communication that Jensen recommended for art: Look to "the quality of the experience, rather than the quality of the artifact." In a sense, the modern, mechanical definition of communication as the transfer of ideas (see Peters, 1989, 1999) was a communication-as-artifact definition—communication as tool, weapon, vehicle, and so on. The needed new definition is communi-

---

[6]In making the point that intelligence is made in interaction, Cronen and Chetro-Szivos (chap. 2, this volume) noted that "Wittgenstein came to the same position independently a little less than three decades later." The authors then playfully asked, "But then, who reads American philosophy?" European intellectuals and philosophers of the 20th century were quite familiar with James. In part this was because James spent considerable time in England (where his brother was living the life of an ex-patriot, of course) and on the continent. In fact, he spent the better part of the 1904 to 1905 school year on a tour of philosophers in Europe, giving lectures and meeting with everyone from Berenson to Bergson (see Lewis, 1991, pp. 522–564). With regard to the more specific case of Wittgenstein, it is interesting to note that he "often referred to James in his lectures, and for a time James's *Psychology* was the one book that he kept in his sparsely furnished rooms" (Thayer, 1981, p. 313).

cation as experience—communication as relationship, both personal and communal. What a rich way this offers for rescuing the notion of *miscommunication*. I have been quite critical of the psychologistic view of communication that this term typically implies (Shepherd, 1999). However, suppose we again say of communication what Jensen and Dewey say of art? That some of it is "shoddily made, dishonestly offered, designed to pander" and so forth; that some of it "offers a degraded experience." As such, some tries at the experience of communication, indeed many such tries, are like bad art is to Jensen—missed opportunities, possibilities deflected or denied. We might reasonably call such attempts *miscommunication*—missed attempts to commune.

Reclaiming the idea of miscommunication in this way is potentially important because there is danger in all this talk of promise and possibility with no recognition of the real tragedy of opportunities too bare. As West (1993b) cautioned, we "must not be so preoccupied—or obsessed—with possibility that it conceals or represses the ultimate facts of the human predicament" (p. 114). I think this caution is also present in other ways in a number of chapters in this volume, but most noticeably in Craig's (chap. 6) excellent treatment of Dewey and Gadamer. In particular, Craig argued that Gadamer's reclamation of prejudice—his deep appreciation for the power of tradition—offers an important corrective to Dewey's more optimistic view. The historicity of truth is indeed an important insight. Consider, for example, the popular appeal of Gray's (1992) abysmal *Men Are From Mars, Women Are From Venus*. It is surely an awful (un)truth to believe that men and women are aliens, each to the other. Yet many men and women must find the metaphor rather compelling. Surely this has to do with the distressing history of gender construction and the terrible weight of missed, deflected, or denied opportunities to communicate. And what is true of gender might be even truer of race. It cannot be best to believe (and so, in a Jamesian sense, it cannot be true) that a Black man and a White man can never understand one another and never commune. Yet there is something undeniable about the difficulties of transcending race. Again this seems obviously tied to evils that have been preserved. This is a lesson of Gadamer's Bildung and something Craig is right to point us toward. Still it is important to understand that one can be hopeful without being optimistic. That is, I think, an opinion Gadamer shares. For all he believes in the sway of tradition, Gadamer (1989) was still able to write that "language is not its elaborated conventionalism, nor the burden of pre-schematization with which it loads us, but the generative and creative power to unceasingly make this whole once again fluent" (p. 549). Similarly, James' meliorism is a hope-filled doctrine that is nonetheless tempered by already present conditions perhaps not unlike Gadamer's prejudices.

James described his pragmatism as a *melioristic doctrine*. By this he meant that it is a metaphysic of the possible. In *Pragmatism*, he asked: What does it mean to say something is possible? His answer was: "It means not only that there are no preventative conditions present, but that some of the conditions of production of the possible thing actually are here" (1907/1991, p. 124). Consider how *half full* this glass of water is. On the one hand, James' consideration of possibility is a hope-filled one. It suggests that we are always somewhat already along toward accomplishing whatever we consider to be possible. The conditions for the realization of all sorts of good truths are already at [this] hand. On the other hand, we also live with conditions that allow for the realization of all kinds of bad truths or, more rightly because James considered truth to be a species of the good, with untruths. Although the truths we have "verbally built out" might fund a better future, the untruths might also fund a worse one. Thus, for example, sexism and racism are present conditions constraining to some degree future possibilities. This sobering restraint, or sense of the tragic, has always been present in pragmatism; it is also explicitly addressed in the chapter by Perry (chap. 9).

Perry offered a good discussion of why, despite James' association of truth with the merely expedient, we are not free to believe whatever we like and why one truth is not as good as any other. In particular, Perry pointed to the collective character of truth's determination in James' writing—that truth is whatever is expedient in our thinking. Pointing to how the collective constrains (and frees) truth from utter subjectivism allies Perry with Craig and his attraction to Gadamer's strong sense of tradition. Again, it is worth noting that this appreciation has always been present in pragmatism. In the same essay/lecture on "Pragmatism's Conception of Truth," in which James defined *the true* as "only the expedient in the way of *our* thinking," he also wrote the following:

> truth is made largely out of previous truths. Men's beliefs at any time are so much experience funded. But the beliefs are themselves parts of the sum total of the world's experience, and become matter, therefore for the next day's funding operations. (1907/1991, p. 99)

That truth is both funded and malleable is indeed sobering. It issues great responsibility on us all. This is the most compelling point of Perry's good work: Our responsibility is not to simply mirror a preexisting world, but rather to create a new and better one. The knowledge that motivates us, of course, is that the current world is plenty bad; the fear that can turn us into skeptics is that we might hammer out (un)truths that will fund an even darker future.

BUILDING A BETTER AND MORE PLURALISTIC UNIVERSE

> We can *create* the conclusion, then. We can and we may, as it were, jump with both feet off the ground into or towards a world of which we trust the other parts to meet our jump—and *only so* can the *making* of a perfected world of the pluralistic pattern ever take place. Only through our precursive trust in it can it come into being.—James (p. 740)

In bringing Habermas to this volume's table of pragmatists, Jacobson reminded us of the practical character of our collective concern with communication. Communication is an idea full of promise and hope, but it is not ethereal. Dewey (1925) considered communication to be a "wonder by the side of which transubstantiation pales" (p. 138), but a very tangible wonder nonetheless. This is the thrust of Habermas' critical project. As Jacobson (chap. 11, this volume) suggested, Habermas employs the ideal of communication to engage in a "practical critique of society." He applies universal validity claims in an effort to promote the coordination of behavior. Thus, Jacobson's chapter points to the need for acting on communication's promise. Shuler and Tate's chapter serves as an exemplar in this regard.

Shuler and Tate (chap. 10) understand that pragmatism's first impulse is toward building a more pluralistic universe; that to pragmatists from James and Dewey to Rorty and West, a more perfect universe is a more pluralistic universe. Shuler and Tate exemplified this impulse on multiple levels. First, they showed the strong connections between feminist and pragmatist theorizations. Second, relying on Seigfried's (1996) important work, they pointed to women's contributions to the development of pragmatism. Third, they demonstrated the value in refusing to dismiss what is so often treated dismissively—teenage girls and *Seventeen* magazine. In an unpublished abstract of their chapter, Shuler and Tate pointed the way for pragmatist researchers when they wrote,

> the truths we seek and find are truths that we actively participate in creating. If there is nothing absolute about current patriarchal structures of oppression, then the possibility of challenging these structures and creating new discourses of empowerment and social justice exists.

Horne's (chap. 7) treatment of relativism and ethics points us directly toward the personal responsibility that comes with the promise of communication. As she argued, following Rorty, the aesthetics of moral development—of selfhood—rests in the process of self-creation rather than in self-discovery. Each individual is a conclusion in the making, and each individual may add his or her making to whatever the universe might be. James' leap of faith is a bet on the promise of communication. It says that the perfect universe is a pluralistic one and we each build ourselves into a universe in the making, believing others are doing the same. In that process, the very pluralistic nature of our individual existences will make us one as well as many.

CONCLUSION

James' depression of 1869 to 1870 was in response to his insight about the tragic implications of modernity's solipsism. He articulated this insight many decades later in his *Radical Empiricism*: "My experiences and your experiences are 'with' each other in various external ways, but mine pass into mine, and yours pass into yours in a way in which yours and mine never pass into one another" (p. 197). Note the striking similarity between that passage and the despondent words recorded in his diary entry of December 21, 1869: "I can never embrace them [other forms of life] as a whole or incorporate them with myself." This insight about the ultimate implication of modernity's insistence on the primacy of individual experience led him to the postmodern realization of truth's utter contingency. This is the first half of the story—the half of pragmatism and tragedy. There is, of course, a second half—the one about communication and hope.

James' realization that truth was a human construction forced a need to focus on the process of construction. His pragmatism suggested a philosophical anthropology where being was in the making—where existence could not be discovered, but demanded to be made. This opened the door for theorizing the ontology of communication (see Shepherd, 1993), for defining it as the constitutive process, and for making it the only a priori— the always already idea. This is the door through which the authors of all the preceding chapters have walked. It is the portal that closes on the metaphysical room that disallows for the possibility of transcendence and opens toward the one that gives hope for such. Ricoeur (1976) captured this walk from pragmatism and tragedy to communication and hope as well as anyone:

> Being-together, as the existential condition for the possibility of any dialogical structure of discourse, appears as a way of trespassing or overcoming the fundamental solitude of each human being. . . . My experience cannot directly become your experience. An event belonging to one stream of consciousness cannot be transferred as such into another stream of con-

sciousness. Yet, nevertheless, something passes from me to you. Something is transferred from one sphere of life to another. This something is not the experience as experienced, but its meaning. Here is the miracle. The experience as experienced, as lived, remains private, but its sense, its meaning, becomes public. Communication in this way is the overcoming of the radical noncommunicability of the lived experience as lived. (pp. 15–16)

It is clear to me that the story of pragmatism and communication is a battlefield tale. It is the story of a resistance movement—of humans employing the hope of communication against the manifest tragedies of complete isolation and total uncertainty. Its built-in never-ending nature makes it a particularly useful story. The story instructs us as to how we might better write it. Our collective duty, it seems to me, is twofold. We must first, in a sense, preach the gospel of communication—the *good news* that is so central to this story. As disciples of this discipline we call *communication studies* (Shepherd, 1993), we are charged with providing people with faith in the transcendent powers of communication—that it is possible to become *one* even as we remain *many*. Explicating, defining, theorizing, and showing the constitutive character of communication has been a remarkably recurrent theme in this volume. As a result, these chapters have answered this first duty well.

Our second duty is less conspicuously displayed in these pages, but nonetheless many chapter authors strongly implied it: We must help provide people with the skills necessary for succeeding in this fight against modernity's solipsism and its attending loneliness, as well as against postmodernism's relativism and accompanying meaninglessness. Communication is a "practical discipline," as Craig (chap. 6, this volume) persuasively argued. It is art, as Jensen (chap. 5, this volume) so successfully showed. My story says that we teach communication as a practical art—and skills courses are central to the discipline's curriculum—because we believe people can be trained to more readily and fully experience the transcendence of communication and so not miss the opportunity to do battle with isolation and uncertainty. Our continued role in this story of pragmatism and communication, then, is to provide people with both the theory and skills necessary to construct the truth of ever better existences.

REFERENCES

Anderson, J. A., & Meyer, T. P. (1988). *Mediated communication: A social action perspective.* Newbury Park, CA: Sage.

Bernstein, R. J. (1995). American pragmatism: The conflict of narratives. In H. J. Saatkamp, Jr. (Ed.), *Rorty and pragmatism: The philosopher responds to his critics* (pp. 54–67). Nashville, TN: Vanderbilt University Press.

Carey, J. W. (1989). *Communication as culture*. Boston: Unwin Hyman.

Descartes, R. (1641/1960). *Meditations on first philosophy* (2nd rev. ed.). Indianapolis: The Liberal Arts Press.

Dewey, J. (1925). *Experience and nature*. Peru, IL: Open Court.

Edie, J. M. (1987). *William James and phenomenology*. Bloomington, IN: Indiana University Press.

Gadamer, H. (1989). *Truth and method* (2nd rev. ed.). New York: Crossroad.

Gray, J. (1992). *Men are from mars, women are from venus: A practical guide for improving communication and getting what you want in your relationship*. New York: HarperCollins.

Habermas, J. (1979). *Communication and the evolution of society*. Boston: Beacon.

James, W. (1902/1985). *The varieties of religious experience*. New York: Penguin.

James, W. (1907/1991). *Pragmatism*. Buffalo, NY: Prometheus Books.

Lewis, R. W. B. (1991). *The Jameses: A family narrative*. New York: Farrar, Straus & Giroux.

MacIntyre, A. (1977). Epistemological crises, dramatic narrative and the philosophy of science. *Monist, 60*.

MacIntyre, A. (1981). *After virtue*. Notre Dame, IN: University of Notre Dame Press.

McDermott, J. J. (1977). *The writings of William James: A comprehensive edition*. Chicago: University of Chicago Press.

Nietzsche, F. (1998). *Beyond good and evil*. Oxford: Oxford University Press.

Oxford English Dictionary. (1971). Oxford: Oxford University Press.

Peters, J. D. (1989). John Locke, the individual, and the origin of communication. *Quarterly Journal of Speech, 75*, 387–399.

Peters, J. D. (1999). *Speaking into the air: A history of the idea of communication*. Chicago: University of Chicago Press.

Ricoeur, P. (1976). *Interpretation theory: Discourse and the surplus of meaning*. Fort Worth, TX: TCU Press.

Seigfried, C. H. (1990). *William James's radical reconstruction of philosophy*. Albany, NY: SUNY Press.

Seigfried, C. H. (1996). *Pragmatism and feminism: Reweaving the social fabric*. Chicago: University of Chicago Press.

Shepherd, G. J. (1993). Building a discipline of communication. *Journal of Communication, 43*, 83–91.

Shepherd, G. J. (1998). The trouble with goals. *Communication Studies, 49*, 294–299.

Shepherd, G. J. (1999). Advances in communication theory: A critical review. *Journal of Communication, 49*, 156–164.

Shepherd, G. J. (in press). Community as the interpersonal accomplishment of communication. In G. J. Shepherd & E. W. Rothenbuhler (Eds.), *Communication and community*. Mahwah, NJ: Lawrence Erlbaum Associates.

Thayer, H. S. (1981). *Meaning and action*. Indianapolis, IN: Hackett.

West, C. (1993a). *Keeping faith: Philosophy and race in America*. New York: Routledge.

West, C. (1993b). *Beyond Eurocentrism and multiculturalism: Volume 1. Prophetic thought in postmodern times*. Monroe, ME: Common Courage Press.

Wittgenstein, L. (1958). *Philosophical investigations* (3rd ed.). New York: Macmillan.

Author Index

Subject Index